$35⁰⁰
2/96

D1058610

WITHDRAWN

Becoming Southern

BECOMING SOUTHERN

The Evolution of a Way of Life,
Warren County and Vicksburg,
Mississippi, 1770–1860

CHRISTOPHER MORRIS

New York   Oxford
OXFORD UNIVERSITY PRESS
1995

Oxford University Press

Oxford   New York

Athens   Auckland   Bangkok   Bombay
Calcutta   Cape Town   Dar es Salaam   Delhi
Florence   Hong Kong   Istanbul   Karachi
Kuala Lumpur   Madras   Madrid   Melbourne
Mexico City   Nairobi   Paris   Singapore
Taipei   Tokyo   Toronto

and associated companies in
Berlin   Ibadan

Copyright © 1995 by Christopher Morris

Published by Oxford University Press, Inc.,
200 Madison Avenue, New York, New York 10016

Oxford is a registered trademark of Oxford University Press

Library of Congress Cataloging-in-Publication Data
Morris, Christopher (Christopher Charles)
Becoming southern : The evolution of a way of life,
Warren County and Vicksburg, Mississippi, 1770–1860 /
Christopher Morris,
p.   cm.   Includes bibliographical references (p.   ) and index.
ISBN 0-19-508366-0
1. Warren County (Miss.)—History.
2. Warren County (Miss.)—Social conditions.
3. Vicksburg (Miss.)—History.
4. Vicksburg (Miss.)—Social conditions.
I. Title.
F347.W29M67   1994   976.2'29—dc20   93-37916

1 3 5 7 9 8 6 4 2

Printed in the United States of America
on acid-free paper

For Stephanie

PREFACE

This is the story of how one place—Warren County, Mississippi—became a Southern place. It was not always thus. Once this small piece of land and the society upon it was Native American, then French, then Spanish, then English, and when it became a part of the United States, when it became American, it was really more Western than Southern. Only after a long process of economic, social, and cultural evolution did the people of European and African descent, who at the end of the eighteenth and beginning of the nineteenth century made it their home, develop a way of life that contemporary Americans and later historians identified as Southern.

A few years ago I presented some of my work on Warren County at a session at one of the many annual historical conventions. A commentator offered me the sort of criticism that can make a beginning scholar consider career alternatives. He suggested, not quite so bluntly, that I was wasting my time. We need to understand Mississippi society during the heyday of slavery and King Cotton—he scolded me—when it was definitely Southern. How it became Southern is not important; it was inevitable.

That criticism forced me to consider some of my assumptions about the historical process, and after doing so I realized that my disagreement with my colleague was total. Nothing is inevitable, not even Mississippi's becoming Southern. If I may paraphrase paleontologist Stephen Jay Gould: While we may speak in terms of life's or history's probabilities, we have to be prepared for the contingencies. Of course, that is what makes history so much fun, at least for me. I am not willing to take it for granted that Warren County, Mississippi, was destined to become Southern. I want to know how and why; this book offers some answers.

I am pleased to acknowledge the assistance, advice, and encouragement of a number of people, and to thank them for their kindness. Sam Hill and Helen Hill, who happened to be visiting Mississippi for a semester when I made my first research trip gave me a place to stay in Jackson. Helen drove me to Vicksburg on that first unforgettable visit to what would be my home away from home. At Vicksburg the staff at the Old

Court House Museum received me with open arms. Gordon Cotton's and Blanche Terry's knowledge of Warren County history and of the local documents proved invaluable. Several other people in Mississippi took an interest in my work and helped me to discover their past. Special thanks go to Dee and John Leigh Hyland for being so forthcoming with their family history. Clinton Bagley took time out from his own research to guide me through the records in the Adams County Courthouse in Natchez, and Charles L. Sullivan did likewise with the massive Claiborne Collection in the Mississippi Department of Archives and History in Jackson. The staff at the Archives was wonderfully helpful. In particular I want to thank Anne Lipscomb.

My research travels also took me to libraries outside of Mississippi. Allison Beck, of the Barker Texas History Center at the University of Texas, helped me wade through much of the as yet largely uncatalogued Natchez Trace Collection. She brought several important documents to my attention that I would never have seen otherwise. I also want to thank the staff at the Hill Library at Louisiana State University, the Southern Historical Collection at Chapel Hill, the Virginia Historical Society in Richmond, the Pace Library at the University of West Florida, and the P. K. Yonge Library at the University of Florida.

Several people read and commented on earlier versions of some chapters. I want to thank Cheryll Ann Cody and Jack S. Blocker, Jr., for their comments on an earlier version of Chapter 7. Edward Ayres and Stephen Ashe provided valuable comments on an earlier version of Chapter 5, as did Daniel C. Littlefield and Harold Woodman for Chapter 2. Ronald P. Formisano offered a careful reading of Chapter 8. Charles Zeldon helped me see what I wanted to say in Chapter 10. Jeffrey Adler, Marvin Harris, Murdo MacLeod, Darrett B. Rutman, and Bertram Wyatt-Brown read and commented on every chapter. At a particularly urgent moment when I needed a fresh reading, Michael Fellman put aside his work to come to my aid. At the University of Florida, Jeff Brautigam, Jack Henderson, Michael Justus, Jane Landers, Steve Noll, Eric Rise, Scott Sheffield, Jeremy Stahl, Diane Stubbins, Dave Tegeder, Joe Thompson, and Lou Williams all heard parts of this work during its early stages, in classes and colloquia. They always gave me insightful criticism brought from several fields of research, but I am most thankful to them for pushing me to "just get done." I want to thank Karen Wolny for seeing the manuscript through the many stages of the publication process, and Stephanie Sakson for her careful copyediting.

Funding for researching and writing came from the Department of History at the University of Florida. I also spent the better part of a year living and researching in Mississippi with the support of a doctoral fellowship from the Social Sciences and Humanities Research Council of Canada.

Gordon Cotton, keeper of the oral history of Warren County, gave me a place to stay, showed me around the county, and put me on the path of more fascinating stories than I could find room for in a long manuscript. I am grateful for his friendship and cherish the memories of my days as the scholar-in-residence at Campbell's Swamp.

When I first arrived at the University of Florida Bertram Wyatt-Brown gave me his old typewriter and put me to work. He never let up. Darrett Rutman was just as demanding. If there is something of themselves reflected in my work then I have at least paid a part of the debt I owe them for their comments, advice, encouragement, and support.

Final thanks go to my parents, who, if not always sure of what I was doing, exactly, nevertheless kept all doubts to themselves and gave me all the support in the world. And to Stephanie Cole. Her knowledge, insight, and understanding makes living with my sharpest editor and toughest critic an absolute delight.

Arlington, Texas   C. M.
April 1993

CONTENTS

INTRODUCTION: THE EVOLUTION OF OLD SOUTH CIVILIZATION

The messenger found him in his rose garden, or so the story is told. With characteristic stoicism Jefferson Davis accepted the news of his selection as president of the new Confederate States of America. The next morning he bade farewell to family and neighbors, to the people who had kept his home for much of his adult life, and then, after nearly missing the steamer to Vicksburg, began a roundabout journey to Montgomery.

That he might never live in Warren County again probably did not occur to Davis. No doubt more urgent matters occupied his thoughts. Still, as he rode upriver he may have surveyed the countryside, forming a mental picture to last through the trying years ahead, a picture of the community that was the South he knew best, the South that he would lead through four years of war.

Hurricane plantation, the home of his older brother Joseph, sat just beyond the bank on the right as the *Natchez* paddled upstream. Still probably the finest mansion around, there were now rivals to its magnificence where only a short while ago had stood crude log dwellings, or else nothing at all. Cotton fields, protected behind a new system of levees that bordered the river, spread out over land that had once been flood plain and cypress swamp. Past Hurricane and around a sharp bend, Davis next would have spied Palmyra plantation, which had once belonged to former Governor John A. Quitman, whose father-in-law had acquired the land in a series of purchases from several homesteading families from New England. About ten miles beyond Palmyra sat Warrenton, a village that years ago had been the county seat and center of local trade. Now most steamboats, including the *Natchez*, passed it by. Another ten miles brought the riverboat to Vicksburg, city of a hundred hills. Perched high on the bluff, overlooking miles of river and Louisiana lowlands, sat the Warren County courthouse. Built by slaves, with its great columns on four sides, the imposing structure symbolized, as it does today, the civilization that was the Old South. Yet this was a civilization only recently come to this part of the world. The courthouse itself was so new that the grounds around it had yet to be land-scaped. Little more than a generation earlier Davis's brother Samuel had hacked a plantation out of wilderness just a few miles from where the president-elect disembarked and prepared to address a gathering crowd. In Warren County the Old South was really quite new. It had only just arrived. Very shortly it would vanish, forever.

Perhaps no state represented the Old South and all that it stood for more than did Mississippi. The state was both before and after the Civil War the leading producer of cotton in the country. In 1860 its slave population outnumbered its white population. The president of the Confederacy made his home in Mississippi. The state epitomized the South, and perhaps more than any other it still does. Yet, a close examination of the economic and social history of the region around Vicksburg demonstrates that the most "Southern" of the Southern states was not always so. Initially, life in Mississippi differed little from life in such Northwestern territories as Ohio and Illinois, and could not have been more different from the older regions of the Southeast, the plantation districts of Virginia and the Carolinas.

Of course, Mississippi, and Warren County, did become plantation societies. But Virginia and Carolina planters, and their sons and daughters, did not simply transplant a fully conceived society in the red clays and black bottoms to the west, although some certainly set out to do just that. The society that developed in Warren County arose out of the material conditions presented by both local context and that place's situation within the world of the late eighteenth and early nineteenth century. Locally, material conditions constantly changed as people adapted their behavior to their environment, then changed their environment as they struggled to make a living, which forced them to alter patterns of behavior. All the while they adjusted and readjusted their world view, their understanding of the way the world worked, to make it conform to life as they lived it.

Thus, the Old South, like any society, was forever in the process of becoming something else. Yet historians often forget how dynamic the Southern states were in the years before the Civil War. This is largely a product of their efforts to differentiate South from North in the decade or two immediately preceding the Civil War. The perpetually static South, they remind us, remained traditional, rural, agricultural, while the rapidly changing North modernized, urbanized, industrialized. Still, for a place that supposedly stood still, the real South has proven hard to pin down. Eugene D. Genovese finds wealthy cotton planters on the Carolina and Georgia coasts and identifies them as pre-capitalistic, hegemonic, paternalistic. James Oakes looks at the smaller slaveholders of the central cotton regions of Georgia, Alabama, and Mississippi and describes them as capitalistic, democratic, liberal. Steven Hahn locates in the South's upcountry communities of noncommercial, individualistic, republican farmers who lived in stark contrast to the planters of Georgia's black belt.[1]

There were, as William Freehling reminds us, many Souths.[2] But the South was more than an amalgam of distinct regions. It was a continually developing society. We understand well how the South varied from place to place. We are not so sure of how it varied over time. Few studies present us with a picture of an evolving South. Fewer still reach back from the late antebellum years into the beginnings of Southern society in the eighteenth century.[3] The traditional political barriers that divide American history into colonial, revolutionary, early Republic, and antebellum periods endure two decades after the birth of the "new" social history promised to tear them down. Genovese acknowledges but does not explore the small slaveholder origins of the wealthy planters he studies. Oakes ends his investigation without considering that the more newly developed regions he studies were in the process of becoming wealthy plantation communities like those in the South's oldest plantation districts. Steven Hahn's study presents a moving picture of change, as market forces transformed yeoman communities into cotton plantations. Yet he tells us that the yeoman resisted change with all their might, that if upcountry society was not static then the people at least were.

The tendency to view the Old South as unchanging also stems from the differing approaches of historians to their craft. On the one hand abstractionists claim that to understand the South we must unlock the minds of the people who lived there and view their world subjectively, as they did. These scholars typically emphasize ethics, ideologies, meanings, and "Southern values." On the other hand, substantialists locate the roots of Southern culture in objectively identifiable and measurable material conditions such as soil quality, climatic variation, miles of navigable rivers, cotton and corn yields, income, nutritional value of diets, and wealth distribution, which they claim determined behavior.[4]

Despite their differing approaches, few of the historians in either camp would deny that they have uncovered two Souths that were somehow connected. Yet they display much confusion over the relationship between the South as it was lived and the South as it was understood by those who lived there. Abstractionists hold firmly to the assumption that behavior is merely an outward reflection of thought, which they see as the essence of culture. They tend to ignore or minimize the evolving material context and the dynamics in which Southerners lived over the course of three centuries. Culture is for these historians unchanging almost by definition. For their part, substantialists, despite their concern for behavior and material conditions, tend to begin with the same assumption about the priority of ideas. Too often they simply look for a material context that corresponds to the beliefs and values they presume existed. But it is not surprising that they, too, tend to present static pictures and, amazingly, do so sometimes against the backdrop of a changing material and social context.

If there is a bridge between life and mind abstractionists rarely cross it. They feel no need to. They are certain that what lies on the other side is only a reflection of their present position. All too often substantialists prove them right, for when they cross the bridge they generally find what they set out to find, namely, a life that reflected the mind.

Southern life and mind were surely connected. There was a bridge. However, the tendency to begin with the mind and then look for the material and social context that reflected it has created much confusion, muddled even more when historians mingle their own perspectives with those of the people they study. Both vantage points, what anthropologists refer to as emics and etics, are best kept distinct.[5]

The bridge spanning Southern life and mind is better approached from the life side. The nature of historical evidence allows us to be more certain of what people did than of what they thought. And to understand how Southerners lived, before we cross over to discover their perceptions of how they lived, we might begin by observing them in their evolving little communities. If we think of the community as a social form arising from what Marvin Harris calls "the encounter between womb and belly and earth and water," then community necessarily becomes a primary unit of biological and cultural reproduction and transmission. For anyone interested in understanding a culture—the South's, for instance—the little community is a worthwhile place to start.[6]

The essence of community consists of the relationships people form so that they can produce and reproduce their ways of life.[7] Tracking their patterns should be a primary objective of a local study. These patterns vary with material context. Sex ratio, population density, ease of transportation, terrain, climate, and mode of production all shape the ways in which men and women come together to work and procreate. Nineteenth-century Americans, by clearing forests, building roads, killing off wildlife, exhausting the soil, or causing erosion, altered their material environment in ways that forced them continually to readjust their patterns of association so that they could continue to meet their primary objectives with an ease they had come to expect.[8] The Southern community, therefore, was dynamic. Moreover, each individual related uniquely to the material context. Even in a perfectly egalitarian society where everyone has equal access to all resources, differences would arise through variations in physical and mental capacities brought by each person to his or her world. Politics, power, relative advantage and disadvantage, then, characterized and shaped interaction. Politics, too, were dynamic.[9]

Interpersonal relationships can be observed, as can the material conditions that are their context. But how are we to understand a society as perceived and expressed in ideologies? How are we to cross to the mind side of the bridge? Reading minds, especially those of people long dead, is not easy. This is not to suggest that we abandon all efforts to explore values and beliefs. Far from it. But the task is risky because the existence of the bridge cannot be known for certain, but only posited theoretically.

A hypothesis: The material context of a given place elicits from each individual numerous behavioral responses, such as observable patterns of human interaction, that in turn constantly alter conditions, all of which are mentally catalogued so that they can feed back into the model in the form of ideas of practical and impractical behavior. Conditions and requisite behavior will tend to filter out pre-existing ideas carried into a locale. Useless notions will fall by the wayside, brand new ones will emerge to correspond with action, while others will undergo some degree of alteration, perhaps by fulfilling a new function even while appearing, deceptively, to keep their original form. In short, as a society evolves materially and socially so too will mental constructs evolve. Culture, in both its behavioral and mental streams, is thus dynamic.[10]

While the process of cultural evolution is universal, the ingredients in this equation, and so the outcome, can vary considerably over time and place. In some communities the process of development can even be arrested or reversed.[11] At any point in the nineteenth century, then, the South, like the rest of America, consisted of thousands of little communities all located somewhere along a moving plane of development.

This study looks at the development of one of those communities, Jefferson Davis's Warren County, Mississippi, the northernmost of the five old river counties located in the state's southwestern corner. Formally established in 1810, Warren County developed as part of a wealthy cotton plantation district that spanned most of west-central Mississippi. Like most of the counties in that part of the South by the start of the Civil War, slaves comprised a majority of the population. The combination of cotton and slaves might be enough to suggest Warren County was "typical" of the South, or at least the Cotton South; the presence of a town of over 8000 inhabitants—Vicksburg—shatters such pretentions. However, Warren County's typicality, the extent to which it was or was not a microcosm of the South, is quite irrelevant.

As a laboratory for a study of social and cultural process it is well suited, for several reasons. First, located in Mississippi, in the Old Southwest, Warren County's development can be studied more or less apart from the distorting shadow of the older societies along the Atlantic seaboard, and as part of a region for too long ignored by historians who look to the South and see only South Carolina and Virginia. Second, initial settlement predated the boom that followed Whitney's invention of the cotton gin and thus cannot be explained simply as a consequence of that invention. Nevertheless, the gin accelerated the county's development tremendously. Third, Vicksburg, laid out on cotton fields in 1819, permits an investigation of the urban process within a developing plantation society. Fourth, by 1860 some Warren County residents were just approaching the level of affluence for which older regions of the South were renowned. Yet little more than half a century earlier the first settlers were stealing land from Native Americans, setting hogs and cattle loose in the forest, and raising log cabins. Thus, several Souths had their moments in Warren County. Fifth, the speed with which Warren County developed, from log cabin to mansion, makes for a more manageable study than a place such as the region around Natchez, where the same process unfolded but over a longer period of time. Sixth, the documentary record of antebellum Warren County allowed for a detailed study of material, social, and cultural development. Evidence gleaned from public records and assembled in the form of more than 6000 cases provides the main database for the study. In addition, a substantial body of more qualitative sources—diaries, letters, newspapers, transcripts of criminal and civil suits—offered insights into the possible perceptions and meanings Warren County residents gave to the behavior observable through quantitative analysis.[12]

From the time of the American Revolution to the breakup of the Union pioneer farmers and herders built a slave and cotton plantation society in the piece of territory that became Warren County, Mississippi. At first this place resembled what were at the time the nation's other Western regions, such as Illinois and Ohio, more than the older plantation districts of Virginia and the Carolinas. Over the first half of the nineteenth century, however, the region around present-day Vicksburg developed into a slave and cotton plantation society.

Three distinct stages marked Warren County's economic and social development. From the mid-1770s to 1790 homesteaders lived by extensive exploitation of local resources, practiced slash-and-burn agriculture, and participated only minimally in a national or international market. During the last decade of the century some homesteaders began to raise large herds of cattle for sale in a regional market. After 1810 or so those who had raised cattle began to acquire slaves and plant cotton. It is significant that farmers with small or no cattle herds did not choose to plant cotton until population growth, the disappearance of wildlife, and the rolling back of the forests brought about the demise of the pioneer economy and thus forced them eventually to take up cotton planting (see table below).

Changing material conditions and economic development stimulated

Population of Warren County, 1778–1860

	1778	1792	1800	1810	1820	1830	1840	1850	1860
Free Whites	86	248	170	705	1401	3356	5213	5999	6918
Enslaved Blacks	14	82	48	473	1287	4370	10493	9254	10524
Free Blacks			0		5	22	104	25	27

Source: For 1778, see Chapter 1, note 23. Spanish Census of the Spanish District, 1792, MDAH. Abstract of Census of Mississippi Territory, 1801, Pickering County, and Census of Warren County, 1810, RG 28, microfilm 546, MDAH. U.S. Census, Population Schedules, 1820, 1830, 1840, 1850, 1860, and Slave Schedules, 1850, 1860, for Warren County, Mississippi.

changes in the character of social relations. Growing reliance on the market attracted attention to the larger world, reducing interaction among neighbors. Local patterns of cooperation broke down, while struggles for increasingly scarce resources frequently turned violent. Individuals came to depend on extended kin networks to marshall collective resources, which placed tremendous power in men, usually older, who had legal control over family property. Changes in material conditions altered relations between men and women. Slave labor reduced the economic contribution of women to the household enterprise and increased their dependence on the men who owned the slaves. Masters worked slaves harder as they struggled to raise more cotton. Perhaps some slaves took solace in the fact that there were increasingly more blacks around, more opportunities to form families, to put some distance between themselves and their oppressors. But in forming stable families they actually contributed to the productive capacity of their masters' households, and to the power of the whites who kept them in bonds. Slaveholders' prosperity modified their relations with less prosperous neighbors. Poorer farmers came to them to borrow slaves or to have cotton ginned and marketed. This planters were happy to do, but they expected certain favors in return, such as allegiance on election day. In time villages appeared, and eventually a city of 8000 people—Vicksburg—grew to rival the influence of the planters who held sway in the countryside.

As president-elect Davis stood on the levee and prepared to offer a short speech, the river lapping at the bank behind him, his friends and neighbors gathered before him, he perhaps reflected on the history of Warren County, his South. That history began in an earlier revolution.[13]

Becoming Southern

1

PIONEERS OF THE
LOOSA CHITTO

The east side of the Mississippi, from the Yazoo River south past Natchez, is bordered by a narrow strip of flood land that quickly rises 75 to 200 feet above the bottom. The black alluvial soil below the bluffs is some of the most fertile in North America. The hills, irregular, steep, and divided by narrow, deep ravines, consist of a fine topsoil collected from the prairies in the Far West by centuries of winds that jettisoned their cargo when the Mississippi ridge forced them abruptly upward. The fine, yellowish silt, called loess, although acidic, is nevertheless excellent for farming, except that its powdery quality renders it extremely susceptible to erosion. Only the dense thickets of cane, with their mesh of entangled roots, aided by the canopy of a walnut, oak, and magnolia forest, hold the soil and prevent rains from carrying it away in creeks that carve their way through the hills.[1]

Europeans first arrived in this corner of the world with Hernando de Soto in the early 1540s, in time to witness the final days of the Natchez civilization, the last of the ancient Mississippians, whose miles of cornfields "thickly set with great towns" had all but vanished by the time LaSalle arrived a century and a half later.[2] During the 1700s the French established forts in the Lower Mississippi Valley (Figure 1.1). The Natchez had by then been so reduced in numbers by Old World diseases that they only briefly figured in the invaders' plans for an inland fur trading empire.[3] The white men simply took whatever land they desired as though it were vacant, which, compared with de Soto's day, it was. In one final gasp of life the Natchez massacred the inhabitants of Fort Rosalie and wiped out Fort St. Pierre on the Yazoo Bluff; the French retaliated, chasing survivors into the woods, where they disappeared forever. When the English took command of the east side of the river, the Choctaw, who had eagerly assisted the French in their war on the

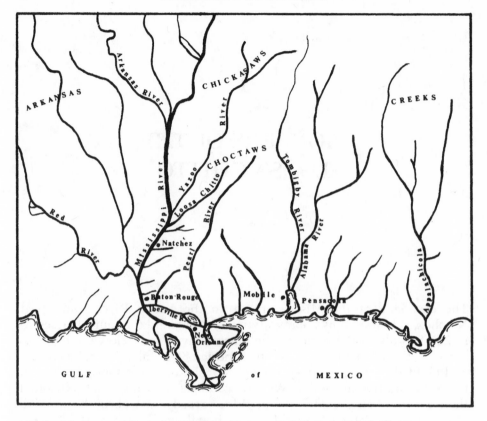

Figure 1.1 Lower Mississippi Valley. (*Source:* Robin F. A. Fabel, *The Economy of British West Florida, 1763–1783* [Tuscaloosa and London, 1988].)

Natchez, had moved into the territory left by the vanquished nation. They, too, now faced extermination.[4]

At the beginning of the eighteenth century, the Choctaw and other nations in the Mississippi and Gulf regions supplied Europeans with furs, as well as corn, beans, squashes, and meat, in exchange for manufactures and liquor. By the end of the century, the pattern had reversed; Native Americans depended on Europeans for food. The deerskin and hide trade had, gradually at first, depleted the forests of the wildlife that had been a most plentiful source of sustenance. The more scarce deer and bear became, the more Native Americans relied on trade with whites to maintain their standard of living, which in turn only accelerated the skin trade. As the Indians moved out of empty forests, white homesteaders moved in. By the 1770s, the Choctaw were fast running out of room. Northward lay the hunting grounds of the Chickasaw, whose situation was no better. Still further north, the fur trade along the Great Lakes had pushed the nations of that region into the land around the confluence of the Ohio and Mississippi rivers. From the south came an onslaught of white settlers.[5]

The Lower Mississippi Valley had several claimants, and spent most of its colonial history being shuttled among them. At the beginning of the eighteenth century, France controlled the whole valley. Following military defeat in 1763, however, the French ceded all their North American possessions to colonial rivals. England acquired the east side, and governed it as part of the colony of West Florida. Spain, in return for relinquishing Florida to the British, received the west side of the river and New Orleans. In 1779 the Spanish, capitalizing on Britain's troubles with her rebellious colonies, seized Natchez and the east side of the Mississippi up to the Yazoo River. Until the century's end the Natchez region remained a part of Spanish Louisiana. In 1795 the United States took possession of the east side of the Lower Mississippi as far south as the Iberville River, at least officially; the Spanish did not actually leave for another three years. Most of Louisiana, including New Orleans, Spain ceded back to France three years before the Louisiana Purchase, when the whole valley came under the control of the United States. It is thus not surprising that, with all the changing of hands, the borders of the Mississippi were settled slowly. Above New Orleans the land was mostly vacant of European inhabitants until the years of British dominion. After 1763, a steady stream of migrants from England's Atlantic colonies flowed into the area around Natchez. People kept coming even after Spain's capture of the Mississippi's east side. It was at this time, principally during the years from 1775 to 1795, that European settlers built the first permanent homes in what was to become Warren County.[6]

The pioneers—some with families, some with slaves, some alone—cleared fields and built cabins along the Loosa Chitto, a river that emptied into the Mississippi sixty or so miles above Natchez, and which later represented Warren County's southeastern border. They came with little more than a few tools, perhaps some livestock, and some ideas about the kind of life they wanted to carve out of the wilderness for themselves and their families. Yet the wilderness had its own ways; its demands were not easily met. Those with experience in the backcountry of Virginia or New England no doubt adjusted to their new surroundings more quickly and easily than others. But experience only separated pioneers briefly, when they first arrived, before everyone had struggled, adapted, and learned to survive in their new environment. In these early years the pioneer economy and society that appeared on the Loosa Chitto owed less to the past experiences of the people who came there and more to the moment. Initially, the outside world, the world left behind by the men and women who journeyed to this place, was only barely visible.[7]

The outside world *was* visible, however. Pioneering, although it surely seemed like it entailed leaving the rest of the world behind altogether, actually extended the civilization of the center to the periphery.

Indeed, the long tentacles of the European economic system had already touched this part of the world in the form of the fur trade, long before settlers planted their first crops. Government and politics, too, soon made themselves felt even in this distant corner. Thus, the energy that drove Warren County's process of economic, social, and cultural evolution had two sources. One radiated from within the locale, as people confronted and continually altered their local environment. The other dynamic force came from the wide and always moving world in which this small place was situated. Context was at once local and global, but the two were often indistinguishable.

The Proclamation of 1763 forbade settlers in Britain's North American colonies from locating beyond the headwaters of the rivers that flowed into the Atlantic. British West Florida stood as the exception to this restriction. Thousands of homesteaders from older regions who might otherwise have headed due west over the Blue Ridge and into the Ohio Valley migrated instead to the Southwest. The British colonial administrators, eager to encourage settlement in the new colony so that England's hold on it might be secured against the Spanish presence in New Orleans and on the west bank of the Mississippi River, enticed the hesitant with a liberal land grant policy.[8] In order to enhance this scheme, royal officials made large donations to individuals and organizations who promised to populate them soon with English subjects or foreign Protestants.

Steady migration continued through the Revolution and Spain's reclaiming of the territory in 1778, raising the number of inhabitants along the east side of the Lower Mississippi. In 1770 approximately 500 whites lived around Natchez, but by 1790 the population had grown to about 2000 whites plus half as many blacks, most of them slaves.[9] All thirteen of the Atlantic colonies sent voyagers to the Mississippi on flatboats down the Ohio from the backcountries of Pennsylvania and Virginia, by ship along the coast and around the peninsula into the Gulf of Mexico, or overland from Georgia through Creek Indian country. Most traveled in bunches of several families, bringing with them little more than the essentials needed to start a homestead—a gun, an axe, two or three spades, maybe a cow, and perhaps a plough. The great expanse of wilderness that enclosed the Lower Mississippi settlements formed no barrier against the "ambulatory spirit" of the newcomers. "One carbine and a little flour and corn in a sack suffice for an American to cross the forests alone for one month," explained the Spanish governor of Louisiana. "With the carbine he kills oxen and deer to eat, and defends himself against the savages." But the numbers of migrants spilling into his territory perhaps gave the governor a false impression of the ease and facility with which they made their trek. Eliza Williams, who as a girl journeyed down the Tennessee and Mississippi rivers to Natchez, recalled how "Indians frequently came on board with game, to barter for such articles as were provided for the purpose. And when all axes were disposed of except one that was kept for the use of the two boats, the Indians became so enraged at not being allowed to get it, that they went down a few miles, and with an armed party fired on our boat and killed one of the oarsmen, and wounded two others, then ran up the hill and sounded their war whoop." The kernel of truth lay between these caricatures.[10]

Behind the exodus to West Florida lay the same forces that pushed and pulled Europeans around the Old World, then to America's shore, inland to the Appalachians, and now to the lower Mississippi Basin. As populations grew and resources diminished in the older settled areas, life in a distant and largely unknown territory seemed more appealing to anyone who perceived fewer opportunities to live than they or their parents had in earlier times. Faced with either barren or high-priced land, residents in the Atlantic colonies itched for new opportunities.[11] Of course, the growing conflict with England contributed to the migration impulse, a point not missed by the Crown, which sought to make Florida a Loyalist haven.[12] Patrick Doyle, who settled on the Big Black River, claimed in his petition for a grant of land that he left Charleston, South Carolina, "to get clear of the disturbance coming to the Northward." His neighbor John Felt, one of the Connecticut migrants, made the same claim in exactly the same words, suggesting that such pretensions could be less a sincere expression of loyalty than an ingenuous if formulaic attempt to expedite the process of acquiring land. Almost as an afterthought, Benjamin Barber attached to his petition an obsequious reminder that he was "ready to give all the assistance in his power to repulse all attempts that shall be made to take possession of this Province." There is at least a ring of truth to some of the claims. Henry Dwight told how a mob ran him out of town in New England. On the whole, however, loyalism offered at best a secondary reason for relocating along the Mississippi.[13] Indeed, the flow of migrants commenced before conflict between the colonies and England and continued long after the creation of the United States. In the 1760s, the so-called Company of Military Adventurers, a group of farmers and veterans of the French and Indian Wars from Connecticut, made plans to move to the Lower Mississippi. Ten years passed after the first Treaty of Paris before any of them actually made the journey and became the first settlers of the Loosa Chitto.[14]

Impulses more fundamental than loyalty to a distant monarch motivated people like Matthew Phelps, one of the Adventurers who sought a new beginning in West Florida. Born in Harwington, Connecticut, Phelps was an orphan by the age of eight, left to the care "of one and of another of his relations, as his necessities required or as their humanity prompted." His father had provided him an estate consisting of a house as well as "a small capital of about one hundred and fifty pounds." At age twenty he married, whereupon he received "but a trifling matter of property, except a decent supply of furniture for his house." Soon after the wedding he sold his home and moved his family to Norfolk. There he opened a store, and "by application to his business maintained his family with tolerable decency for some time." As the size of his family grew, Phelps's business "gradually declined, and occasioned a degree of anxious solicitude about the prospects of future support for his wife and tender offspring." He had to do something, and after speaking with several people who were preparing to move to the Mississippi, "he had but little doubt of its being advantageous to him to remove thither." He undertook a preliminary visit to West Florida before transporting his wife and children. Conflict with Britain, however, interfered with Phelps's plans. "I ultimately determined to give up the design for the present, rather choosing to risk the loss of my property . . . than to expose the lives of a wife and rising family." Unable to provide an adequate living, Phelps had to act, whatever the risks. He decided again to move, this time to Vermont. After journeying as far as Westfield, Massachusetts, he abruptly changed his mind and took his family to Mississippi. As they journeyed up river Mrs. Phelps and her newborn baby contracted a fever and died. A few days later Phelps's boat capsized in a whirlpool, and his two young boys drowned. He arrived at his new home alone.[15]

Matthew Phelps sought only to provide for his family, refusing to allow even the Revolution to interfere with his prime objective. His effort led him to Mississippi, but it did not seem to matter to him where he went so long as he left the older colonies of Connecticut and Massachusetts, so long as he went somewhere. Were it not for a spring thaw that made travel through the Green Mountains difficult he might just as well have gone to Vermont. Peter Chester, West Florida's governor, understood people like Matthew Phelps. Their desire "to better their circumstances," he wrote, created "the natural disposition for emigration that prevails in all the old colonies." Chester urged his king to take advantage of that disposition for emigration to release social tension in the older colonies and to populate the new colony along the Gulf of Mexico.[16]

The families that left eastern farms and seaports took little with them. They arrived in the Mississippi Valley sometimes with even less. The fate of the Phelps family represents an extreme case of the risks involved. Those more fortunate kept their lives, if little else. Aware of their condition, Chester appealed to his superiors for permission to give the newcomers aid. "When they first arrive on the Mississippi, they are with their wives and children destitute of almost every thing, and without a little assistance from hence of powder, shot, salt and corn, which it will be unavoidable to give them, they will be driven to the greatest distress during the winter." Chester received permission to hand out provisions at the colony's expense to the families that needed them most.[17]

Upon arrival in British West Florida, family heads and single individuals started the long and involved process of acquiring a freehold. Most applied for a family right—100 acres for the family head, plus 50 acres for each remaining family member, including slaves. Technically, the British Crown granted land for free. Officials, nevertheless, charged large and often prohibitive sums for their indispensable services in expediting initial petitions, surveying tracts, drawing plats, and filing claims. Thaddeus Lyman, one of the leaders of the Military Adventurers, paid a fee of 3000 acres to the men who helped him secure his father's grant near the Big Black River.[18] Moreover, their duties put government office-holders and their associates in a good position to discover and purchase prime land, leaving poorer quality acreage to homesteaders unable or unwilling to pay the speculators' prices. Indeed, the British governor of West Florida worried that large, empty tracts tied up in the hands of speculators, and distinctly avoided by newcomers who sought titles of their own, effectively removed much of the best land from develop-ment.[19] On the whole, however, speculation did little to affect the process of settlement along the Mississippi.[20] There was simply too much good vacant land available by grant of family right, or if one could not afford the fees, by squatting. When Phineus Lyman, the leader of the Military Adventurers, received 20,000 acres in one tract along the Bayou Pierre, just below the Loosa Chitto, he knew of a hundred New England families prepared to settle it. For years after his death in 1774, however, the land sat mostly empty, his followers scattered around its edges on grants of their own.

Acquiring title to land during the Spanish period proved somewhat easier. Spain recognized claims held under the British and continued to give away land on a family right basis. Spanish officials were more eager than their British counterparts had been to populate the colony, and they hastened the process of filing claims and registering titles to all who swore an oath to His Most Catholic Majesty.

The first white families to settle in the region that became Warren County claimed acreage covering a fairly flat stretch of high ground along the Loosa Chitto, near a place the Choctaw called "nanachehaw," about twenty-five miles from the river's mouth on the Mississippi (Fig-ure 1.2). They all came from the Atlantic colonies, although from no sin-gle colony or region in particular. Their backgrounds and family status were as varied as their places of origin. Clustered together on a concen-tration of good farm land, along a winding river that sooner or later snaked by almost everyone's door, the Loosa Chitto community, like the last link in a great long chain, sat at the farthest reaches of Britain's crumbling North American empire.

Following the river through the community in 1778, beginning about fifteen miles upstream from the Mississippi, where high ground first ap-proached the Big Black from the left, a traveler headed upriver would have come first upon the home of Benjamin Day, a hatmaker and wool merchant from Massachusetts. Day lived with his wife, ten children, and three slaves. The improvements of Jeremiah Routh, "a very poor man, and scarcely able to maintain his numerous family," lay a few turns of the river upstream on the right, adjoining Oliver Lyman's settlement. Just beyond Routh and Lyman lived Henry Dwight, another New Englander, and his two slaves. Past a long stretch of cypress swamp, the river turned

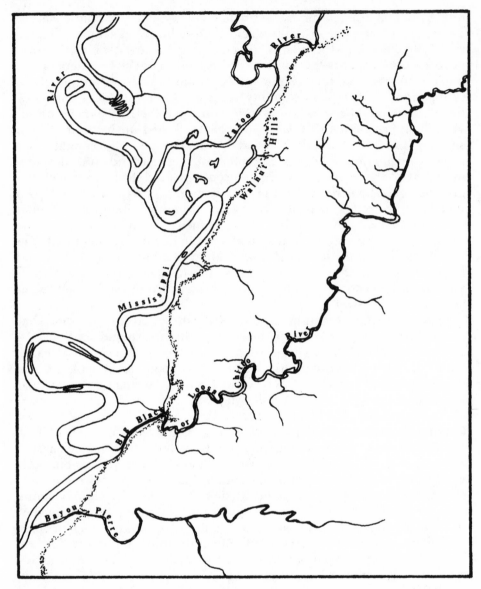

Figure 1.2 Mississippi River from the Yazoo River to the Loosa Chitto River.

sharply northward when it again struck high ground. George Grant owned 2000 acres here, but he never showed up to take possession, so Patrick Doyle, late of South Carolina, "pitched" himself upon it. A cluster of families lived on the ridge where it reappeared on the left: Abraham Knapp, Ithamar Andrews, and Benjamin Barber all worked small plots by themselves. John Stowers, and his son of the same name, were the first into the area. They hailed from Virginia. Behind the Stowers New

Englander John Felt, his wife and child, and Thaddeus Lyman, owner of seven slaves, worked their improvements. Continuing upstream, a traveler would have found the next homestead on the left, at a place called Nanchets, and which belonged to yet another Lyman, named Thompson. The Lyman sisters, Experience and Eleanor, lived through the woods on the right, fronting the river on the other side of a peninsula. The small fields worked by Hezekiah Rue and Abijah Leonard—the latter journeyed from Massachusetts with the Days—lay nearby. Benjamin James owned the place upriver from Thompson Lyman, and just past him Matthew Phelps farmed on the hundred acres he had received for himself plus the other 250 acres he had received for his wife and children, who never lived to see their new home.[21]

Near what must have seemed like the edge of the world, these pioneers of the Loosa Chitto lived in single-family households. They survived by raising a few hogs, planting small fields with corn and vegetables. Hunting, trapping, and felling timber provided supplementary income, perhaps in cash. Indoors, at night, they made clothes, bullets, and whatever else they needed and could make themselves. Isolation made interdependence a necessity; neighbors exchanged the fruits of their labors and reciprocated favors and kind treatment. Perhaps this was not the life that some of them had bargained for when they left their homes in the Atlantic colonies, and yet it had its advantages. Land was plentiful and fertile, and with luck and not too much work, once they felled some trees and planted the ground, farmers prospered. Even the precariousness of life had a way of bringing out the best in people, reflecting, as Matthew Phelps put it, "honor on the human character."[22] Of course, isolation was never complete. Although community members worked out their own systems for exchanging local produce and property as well as for maintaining order, formal and supra-local structures existed too. Trade networks brought the material comforts of the center to even the farthest peripheries of the European world. Similarly, remote settlements like the one on the Loosa Chitto did not escape the touch of government and national as well as international politics.

On average, the two dozen or so households contained five or six persons, mostly members of a nuclear family, although at least five households included a slave. Seven blacks, probably the largest holding, belonged to Thaddeus Lyman. Household size ranged from one to fifteen residents. Over the next twenty years families came and went, but the size of the settlement and the make-up of its households stayed constant, with the exception that the largest slaveholding approached ten blacks. Nevertheless, by the mid-1790s, few family heads owned any slaves at all.[23]

There was no church. Nor were there public buildings. Official business, the registering of deeds, wills, and the filing of small suits for debt, meant a journey to Natchez or Pensacola, although Thaddeus Lyman, and later Tobius Brashears, as justices of the peace, expedited some business for their neighbors.[24] Nelly Price operated the nearest store, fifteen overland miles away at Grand Gulf, where the Big Black emptied into the Mississippi.[25] Residents lived in and around a few small dwellings that lent an appearance of impermanence to the wilderness clearings. In petitions and surveys people almost always described the location of their homes by giving the distance from the Mississippi, the one landmark everyone recognized. Often they mentioned the name of an adjacent neighbor, but the only other reference points were, like the Mississippi, natural, or at least they predated the entry into the area of these inhabitants. Several residents, for example, gave the position of their land relative to the "nanachehaw hills." A few mentioned the "Nanchets improvements," which may have been fields left by the Natchez. Sense of place, that is, some notion of where in the world one lived, was closely tied to nature, and understandably so. At this early stage of development the signs of human existence were few and fragile; nature must have seemed ageless and everlasting. This is not to suggest that the land was untouched. Quite the contrary: the influence of Europeans in North America long preceded the arrival of the first permanent settlers on the Loosa Chitto. Diseases had thinned the Native American population. Europe's thirst for leather had depleted the deer population. But the most visible signs of human activity—buildings, fields, roads— did not exist. In short, the Loosa Chitto families needed only to glance about them to be reminded that they lived on the very edge of the European world.

The nearest place of similar size to the Loosa Chitto community lay almost a half-day's hike to the south, along the Bayou Pierre. Sixty miles further stood the village of Natchez, with its "ten log houses and two frame houses" bordering recently surveyed and still mostly vacant streets.[26] To the north for hundreds of miles lay nothing but a small Spanish post on the Arkansas River, scattered villages of Native Americans, and the few white or half-breed traders who lived among them.

Immediately upon arrival, settlers began to make their mark on the wilderness by turning loose their hogs to forage among the trees and by preparing small plots to plant with corn. Nearly every household brought with them, or very shortly acquired, a cow to produce milk and butter and an ox to pull a plough. Horses, useful primarily for transportation, were something of a luxury, although most households eventually acquired at least one. But the essential ingredients to successful homesteading lay in the combination of hogs and corn. Swine thrived among the hardwood trees, living off acorns and roots. They provided a ready food source with virtually no exertion of energy on the part of the farmer. Corn provided a meal for bread, and any remaining surplus fattened hogs nicely before slaughter.[27] Supplemented by wild game, vegetables, especially pumpkins and squashes, and perhaps some fruit— peach trees grew particularly well—households obtained a subsistence quickly, and on small parcels of land.[28] John Calhoon and his family of three managed, in their first year, to plant some peach stones and clear half an acre for cultivation, enough, apparently, to see them through a winter. William Selkrig cleared and fenced three acres and erected a house, all in one year. By the next year he had time to supplement his income by overseeing a neighbor's place. In 1773, John Stowers arrived on the Big Black penniless, his worldly possessions consisting of a gun and an axe. Four years later, Stowers, "on the unremitting industry of himself and son . . . had gained a desirable competency, and was now enabled to live comfortably." Among his possessions he counted a house, some cows, a couple of steers, a store of hogs, and an assortment of farming utensils. Matthew Phelps also arrived penniless, near death from fever, and heartbroken at the loss of his wife and children. As partial compensation, however, he quickly learned that making a living in the Lower Mississippi Valley could in fact be as easy as he had, in an initial rush of enthusiasm, dreamed. Borrowing some livestock and tools from Stowers, he set to work planting "crops." By the year's end Phelps marketed enough "pork, and such other produce as I could conveniently spare," to repay his neighbor.[29]

The apparent ease with which homesteaders raised a sufficiency of corn and hogs provided them with time for other endeavors, such as felling timber for sale in New Orleans, or experimenting with unfamiliar but marketable crops such as cotton and tobacco. Another important consequence of undemanding agriculture, however, was that it left farmers free not only to produce a surplus for market but to make the long treks necessary just to get there. Indeed, the most serious risks to life and produce occurred after the harvest, as the farmer set out in a pirogue down a swirling and snag-infested river, or on foot over a rugged path wishfully called a road. In this context, subsistence agriculture did not necessarily dissuade farmers from producing for market; instead, it was a necessary precondition. With essential foodstuffs secured, the risks of commercial activity became more acceptable, and the offerings of the marketplace—sugar, coffee, clothes—became more desirable. At no time were the Loosa Chitto households commercially isolated.

Nevertheless, in the Lower Mississippi Valley commercialization advanced slowly beyond a primitive stage of development, though not for any lack of will on the part of the region's inhabitants. The barriers separating Mississippi farmers from markets were natural and political, not mental or conceptual. While a British possession, West Florida exported few agricultural products. Planters below Natchez grew indigo with some success. Tobacco grew well in the district around Natchez, but partly because of distance from world markets, and partly because of a shortage of labor, it became a viable staple only after the Revolution interrupted the tobacco trade between the Chesapeake and Europe. By the late 1770s, Natchez planters grew tobacco for sale in New Orleans and England. After Spain took control of West Florida, granting the colony a tobacco monopoly within its empire, the weed became the mainstay of the Natchez district economy until replaced by cotton in the 1790s.

Farmers along the Loosa Chitto, however, throughout most of the colonial period, concentrated on raising a subsistence of corn and pork, rather than on raising commodities for distant markets not easily accessed. Still, they depended on being able to sell small surpluses of grain and meat to local buyers in order to purchase items such as gunpowder and salt, but these markets were never fully developed. Initially, demand for food crops in West Florida was virtually nonexistent. Nearby farms easily supplied residents of the few small towns in the colony. Even New Orleans, the largest single market, obtained all it needed in nearby Spanish Louisiana. Moreover, as a Spanish possession, the Crescent City's trade fell victim to the whims of officials who periodically slapped large duties on imports. In April 1777, Spanish governor Galvez closed New Orleans entirely to British trade. Although in practice trade regulations proved difficult to enforce, nevertheless, their presence only added to the unpredictability of the market.[30]

The export economy of West Florida consisted mostly of the fur trade and the shipment of timber to the West Indies. Although the commercial viability of both was subject to the uncertainties of international trade relations, they served homesteaders as readily available marketable products. Several Big Black settlers, immediately upon arrival, selected a good spot for a sawmill, with the intention of selling lumber to the Spanish.[31] There is no record to indicate that the mill was ever built, but they may well have floated rafts of logs downriver for cutting in New Orleans, a practice common in other settlements. During the 1770s William Dunbar, a prominent Natchez landholder, earned much of his income by felling timber and producing barrel staves for sale to the British and the Spanish.[32] By 1790, or shortly thereafter, Daniel Burnet had a sawmill operating on his land on Bayou Pierre, a few miles from the Big Black.[33]

To small farmers faced with a limited market for foodstuffs, the fur trade presented a valuable opportunity to exchange for items not produced by the household. John Watkins's estate inventory, the only one remaining from the 1770s, lists two traps. Inventories from the 1790s, when demand for agricultural products was greater, indicate that by that time residents were occupied primarily with farming. Nevertheless, the skin trade, if not actual hunting and trapping, provided households, especially during winter months, with an important source of income. Benjamin Day, for example, earned some extra cash by tanning skins for some of his neighbors. Jacques Rapalje, who operated as a middleman between Choctaw hunters and Indian trader John Turnbull, became so involved in the business of exchanging hides that he compiled an extensive Choctaw dictionary in his account book. In the spring of 1794 he paid off his account at Turnbull's store with the usual corn, pork, beef, and peas. In addition, however, and accounting for more than half the total value of the trade, Rapalje presented his creditor with 79 deer skins, 10 otter skins, and 4 bear hides. He made another payment soon after with more of the same, plus raccoon, wild cat, and fox pelts. Furs also served as a medium of exchange, useful in a cash-scarce economy. Skins of different kinds and qualities were valued in terms of "hides," apparently a leather container of gunpowder. Thus, for example, a Choctaw hunter purchased from a Big Black farmer 4 kegs of rum, 2 blankets, 2 flaps [*sic*], and 6 empty kegs, worth a total of 76 hides; while another paid his debt with 4 bear skins, valued at 2 hides.[34]

On the whole, however, Rapalje and the other farmers on the Big Black depended for their livelihood on tilling the soil and selling or bartering its fruits. Loosa Chitto husbandmen had little to sell but corn and pork. Surpluses of these they took to Eleanor Price's store at Grand Gulf and later to the trading post John Turnbull operated—with the permission of the Spanish—at Fort Nogales on the Walnut Hills. Price's store was only fifteen miles down the Big Black River. Nogales was a little farther, requiring at least a long day's hike, and it took longer if one were driving livestock. But the nearest alternatives lay at great distances to the south. Price and Turnbull conducted most of their business with Choctaw hunters, exchanging rum and gunpowder for hides. Indeed, Turnbull's connections with the Choctaw were quite extensive, having lived among them as a trader for a number of years, during which he fathered at least two children.[35] Price, a free black woman, had come to the Natchez district presumably from one of the English Atlantic colonies, perhaps as an escaped slave. She first opened a store at Grand Gulf in partnership with John Fitzgerald, a prosperous merchant at Manchac, but after he withdrew his support when the two had a falling out she took on one Miguel Lopez as a partner and managed to maintain her business. Like Turnbull, she lived primarily off of the skin trade. Nevertheless, both provided a service for local farmers, exchanging tools, implements, and various other "sundries" for agricultural products, which they shipped downriver, or sold to Native Americans and traders heading north into the wilderness.[36]

Jacques Rapalje, who lived on the Loosa Chitto from 1789 to his death eight years later, found nearly all he needed, from blankets and brass kettles to cloth and coffee, at Turnbull's Walnut Hills trading post. Turnbull shipped in his supplies from Baton Rouge, where he kept a plantation, and New Orleans, thus saving Rapalje the effort of traveling to more distant markets, which he rarely did.[37] Other merchants provided a similar service. Ebenezer Dayton, a Natchez butcher and tanner, kept a pen and slaughterhouse at the Walnut Hills, where he collected cattle from local husbandmen, slaughtered them, and shipped the carcasses to his shop downriver for further processing and sale.[38] Merchants like Turnbull, Price, and Dayton, when they brought the market into a remote area, contributed to the physical isolation of local farmers like Rapalje, who no longer had much need to take their business to distant places. Along the Loosa Chitto local trade predominated.

Jacques and Isaac Rapalje's account book indicates two parallel networks of local exchange. First, an apparently friendly, noncommercial circle involving near residents helped neighbors endure temporary

shortages. With five families in the vicinity, the Rapaljes lent and borrowed small quantities of food and material. "Lent Hardy Perry 4 quarts
Salt 1 pint Sugar," reads one entry, which is marked "returned," the last
notation added, presumably, at a later date. Another: "Lent Mrs. Stowers
2 cups of sugar 2 cups in honey," also marked "returned."[39] The Rapaljes
were less likely to record instances when they borrowed, presumably
leaving that task to the lender. One entry suggests that they did in fact
participate as receivers in this local exchange system. One of the Rapaljes borrowed 17 ounces of thread from Mrs. MacChristy, and later returned it to her.[40] Some loans they marked "paid," perhaps indicating a
cash payment, although the entry might have denoted payment in kind
other than an exact return of the items borrowed. Early in November
1793, William Bassett borrowed coffee and sugar. A month later he
asked for and received a little more of each, plus a yard and a quarter of
cloth. Shortly thereafter he "paid" his debt, and then proceeded to borrow more: "1 bowl of coffee 2 ditto of sugar." Bassett accepted loans five
times over the next two months, all in small amounts, periodically paying what he owed with cash or kind.[41]

Although the Rapaljes carefully recorded the amount of each item
they lent, indicating an awareness of self-interest, the objective of these
transactions was not monetary profit. The account book shows no cash
values for merchandise lent or borrowed. Moreover, only a handful of
families, all from the immediate vicinity, participated in this network at
all, and only two regularly. Finally, the items exchanged, always measured in small quantities—a cup of sugar, a few ounces of thread—allowed individuals within the neighborhood to minimize trips to distant
trading posts. Convenience, not cash, was the premium. In a context of
relative market isolation, reciprocal exchanges of a few items in small
quantities served individual self-interests.

Most of the entries in the account book are more business-like, less
personal in tone. They indicate a second network of exchange relations,
although not one that extended any farther geographically, infrequent
trips to distant markets notwithstanding. Except for the occasional deals
with passers-by, this network, like the first, involved only a handful of
people from the Loosa Chitto area. The variety of items exchanged, however, was much greater, as were the quantities. And although the Rapaljes appear to have traded for kind as often as for cash, nevertheless, for
all the transactions in this network they carefully recorded a monetary
figure. Furthermore, whenever they purchased goods they had the seller
sign a receipt proving payment. For example, John Estes signed when he
received in Spanish currency $124.5.00 "in full for a Plow Shear & cot-
ten Corn Some Hogs and for Sundry Tubs Fowls etc."[42]

Only a few entries in the account book give a date. Calculating the
difference between the price paid and received for a given item in a
given year is thus impossible. On the whole, however, the Rapaljes seem
to have bought cheap and sold dear, relatively speaking. For example,

over the eight-year period spanned by the account book, they marked up the price of sugar and coffee an average of six cents per pound over what they paid for them. Limited information on prices requires that this point be made cautiously. In addition, commodity values fluctuated very little within the community, suggesting limited response to local supply and demand, although this, too, may reflect source limitations.[43] Nevertheless, the commercial exchange network differed qualitatively from the borrowing and lending circle; participants in each did not overlap. The Rapaljes lent to some and sold to others, perhaps because the interests served by each type of exchange did not always correspond. Concern for profit could injure friendships, while unlimited consideration for friends was bad for business. Only their relationship with John Stowers, the Rapaljes' nearest neighbor, and probably their closest friend, was secure enough to withstand possible tensions between exchange for profit and for use. He alone participated in both circles. Furthermore, women participated regularly as borrowers but rarely appeared as buyers, suggesting a division of labor that extended from the household into local exchange networks. Although men and women both worked in the home, the income-producing activities of housewives ceased at the doorstep, while those of their husbands extended to the outside world. Women were not, however, shut up in their houses but engaged actively in local exchange of a more social nature.[44]

The two local networks of distribution, one social, the other economic—although such a distinction may not be appropriate since each contained elements of both—arose simultaneously from the Loosa Chitto community's uncertain relationship with the outside world. The former represented, on one hand, a cooperative effort to assist individual households to cope with their remoteness from the market. By distributing small quantities of select commodities available locally it reduced the inconvenience of temporary shortages and the frequency of trips to a distant market. The latter, on the other hand, by its very existence demonstrated that isolation from markets was never absolute but only a matter of degree. Moreover, no amount of communal cooperation could shield households from price fluctuations and fraudulent merchants, against which the best security was accurate bookkeeping, the close tallying of credits and debits, the signing and filing of receipts.

Scholars are divided over the meaning of local exchange. Economic historians hold up commercial networks as the inevitable and rational result of market penetration rooted in the innate and timeless concern of even the most isolated American farmers for profit. Some social historians apply a more sentimental interpretation to past civilizations and champion social networks as heroic barriers built by traditional-minded people against the disruptive and even oppressive forces of modernization, declension, commercialism, and capitalism. Pre-modern and pre-capitalist rural people, they suggest, participated in the market cautiously, and only as a last-ditch effort to preserve their cherished traditional patterns of exchange. Both interpretations are drawn from preconceived notions about the way eighteenth-century Americans thought.[45]

A close study of commercial patterns suggests a more persuasive interpretation. Neither communalism nor individual pursuit of profit were ends in themselves. Rather, they were *means* to ends. Loosa Chitto households cooperated by borrowing and lending because the nearest store was an arduous two day's hike away. They were responding not to traditional values but to geography. Similarly, farmers ventured into the marketplace because they could not produce at home all they required or wanted. But the market was a risky place. Bookkeeping—the careful calculation of monetary costs and benefits—arose, like the cooperative network, because it provided some security in the face of conditions otherwise beyond one's control. In short, both networks reflected first and foremost local conditions and the community's relation to the outside world, not a particular attitude toward the market.

Two parallel systems of authority, one signifying the community's place within a larger political and economic entity, the other underscoring its remoteness from seats of power and trade, also evolved within the Loosa Chitto settlement. Relationships between neighbors, within the community, were face-to-face, personal. Reputation mattered. There was a certain sense of honor in Jeremiah Routh's poetic appeal for leniency from creditors—"He can prove by his neighbors that although poor he has always maintained a large family of children by the sweet [sic] of his brow and paid his debts until now."[46] But as the very existence of court records demonstrates, outside authorities played an important role in mediating relations even in so remote a place as the Big Black. In 1774 the planters around Natchez petitioned the Governor's Council to set up a court to handle the collection of debts. The economy was growing, albeit slowly, as the center of trade in the colony shifted from the Pensacola-Mobile region to the little town on the Mississippi River.[47] Within a regional trade system that brought strangers together into creditor-debtor relationships, personal reputation carried little weight. Authority, therefore, had to be formalized. Both systems, however, operated simultaneously.

While the need to formalize relationships may have been less pressing within the Loosa Chitto community than elsewhere in the colony, once the court began to meet at Natchez it offered some advantages over the informal arrangements worked out between neighbors in the court's absence. For example, the court was better equipped to handle cases in which debtors absconded, disappearing beyond the pale of local, informal authority.[48] More important, the formal authority of the courts mediated relations that extended beyond the community and the pale of local structures that rested on personal honor. For example, a reputation as a hard worker who always paid debts stood one in good stead with neighbors, with people whom one knew personally. Distant, unknown associates felt more comfortable with the security provided by the court. Moreoever, personal reputation was not everything. Even the most honorable and well-intentioned man, like Jeremiah Routh, could easily lose control over his affairs simply because life was very unpredictable. Routh's honesty did not protect his farm from pillaging by Choctaw warriors. The predictability of the court, however, gave his creditors added security. It also allowed them to depersonalize what otherwise was a very personal matter; to collect compensation without holding Routh responsible for something—the attack on his farm—that was beyond his control. The greatest problem with personal reputation as a basis for authority was that people tended to become very touchy. Attacks on their integrity or motives were received, and answered, personally. But lodging a suit and letting a judge decide the matter placed some distance between confronting parties. Creditors did not challenge a debtor's honor as directly as they would have if they knocked on his door and demanded payment. Similarly, debtors came away from lawsuits with their self-esteem intact, confident that a judgment had been executed against them by an unknown officer of a distant court who could not have based his decision on reputation, and who therefore could not be understood as having attacked that reputation. The court, in short, did not replace local systems of face-to-face authority. Quite the contrary, it helped them to continue.[49]

A similar relationship existed between outside formal and local informal rights to property. When Matthew Phelps first appeared on the Big Black, he secured a tract of land that suited him, "by paying to a resident fifty dollars to relinquish his possession in my favor which *by the custom of the country* ensured a title to me." He then returned to New England to collect his family. Phelps arrived two and a half years later to find "that the title to my land had, according to *the usuage [sic] of the country*, reverted to another, and strangers had become, rightfully as it respected them, possessed of the property on the soil which once vested in me."[50] Phelps had purchased title from a squatter, which, according to custom, made the land his. But, again according to custom, in his long absence he lost his title. Squatters' rights, in which Phelps placed such confidence, evolved as the only viable way to establish and hold a claim. The land office was miles away in Pensacola, and legal title took time and money to process. The procedure of acquiring legal title, however, did not replace custom; it worked with it. So long as the formal process remained slow and expensive, custom continued to serve a useful function, and so long as custom remained insecure, landowners sought legal title, as Phelps eventually did. In some cases, families had to market at least one crop to raise the fees necessary when applying for a family right. Unable to "pay the expenses of taking up a piece of land," Jeremiah Routh squatted, acquiring legal title only after Anthony Hutchins, a prosperous Natchez landowner and speculator, offered to pay the costs in return for half of Routh's entitlement.[51]

The resemblance between the pioneers' system of squatters' rights and the Native American tradition of usufruct rights was not coincidental. Both property systems appeared in face-to-face societies established in the wilderness. People unfamiliar with pioneer communities found the attitudes toward private property of some whites no less puzzling than those of Native Americans. Elihu Hall Bay acquired upwards of 25,000 acres along the Mississippi while serving in the office of the governor of British West Florida. Later, as a South Carolina judge, he attempted to dispose of his speculations. Proving his title to land situated in territory held successively by England, Spain, the state of Georgia, and the Mississippi Territory presented him with legal difficulties made worse by the fiasco of the Yazoo Land Company. But Bay was a judge with faith in a legal system that would protect the property of anyone possessing bona fide deeds as he did. He discovered that the law had little authority in distant Mississippi pioneer settlements, where title fell to whoever settled the land, which if vacated became untitled once again. Squatters refused Bay's offers to sell them his land at a price he thought fair. Claiming that the South Carolinian had never settled upon it and had thus relinquished his title, the Mississippians purchased title from the county at a local sheriff's auction. Bay, "at a loss as to the Precise Grounds or authority under which this Sale (bare faced as it was) was made," instructed his attorneys to protest the subdivision and sale of his lands, "otherwise I shall be ruined by the Sh[eri]ffs of the different Counties." But at least one of Bay's lawyers understood what had happened: "Considering your age and distance from here and the difficulties of making a survey and of collecting the Evidence for a Successful Trial and the nature of your Claim I would recommend a Compromise on the Terms" the local authorities propose. Colonel Sessions, sheriff of Claiborne County, which included the territory that later became Warren County, "will not take any trouble about the Business, as his neighbors are to be affected by it." As to Bay's survey, his lawyer informed him "that you could not now find your beginning corner—it is possible they have all been destroyed—these are influential men—and I think all the others who interfere with your survey will follow their Example." Bay accepted the *fait accompli* and instructed his agent to accept whatever local authorities would offer.[52]

In one sense, then, two communities appeared on the Loosa Chitto. There was an interior community of interdependent households that concentrated on raising a subsistence of food, taking only small surpluses to local markets and purchasing items not available within the community, exchanging commodities locally so as to minimize each household's need to interact with the outside world—an interior community with its own ways of determining how one established a claim to a piece of land, who was worthy of a neighbor's assistance, of how things were done. At the same time there was an exterior community in constant interaction with the rest of the world, initially by virtue of having been settled by people from elsewhere, but henceforth by regular contact with world markets, as in the case of the fur trade, and as part of a larger political entity that imposed its authority if not always successfully from distant places. From the late eighteenth century through to the middle of the next, these two communities coexisted and developed symbiotically, although over time there occurred a distinct shift in emphasis from interior to exterior.

In the spring of 1778, recalled Matthew Phelps, "the distresses of the revolutionary war began to afflict our remote settlements, and on a sudden put a stop to the efforts of honest industry, and agricultural enterprise among us."[53] The British had since the beginning of conflict worried about holding their shaky West Florida outpost, and with good reason. Sparsely settled, poorly defended by only a few hundred troops, and adjoining the much more populous Spanish Louisiana, the colony seemed indefensible, especially if Spain were to join the fray alongside France. England hoped to keep the conflict a domestic affair. Spain concurred, reluctant to risk angering the British, whose trade had become vital to Spanish New World possessions. But the necessity of remaining neutral seemed more apparent from the vantage point of Madrid than it did from New Orleans, where Governor Bernardo de Galvez entertained American proposals for a Spanish-supported raid on British West Florida. Plans eventually materialized in the form of James Willing's expedition down the Mississippi. Looting and sacking plantations, then withdrawing below the Spanish line only to strike again, Willing brought the Revolution to the Mississippi.[54]

War and the Royal Navy's blockade of New Orleans brought trade to a standstill. Farmers had no way to market their produce. The flow of credit ceased as hard-pressed lenders called in loans even at the risk of ruining debtors. Making matters worse, Native Americans took advantage of the general disruption in authority to pillage homesteads near their territory. John Farquhar "was compelled to give up his property to his creditors on account of the failure of his crop." Claiming he "had done everything in his power to do justice to his creditors," Farquhar "sold his plantation and had much trouble to make a crop this year on the plantation on which he is now settled; he asks that his creditors wait until the end of the present crop when he will divide the whole" among them. Jeremiah Routh told his creditors how the "Indians have stolen every one of his horses and reduced him to giving his last cow to pay a debt to a certain Thomas Green, his hogs that were not taken by the Indians are running wild in the woods." At the time of "the very unhappy revolution," Choctaw warriors drove Justus King and his brother Caleb from their home. Settling closer to the fort at Natchez, the Kings managed to live off savings while their land sat abandoned for nearly ten years. Willing's raiders actually carried off William Selkrig, and in his absence Native Americans plundered his farm. He never returned to it.[55]

By the signing of the second Treaty of Paris in 1783, most of the Big Black families were gone. The Lymans, supporters of the British during the war, fled the Spanish, who by then controlled the district. For the time being Matthew Phelps gave up farming, enlisted with the British, and eventually returned to New England, settling in Vermont. There he remarried and started another family. Indians killed John Felt. Most of the remaining settlers moved closer to Natchez, near the protection of Fort Panmure. By the war's end following the Spanish seizure of the Natchez district in 1779, only John Stowers remained on the Big Black, although even he apparently kept another home thirty or so miles to the south at Fairchild's Creek. But the war's interruption proved brief. With peace, migration to West Florida started again, and newcomers arrived to replace those who had left. They brought hogs and a few cattle, took up planting corn on the same plots of cleared land, and lived in households of the same size. The Revolution changed only the names of the families that lived along the Loosa Chitto. It disrupted lives, but not life, within the community.[56]

2

ECONOMIC TRANSFORMATION AND THE RISE OF THE PLANTERS' WORLD

If the Revolution did not directly alter ways of life along the Loosa Chitto, geopolitical changes following American Independence most certainly did. In particular, a combination of circumstances shifted an economy that tended to be more community- and subsistence-oriented to one that tended to be more individualistic and commercial in bearing. This slow but discernible shift in economic emphasis transformed social relations and altered the very nature of the Loosa Chitto and surrounding communities.

The process began when the Spanish opened their markets in New Orleans and the Caribbean to West Florida farmers, officially for the first time. Meanwhile, they continued to restrict as much as possible the flow of goods into their territory from the United States, thus giving Natchez area producers an advantage over their counterparts in Ohio and Kentucky.[1] Most immediately, Spain, holding tenuously to the Natchez District, shored its defenses against the newly formed United States by constructing forts and stationing more soldiers in the area, with two effects. First, the Spanish governor of the Natchez District, Manuel Gayoso de Lemos, negotiated with the Choctaw for the right to build a fort high on the Walnut Hills overlooking the Mississippi River, thereby pushing the border between people of European descent and Native Americans permanently north of the Big Black River to the Yazoo River, opening more territory for settlement and placing the old boundary more safely within Spanish territory. Second, the presence of more soldiers and their supporters provided local husbandmen with additional consumers for their produce, especially livestock. The Spanish army's hunger for meat made beef a locally marketable product. Cattle herding, however, proved to be only the first small step in the rise of commercial agriculture, for it enabled farmers to purchase slaves and take advantage of even greater opportunities eventually presented by the cotton market. And cotton changed everything.

In 1790, Gayoso received permission from the Baron de Carondelet, governor of Louisiana, to commence building Fort Nogales. That year Gayoso hired thirty carpenters, most of them citizens of Natchez. Within a month they had cleared sixty acres, built five palisades with twelve cannons in place, nearly completed a warehouse for groceries and ammunitions, and started on a house for the commandant. By September of the next year, several buildings, including a bakery and butcher shop, stood on the bluff. Stone masons then took over from carpenters, as construction continued on the brick fortifications that eventually replaced the hastily erected wooden enclosures. In addition, Gayoso had his men clear "a communication road and fences, six leagues long, from Los Nogales to Black River." By January the completed fort housed sixty soldiers.[2]

The commandant and his troops lived off of local resources. His superior in New Orleans, promising to send only rice, suggested he contract for beef. Farmers from the area responded immediately to this new opportunity, driving cattle along the new road for sale at the fort, or to Ebenezer Dayton's slaughterhouse when it opened in the mid-1790s.[3] Soon, herds of wandering steers became a nuisance all over the Natchez District. In a proclamation issued in February 1793, Gayoso decreed the region's first stock laws, setting a minimum height for fences around planted fields, regulating slaughtering procedures, registering brands, requiring all herders to maintain a "public pasture" on their property with a strong stockade for the impounding of strays and the sorting of cattle belonging to different people. On the Big Black, Garret Rapalje and Tobias Brashears gathered their neighbors and erected such a pound. The governor established a scale of fines to enforce the new regulations. Although the presence of the Spanish military presented husbandmen with new opportunities, it also meant that relations within local communities were sometimes strained, particularly when cattle bound for market wandered into the gardens of more subsistence-oriented agriculturalists. Moreover, by reaching out of the locales to participate in a growing market, farm settlements invited the regulation of a government no longer so remote, and in whose interest it was to promote regional livestock trade over local exchange. In a pattern that would repeat itself over the next several generations, political organization fast followed economic expansion and development.[4]

Production for market had other consequences. Like never before, farmers found themselves caught in a growing web of indebtedness. Cash had always been short. Economic growth only worsened the situation. Debt encouraged further production for market, which only led to further indebtedness. This cycle, too, would be repeated. By February

1792, the number of court executions against debtors threatened commerce within the Natchez District. Gayoso responded by proclaiming the region's first, but not last, debtor relief laws, suspending all executions, although requiring that property be mortgaged to current creditors.[5] At the same time, the trickle, and then stream of agricultural products shipped down the Mississippi River by Ohio Valley farmers swelled to a flood, presenting Natchez District products with tough competition. An international border regulated by customs collection officers at Fort Nogales, and later at Loftus Bluff, restricted, but did not prevent, the development of a larger regional trade system, with local specialization based on competitive advantage.

For Lower Mississippi inhabitants, competition from Ohio and Kentucky nearly proved ruinous. The trade from the North ended the momentarily profitable tobacco business at Natchez, and cut into the local corn and pork market.[6] In short, as late as 1795 the chances seemed slim that agriculture and animal husbandry along the Loosa Chitto would ever develop much beyond what it had been twenty years earlier—production for local subsistence with small surpluses of a few items finding their way to market often enough to supply the community with items not produced in the home. Cattle herders best withstood competition from Ohio and Kentucky. While advantages in soil and climate gave Ohio Valley farmers an edge over their Lower Mississippi Valley counterparts, they suffered from their great distance from New Orleans. Ohio Valley meat survived the long journey to market without spoiling only when cured and packed in barrels. This presented Northern farmers with several problems, not the least of which was their lack of a natural source of salt for packing. Consumers, moreover, preferred fresh beef over the cured variety, a demand local producers in the Lower Mississippi were able to meet by walking steers to market and selling them on the hoof.[7] Consumer preference for fresh meat did not extend to pork, however, and Mississippi farmers faced direct competition from northern producers of bacon and ham.

The first commercial farmers, that is to say farmers who produced primarily though not exclusively for a market rather than for their own consumption, in the region extending from the Loosa Chitto to the Walnut Hills, then, were cattle herders who sold their steers to Spanish soldiers and bureaucrats at Nogales and Natchez. However, Loosa Chitto herders were not part of some ancient tradition that extended back in time and across the continent to the backcountry of the eastern states, or across the Atlantic to Celtic Scotland, as some historians have argued.[8] Livestock farming arose as a response both to local conditions and needs and to the locale's place within a regional and ultimately a world economic system. The first homesteaders along the Loosa Chitto initially raised hogs because they thrived with a minimum of attention in southern hardwood forests, and thus provided an abundant source of meat. A product easily raised in surplus, hogs became an early marketable commodity. A combination of developments outside the Natchez

District, however—the opening of New Orleans and the Caribbean trade to Natchez producers, growing tensions between Spain and the United States and the subsequent militarization of the Lower Mississippi, the opening of the Ohio Valley to American farmers, and finally the flood of Americans into the Lower Mississippi following Spain's evacuation—created a growing demand for beef that Loosa Chitto homesteaders were well situated to meet. Similar developments, both locally and beyond the immediate vicinity, eventually turned cattle herders into cotton planters.

Through the 1790s, as the pace of migration into the Mississippi Valley accelerated while the Spanish prepared to turn the Natchez District over to the United States, the market for beef expanded. By 1800 the wealthiest and most prominent families in the region tended herds of a hundred or more steers. While households continued to raise hogs for home consumption, as a marketable product they gave way to cattle. For example, in 1792 Tobius Brashears kept 140 hogs and 10 cattle. Ten years later he paid taxes on 100 cattle, and at his death a few years following his herd numbered 150 head, while his drove of hogs had shrunk to a mere 13 sows and pigs. Brashears responded to the combination of a growing demand for fresh beef and competition from northern producers of pork by taking up cattle herding.[9]

As a commercial enterprise raising livestock offered a special advantage to homesteaders in newly settled areas; herding required a minimum of labor.[10] On average, a single hand could tend approximately thirty cattle.[11] A father with two children of age ten or so could maintain a herd of nearly one hundred head and take twenty to market each year.[12] Open-range grazing on the huge expanses of still unsettled land, moreover, meant that farm size did not limit herd size. At five dollars a head, cattle herding could be very rewarding.[13]

Given the ease of tending cattle, it is thus surprising that the Loosa Chitto's cattlemen were the region's first slaveholders. Herders did not really need slave laborers. But raising cattle was profitable. Herders, better than anyone else, could afford slaves. Moreover, slaves were readily available in the eastern colonies and states from which settlers came, and at the slave markets to the south, at Natchez and New Orleans. But among the Loosa Chitto homesteaders slaves were more useful as extra hands in maintaining the family farm than as investments aimed at increasing farm income. This may be a fine distinction, but it is an important one. The primary objective of the household head, cattle herders included, was to ensure a comfortable living for his or her family. Like an ox or a plow or a hired hand, a slave sometimes proved useful to this end. Being an owner of slaves was not an end in itself; it was a means of guaranteeing the survival of the household enterprise. In time farming successfully without slave labor became more difficult; providing a comfortable life for one's family increasingly required owning slaves. Only when slaveownership and the task of maintaining an accustomed standard of living became associated did slaveownership then become an end in itself.

What pioneer farmers really needed, in other words, was the occasional assistance of an extra hand. The abundance of land lured away young whites who might otherwise have offered their services as wage laborers, and who instead only added to the demand for labor. In other regions of the country farmers solved this problem through cooperative labor exchanges—neighborhood barn raisings offer perhaps the most famous example—when several households pooled their labor resources to meet the needs of individual members of the group. This sort of activity occurred along the Loosa Chitto, to be sure, but Mississippi settlers because of their proximity to slave markets around New Orleans and the Caribbean had an alternative means of meeting their labor requirements not available to farmers farther north, although one should not forget that slaves worked some of the early farms in Illinois, too, for example. Slaves, therefore, were integrated into homesteading communities and adapted by farmers to suit the needs of their household and local economies.[14]

Black slaves entered the local neighborhood as the property of some white residents. Initially they were few in number. Once one or two white members of the community purchased slaves the urgency for others to do so lessened, for they could meet all their labor requirements by hiring their neighbor's slaves. And the first farmers to purchase slaves could rest assured that they were not going to add an extra burden to their households so long as they had neighbors who would take slaves off their hands when not needed. Once in the neighborhood slaves functioned in the local economy very much as wage laborers, except that their condition was permanent. They drifted from household to household working for cash or kind whenever their labor was needed. The owner's requirements came first, but masters could not keep their hands busy all or even most of the year, and when they had no use for them they turned them out to find work elsewhere, or to otherwise raise their own subsistence. Following the Haitian Revolution the Spanish governor of Louisiana worried that his colony's slave population was too idle. To remedy this problem he urged slaveowners "to assign Fields to their slaves, for their own cultivation, and to their use, which will not only put them more at their ease, but also increase the mass of the productions of the province, and advantageously employ the time they might otherwise spend in riots, and debauchery."[15] Thus, from the perspective of the whites, slaves were a communal resource they shared much as implements, draft animals, and their own labor. From the perspective of the slaves, the whole community, not one particular farm, formed the context of their existence.

Selections from Jacques Rapalje's notebook illustrate the pattern of slave hiring in the neighborhood of the Big Black before the cotton boom. Terms were short, usually a month but sometimes a day. Wages were calculated in dollars, although usually paid in kind. Hired slaves performed a variety of tasks, usually heavy labor, from field work to splitting rails. In April 1796, for example, Rapalje hired Dick, a slave who belonged to neighbor James Frazier, for ten dollars per month, which Rapalje paid in corn and seed cotton. At about the same time Rapalje agreed to pay "Negroes Isaac & Jack"—their owner is not named, and they apparently just showed up looking for work—pork and deer skins for "making 500 rails." "Mr. Perries Jack began to work here the 1 November"; he earned ten dollars a month, at least part of which Rapalje paid in cash. George received credit for two weeks of work. For a single day during the November harvest time, Rapalje hired seven slaves from a Mr. Vashera to finish hauling the corn crop. In 1802 Isaac Rapalje "Hired of Stephen Gibson one Nigro Wench and 3 Children at five Dollars per Month began the first of June to work till the first of November."[16] Payments in kind indicate that hired slaves worked only for their own subsistence, and not for their owners' profit. During lulls in the agricultural cycle, when masters had nothing for their hands to do, and no wish to feed and board them for doing nothing, slaves sought their keep elsewhere.[17]

The proximity of slave labor markets to a pioneer economy in which homesteaders quickly accumulated capital combined to put a Southern stamp on the gradual change in emphasis from subsistence to staple agriculture in the Mississippi Valley. Backcountry homesteaders generated capital in a variety of ways: improving land; selling timber; hunting and trading furs and skins; supplementing diets with game and food sources gathered in the forest, which left them with a larger marketable surplus of corn; making tools and furniture; and constructing buildings. The process tended to follow a series of steps, with the capital raised in one applied to the next. For example, families often squatted on land, and hunted and gathered and raised a first crop sufficient to pay the costs of acquiring title. Once the land was theirs, they could continue to improve it, enhancing its value, and either sell or use it as collateral with creditors, who provided farmers with tools and hardware. Providing a neighbor with a little work, or perhaps the use of some tools, might bring a sow in return, which would forage in the woods, mix with local stock and multiply. Small sales of pork and bacon further added to family coffers. Before long the family could claim among the community herd that grazed in the swamps near the river a cow or two, which would provide them with oxen to pull a plough and, eventually, with a small herd of their own. Income earned by raising cattle could be used to purchase a slave.[18]

Slaves thus preceded cotton into the Loosa Chitto by nearly a quarter of a century. African and African-American slave labor, however, was only one more among many productive resources used by white pioneer farmers in their struggle against the wilderness, the conditions of which shaped this evolving society, including patterns of free and slave labor, just as it shaped pioneer societies elsewhere. But once the cotton market presented new opportunities, those farmers who owned slaves were well positioned to take advantage of those opportunities. And the farmers most likely to own slaves were those who possessed the largest cattle herds.

In 1795, a man named John Barclay introduced into the Natchez District a cotton gin. Local landholders immediately contracted mechanics to construct similar machines.[19] By the end of the decade, if not sooner, Benjamin Steele and Anthony Glass operated a gin, apparently the area's first, on the Loosa Chitto just below the Rapalje settlement.[20] Each year cotton farms appeared a little farther up the Mississippi River from the Big Black. By 1806 a settlement of "about twenty New England families" reportedly raised "great quantities of cotton, and [made] some portion of it into thread."[21] Another year and the plant reached the Walnut Hills, as "flowering, verdant, and lofty trees" gave way to fields of cotton and corn, "whose rows are so varied in direction by the numerous hillocks and gullies on the side of the hills, as to give great beauty and variety to the whole, which, in the spring season look like one extensive garden."[22] By 1835, the region along the Mississippi between the Big Black and Yazoo rivers—Warren County—produced annually between 25,000 and 30,000 bales of cotton. The 1840 census reported a total in excess of 32,000 bales, the second highest county total in the state of Mississippi.[23]

Prior to the appearance of the cotton gin in the Mississippi Valley, Loosa Chitto farmers if they grew any at all limited their cultivation of the crop to one or two hundred pounds—after the seeds had been extracted—an amount requiring less than an acre of land. The labor required to remove seeds by hand made short-staple cotton cultivation in larger amounts unfeasible. John Hutchins, who lived near Natchez, recalled how the women of his neighborhood used every spare moment to prepare cotton for spinning. When they went to visit a neighbor they "would fill their aprons with cotton to amuse themselves with on the road by picking out the seed."[24] Eli Whitney's invention dramatically changed this scenario, raising the limit of production to the picking, rather than seed-extracting, capacity of available hands and thereby permitting small farmers to respond positively to the high price of cotton. By replacing corn with cotton, Loosa Chitto households could have easily doubled the market value of the crop they produced on a per-acre basis.[25] Not everyone took up its cultivation, however. Indeed, while some households immediately began to grow and market the new crop, others showed a marked lack of interest in it. The transition to cotton cultivation, the gradual shift away from simple homesteading toward staple agriculture, cannot be explained simply as the consequence of the invention of the ginning machine, a response to high prices, or access to the cotton market, necessary as those developments were.

On the one hand, there was little reason for pioneer farmers along the Lower Mississippi River to plant cotton. The ease with which they met most of their subsistence needs may have worked to keep production for market to a minimum. In one day a single family practicing slash-and-burn agriculture could deaden several acres of forest sufficient for planting a first crop. By removing rings of bark they killed trees quickly and then burned away underbrush, leaving a layer of ash for fertilizer. Although the trunks of large trees remained standing, rotting away over the next year or two, plenty of sunlight reached the fresh and weed-free soil below.[26] During the initial settlement period when uncleared land was in abundance only the shortage of mills for making meal limited the surplus production of corn.[27] The family head could tend to at least six or seven acres of corn and peas, a garden of pumpkins and squashes, a small orchard, a drove of hogs, and a herd of thirty cattle.[28] The initial high productivity of new land diminished after one or two sessions, but when yields declined backcountry farmers simply slashed and burned a few more acres of forest and planted anew. In this manner they provided plenty of food for their families and had enough corn remaining to fatten nicely the several hogs which, along with five or six cattle, they marketed every year. Livestock alone could bring an annual income of a hundred dollars for supplies and manufactures, no small sum in a time when cloth enough to outfit his whole family could be had for only ten dollars, a pound of shot plus another of powder for sixty cents, two hatchets for a dollar, a brass kettle for almost half that price, and sugar and coffee for fifty cents per pound.[29] Upon the physical maturing of a son and his assumption of a full work load the household could have doubled its agricultural output, but since subsistence was already secured, this increase was all surplus. In short, homesteaders met subsistence requirements with relative ease, provided, of course, natural disasters and sickness, both beyond their control, did not intervene.[30]

On the other hand, the more valuable the crop grown for the national and international market the greater the rewards in the form of consumer goods not produced locally.[31] True, cotton planting may have entailed certain risks that would have seemed particularly unnecessary in light of the ease with which most subsistence needs could be met.[32] Families that relied on the market for their livelihood, rather than on food raised in their own fields, risked their land and property, their very survival, on the chance that the market would bring an income sufficient to purchase food they could have raised at home. This was a gamble that few small farmers with little personal property to sell in the event of a drop in cotton prices chose to take. Instead, they devoted labor and land to raising enough food to guarantee that their families could eat and only then applied what resources remained to the cultivation of a staple crop.

Individuals not familiar with cotton agriculture faced the additional risks brought by their own inexperience. Although most had probably grown a little cotton for home use prior to even their considering growing it for sale, the problems of one novice may not have been isolated. The first season Richard Harrision "ever attempted making a crop of cotton," he delayed picking until too late in the fall, "after the leaves and snow had fallen and mixed with it." Once baled, the already damaged crop then sat "on an open boat where it lay several days exposed to excessive rains." Needless to say, Harrison's "first essay was not sent to the market as prime cotton," and was condemned by inspectors.[33] However, so long as one did not borrow against a crop, and continued to cultivate subsistence requirements, then lack of experience did not really present serious problems to the farmer who experimented with new crops.[34]

The notion of risk, as agricultural historians use the term, is not really appropriate for pioneer communities. It explains better a context in which cotton and corn competed for the same land, where farmers by planting cotton necessarily reduced the amount of land available for their subsistence crop of corn.[35] In a recently and sparsely settled area landowners did not face this dilemma. Risk, therefore, cannot account for the reluctance of some Loosa Chitto homesteaders to plant cotton. They had the extra time, energy, and resources beyond those necessary for maintaining subsistence levels to devote to cotton production. By further diversifying their crop selection cotton could actually have reduced the risk of catastrophe by providing the household with the means to purchase grain if torrential rains destroyed the corn while it was sprouting, or if an early frost ruined it before it had milked, the latter, admittedly, an uncommon event in Mississippi. And cotton more than corn brought the benefits of the market into the farm household in the form of consumer goods, those necessary for production as well as luxuries.

Two questions arise: If cotton promised the rewards of participation in an international market without the risks that often went with planting a staple crop, why did Mississippi Valley farmers with access to a gin and press not take up its cultivation with great gusto, especially during the years before 1820 when cotton prices were so high? Conversely, if most subsistence needs could be met so easily, why did anyone bother planting cotton at all? Pioneer farmers, it would seem, were pulled in opposite directions. However, the lure of the market and the security of subsistence production were not necessarily contradictory. Some homesteaders took up cotton planting precisely because they could integrate it into their local subsistence economy and lifestyle. Farmers with a herd of a hundred or so cattle who either had slaves or could afford to buy some were able to plant cotton with minimal financial costs or risks to their household subsistence. As important, they could plant cotton for market without disrupting their time and work rhythms, without sacrificing the more qualitative advantages of life on a small farm.

In sparsely settled regions cotton and corn did not compete for land, contend for the farmer's energy, or contest for attention during the crucial moments of planting and harvesting. The seasonal cycles of the two crops differed. Cotton, planted in the very early spring, or even late winter, required little attention until picking time in September and October, while the long Southern growing season meant that corn planting could be left until later in the spring, and then harvested in the late fall or early winter.[36] A single, healthy farmer could have planted five or six acres of cotton in addition to and without risking the corn that provided his household's subsistence. Moreover, the energy of each additional laborer would have enabled the production of that much more cotton. A family of six, with a father and son working in the fields, could have worked the six acres of corn necessary to feed the household, plus an additional ten acres of cotton.[37] A family of eight, with three adult men, could have cultivated twenty acres of cotton without reducing their food crops. The logic of formal economics suggests that families with available land, and with their subsistence levels of food production secure, should have responded to growing market opportunities for cotton according to the number of hands available to work in the fields. Yet, formal economics to the contrary, this is not what such families did. Regardless of household size or the number of family members available to work in fields farmers did not plant cotton unless they owned slaves.[38]

Nonslaveholding households could have planted cotton for the market and still have provided most of their own subsistence needs, but not without reducing their nonagricultural activities, particularly their leisure or nonproductive time. Economic historians rarely weigh the costs in time and energy of extra work against the benefits of staple production. More often they assume the maximization of all resources, including labor. Yet, a household head, to maximize, or even just increase, cotton output without reducing subsistence levels of corn would also have to increase, perhaps even double, the total amount of time given to work in the fields.[39]

The relationship between work and cotton cultivation can be expressed by the model illustrated in Figure 2.1. A nonslaveholding household head who tends without help from family members acreage enough to maintain a subsistence in corn works at a level represented by point C. If, in addition, he plants as much land in cotton as he possibly can his total work load rises to point A. With each additional field hand in the household, such as mature sons, the total amount of work per hand required to maximize cotton output declines along the line A-B. But the total amount of work required to maintain nothing more than a subsistence also declines with additional hands, along the line C-D. The two lines, therefore, represent levels of maximum and minimum agricultural work. Presumably, actual work levels of Mississippi farmers fell somewhere between the two.

The reluctance of nonslaveholders to work harder and plant more cotton when the cotton gin and the market provided them with the opportunity to do so suggests that there was a limit to the amount of agricultural work they were willing to do. We may define that acceptable level of work at point C, that required by a subsistence farmer feeding a

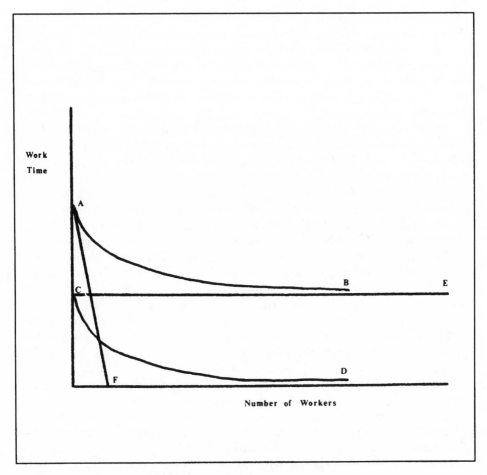

Figure 2.1 Relationship between work and cotton planting.

wife and two or three children. That was the level of work that young household heads voluntarily accepted when they took up homesteading. They might work less, perhaps when sons matured and contributed their labor to the household enterprise, but they would not work more. Of course, if a father were willing to continue to work as hard as he always had then as his children matured a larger proportion of time and energy could have been expended on cotton cultivation without raising total work levels per household member above point C. The area between lines C-E and C-D, therefore, represents the work per hand that could be devoted to cotton without raising work levels above the acceptable level. Note that as the number of workers increases, the level of work necessary to maximize cotton output approaches the acceptable level of work. A nonslaveholding family with fifteen or more hands could nearly maxi-

mize cotton output without working more than that required by a subsistence farmer working at level C. In reality, of course, few if any nonslaveholding households were so large. A more likely family of eight,
including a father and three mature sons, could have produced some
cotton without working above the acceptable level. They would have to
have been willing, however, to increase their work loads substantially to
maximize cotton output.

In short, while nonslaveholding families conceivably could produce
small amounts of cotton, though evidence indicates few in fact did, additional work loads served as a strong disincentive against the maximization of cotton production. An individual's inclination to minimize agricultural labor would have become even stronger with age and the
deterioration of health. Fathers, for example, might have chosen to cut
back on their work loads as sons came of age, rather than take advantage
of additional family labor to increase the household's cotton production.

For slaveholders the scenario was entirely different. Slaves did not
choose their own acceptable level of work, but could be forced to maximize as nearly as possible their labor output. For slaveholders, the work
required by the master in order to maximize cotton output drops
quickly, along line A-F, so that even one or two slaves would allow the
maximization of cotton output without requiring any additional labor
input by the slaveowner. At point F the master does not have to work in
the fields at all, except perhaps as overseer.

The model has other implications. For example, the relationship between a father who wished to maximize household cotton output and
his sons who enjoyed their leisure would have been strained. Of course,
this was precisely the tension, only on a larger scale, that arose when
slaveholders forced hands to maximize their labor output. The acceptable level of work for slaves, who enjoyed none of the benefits of work
beyond the bare subsistence level, if that, would have been well below
that of whites on nonslaveholding farms.[40] Therefore, the success of individual masters to a large extent hinged on their ability to develop effective incentives, whether negative or positive, that encouraged their
hands to work.

Available resources, market accessibility, prices, and degree of risk
all account for only a small amount of the variation in cotton production. The best single predictor of cotton output was size of slaveholding.
Because its agricultural cycle did not interfere with the corn cycle, cotton demanded an increase in the amount of labor per person if output
were to be increased. To masters cotton offered a means to keep their
slaves busy for most of the year. To nonslaveholders cotton only meant
more agricultural work after the corn crop was tended, and less time
spent fishing, hunting, making clothes, mending fences, constructing
out-buildings, visiting, or simply loafing.

Thus, pioneer homesteaders took up commercial staple agriculture
in earnest when they were satisfied that two conditions could be met:

First, they had to be able to afford the initial costs of cotton planting and marketing. In particular, this meant they had to afford the expense of a gin and press. Of course, this cost was not born individually but was spread between neighbors, either directly when they invested in implements as partners, or indirectly when they paid for access to privately owned machines. Nevertheless, capital for initial costs had to be raised somehow. Second, assuming they had access to a local gin and press farmers still had to be assured that they could continue to live in the manner to which they were accustomed, that cotton would not be detrimental to their lifestyle. Cotton planting promised additional income to increase one's standard of living, or at the very least secure it at its present level. Thus its appeal. No farmer, however, was willing to place their means of livelihood at the mercy of the cotton market. They would look after their own subsistence needs first, plant cotton second.

Cattle herders, because they owned slaves or could afford to buy some, were in the best position to satisfy both requirements. They could raise the initial capital required to plant cotton and ship it to market. Slave labor allowed them to continue to provide their subsistence needs in corn while also raising cotton but without disrupting work rhythms. But nonslaveholders, if they were to plant cotton without reducing their subsistence levels of corn, had to spend more time digging in the dirt. Compensation for their extra effort would have come from the items they could have purchased with the cash acquired from the sale of a bale or two of cotton. However, this was a tradeoff that few nonslaveholding households made, especially when presented with other marketable alternatives to cotton, principally hogs and cattle, that sufficed to provide them with the few necessary items they could not produce themselves, and even such luxuries as coffee.

The growth in demand for fresh beef, and the concurrent rise in competition from Ohio Valley grain and pork producers, made cattle herding the easiest way to raise the most capital. Cattle, thriving with a minimum of attention in the cane breaks and grassy marshes of the Mississippi Valley, became, in effect, a profitable "cash crop" that underwrote the costs of slave labor, thereby opening the door to cotton agriculture. But it was the nature of the pioneer economy, based on extensive use of natural resources, slash-and-burn agriculture, and cooperation between neighbors, that allowed families who arrived with little more than a gun, an axe, some corn and pumpkin seed, and the clothes on their backs, to become prosperous farmers, herders, and eventually even cotton planters. The backcountry economy did not contradict, restrict, impede, or conflict with the spread of staples agriculture. Given the right conditions it led directly and even smoothly to it.

Historians have understood the antebellum Southern economy in one of two ways. The first view holds that the South was essentially a capitalist society of profit-maximizing, cost-minimizing slaveholders and poorer farmers on the make. This view builds on an old interpretation of American history as essentially the loosening of environmental bonds and the playing out of the original settlers' dream of material prosperity and huge profits.[41] According to a second view, Southerners were not capitalists at all, or at least large portions of the population were not primarily profit-motivated, but instead strived to maintain a more traditional social order sometimes even at a financial cost.[42]

There is little point merely in identifying the capitalist and pre-capitalist traits of Southern, or for that matter Northern, society. Both were present though in unequal and changing proportions from the seventeenth into the twentieth century. Moreover, regional economies and societies more or less capitalistic were not necessarily at odds. Thus to describe capitalism and markets as having penetrated or invaded isolated Western and Southern communities is naive. Capitalism emerged as much within as outside the American countryside. The crucial questions, therefore, should concern the transitional process itself—how it occurred, how it affected the people who lived through it, and how in turn those people shaped the process.[43] Only in retrospect does the gradual transition from subsistence to staple agriculture seem abrupt or revolutionary. Yet, initially, cotton planting offered one among several means of preserving the small-farm lifestyle. Thus there was no immediate clash between opposing ways of life, even if over the long term fundamental changes in behavior and attitudes did occur. The commercialization of the Mississippi countryside was characterized by a meshing of two economies as one more local and subsistence in bearing articulated with another more market- and profit-oriented. For the moment, at least, both coexisted and were indistinguishable.

The ambitions and expectations of the Loosa Chitto farmers helped shape the gradual transition toward production for market, although the strength of their influence existed within a changing material context. For example, homesteaders did not have to work long hours for days on end just to meet their subsistence needs. Periods of nonagricultural activity regularly broke the routine of field work. Thus some farmers may have resisted cotton because it extended the planting season, lengthened the harvest, and disrupted familiar patterns and expectations—unless slaves were available to do that extra work.[44] Of course, once under way the growth of slavery and the transition to cotton agriculture entailed the decline of the pioneer economy, forcing people to plant cotton regardless of their predilections. Conversely, some farmers perhaps harbored ambitions that lay dormant, stifled by pioneer conditions, but which became manifest as the economy developed and as new opportunities presented themselves.

Few people probably aspired to more than Phineus Lyman, the first Loosa Chitto landowner who in 1770 foresaw a new colony with its capital on the Big Black where he would preside as governor, and with a grand public college to teach, among other things, the secrets of agriculture to the children of Native Americans, French, and English.[45] The expectations of others were more modest. One man, frustrated after years of struggling on a farm in New York, took his wife to Mississippi, where he thought the two of them could live more easily and comfortably by running a mill.[46] Matthew Phelps later recalled that when he first saw the Big Black the place seemed full of promise for one whose only desire was to provide a comfortable living for himself and family. "The soil appeared to me to be remarkably good, the situation of the place delightful, the ease of transportation of produce to market very apparent, and the probability of New Orleans forever forming a mart of trade, sufficient for the country around, scarce admitted of a doubt in my mind." The "superior prospect of soon becoming possessed of a desirable competence," he continued, put to rest any lingering doubts about the "reputed unhealthiness of the climate."[47]

Initially, however, expectations of migrants to the Mississippi Valley did not matter much, except in selecting or influencing very generally who came and who stayed, and even in this instance the only criterium seemed to be a vague notion that the place of destination offered more—a feeling that apparently motivated people from everywhere, from all walks of life. But the wilderness proved a great equalizer. Whether one owned 20,000 acres, like Phineus Lyman, or 200, like John Stowers, whether one was a prosperous Massachusetts merchant like Benjamin Day, or a struggling Connecticut storekeeper like Matthew Phelps, on the Loosa Chitto all lived as simple homesteaders, planting corn on small plots, herding hogs, driving cattle, raising families in crude dwellings, trading mostly with neighbors, accumulating a minimum of comforts. The story of the Rapalje family illustrates the point.

In 1774, Garret Rapalje, a prosperous New York merchant with connections in the colonial government of British West Florida, sent his son Jacques to Pensacola to request a grant of land. The Rapaljes received 25,000 acres, which they settled with New Yorkers and a shipload of slaves brought from Guinea. The proceeds from the division and sale of the grant went toward the purchase of a working plantation near Baton Rouge, on which the elder Rapalje and his several sons intended to settle themselves as landed gentlemen. Shortly after their arrival on the Mississippi, Garret and his son Jacques returned to New York to collect remaining family members. The Revolutionary War intervened, however. Unable to receive permission to leave New York, Garret entrusted the Baton Rouge plantation to a younger son who had remained behind. Thirteen years later Garret and Jacques returned to the Mississippi, only to find their property greatly reduced by sales for debt, and the younger Rapalje unwilling to relinquish title to his elders. Undaunted, and still well connected, Jacques and Isaac, another brother, received grants from the Spanish government, totaling 1600 acres along the Big Black, where they eventually settled, while their father took up residence

nearby on an abandoned farm on the Walnut Hills. The brothers managed better than their father, who built a small house and planted potatoes until, exasperated, he returned to New York to die. Yet prosperity
still proved elusive. Over his remaining few years Jacques scraped a tiny
section of his 900-acre tract, and then died, bankrupt and in debt, leaving Isaac to continue their dream. As late as 1805, the heir to the Rapalje
family's thirty-year endeavor to build a landed estate lived in a small
cabin with the slave and the free black who worked beside him in his
small field.[48]

Clearly, material realities on the peripheries of Euro-American civilization could dash the dreams of even the most resolute individuals. Aspirations could not have been inconsequential, however, although the
historical record only hints at what they were. Isaac Rapalje was probably an ambitious man. And if he was, though he lived in a small cabin in
the wilderness, he may not have considered his family's search for
wealth and status to have ended in failure. Quite the reverse. Evidence
indicates that he perceived himself to have, in some sense, arrived as a
landed gentleman even as he planted corn and herded cattle like any dirt
farmer. Thus he referred to himself as Don Rapalje, and later by the title
of Captain. He also gave a name to his home—Nanachehaw—a Choctaw
word that lent a ring of timeless permanence to his recent and fragile existence. To be sure, if he had a dream of acquiring the status of a landed
gentleman he must have tailored it drastically to conform to reality. Survival demanded as much. But when opportunity presented itself—to
plant cotton for profits greater than he had ever experienced, to become
a master who no longer toiled in the hot Mississippi sun but who instead
lorded over his chattels like a true landed gentleman—he was ready to
seize it without a moment's hesitation.

When Jacques Rapalje died his many creditors saw to it that appraisers made an accurate inventory of his estate. They did not find much:
some farming utensils, household furniture, a large spinning wheel, two
muskets, three pairs of breeches. They also noted the crop, in storage
and in the ground: 25 acres of corn, a few more of potatoes, and "about
twelve hundred pounds of Cotton of the last Crop in the seed." By 1835
George Rapalje, Jacques's nephew and Isaac's son, was one of Warren
County's wealthiest and most influential cotton planters.[49]

No one who lived along the Loosa Chitto and the Walnut Hills at the
end of the eighteenth century could have been oblivious to the ways and
means of life elsewhere. All had come from the Eastern states, and some
from Europe. They knew how people lived in New York City, in western
Connecticut, along the Carolina coast, and in the Virginia backcountry.
Much closer to home were Natchez, Baton Rouge, and New Orleans,
where visiting Loosa Chitto farmers could not have escaped noting that
there was more to life than a log cabin, corn, and cattle. As members of,
and witnesses to, a mesh of regional, national, and ethnic cultures they

carried in their heads a variety of lifestyles. Their experiences and ideas suggested who or what they might become, and perhaps even how they thought of themselves; the realities of life in the Mississippi Valley in the world of the late eighteenth century dictated what could be, and sometimes what must be. For the people of the Loosa Chitto, like Don Rapalje, lord and master of all the cattle and corn he and his two black laborers could tend, life was an inseparable blend of the real and the imagined.

Mississippi Valley herders, at least those who could afford the expense, took up slaveholding and cotton planting perhaps because they understood they had little to lose and much to gain. They would have seen exactly how much they stood to gain every time they journeyed downriver to the land of the Louisiana sugar planter, or east to the Carolina coast. They saw what could be theirs every time they walked into a store stocked with silver cups, looking glasses, fine imported clothing. And who in 1800 had ever suffered by planting a little cotton? Future generations would know better.[50]

Of course, nonslaveholding subsistence farmers knew about consumer goods. They, too, lived within a Euro-American cultural context characterized in part by the things people owned. Yet different people apparently had different wants and different levels of satisfaction. Nonslaveholders perhaps thought about exerting themselves to plant cotton but then quickly decided there was little they wanted that they did not already have. Slaveholders or cattle herders who could afford to buy a slave or two thought about planting cotton and decided there was plenty more they wanted. Both groups already had enough to maintain themselves comfortably: food, a place to live, clothes, tools, tobacco, coffee, and rum. Yet nonslaveholders tended to be satisfied while slaveholders wanted more. The different capacity of each group to want more, however, followed their different capacities to get more for less.

In time even nonslaveholders began to plant cotton, although not necessarily because they had somehow become enamored with the market or consumer goods. They may well have expected to spend all their years raising little more than a subsistence, a "desirable competence," as Matthew Phelps put it, and they might have been content to do so if it had turned out that that was all they could do. But the life of a subsistence farmer became more difficult with each passing year. As wildlife vanished and with it the skin trade, as farm products flooded into the Lower Mississippi from the Ohio Valley, cattle, and then cotton, a plant so well suited for Southwestern soil and climate, and viable once the seeds could be removed from its sticky fibers with relative ease, appeared more attractive to small farmers desiring only to continue the standard of life to which they had long been accustomed. In other words, not everyone who farmed cotton took to its production with an eye to replacing a

life of simple homesteading with one of gentlemanly leisure and opu-
lence. Even the simple life demanded that one produce something marketable, if only to purchase the items that kept life simple.

Just as the wilderness had forced gentlemen to live like simple farmers, changes in the material conditions that supported the pioneer
economy encouraged simple farmers to plant cotton. Some, perhaps
because they were sons of Eastern planters of merchants, doubtless
turned to cotton production because they were predisposed to do so.
They had grown up in a commercial world. Moreover, if commercial
aspirations had already gotten them into debt, as they had Jacques Rapalje, then they had all the more reason to raise a crop that promised
them much needed cash or credit. But even small, mostly subsistence
farmers increasingly looked to cotton, just as they had earlier to animal
skins and furs, as a marketable commodity that provided the means of
acquiring necessities and consumer goods not produced on the farm.
In planting cotton, however, they need not have been striving to get
rich, but only striving to maintain a standard of living, a standard that
had rested on extensive exploitation of natural resources, which, as
they diminished, had to be replaced. But the intensification of production that cotton represented required greater planning, more hard
labor. An increase in work also represented a negative change in the
standard of living, which the husbandmen of the Loosa Chitto fended
off by purchasing or, as the number of slaveholders grew, by renting
slaves.[51]

By 1800 the wildlife had disappeared from the forests near the Loosa
Chitto and the Walnut Hills. Choctaw hunters, who lived by trading
skins for rum, were leaving the area and roaming the territory on the
west side of the Mississippi River, but apparently with little success. The
Spanish Commissioner to the Choctaws and Chickasaws reported that
the Indians "are in a most wretched condition this year," and that they
would journey to the annual gift-giving ceremonies with the Spanish in
great numbers. This year, not just the braves, but "even the old women
went to get the presents," for "they are dying of hunger."[52]

Thus, as the deer vanished, so too did the Choctaw and Chickasaw,
although not so quietly. The decade of the 1790s was marked by war-
fare, as starving Indians raided farms and, in particular, the cattle herds
that wandered among the trees and grasses near the river's edge. White
settlers responded by building block houses and organizing militias,
both for protection and vengeance, and in the end they won out. But
theirs was not a military victory. The fate of the Indians was sealed with
the shooting of the first deer for trade, an act so harmless on its own,
and apparently so sensible because it cost that hunter nothing, and
brought him abundant material rewards from European merchants.
Begun as purely an addition to the subsistence economy of the Native
Americans, the skin trade cut into that subsistence as the game dimin-

ished. Soon they traded not for luxuries, but for food. And when the deer disappeared and they had nothing left to trade, they starved. At the mercy of a government and economy controlled by whites, they tried to take up agriculture, even cotton planting, but ended up trading away their land. In 1837, with sorrowful resignation, they walked the long trail to Oklahoma.[53]

As quickly as the Indians vacated the region around the Loosa Chitto and the Walnut Hills, whites moved in, at first replacing wildlife with hogs and cattle, then replacing even the trees with fields of cotton. Like the Indians before them, the first settlers lived off the resources of the forest. As natural resources diminished, they turned more to commercial agriculture. In a pattern similar to the one that ended the Choctaw's way of life, the planting of staples for market brought to an end the pioneer economy and society. The decline of the skin trade increased the importance of livestock as a source of food and as a marketable commodity. Most important, cattle herding enabled farmers to purchase a slave or two and take up cotton planting. Cotton raised their standard of living. It gave them access to metropolitan culture. But as more people planted cotton, the cattle ranges shrunk, a problem that accelerated as people flooded into the Mississippi Valley. Once a luxury planted after a subsistence in meat and corn was secured, cotton became an integral and indispensable source of household income, replacing the large herds of cattle. For households with several slaves already, this presented no problem, for they planted more and more cotton. Farmers with few or no slaves, however, missed an opportunity of ever becoming wealthy cotton planters, once open-range cattle herding became impossible. They still planted cotton; everyone did. But income from cotton no longer went toward luxuries. It purchased food and other essentials. And as the forests receded, as rains eroded the naked soil, as year after year of planting depleted the ground of its life-giving potential, households struggled even more to maintain their standard of living. As a result, they planted ever more cotton, which only accelerated the process.[54]

Within the space of a generation, two or three decades, the pioneer homesteads along the Loosa Chitto and the Walnut Hills were replaced by cotton farms and plantations of various sizes. With this transformation came corresponding changes in the character of relations between the people. Reliance on the market drew families out of their neighborhoods and away from each other. It altered the responsibilities of men and women for production within the home, and thereby rearranged relations between husbands and wives. As slaveholders continued to prosper, their associations with less prosperous neighbors were modified. And as cotton planting became a way of life, instead of a secondary occupation, the existence of the slaves, the people who raised the all-important crop, was transformed too. Material transformation provided context for the evolution of Southern society; more than that, it was its source.

3

RELATIONS WITHIN HOUSEHOLDS: WHITE FAMILIES

In 1820 Isaac Rapalje was over fifty years old. We can imagine the old farmer sitting on his horse, surveying his fields and reflecting on the past quarter-century since his arrival just before the Spaniards' departure. Changes in the land around him must have been striking. Cotton fields had replaced much of the forest and pasture. The fields themselves were much larger than the corn plots cultivated in earlier days. Between the rows once worked mostly by white families moved gangs of black slaves. Not that there were fewer whites than there used to be. There were plenty of newcomers, and plenty more arriving every year. Some brought slaves in great numbers, cut down trees, and destroyed the forest where in earlier days the old farmer had let his hogs and cattle wander. But it was not only the newcomers who had changed the land, Rapalje would have mused. He and other pioneers now owned lots of slaves and planted cotton, too. The old days were gone. Life was different now.

Warren County changed dramatically over the short space of a lifetime, or at least on the surface so it would seem, to the historian as well as to the contemporary observer. Population grew rapidly from some 200 people at the beginning of the century to over 7000 by the end of the third decade. Once situated at the end of the world, the county was only an easy steamboat ride from New Orleans. The wares of merchants, once practically out of reach, filled the shops that lined the street of the county's two towns. Less perceptible, however, to historians, and perhaps to early nineteenth-century Mississippians too, were the often subtle and profound changes that occurred in relations between people, changes connected to more obvious material transformations. This chapter examines relations within rural households, in particular between husbands and wives.

In December 1836, Methodist preacher Randal Gibson died. His funeral, held at Asbury Chapel near the Gibson home in Warren County, presented friend and fellow preacher the Reverend William Winans with an occasion to reflect on Gibson's life, which he held up as a model to the community. Winans began, of course, with a few words of scripture. Acts 11:24: "He was a good man." The preacher then proceeded to offer a definition of Christian manhood, using Gibson as his example. As a slaveholder Gibson had strived to fulfill his obligations to his servants: "To supply their wants, to soothe their sorrows, to render as light the burden of their condition as circumstances would permit." In return he expected hard work and obedience. Similarly, as a father he had shown nothing but tender affections toward his children, had provided for their education and for their future by bestowing them with a "respectable" competency. In return he demanded and received nothing less than "absolute dominion" over them. As a husband Gibson gave his wife love, tenderness, and friendship. She in turn "manifested such entire deference, without any thing approaching to servility," yet she "seemed to live for and to live in her husband's countenance." Members of the audience surely nodded in agreement, for Winans spoke words they wanted to hear, wanted to believe. The reciprocal order he held up as an ideal—masters, husbands and fathers who loved, protected, and provided for dependents, who responded with absolute obedience—largely reflected the reality of life within their households. This was 1836. A generation or two earlier and such words would have made little sense to many of the people of this same community.[1]

In Warren County population growth and eventual transition to staple agriculture enlarged households, changed their racial composition, and altered relations between its members. In the early pioneer homes women provided essential labor and skills, contributing to the productive capacity of the household. However, changes in the ratio between men and women, as well as the increasing availability of purchased goods, altered relations between husbands and wives by tilting the balance of power toward the man. Slavery also enhanced the master's power over all other household members, white and black. Moreover, with larger slaveholdings came an increase in the social distance between slaveowners and servants. Overall, households, both slaveholding and nonslaveholding, evolved from relatively simple egalitarian social units organized mainly for production to more complex patriarchal arrangements that also functioned to preserve and transmit property and status. Paternalistic notions of family, gender, and slavery, such as those expressed by the Reverend Winans, followed material and social change.

Northern households during the century after the Revolution are better understood than those in the South, although many questions remain unanswered for both regions. The combined work of recent historians, particularly of those whose focus has been on women, points to significant regional differences. In pre-Revolutionary America, North and South, households functioned as the basic unit of production and reproduction. Men and women worked at home, and both made vital contributions to the production process that enabled the household to survive. Gradual commercialization of the countryside and the advent of factory production in the years after the Revolution, however, altered this arrangement in certain regions of the North, along the seaboard in particular, removing manufacturing from home to factory, creating separate spheres of responsibilities for men and women.[2] The South, historical literature tells us, did not experience the economic transformation that swept the Northeast. Thus domestic arrangements remained unaltered. Southern households continued to produce much of what they needed and wanted. More significant, men worked at home, where they supervised production by family members and slaves. Differences between slaveholding and nonslaveholding households were minimal compared with the differences between a dynamic, modernizing North and a static, traditional South.[3]

The comparison of South with North can easily be overworked. More useful contrasts might be made between West and East, or city and countryside. Petersburg, Virginia, seems "Northern" in many respects while Sangamon County, Illinois, was quite "Southern." To the extent that the Southwest was rural and much of it newly settled, while the Northeast was older and more urban, contrasting the two regions is of some use. Moreover, that the South did not change as quickly or in the same manner as the North does not mean the South did not change. Domestic economies and gender relations evolved not as regional types but rather as part of a common process that unfolded at varying rates within all sections of the country. Differences between North and South, East and West, rural and urban, reflected differences in stages of development along a continuum with perhaps New York City at one end and the most isolated communities in the West at the other.[4]

In Warren County early settlers formed households consisting of what I will call "stem" families—male and female with or without children, and male or female with children. They formed families quickly, too. Single persons comprised 60 percent of all households in 1792 but just 12 percent by 1810. Rapid family formation was typical of Western settlement north and south.[5] Over time, however, household living arrangements became more complex. The percentage of homes inhabited by a white stem family reached 60 percent in 1810, but declined thereafter, accounting for 42 percent in 1850. The percentage of whites who lived in stem family homes also declined over time. Meanwhile, the more complexly organized nonstem households steadily increased, from 20 percent in 1792 to 49 percent in 1850. By 1850 households often contained several families plus non-kin. As they became more complex, living arrangements in Warren County began to take on more of the characteristics of households in older parts of the South.[6]

The first settlers in the Warren County area usually arrived alone or in stem family groups. The presence of single men created the lopsided sex ratio typical of newly settled areas. In 1800 adult men outnumbered adult women by a ratio of three to two.[7] Nevertheless, single men soon married, a majority of them within four years and a third of them before two years passed, taking brides several years younger than themselves.[8] Both the predominance of stem family households and the haste with which people married attest to the importance of marriage and family to homesteading.[9]

Women were in great demand. In a letter he wrote to a single lady in New York, perhaps a widowed sister—the author's relationship to the addressee is not indicated—Jacques Rapalje tried to persuade his correspondent to come to Mississippi: "I can assure you that wrinkles or a small stoop in the shoulders nay even grey hairs are no objection to the making new conquest here if you will transplant yourself a few months in the Clime[.] a woman till five and thirty [is] only looked upon as a raw girl[.] this is a paradise for you." For young farmers a wife was an essential partner and laborer. James Smith claimed his marriage to Sarah Phips "was a marriage of love," and it might well have been. But when business affairs took him from home Sarah took his place in the fields, and she probably worked beside him during the crucial planting and harvest weeks. Another woman worked on her husband's farm in New York for a number of years before they moved to the Bayou Pierre, where they hacked a farm out of a cane brake and tried to build a mill. The husband, a poor farmer with little business sense, struggled constantly, but failed finally after his wife abandoned him. He barely made ends meet when they lived together; the farm and mill stood no chance of succeeding after she left.[10]

Women, however, did not spend all of their time in the fields. They tended hogs and chickens, prepared food, and manufactured items for use in the home—stitching clothes, molding candles, churning butter— and thus enabled the household to achieve a greater degree of self-sufficiency, which in turn reduced the burden of the men. John Hutchins remembered how his father worked the fields and bought and sold flour, but that the family was clothed in homespun "made by our mothers and sisters from the spinning wheel and loom."[11] Single men had little choice but to raise a crop primarily for the market because they needed to purchase what a wife could have made at home. Married men had more options. Although they produced for a market, too, they were not compelled to do so, at least not to the same extent. Marriage, in short, made good sense, at least from the perspective of the man. A skillful housewife reduced the stakes riding on his crop. Domestic production—the labor of women—thus encouraged market development by freeing men to engage in commercial agriculture at their own pace, at their own choosing, based on their judgments of what the market did or did not have to offer.[12]

Evidence of home manufacturing can be found in the earliest surviving estate inventories: lists of looms, spinning wheels, and cards provide

TABLE 3–1. Number and Percent of Probate Inventories with Selected Items, by Households with and Without Spinning and Weaving Equipment

	With		Without	
	Number	Percent	Number	Percent
Slaves	12	67	9	75
Cotton (over 500 lbs., clean)	4	22	1	8
Corn (over 100 bu.)	5	28	1	8
Cattle (10 or more head)	11	61	6	50
Smoothing irons	9	50	1	8
Looking glasses	10	56	3	25
Clocks and watches	3	17	0	0
Silverware	2	11	0	0
Notes in hand	5	28	1	8
Number of inventories	18		12	
Average total value	$3905		$3210	

Source: Warren County Orphans' Court, Minutes Book A, 1818-1824, OCHM. Seven inventories given in the minutes book were excluded from analysis, as they clearly did not belong to a farm or even a working household. One, for example, contained mostly law books.

the best indicators. But these households were not isolated or subsistence enterprises (Table 3–1). A majority raised herds of cattle for market and owned slaves. These were households poised to take advantage of the cotton market when its opportunities materialized. Some were doing so already. Women continued to spin and weave even as their husbands sold more agricultural produce and purchased more tools and luxuries. In 1810, in the midst of a local cotton boom, Warren County households continued to produce a sufficiency, or close to it, in cotton cloth. A decade later, women from some of the wealthiest cotton planting families still spun and wove. Of the 30 farm households inventoried between 1818 and 1824, some 18 contained thread- or cloth-making equipment. Moreover, the total value of these inventories was greater on average than that of the remaining inventories by over 20 percent. Appraisers listed spinning wheels and homespun along with such luxuries as sugar dishes, cream pitchers, cups and saucers, silver watches, and silver spoons. Five inventories also mentioned notes of hand—promissory notes—drawn on neighbors as well as merchants, further indication of the commercial nature of farming.[13]

Occasionally women on small farms produced specifically for a market. For example, during the brief period when Warren County farmers began planting cotton, but before merchants set up shop and opened their doors for business, there seems to have flourished a local trade in cloth. About fifteen or twenty families clustered on the banks of the Mississippi River at a place they named Palmyra raised "great quantities of cotton" and made "some portion of it into thread, which they manufacture into cotton cloth, and sell for a dollar per yard." At the same time they continued to cultivate "such provisions as are necessary for their own consumption."[14]

On the whole, however, housewives worked to maintain the self-sufficient farm household, or at least a household as nearly self-sufficient as possible, so that husbands could respond to the market with more freedom. In other words, within the home production for use articulated with production for exchange. In a sense marriage bound more than two people. It provided a basis for a union of two economies, each identifiable according to how the products were used, as objects for immediate consumption versus commodities for sale, and each clearly divided by gender. But as a strategy for farming, for providing household members with basic needs, as well as with consumer goods and a few luxuries, the two were indistinguishable.[15]

The economic patterns of men and women, discernible if not separate, extended outside the household in the form of the local networks of exchange discussed in Chapter 1. As the primary producers of items for use, women traded goods for use, not profit—a cup of sugar lent to one neighbor, a sack of coffee borrowed from another, with never a mention of monetary value. Men, who took much of what they produced to market, participated in a different circle of exchanges, giving a value to everything, and expecting at least a small profit. But the exchange patterns of men and women were mutually supportive, and, like their respective roles in the production process, together formed a domestic economy organized to reproduce, or improve, the material circumstances of the household.[16]

Relations within the domestic sphere encouraged large families with lots of children. A young population seeking to make a living by independent means, and a high ratio of men to women, which pressured more women to marry and at a young age, were characteristic of recently settled regions and guaranteed a high rate of family formation and child-rearing. To the housewife fell the dangers of giving birth and the burdens of tending young children. Married at nineteen, a woman could expect to see her forty-seventh birthday, but was not likely to see any more. And during those years following marriage, virtually all her adult life, she would always have three or more children at her feet.[17] Elizabeth Clark, for example, married Newit Vick in Virginia shortly before her twentieth birthday. She gave birth to two children before the couple left to make a new home in Jefferson County, Mississippi. There she had three or four more. When they moved to Warren County, though with a large family already, including a son in his early twenties, the couple continued to have children. In 1819 Elizabeth and her husband died of yellow fever, leaving nine sons and daughters, plus an infant less than a year old.[18]

Elizabeth Clark Vick's experience was exceptional, not in the number of children she bore but for living with one man continuously for nearly thirty years. Death and widowhood gave reprieve from childbearing, if only temporarily, to other women. Vianna Smithheart married Lewis Dyer when she was only seventeen years old. Dyer, however, died before they had any children. Vianna waited several years before marrying again, and at the age of twenty-seven gave birth to her first child. She had three more before she was widowed again. Despite being married at a young age, Vianna Smithheart spent nearly half her childbearing years as a widow; she raised only four children.[19]

Spinning and weaving cotton was tedious work. Cutting and dressing meat could be exhausting. But giving birth was downright dangerous. Some 46 percent of all deaths among women over the age of fifteen occurred before they reached their thirty-first birthday. The comparable figure for men was 33 percent. The greatest number of deaths occurred around age twenty, a result of complications during the first birth, with risk decreasing with each child thereafter. Yet despite the very real dangers of childbirth, women continued to have large families.[20]

Although the fertility rate declined steadily over the first half of the nineteenth century, it was always much higher in Warren County than in older areas of the country, though lower than in some new regions.[21] Several explanations can account for the decline in fertility. By shifting the burden of production from white to black household members and at the same time placing a premium on the consolidation of family wealth, slavery may have encouraged planters and their wives to have fewer children, and thus fewer heirs. Also, the balancing of the sex ratio resulted in an older age at first marriage for women, reducing the span of their childbearing years. Moreover, fear of pain and death from childbirth doubtless caused women to dread pregnancy and to reduce the frequency of childbirth if and when they could.[22] But though they declined over time fertility rates remained high. The abundance of resources, land in particular, and the relative ease with which a family could be supported, meant that couples felt little pressure to limit the size of their families. If anything, low survival rates for infants plus the advantages that children offered as they matured into workers would have made family limitation unnecessary if not impractical for nonslaveholding households where the white family produced its own livelihood.[23]

Families were living entities that changed constantly as individual members passed through the life cycle. Single men and women married, had children, and formed nuclear family households. But nuclear families existed only briefly. Spouses died, survivors remarried, bringing stepparents, half brothers and sisters, and cousins together under one roof. The short life expectancy of men and women meant that few parents lived into old age. As a consequence, three-generation households were relatively rare. Nevertheless, extended families of cousins, aunts, and uncles eventually predominated within Warren County households.

In 1810, and at the young age of sixteen, Thomas Wright kept his own household. He owned two slaves, whom he had probably inherited, but as yet he had no land. How he earned a living is not known. Most likely he leased acreage, or hired himself out as an overseer. Before ten years passed Thomas was married and father to a young boy. Another decade passed and Wright headed a nuclear-family household with six children. Shortly thereafter his wife died. Thomas, however, quickly remarried, to Nancy Evans, thus re-establishing the two-parent, though, significantly, not nuclear family. He and Nancy had no children together. Three years later Thomas died. The family unit now consisted of the children and their stepmother. By 1860 all but one of Thomas's heirs lived in households of their own. Now sixty-five years old, Nancy still lived on the family farm. She and her unmarried stepdaughter were joined in their extended-family household by kinsman William Rawls, his wife, and seven children.[24]

The Wright family's experience was typical. Some 91 of the household heads counted by the 1830 census had headed a household in Warren County for at least ten years (Table 3–2). In 1820 nearly 60 percent of the families in those households had one or both parents present, typically a young father, such as Thomas Wright, on average just twenty-five years of age, an even younger mother, and a few children. Ten years later the percentage of stem families had dropped to only 36 percent. Meanwhile, over the decade the average size of the households increased from five to six persons, with grown children, sons- and daughters-in-law, and aunts and uncles all replacing deceased parents and ending the brief period of stem family formation.

In general, short life expectancy undermined the tendency toward stem family formation. Accidental injuries probably caused more deaths in relatively isolated rural societies than in places where medical attention arrived more quickly. People who suffered severe injuries while hunting or working with sharp tools bled to death but might have lived had they received help immediately. Disease, of course, was a common cause of premature death. Nineteenth-century Americans faced a host of potentially fatal illnesses virtually unknown to their late twentieth-century descendants, diseases such as tuberculosis and cholera. In 1832, by

TABLE 3–2. Households Present in 1820 and 1830

	1820	1830
Percent stem-family households	57	36
Mean household size	5	6
Mean number of children in the home	3	3
Number of households (91)		

Source: U.S. Census, Population Schedules 1820, 1830. Children are people under 16 years (1820), and under 15 years (1830).

the first of November, 10 whites and 6 blacks had died of cholera, which that year swept through much of the United States. The Lower Mississippi Valley was notorious for its fevers and generally unhealthy conditions. Its warm climate and stagnant swamp waters bred infectious, deadly strains and the mosquitos to spread them. In the eighteenth-century the region was known for malaria, a disease that usually proved fatal in combination with such other sicknesses as pneumonia. Malaria preyed on older adults whose general state of health had started to decline, on mothers weakened by recent births, and infants. It tended to pass over robust young adults. In the nineteenth century yellow fever replaced malaria as the region's most celebrated killer. Following the 1817 outburst in New Orleans severe epidemics struck with increasing regularity, culminating in the summer of 1853 when thousands died. Parasitic protozoa attacked the liver and caused the skin to turn a yellow color. Victims became feverish and suffered severe headaches. They began to vomit black bile within a day or two of having been bitten by a carrier mosquito, and an agonizing death followed a period of ceaseless retching.[25]

When mothers and fathers died they frequently left young children in need of care. Moreover, orphans often inherited property. Neither they nor their inheritances were dispersed, however. Demographic patterns made that unnecessary. Families tended to be large enough and so spread out in age that by the time parents died their oldest children were, or would soon be, in a position to care for young brothers and sisters. If not, there was often a young uncle who could act as guardian. When Wesley Mathis died he left two minors. Wesley Mathis, Jr., already married and with two children of his own, took his younger brother and sister as his legal wards.[26] The heirs of Pharoah Knowland passed to several guardians, and were split up briefly, though they were never far from immediate family, and were soon reunited. When Knowland died his children remained in the custody of their mother. After the mother's remarriage, the children's uncle requested that he be made their legal guardian, so as to prevent their property from falling into the hands of the stepfather. The court, however, decided to leave the children with their mother, although the oldest, William, being over fourteen years, was permitted to choose his own guardian. He chose his uncle. But William's uncle died within a year, so again he selected a guardian, this time a neighbor and associate of his deceased father, although apparently not a kinsman. When William turned twenty-one, the age of majority for men, he set up his own home and requested and received the guardianship of his younger brother and sister. The children, with their property, were reunited.[27]

Despite disruptions of the stem family caused by premature death, except during the first generation after the arrival of a new family, orphaned children did not typically end up in the care of strangers, or rarely with kin more distant than an uncle. Many close kin lived to serve as guardians; therefore, within the home relations remained close.[28] Nevertheless, the deaths of parents with young children had two consequences, both of which drew outsiders into affairs within the household and contributed to the rise of the Old South's variation on the extended patriarchal family. Each is discussed in more depth in Chapter 5, but they are worth mentioning here.

First, as the Knowland family's experience shows, the question of guardianship was not always easily settled. Potential guardians sometimes quarrelled over custody of orphaned minors. In their desire to protect family property, families generally preferred a male guardian. But raising young children called for a woman. The only woman who could legally serve as guardian was the widowed mother. If both parents were dead then there was generally no problem. An older and married brother, or a married uncle, simply took the children and the estate into his household. While older brothers and uncles were known to challenge one another over the right to serve as guardian of young siblings, or nieces and nephews, more problems arose when a surviving mother remarried. The mother generally received custody of her deceased husband's, that is to say her own, children. She was the only woman who could receive legal control of the property of minors, so long as she remained a widow. If she married again, however, the new husband took legal control of the children's estate, property never intended for him. At this point adult male kin usually stepped in and demanded custody of the children and especially of the estate. The court then had to decide between the minors' personal interests, which were probably better served by leaving them in the care of their mother, and their financial interests, which could be better protected by an uncle or brother rather than an unrelated stepfather. Sometimes the decision split orphaned brothers and sisters, placing the youngest with the mother, the oldest with a male relative. Protracted legal battles only stirred feelings of bitterness between family members.

This is the pattern of events that occurred following the death of Stephen Gibson. His children stayed with their mother even after she remarried to Patrick Sharkey, who then became the legal guardian of Gibson's heirs. James Gibson, however, challenged Sharkey in court. A cousin to the children, leader of this generation of the Gibson family, James believed it his right and duty to look after his deceased uncle's sons and daughters. But the suits and countersuits that followed really concerned the half-dozen slaves Stephen Gibson had left his heirs, for with guardianship of the children came control of their property. James Gibson claimed the slaves as his and took them from Sharkey's home. Sharkey then sued Gibson for slave stealing. Upon his acquittal Gibson sued Sharkey for libel. In the end the two men, with the court's assistance, settled the matter by placing the children and their slaves in the care of a third party.[29]

Second, perhaps the most important consequence of parental loss for the family was its effect on sibling relationships. Historians of the antebellum Southern family have mapped extended kin networks and explored relations between parents and children. But relations between sisters and especially brothers were central to the lives of many Southerners. When fathers died the oldest son assumed the role as family head, if not immediately then as soon as he came of age, and he continued in that capacity for the rest of his life. To his younger brothers and sisters he was not just another brother; he was also a father. The Davis brothers offer an example. When old Sam Davis died he left ten children. The eldest, thirty-year-old Joseph, was a successful Natchez lawyer who had recently begun building a plantation on the river in the south end of Warren County. The youngest child, Jefferson, future president of the Confederacy, was only a boy of sixteen. Joseph immediately assumed the role of family head, and his new home became the family seat. Although most of the children were grown, they always turned to Joseph during time of need. When his sister Amanda was widowed, for example, she and her seven children moved into Hurricane, Joseph's plantation home, where the older brother could provide for her. Joseph's influence was greatest on young Jefferson, encouraging him to attend West Point, eventually settling him upon a section of his estate, and even arranging for the purchase of twenty slaves to get his brother started in the business of cotton planting. Joseph did not act solely out of fraternal obligation. Having never transferred to Jefferson a rightful share of their father's estate he was truly indebted to him. But serving as trustee of his youngest brother's inheritance only emphasized his role as father figure. As neighbor, advisor, confidant, and senior business partner, he continued in that role until his death after the war.[30]

The natural course of the life cycle, early death in particular, forced modifications on family structures. At the same time, certain demographic patterns, such as large family size, worked to sustain the close relationship between immediate kin, even after they were grown and no longer sharing a home. Over time extended family networks linked the residents of individual households. While single families continued to live under many roofs, the context of family life expanded from the household to include the surrounding neighborhood.

This change occurred for two reasons. The first was simply time itself. The tendency of children to marry and settle close to home turned rural neighborhoods of disconnected families into a mesh of kinship. Over time one acquired more aunts and uncles and cousins. And the loss of a father, through age or accident, brought extended kin, male relations in particular, into the stem family.

The second cause for change in family relations was the growing importance of maintaining and transmitting, rather than just producing, wealth, as resources, primarily land but also labor, became more scarce and expensive. The protection of property, and increasingly of the status that gave individuals claim to property and authority, put a new edge on family relations and on their relative positions of power. Demographic patterns made it possible for extended relations to involve themselves in the affairs of the single-family household. Concerns over property and status gave them a strong reason to do so. During the period from 1820 to 1850 in Warren County the extended patriarchal family increasingly became an arena for social and political interaction.

Kinship and neighborhood are the subjects of a later chapter, but the growth of a patriarchal power clearly altered relations within the household, in particular relations between husbands and wives. The home continued as the center of production and consumption. But over time it became the domain of the men who controlled its resources. At the same time, the power of women relative to men diminished, especially in homes where slave labor, controlled by the patriarch, displaced them as producers and as economic assets to the household enterprise. Even in nonslaveowning households a gradual shift to production for market, a male domain, rather than for use must have engendered a corresponding shift in the nature of domestic manufacturing and thus in the economic contribution, and power, of wives.

In 1810, Warren County farm households, that is, households with three or more acres, a standard set by the 1860 census, produced on average $206 worth of cotton goods. By 1840 the average had fallen to only $15, and not just for cotton products but for all household manufactures. By 1860 the average had risen to $131 for all household manufactures; however, this did not reflect a return to production by housewives. Masters learned they could make better use of their slaves between agricultural cycles by putting them to work making such items as baskets and clothes. By the time of the Civil War spinning and weaving were nearly lost arts that had to be relearned to meet wartime scarcities.[31]

The most dramatic change occurred within households that acquired slaves, for on nonslaveowning farms wives and daughters continued to provide a vital source of labor.[32] Accounts of how Warren County plantation women spent their days are scarce, but those that do exist suggest that by the late antebellem period such women contributed less to the household's productive enterprise than did women on earlier pioneer farms and on contemporary nonslaveholding farms. Ellen Hyland read and sewed while her husband was off in the fields supervising his slaves. "We have a tolerable good library though not a great variety of books." When he returned in the evening "we generally take a long stroll through the pasture William with his gun although the only game we start is rabbits." Tasks such as pickling and smoking were left to slaves, as was the cooking. "Our cook is very good for plain cooking or anything that she has ever attempted particularly *cornbread and coffee*." With little to do, Ellen, an educated preacher's daughter, found life on her husband's plantation rather tedious. "There is nothing to interest you here," she wrote her sister, explaining why she had little to say in her letters, "the summer has been almost insufferably dull." "We are as dull as usual, the bustling world beyond us seems to be in a strange turmoil to us in our state of perfect quiescence." "I have not a single item of news as Bogue Desha"— the plantation—"is unusually dull and devoid of interest." Other plantation women expressed the same sentiments. Carrie Kiger spent much of the year away from home, visiting family and friends in New Orleans and Virginia. The plantation, she wrote, "is very lonely at times, but we try to be as cheerful and contented as possible, and I expect succeed better than many would, under the same circumstances."[33]

Of course women who wished to keep themselves busy found plenty of work to do. Some spent hours sewing clothes for their family and servants, typically with cloth made by slaves or else purchased. Others took a keen interest in household chores and though they did not actually dirty their own hands they nevertheless closely supervised their servants, a burden mistresses easily exaggerated in their minds, convinced as they were of black incompetence and laziness. Sophia Hill Dabney managed nearly thirty house servants at Burleigh plantation, across the Big Black River in Hinds County. But her servants did all the actual cooking, cleaning, washing, and even wet-nursing. Still other plantation women mixed work and pleasure. Mary Blackman, for example, could simultaneously entertain an old friend, read, and watch slaves barbecue meat for an upcoming political rally that her husband was to help host.[34]

However, the work done by plantation women was not essential to household production, any more than was the work of their slaveholding husbands. Both could have absented themselves from their homes, as many frequently did, without significantly affecting their businesses. This distinguished planter men and women, however hard they in fact worked, from the simple farmers whose backbreaking labor was absolutely crucial to their domestic economy. And plantation households differed from small farms in another respect. Ownership and ultimate authority over the slaves distinguished the master, no matter how little he actually worked, from his sometimes hardworking wife. As slaveowners, men continued to contribute to the domestic economy even as they withdrew their own labor. Women possessed only their own labor and talents, valuable on small farms but easily replaced on plantations.[35]

This context, of course, was the often unnoticed reality behind the myth of the plantation belle, as presented for example in a painting of Sarah Vick, who lived on a plantation near Vicksburg. Upon a handsome mount sits Sarah, side-saddle, a picture of gentility and beauty, her long and flowing dress nearly touching the ground. She has on riding gloves and in her left hands clutches a crop poised as if to strike the slave who feeds the horse, rather than the steed itself. The slave, in sharp contrast to Sarah, is dressed in working clothes, complete with apron and cap. There is no question about which of the two contributed most to the productive enterprise of the plantation. Many plantation women did indeed work hard. Some contemporary observers and historians have thus concluded that the myth of the Southern belle was just that. But they have underestimated the extent to which the myth actually reflected the reality that on slaveholding plantations, white women such as Sarah Vick, whether they worked hard or spent their days enjoying equestrian leisure, were economically superfluous.[36]

Changing relations between husbands and wives is evident in the abandonment and divorce cases filed between 1800 and 1860. Throughout this period there were probably the usual numbers of unhappy marriages. What altered, however, was the means by which women freed themselves of a bad situation. All women depended on men to provide their livelihood because men owned the land and in a growing number of households the slaves as well. But they were not necessarily dependent on specific individuals, and might shift their dependence from father to husband to lover and back again. Conditions during the early years gave them some power over their circumstances. Moreover, at least during the pioneer phase of settlement, men depended on women, too, and on their labor in particular. Slavery, however, reduced the productive, though significantly not the reproductive, usefulness of white women as a whole. At the same time, a balancing of the sex ratio reduced men's dependence on individual women.[37]

Little has been written about divorce in the Old South, the general understanding being that it was too rare or exceptional to warrant investigation by historians interested in the more common experiences of Southern men and women. This position is easily supported. One study of divorce based on suits brought before the supreme courts of eight Southern states over a period of sixty years uncovered only 109 cases.[38] There are indications, however, that divorce was more common than historians have supposed. In Warren County, for example, the court granted nineteen divorces during the nine years for which there are complete records. More important than the number of divorces, however, is the evidence the suits offer about changing relations between men and women.

Historians usually focus on plaintiffs and the treatment they received while at the mercy of the judicial system. This inevitably places all responsibility for divorce on the law and on the men who interpreted it. Thus, historian Jane Censer sees in divorce cases clear evidence of the sad lot of Southern women, but concludes on a positive note, identifying in jurors a growing appreciation of Southern womanhood and of their sense of responsibility to protect women who fit the ideal. Contrary to Censer, Bertram Wyatt-Brown sees in the courts no enlightened concern for suffering women, but only a consistent desire to protect male honor, which occasionally and quite secondarily meant rescuing a wife in distress.[39] Both, however, agree that women's fate rested with male authorities.

That the court offered women little chance of ending their marriage is clear. Although female plaintiffs enjoyed more success than male counterparts, the number of divorces was small and the grounds limited. Wife beating, for example, was not legal cause for separation. Nevertheless, women were not always so dependent on either the law or the men who interpreted it as historians often suggest. When pressed they could and did take matters into their own hands to win freedom from an unsatisfactory marriage.

Legal grounds for divorce in Mississippi at the time of statehood, as elsewhere, were bigamy, impotence, adultery, and desertion, the latter two being most common.[40] In the years before 1820 women who wished to dissolve their marriage simply ran off, usually with the assistance of third parties, men who stood up for them in court and to whom they sometimes remarried. Property law kept women dependent on men, but the imbalance in the sex ratio—the surplus of adult single males looking for a wife—enabled them to transfer that dependence to someone besides their husbands.[41]

Examples of wives deserting husbands abound. Although he eventually settled in Warren County, James Dromgoole initially made a home for himself and his wife Frankey at Chickasaw Bluff, near present-day Memphis. In 1800 Dromgoole went to the Cumberland settlement, or Nashville, on business, only to return to find that Frankey had sold his land and gone to the Mississippi Territory "where her conduct . . . has been very unbecoming, and incompatible with the Chastity of the Marriage State." Gabriel Osteen, in another example, had been settled in the Mississippi Territory only three weeks when his wife left him, he presumed with another man. When Osteen petitioned for divorce he had not seen her for over a year. A Bayou Pierre miller's marriage of twenty years ended when his wife ran to the Spanish territory with a young laborer who had been in his employ. He pleaded with his wife to return, promising to forgive her, but to no avail.[42]

Husbands, of course, abandoned wives, too. In 1807 Eliza Jones and John Simpkins married at or near the Big Black River. By 1811 they had two children. In the fall of that year John left Eliza and moved to South Carolina where he married another woman by whom he had several children. Eliza, however, had no problem enlisting the assistance of another man. Represented in court by her "next friend" William Goodwin, she sought and received a divorce, then promptly married Goodwin. Richard Williams deserted his wife for another woman after ten years of marriage, leaving her in "needy & distressful circumstances." And Samuel Barkley, within a month after marrying Elizabeth Glass, fled Mississippi with another woman, also leaving his wife in "needy & distressful circumstances." Elizabeth's situation was not so dire, however.

She belonged to one of the most prominent families in the county, and her uncle, a planter who also happened to be sheriff, served as her "next friend." Divorce was granted in all these cases of desertion, whether initiated by the husband or the wife.[43]

Women seemed quite as willing as men to take matters into their own hands, ending unhappy marriages by fleeing or taking up with another. Furthermore, the court played a rather passive role in the early divorce cases, merely acknowledging what the parties had already worked out themselves. There were no attempts by jurors to find absent mates; neither did they order couples to settle their differences without separation. They did not seem particularly interested in finding fault. Thus, marriages ended peaceably, or at least consensually.

After eight years of marriage Mary Blackman decided she had had enough. She left her husband and moved in with a neighbor, Samuel Cloyd, swearing never to return. Two years later her husband sued for divorce, which the court granted. Mary immediately married Cloyd and continued to live practically next door to her ex-husband. Another couple, William and Mary Lewis, also ended their marriage amicably. After a series of separations, each followed by a reconciliation, Mary finally sued for divorce, claiming only verbal abuse. William argued in rebuttal that the marriage had foundered on his wife's "unhappy temper & disposition." There were no accusations of adultery. Neither abandoned the other. Indeed, there were no real legal grounds for divorce, except that William and Mary had decided the marriage was not going to work. The court agreed, and they each went their separate ways. In this case, Mary did not require the assistance of a third party. She had been a widow when she married William, and retained her dowry through her second marriage and after her divorce. With $3000, a horse, and a slave, Mary was quite independent.[44]

By the end of the antebellum period, conditions had changed. Wives who wished to be free of their husbands took their chances in court, rather than running off. In the five years from 1857 to 1861, twelve women sued for divorce, more than in the previous 38 years. Ten divorces were granted. Only five men sought an end to their marriage, and only three received one. In part, this reflected what historians have characterized as a liberalizing of divorce laws. In Mississippi, for example, extreme cruelty in 1822 and, later, habitual drunkenness became grounds for divorce, or at least for legal separation. In addition, in 1840 the period of desertion that justified divorce was reduced from five to three years. Such "liberal" laws, however, only served to recognize the precarious predicament of married women, who were at the mercy of their husbands. Unfortunately for so many wives, however, judges, especially those in Mississippi, interpreted divorce law very narrowly.[45] Women increasingly sought redress in court, but not because judges were more open to them; they no longer had any alternative. Slavery rendered plantation women less essential to the household enterprise, while a balancing of the sex ratio lowered the economic worth of individual women in the eyes of all men, slaveholders and nonslaveholders alike. Put simply, if harshly, individual women were easily replaced, by slaves and by other women; their power in relations with men diminished accordingly. Only in the poorest of households did women continue to flee husbands. Unattached women became anomalies to be regarded with suspicion. Female vagrants much more than their male counterparts frightened male authorities who had "their" women dependent and in their control.[46] The courts, however, mediated relations between husbands and wives to a greater degree, stepping in to reduce the dangers inherent in lopsided marital relationships. Perceptive judges understood that while men exercised authority over their women they were not to abuse it so much that they threatened the very institution of marriage. They presented their views in opinions that helped articulate for all citizens the paternalistic notions that functioned to counter a patriarchal society's self-destructive tendencies.

One case in particular shows the constraints on married women by the 1850s, and the court's response to the new arrangements between men and women. In 1824 Matilda Cox, seventeen-year-old daughter of a wealthy Natchez land speculator, married James Cotton, a young man of twenty-two. Little is known about James, except that he was poor. Perhaps he was a handsome and charismatic lad, for he had none of the material charms that might explain his success in winning Matilda's hand. Whether the bride's father was quite so swept away is not known. In any case, there is no indication that he did anything to stop the wedding. For the next fourteen years James struggled to support his family, which by 1835, when they first appeared in the Warren County record, included three children. Three years later, about the time Matilda's mother died, James purchased a small farm, fully equipped and including a couple of slaves. He had trouble meeting mortgage payments, and ultimately lost his field hands along with some personal property, but finally paid most of his debts after selling his in-laws' land in Adams County. Depleting the last of Matilda's resources, James purchased a slave, placing him out of the reach of creditors by putting him in the name of his son Edward. James and Matilda continued to live on their farm, planting cotton, mostly, which they sold to pay off lingering debts, and to pay the rent on the slaves that worked the fields.[47]

The early 1840s were depression years, and James and Matilda never seemed to get ahead. Cotton prices remained low, yet James kept planting it; no one would lend him any money unless he did. He was not a good farmer. Nevertheless, many of his problems were not of his own doing. Opportunities for success for men with little or no property were disappearing. James seems not to have realized that the "flush times" were over. Nevertheless, he did not handle failure well at all, and that only made things worse for him and his family.

By the end of the decade James had given up farming for drinking.

Still, he continued to rent slaves, half a dozen at a time, perhaps piling up debts once again, although there is some suggestion that a few neighbors and friends, concerned about the welfare of Matilda and the children, may have sent hands over to help out. In any case, James no longer cared; he frequently disappeared for long spells. "In relation to his working on the farm or in the field himself," son Edward remembered of his father during these years, "he done but little." Matilda now supported the family, "and by her own personal labor." It seems that the more Matilda had to work the more James resented her. And the more James drank, the more Matilda resented him for reducing her to poverty. He had always been poor; she, however, had not. At this point, according to James, Matilda ceased allowing him "the privileges of a husband." He responded with violence.

According to Edward, James succumbed to severe spells of drunkenness and rage, on one occasion clubbing Matilda "with a stick, capable or sufficient to cause dangerous wounds or death." He whipped her with a cowhide and "made attempts to cut her throat with a knife." He threw gunpowder into the fireplace next to where she sat, "the quantity of Powder being sufficient to occasion by explosion personal injury and damage." Once, James broke Matilda's arm as he threw her out the door. He "threatened to kill her when she was asleep, to blow up the House with Powder, using the worst kind of language when speaking to her," finally "compelling her to seek Protection from the Officers of the Law, from whom he fled, and remained away several Months."

But however much Matilda may have feared for her life, and justifiably so, it was not the violence that ultimately drove her to seek a divorce, but the loss of the farm. James, who by this time no longer lived with his family, sold all the land to a neighbor, leaving his wife and children homeless. With two children still in her care, Matilda refused to surrender the house but continued to feed her family by working the small garden. The neighbor and new owner, one Benjamin Johnson, doubtless was aware of the woman's predicament, for he made no attempt to evict her. In an earlier time, before relations with her husband got so out of control, Matilda might have fled to the protection of a single man desiring a hard-working woman and companion. Now, however, she had to stay in the home. There was nowhere else to go. When she lost her home, desperate and alone, she could only throw herself on the mercy of the court.

The legal grounds for divorce in this case were James Cotton's extreme cruelty and drunkenness. Wife-beating was, of course, nothing new.[48] But so long as a woman could seek her own safety, she did not require the assistance of the law, and some of the women who in earlier years had deserted their husbands might well have fled in fear of their lives. The point is that they were able to flee. In later years women no longer had much choice but to remain at home, no matter how bad their situation, and seek redress in the court. The 1822 act by the legislature extending divorce to cases of extreme cruelty was, in part, recognition of the changing situation in the home. But the new law allowed for only a partial divorce, what in legal parlance was called divorce *a mensa et thoro*—from bed and board—a separation that granted neither party the right to remarry.[49] Furthermore, judges resisted interfering in domestic affairs. "Family broils and dissensions cannot be investigated before the tribunals of the country," wrote Mississippi High Court Justice Ellis in 1824, "without casting a shade over the character of those who are unfortunately engaged in the controversy. To screen from public reproach those who may be thus unhappily situated, let the husband be permitted to exercise the right of moderate chastisement, in cases of great emergency, and use salutary restraints in every case of misbehavior, without being subjected to vexatious prosecutions, resulting in the mutual discredit and shame of all parties concerned." This was paternalism with a vengeance.[50]

Despite a "liberalized" law that granted divorce in cases of extreme cruelty, however, Matilda could not simply show up before a judge, display her scars, and expect justice. She, or at least her lawyers, knew better. Much of her case rested on her being able to demonstrate that she had done all she could, and "by her own personal labor," as Edward stated, to keep the household enterprise going, while her spendthrift and drunken husband had not done "what he could or ought reasonably to have done, in order to provide for and support his family." In selling the farm James provided the proof Matilda needed. Reluctant to interfere in family affairs, there were nevertheless occasions, and this was one, when the court had to protect a woman and her family to prevent their becoming a burden to society, perhaps even to save their lives. Conditions conspired to leave wives utterly dependent on their husbands, who, accordingly, proclaimed themselves the protectors of their women. This is the context within which husbands and wives internalized notions of honor and paternalistic duty, which functioned to soften the harsh reality of gender relations. But paternalism sometimes went awry. When it did the legal authorities—other men—had to step in to set it right. In other words, the growing dependency of women on their men engendered a new understanding of the obligation of men to their dependents. James Cotton had failed in his obligation to Matilda; the men of the court did not. On St. Valentine's Day in 1856 Matilda received her divorce *a mensa et thoro*. Word of the court's final decision arrived anticlimactically, however; James had died a few months earlier.[51]

Women may have been dependent, but they were not helpless. Matilda Cotton adapted to her circumstances as best she could, in her case by maneuvering conservative justices into protecting her. It was no coincidence that the testimony she used most effectively in making her case was that of her son Edward, a young man in his early twenties who understood the obligations of a husband and father, and who knew only too well how his father had failed. Matilda also benefited from the judge's same sensitivity to the duties of honorable men. For the real issue in this patriarchal and paternalistic culture that had settled on Warren County by the late antebellum period was honor, not cruelty. Honorable men sometimes beat their wives; they were not considered cruel. But James Cotton was not an honorable man. Matilda convinced the court of that fact, and thus in the end saved herself by using her position of weakness to her best advantage.

On the early pioneer and nonslaveholding farms, the head of the household had exclusive control of the land, but not the labor, which was shared by the other adult members of his family, although directed by him. The rare woman who owned land—widows received a third of their husband's estate—usually turned it over to male administrators, often court-appointed guardians of minor children or else to new husbands. Both kinship and economic interdependence united the members of such households, at least while land was abundant and labor scarce. Sons could leave at a young age to set up their own homes, and they would want young women to join them. But as the population grew and land became more scarce, the balance of power within the household shifted in favor of the landowner, and against family members whose labor became relatively less valuable. This process did not require slavery; it unfolded in the free North, too.[52] But slavery certainly exaggerated its effects on social relations. On slaveholding farms the head of the household controlled both land and labor and was thus rendered economically independent of his wife and children, who became all the more dependent on him. In a context in which men possessed extraordinary power over their dependents the commitment to paternalism and family honor was that much stronger, as it had to be.

The process that created male power and honor remained incomplete, however, in the majority of households that did not own slaves. Thus, gender as both experience and ideal was wrapped up in the process of class formation. Yeoman farmers and small slaveholders, men like James Cotton, found themselves held by court, community, and family to a paternalistic planter ideal of manhood, the ideal articulated so clearly by the Reverend Winans, that they sometimes found it difficult to live up to without control of the material underpinnings of that ideal. Successful farmers who managed to provide for dependent wives and children could share the ideology of their slaveholding neighbors.[53] Unsuccessful farmers faced a difficult struggle, not just against their own lack of skill as farmers, or bad cotton prices, or poor land, but against a community that could not understand their failure to fulfil their paternalistic obligations, to act honorably. Such a man was James Cotton, an incompetent farmer who self-destructed in a storm of drunkenness and brutality.

Changes in the relationship between masters and slaves paralleled those between men and women. Patriarchal power rooted in control of material resources as well as paternalistic ideals expressed by community leaders brought the slaves both figuratively and actually into the homes of their masters, and brought the masters into the homes of the slaves.

4

HOUSEHOLDS WITHIN HOUSEHOLDS: MASTERS AND SLAVES

Henry Jones lived with his master on a farm near Natchez. His wife, Diana, lived nearby. When sold and carried to a farm on the Big Black, Jones determined to run away. He asked Diana to go with him, but she refused, perhaps out of fear of her master, who suspected Jones's scheme and had already questioned her about it. Or perhaps she simply accepted the undeniable authority of her master. In any case, she would have nothing more to do with her husband. Enraged, Jones lashed out violently, not at the master who had persuaded the woman to stay, nor at his new master who was taking him away, but at Diana. He caught her early one morning as she was milking cows, kicked her in the stomach, knocked her in the head, and fatally plunged a knife eight inches into her right breast.[1]

Henry's destructive outburst illustrated the harsh reality of life for the slaves. Too often studies of the slave community place "ole massa" in the background, bringing him to the foreground only during work hours, or in the familiar scene at the whipping post. But as Henry well knew the master's shadow hung over each slave every minute of every day of their lives. The worlds of Southern blacks and whites were not built independently but within a social context that brought both together—unequally. The meeting of master and slave—and the household is one place where they met regularly—reverberated throughout the slave quarters, shaping relations within the black community, within slave families. That this murder happened just as cotton planting was taking hold along the Lower Mississippi River is significant, for masters were beginning to interfere in the lives of slaves much more than they had previously. Men like Henry Jones could not adjust to this change.[2]

TABLE 4–1. Origin of Slaves Sold at Natchez

	Percentage
Africa	58
West Indies	10
North America	32
N = 534	

Source: Records of slave sales recorded at Natchez for the period 1782-1797, and abstracted in May Wilson McBee, Natchez Court Records, 1767-1805: Abstracts of Early Records (Baltimore, 1979).

Little is known about the background of the first blacks to live in the Warren County area, but if they were representative of Natchez District slaves generally, then they were a motley lot, differing one from another in their place of origin, culture, and language (Table 4–1). Settlers brought some of them from the Eastern Seaboard colonies. Traders brought others from Africa or purchased them in the West Indies for sale at the slave market in New Orleans. The black population of Natchez thus reflected the farflung world built by Europe's merchants, sailors, and men on the make, who carried to this small place people from all over the west coast of Africa, English, French, and Spanish colonies on the islands of the Caribbean, as well as Florida and Louisiana, and the United States from New England to Georgia.[3]

As a rule Spain itself never imported Africans into its New World colonies, but instead granted monopoly privileges to a succession of other European slave-trading nations, beginning with the Portuguese, followed by the Dutch, French, and, finally, the English. By the last half of the eighteenth century, however, the right to sell slaves to Spanish colonies had been thrown open, although the English continued to supply the greatest share. As most of the African-born slaves of Spanish Natchez passed through Jamaica, their place of origin reflected the preference of Jamaican planters for the southern Nigerian peoples, the Ibo in particular, of the Gold Coast and the Bight of Benin. In language and political formation, these herders and farmers who lived in small, independent communities along the Niger River differed from the Bantu-speaking peoples from the monarchical states of Angola, and from the Gambias preferred by the planters of South Carolina, although they shared cultural traits with the Biafrans carried to Virginia.[4]

The majority of African-born slaves of Spanish Natchez probably shared similar languages, religions, and concepts of family formation. But not all slaves in the region were African-born. Incoming whites brought blacks born in Virginia, Maryland, and the Carolinas. Also present were Creoles from Louisiana, and the islands, Jamaica mostly, but also Barbados, Saint Domingue, and Martinique. Thus, in 1790 the black population of Natchez was a mix of newly arrived Africans just learning what life would be like in their new home, and African Americans familiar with European, though not necessarily English culture. Nearly all, like the white population, were new to Mississippi.

The flow of slaves into the Lower Mississippi nearly stopped with the disruptions in the Caribbean trade caused by the Haitian Revolution in 1791, and did not pick up again until after the departure of the Spanish.[5] That year marked the end of direct African influence on African-American culture in Natchez. By the time the United States took over the district the overseas trade had ended in all states except South Carolina. Until congressional prohibition of the overseas slave trade in 1807, the same year the English ceased their trade, some planters imported Africans. But the great majority of incoming slaves were born in the United States, in Virginia, Maryland, the Carolinas, and Georgia.

The diversity of cultures and experiences probably slowed the formation of a separate black society or community, at least until the end of the overseas trade. Thereafter, the differences that separated the many ethnic groups within the slave population would have faded as the experience of slavery melded all African Americans into a single people.[6] However, no less so for blacks than for whites, local circumstances, population patterns, and the nature of the pre-plantation economy in particular more than common experiences and inherited cultures shaped the lives of the slaves along the Mississippi.

Large plantations had formed near Natchez by the late eighteenth and early nineteenth century. However, they had not yet made their appearance in the Warren County area, where many farmers if they used slave labor at all relied primarily on occasional hands hired from the few local slaveowners. Slaves thus spent most of the year living on their own and working for someone other than their owners. As a consequence, whites never really integrated blacks into their households. Before 1800, slaves accounted for one-sixth to one-third of the population that settled along the Loosa Chitto and the Walnut Hills. They could be found in only a minority of households, about one in five, where they lived in small holdings of four or five.[7] Among adult slaves, men outnumbered women by a ratio of three to two. Nevertheless, nearly all slaveholding households had slaves of both sexes, and a majority had children as well. The presence of men, women, and children indicates family groups, although such a conclusion must remain tentative, for they might well have been unrelated. One in five adult slavewomen sold in the Loosa Chitto region during the years of Spanish administration took a young child to her new master's home, but no adult male or likely father went with them. If, however, the slaves did live in two-parent families, those families nevertheless were unusual in their composition.[8] Children under the age of fifteen, scattered over ten households, totaled 27, and yet there were six men and only one adult woman under fifty years of

TABLE 4–2. Percentage of Slave Population by Age Group

	0–14	15–49	50+
Big Black and Bayou Pierre	32.9	15.9	51.2
Natchez District	36.1	58.9	4.9

Source: Spanish Census of Natchez District, 1792, MDAH; Antonio Acosta Rodriguez, *La Po-blacion de Luisiana Espanola (1763-1803)* (Madrid, 1979), 273.

age (Table 4–2). The women over age fifty probably were the mothers of these children, born to them late in their childbearing years. But surely they were not their first children. Yet sons and daughters born earlier were not present. Only a small fraction of farmers owned any slaves at all. Those who did purchased and kept just the very young and the very old, separating them from higher priced laborers who worked plantations elsewhere.

By 1815 or so the sometimes haphazard, informal hiring pattern of pioneer days developed into a more organized market as masters carefully managed their slaves' time. Thus, blacks suffered a corresponding decline in what little control they had over their own lives. In particular, they lost much of the power they had to earn their own subsistence independently of their owners. As hiring out became a means by which masters could add to their incomes, slaveowners reclaimed the authority they granted earlier to slaves, if only by default, to bargain for a rate and to collect payment. Abruptly reminded of their true condition, blacks no longer received direct compensation for their labors as they frequently had during the early years of settlement, but depended for their livelihood on the whites who owned their time.

"Since our conversation of the score of Negro Hire," wrote merchant David Hunt to a client in Warren County, "I have seen Mr. Hamilton and find he is in want of several negroes." Should "you & he agree on terms it will answer our purpose." In the developing rental market, merchants sometimes acted as brokers, bringing slaveholders and slave renters together. Hunt also hired slaves for his own uses: "I will give you Twelve Dollars pr. month for a negroe Fellow who is a good ax man and will attend to his business without an overseer." Should "you accede to this proposition pleas give the Boy a pass or send him in a Boat to the Gulf in the course of the Ensewing week or advise me of your determination that I may look out else ware."[9]

At least the practice of hiring, which by 1830 involved 17 percent of the slave population, enabled slaves to escape the authority of a single master and to experience conditions elsewhere, which could be better or worse (Table 4–3). Moreover, there is evidence that some slaves continued to influence masters' decisions regarding who would be hired out

TABLE 4–3. Incidence of Slave Hiring, 1810–1860

	1810	*1820*	*1830*	*1860*
Percentage of slaveholders who rent	12	34	34	20
Percentage of total number of slaves hired out	10	9	17	9

Source: See Appendix F.

and where. But this hardly compensated for the more serious losses slaves suffered as cotton cultivation placed a great demand on their labor. Moreover, the most profound consequences of the intensification of cotton production—masters' increased interference in relations among slaves themselves—were already becoming more acute. A letter written by Daniel Burnet, who lived on the Bayou Pierre a few miles from the Big Black, is suggestive. Burnet describes how he visited Mrs. Evans, who currently employed his slave Jacob, and ordered the servant to proceed to the farm of a Mr. Barnes and begin working there. Jacob must have had a horrifying previous experience with Barnes, for he clearly did not wish to go. Burnet, however, insisted. Jacob turned to another slave for help. He prevailed "on Frederick to take his place for the Ballance of his time," a solution which Burnet and Barnes accepted.[10]

Even the incidence of slave hiring declined as slaveowners found plenty for their hands to do at home. With it went what benefits remained from the earlier period: the experience of working for more than one master, the opportunity to move from farm to farm, the sense of independence and self-responsibility that the hiring-out system encouraged. Hiring out peaked around 1830, as the cotton boom and so called "flush times" accelerated, straining local slave labor resources. Thereafter the influx of blacks brought from the Eastern states expanded the supply of slaves for sale and reduced the need to hire out. As more farmers purchased slaves for their own use they treated them as full-time participants in the productive functions of their household, and acquired an interest in all aspects of their servants' lives. At the same time, slaves formed their own households to provide as best they could for themselves and their children, an endeavor that overlapped and meshed with the objectives of their masters.

Slaveholders had no reason to discourage black household formation. If it resulted in a high rate of birth they had every reason to encourage it for increasing the value of their estates. Slaves lived in white households as producers. If by forming their own homes they did not interfere with that end—even better if they contributed to it—then masters let them be. There always existed, therefore, the potential for conflict between white households and the black households within, between the efforts of slaves to protect and provide for themselves, and the business

TABLE 4–4. Slave Population, Warren County, Mississippi, 1792–1860

	1792	1800	1810	1820	1830	1840	1850	1860
Number of slaves	82	48	473	1287	4370	9428	7720	8246
Slaves per white	.33	.28	.67	.92	1.30	2.90	2.24	2.21
Males per 100 females	133	—	—	121	103	100	94	141
Average slaveholding size	4–5	—	6	10	11	14	12	13
Percentage of slaves in holdings larger than ten	21	—	58	65	77	—	88	91

Sources: Spanish Census, Natchez District, MDAH; Second Census, Schedule of the Whole Number of Persons in the Mississippi Territory; U.S. Census, Population Schedules, Warren County, 1810, RG 28, microfilm 546, MDAH; U.S. Census, Population Schedules, Warren County, 1820, 1830, 1840.

Note: The figures for 1792 include the Bayou Pierre households near the Big Black River, in what became Claiborne County. The figures for 1840, 1850, and 1860 do not include Vicksburg, the slave population of which is treated in Chapter 7.

of the master. But the black family, and the slave household that maintained it, persisted within the masters' homes because the interests of each were not totally antithetical.

From 1810 until the panic of 1839 people poured into Warren County. Whites seeking a fortune in the cotton trade brought slaves to work the crop. As Table 4–4 shows, during these years the black population soon outnumbered the white. The average size of slaveholding doubled. The percentage of slaves who found themselves in holdings of more than ten tripled. The opportunity for marriage increased with the density of population and with the balancing of the sex ratio. Although slaves continued to find partners beyond the boundaries of their masters' households, as the slave population within the immediate vicinity increased they did not have to look far afield. Moreover, the growing size of slaveholdings enhanced the opportunities for slaves to marry on the farms where they lived. By 1830 one in five Warren County households included a slave mother and child, or even a complete nuclear family.[11]

The significance of familial integrity to enslaved African Americans is evident from its durability over the course of more than two centuries of slavery. In their struggle to survive, blacks found strength and solace in the kinship networks they maintained, oftentimes only in the memory of a lost relation kept alive in a name passed on to a newborn child. Moreover, the strength of the black family may well have urged masters to accommodate it more than they might have otherwise. The black family survived the ordeal of slavery because African Americans adapted it to the demands imposed by the ruling race. In so doing, however, they turned their families into an integral feature of the institution that kept them in bonds.[12]

Within the master's household, slaves served one purpose: to contribute to the material well-being of the white inhabitants. As property, living assets whose value their owners measured monetarily, they performed this function when they reproduced themselves. As human beings, however, they would not be bred like cattle. Confronted on the one hand with the need to see their property increase, and on the other hand with the fact of slave humanity, masters not only permitted but encouraged slaves to form households and families so that they might live and reproduce as people.

Warren County slaveholders, like their counterparts across the South, housed their servants in family cabins rather than barracks. They provided them with a household setting, in other words, so that couples could live together in some privacy as husband and wife. But if the prospect of a household of one's own was not enough to encourage slaves to marry, shrewd masters ensured that the event was celebrated.[13] Basil Kiger, owner of Buena Vista plantation at Eagle Bend, just upriver from Vicksburg, provided the couple with fancy clothes. Sometimes a bride wore a white dress and a groom a handsome coat. All such apparel were hand-me-downs from the master's and his wife's wardrobe. In addition, he gave all his slaves a feast in the dining room of his "big house." Much of the food, however, probably came from the slaves' own gardens. Describing the festivities of one wedding to his wife, Kiger noted that the table "seemed to be quite bountifully supplied the variety however was not very great consisting principally of *Hog, Shoat, pork,* & *Pig,* with any quantity of cakes & whiskey." "They had their dance in the Hall," he continued, "Old Charles Fiddling who at times I really feared would wear a hole through the floor with his foot. I fell asleep about 2 oclock leaving them still at it in high glee." Kiger took great delight and pride in the happiness his slaves displayed on such occasions. "You know," he wrote his wife at another time, "it is against my principal to sell but were I disposed to do so an offer of 10000 dollars would not buy them tomorrow." But the real source of Kiger's joy showed through in his next sentence: "I learn through Meredith who learns through Dolly that matches are rapidly being made up and that they are desirous [of] knowing my wishes as to whether I desire them to wait till Christmas" before marrying. "Isaac, Stape, Yellow Bill, Lazy Bill & even Zeke I am informed have made their selections. . . . It does my heart good to see them so cheerful & happy."[14] Kiger claimed some success in inducing his slaves to find husbands or wives, boasting of how he had talked Zeke into picking two hundred pounds of cotton a day by threatening not to allow the slave to marry if he failed to maintain this heroic pace. But Kiger had a stake in his slaves' marriages; Zeke need not have worried.

The greatest incentive to family formation, at least for the women, was the prospect of a reduced work load. From the slaveowner's perspective, this had the added benefit of enhancing the chances of conception and a healthy birth. Slave breeding, therefore, was as much the

business of every master as raising a crop. By investing in one, he di-
vested in the other. He could either push his women hard in the fields
and suffer a lower birth rate, or reduce their work load, increase the
number of births, but take fewer bales of cotton to market. It required
cold calculation, clear perceptions of the payoffs of short-term cotton
prices versus long-term slave prices. Such a business left them no room
to doubt the value of the slave family, or of the lives they trucked.

Around 1827 or so Judge Alexander Covington and his nephew Edmund left Natchez and settled on adjoining acreage totaling nearly 2000
acres in the south end of Warren County, near the Big Black River. Edmund took charge of the nearly forty slaves, the judge being too old for
physical exertion, and proceeded to turn the forest into cotton and corn
fields. However, much of the land they had chosen, broken by numerous
hills and hollows, quickly proved itself unsuitable for agriculture. When
cleared the slopes would not hold the topsoil, while the low-lying areas,
small and marshy, were "not susceptible of cultivation." Their plans for
cotton planting spoiled by the limitations of their land, the Covingtons
adopted a new business strategy: "The policy is not to make large crops
but to raise young negroes."[15] As far as the Covingtons were concerned,
and their neighbors too, the decision to concentrate on raising slaves
rather than on planting was strictly business. Questions of humanity did
not interfere in the matter, no more than if they had elected to cultivate
more acres in corn, or to try a different variety of cotton. Edmund Covington died in 1833. Over the next six years his wife's brother, Isaac
Roberts, and his wife's brother-in-law, the well-known Natchez planter
and naturalist Benjamin L. C. Wailes, disputed over who should admin-
ister the estate. The final decision rested on the court's judgment regarding which of the two men was most skillful at running the business Edmund had left, that is to say, at raising slaves. The expert testimony of
neighbors and overseers offer excellent insight into the practice of slave
breeding.

To increase the number of births on their plantations, a successful
slave-raising operation required, according to witnesses, that servants be
well fed and clothed, and provided with "comfortable dwellings." Most
important, the work load of women between the ages of fifteen and forty
had to be reduced. "If negro women are driven hard," observed a neighbor, "they will not increase so well." Tobius Stephens, another neighbor,
agreed, and suggested rating "breeding women" at half a hand: "If
breeding women are worked hard on the hills, it is likely to produce
abortion & sickness." A witness for the plaintiff thought the current administrator had not managed the plantation very well, and offered as evidence his observation of women working in fields.[16]

Despite the testimony of the last witness, the court decided for
Wailes, who remained as administrator, for he had succeeded quite remarkably in increasing the number of slave births, and thus the value of
the plantation. A March 1836 inventory of slaves showed seven recent

births in a slaveholding of 55, for a crude birth rate of 13 percent. Another inventory taken in March three years later listed 60 slaves, including two recent births. The overseer reported eight more births by November of that year, for a crude birth rate of 15 percent, more than double the national average for slaves.[17]

Historians have generally assumed that slave breeding was, as a rule, not practiced by Southern planters. While acknowledging that there were exceptions, most would agree with Robert Fogel's conclusion that when masters interfered in the family lives of their slaves the effect was usually a lower, not higher, birth rate. Economic incentives led slaveholders to concentrate on raising staples and fashioning a disciplined, hardworking labor force, which conflicted with slave family formation. They sold husbands and children, restricted marriages to the boundaries of the plantation where slaves could be more strictly supervised, and pushed their workers hard in the fields. Masters did provide family housing, but had little incentive to do much more to increase the number of slave births, for on the whole, historians have argued, the slave family was essentially inimical, or at least irrelevant, to the interests of slaveholders.[18]

But historians have not fully comprehended the extent to which masters *and* slaves shared an interest in slave family formation, nor have they understood the implications of this common interest for the meaning of slavery as an institution based on human lives. Masters who raised slaves did not practice eugenic manipulation, a charge leveled by Northern abolitionists. They understood the humanity of their slaves in a way that their Northern antagonists did not. Nor did their efforts to increase fertility cause them to disrupt slave family life, indeed, quite the reverse. Masters strove to create conditions that would encourage family formation and thereby raise fertility. This was no trivial matter to them. They figured the reproductive success of their labor force into calculations of profit and loss, they made decisions about whether to pick more cotton or raise more slaves, and they called this the business of slave breeding. Masters had much to gain by attempting to increase the birth rate of their slaves, and so they endeavored to do just that. Fortunately for them the slaves wanted to form families and to raise children, although for the entirely different purpose of fashioning a life apart from whites and the everyday hardships of a life in bondage. Nevertheless, this articulation of interests between masters and slaves was the basis of whites' slave-breeding practices. Masters did not dehumanize their slaves; they lived off of, indeed they counted on, the very humanity of the people they oppressed.

Slaveowners who succeeded in raising the ferility of their female servants stood to increase their household income substantially. By encouraging women to have children Edmund Covington's plantation realized an additional $2000 per adult female slave over a fifteen-year period above what the same women would have earned had they been driven to

pick twice as much cotton.[19] And the slave-raising efforts of the Covingtons were not exceptional. Their neighbors spoke of slave breeding as if
it was as common as planting corn and cotton. A slaveholder named
Crowder who owned twenty or so slaves was reputed to be "an unsuccessful farmer, generally buying his corn and meat, but that he succeeded very well in raising young negroes." Ellen Cragin told an inter-
viewer years after emancipation that her mother was a "breeder," and
that "she had children fast." "It wasn't her work to be in the field," recalled Cragin. Her master "made her breed and then made her work at
the loom," where the work was less physically stressful. Mary Jane
Jones's mother "was a wedding gift to my master at the time of his marriage; was given to him as a kind of nest egg to breed slaves for him, and
just as soon as he carried her home, he bought a slave husband for her
and children came to both families thick and fast."[20]

Raising slaves and cotton were crucial to the business interests of
Southern slaveholders, but they tended to run at cross purposes. The
best managers, therefore, raised both slaves and a staple, giving priority
to whichever promised the greater returns, but not neglecting the other
half of the business any more than necessary. The relationship between
cotton planting and slave raising is illustrated in Figure 4.1. At point 0 a
female slave does no work and has no children, thus brings no return to
her owner's investment. The slaveowner realizes the greatest return at
point D, where his slave does a maximum amount of work and raises a
biological maximum number of children. In actuality, however, female
slaves worked *and* raised children. The master's return on investment,
therefore, fell somewhere along the line 0-D, more precisely, along line
A-D, where A represents the minimum amount of work regardless of
number of children, and the minimum number of children regardless of
amount of work.

If the rate of return from working versus raising slaves were constant, then an increase in one would have meant a proportional decrease
in the other along line F-H. Any point along that line would have been
the slaveowner's objective, for the rate of return would not change. At F
he concentrates on raising slaves by encouraging his slave woman to
have a maximum number of children, and meanwhile gets as much
work out of her as possible without jeopardizing his main objective. At
H he pursues an alternate strategy of working his slave as hard as possible, although he can still expect her to have some children. One would,
however, expect slaveholders to maximize returns in the short term at H
rather than opt for the long-term investment of raising slaves. And yet
the Covingtons gave priority to raising slaves over planting cotton, indicating that the rate of return for hard work versus child-rearing was in
fact not constant (Figure 4.1). The line F-C-H more accurately represents the relationship between working and raising slaves. When the
workload is reduced, the number of children increases more than
enough to compensate for the loss in returns due to less work. The rate

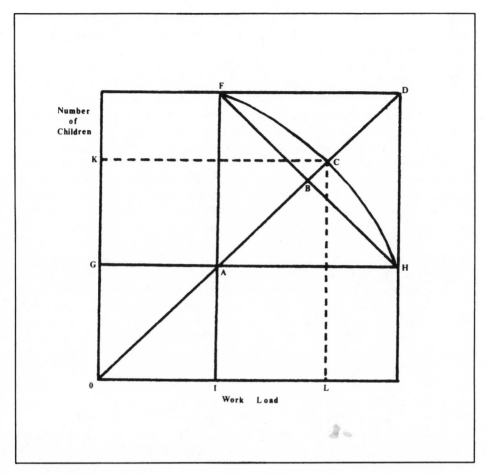

Figure 4.1 Raising slaves versus raising cotton.

of return peaks at point C, and then diminishes at points F and H. The master's objective is C, which is attained by reducing workload to L and raising K children.

Slaveholders probably did not strive for point C all the time, but constantly altered their strategy according to several fluctuating variables. For example, a planter might decide to work his women hard if he expected cotton prices to be high that year, opting for a lower rate of return, but one that paid off in the short term. When prices were low, he might reduce the work load of his women and hope to raise more slaves. If poor soil meant a rapidly diminishing return on labor inputs—the problem faced by the Covingtons—then there would be little point in working female slaves hard in the fields.[21]

Within the slaveholding household, masters used their slaves to maximize their income by squeezing as much labor out of them as possible, but also by encouraging women to have children. In working their servants, slaveowners battled against the wills of the people they kept in bonds. The slaves had no desire to sweat all day for someone else. They did, however, want families and children. By raising slaves, masters used to their advantage some of their servants' own needs and desires. Slave women, loving mothers, seized the opportunity to reduce their work load, to live in their own households, and to raise the families that were so important to them and to their identity as people, only to see their children turned into dollars and cents in a plantation ledger.

Masters did not have to sell slaves to realize the benefits of their workers' own reproduction. There is no indication that the overseers of the Covington plantations measured their success by number of people sold. Indeed, regular disruption of slave families would have been counterproductive. Mothers would have been reluctant to raise children only to have them seized and sent away, never to be seen again. But each newborn slave represented one less worker that the master would have to buy. More important, additional slaves increased the master's assets, which made it easier for him to obtain credit. It is thus not surprising that Warren County planters congratulated themselves for not selling slaves. But these masters were hardly the benevolent, charitable fellows they liked to think they were. They did sell slaves and they did break up families, regularly. Their expressions of concern for the integrity of slave families were not so completely hollow, however. They tried to practice what they preached, although not because they forgot where their real interests lay. Even the most paternalistic masters knew well and measured with care the material rewards of the growing families over which they ruled.[22]

Slaves, of course, were valued most for their labor, and within their masters' households they were the primary producers of food, domestic manufactures, and the commodities sold for cash. Slave work patterns on Warren County's farms and plantations corresponded to what historians have observed across the South.[23] On small farms one slave might be responsible for "every kind of chore from cooking to pulling a plow in the fields," while on large plantations slaveowners organized their workers into a hierarchy of occupational categories.[24] At Nanachehaw plantation in Warren County, for example, twelve slaves worked at domestic tasks while sixty worked in the field. The domestic servants included the gardener, cook, housekeeper, stable hand, and personal servants who worked in the master's house, as well as those who worked for the plantation residents generally, such as the plantation cook, a washer and milker, and the woman who cared for the children. James Allen, the plantation's owner, divided field hands into two main groups, those who worked among the rows of cotton and corn, and those who spent their days felling timber, digging ditches, and draining swamp land. A white overseer supervised all work, with the assistance in the cotton fields of a black driver. In addition, the plantation had a carpenter, a stock keeper, and a cart driver.[25]

Regardless of farm size, however, work for slaves in Mississippi was hard. Born in Virginia but sold to a Warren County slaveholder, Tom Bones found that "for a long time he could not get used to cotton growing as he had been accustomed to wheat and tobacco." Ben Montgomery, also born and raised in Virginia, worked on Joseph Davis's Hurricane plantation. As his son Isaiah later recalled, Ben "did not take kindly to the change from Virginia town life to plantation life, so he ran away." Davis soon recovered him and relieved him from field work. Montgomery learned to read and write, became a skilled mechanic and civil engineer, and eventually ran the plantation store. For the majority of Davis's slaves, however, work remained drudgery for much of the year: cut weeds, pick and chop cotton.[26]

Slaves spent most of their time, but not all of it, working directly for their masters, excepting, of course, the minority who were hired out. They also worked to provide for themselves and their families, both producing and exchanging in an internal economy. Benjamin L. C. Wailes allowed the slaves of Fonsylvania plantation to raise their own chickens, which they marketed along with eggs. In addition, he provided them with land, tools, and draft animals so they could plant corn. Wailes was their largest customer, paying them from $80 to over $100 each year, although he permitted them to conduct some business with other whites. The slaves of Nanachehaw kept, in addition to chickens, a twelve-acre garden of potatoes, as well as hives of bees. The slave economy was more extensive and complexly organized at Buena Vista plantation. The men earned from $5 to $25 per year cutting wood, which they sold to their master, who in turn sold it to passing steamboats. The women raised corn for their families, selling surpluses to other slaves, men mostly, who paid with their income from chopping firewood. Men and women used most of their cash to purchase sugar, molasses, flour, and tobacco from the plantation commissary.[27]

In what was, literally, an internal economy, masters did their best to contain the production and distribution of garden products and manufactured items within the borders of their farms, although it was "customary," noted Samuel Luckett, "after the laying of the crop, for planters to allow their negroes to go to town to sell their chickens &c." In addition, the slaves who drove the wagons of cotton into town generally took advantage of the opportunity to make a few purchases, usually in local grog shops, with some of the money they saved over the year. In December town streets filled with slaves making their Christmas purchases. But for most of the year, for most of the slaves, owners constricted the locus of the slave household economy. Although despite masters' best efforts, some slaves did manage to trade with outsiders, usually after dark with peddlers or transient whites and free blacks.[28]

The gardens might seem to contradict the logic of slavery. To be sure, they provided slaves with a sense, or at least a taste, of independence. Moreover, once the privilege of working a garden and selling its prod-

ucts had been granted, slaves quickly turned it into a right they refused
to relinquish. But the significance of the gardens as a challenge to the
institution of slavery can easily be exaggerated. Economically, the internal economy was not inimical to the interests of the slaveholders. Like
the black family, it became a part of the system. Masters, after all, encouraged their servants to raise part of their own subsistence, provided
them with the time and resources to do so, and supervised their marketing of surpluses. Slaveholders permitted such activity individually
even while, as a group, they sometimes worried about how it undermined their control. As they knew only too well, slaves worked most
productively when they worked for themselves. Rather than battling
this reality, slaveholders used it to reduce their expenditures on products produced elsewhere, to provide their slaves with healthier diets,
and themselves with stronger workers. Indeed, the marketed products
of just one slave could subsidize the costs of his or her maintenance by
as much as 50 percent.[29]

The system succeeded because the time spent tending garden plots,
raising chickens, and making baskets produced more than the extra cotton raised instead would have purchased. The internal slave economy
was integral to, and even partially underwrote, the larger economy that
kept blacks in bondage. There was no overt conflict between the two.
While the slaves cultivated vegetables or raised chickens on their own
during their "leisure" time, they never really received control of the distribution of these products, except within the confines of the plantation. Access to outside markets remained restricted by the white head of the
household. Yet the semblance of freedom enjoyed by slaves who worked
their own gardens served to reduce the frustrations and anger that could
cause them to rebel. Thus, in 1795, following the Haitian revolution, the
Baron de Carondelet, Spanish governor of Louisiana, urged all masters
"to assign Fields to their slaves, for their own cultivation, and to their
use, which will not only put them more at their ease, but also increase
the mass of the productions of the province, and advantageously employ
the time they might otherwise spend in riot and debauchery." The Baron
addressed his remarks primarily to New Orleans-area sugar planters, but
he spoke words of wisdom that future cotton planters never forgot.[30]

Thus, slave men and women lived in households within households,
as it were, forming parts in the larger whole controlled by masters.
Within their own households, slaves formed families, raised children,
and provided as much of a living for themselves as they could under the
circumstances. Yet their households existed within masters' homes, and
by struggling to build family lives for themselves slaves contributed to
owners' productive enterprise, and to their own bondage. Thus, the protection against slavery that black households and families seemed to
provide individual slaves was at best ironic, and at worst a cruel illusion.
When it was in their interests to do so whites respected the integrity of
slave families and homes, and treated them as people. This happened

often enough that slaves counted on being treated in this manner. Then when masters suddenly shattered the illusion, as they inevitably did, they threw the slaves' world into turmoil and confusion.

The social atmosphere within Warren County households was always tense. After all, slavery was an institution of violence. It set the tone for relations between all household members. When not expressed overtly, anger always lurked just beneath the surface. Ellen Cragin was so filled with hatred for her master, who regularly raped and whipped her mother, that she stole a gun and kept it behind the door of her cabin. Every day she told herself that if he whipped her mother again she would shoot the man down, although she never dared to do it. Yet the gun was always there just the same, even if her master never knew. If, however, whites could not know what their slaves were thinking, they had good reason to be fearful. Poisonings and barn burnings attributed to slaves may have been imagined. Or perhaps not. Either way they put an edge on household affairs.[31]

Had relations between masters and slaves been a steady war with battle lines clearly drawn, then both sides could have been certain of their enemies, and of what they had to do to protect themselves. To be sure, there were many moments when such a conflict clearly existed. For example, when an overseer hired by Samuel McCray killed two slaves, only to be acquitted by a jury "on the ground of danger of his own life, from insubordination, and attack by said negroes," other slaves retaliated by setting fire to the corn and corn cribs. In another case a slave named Wesley, while being "chastised," picked up a hoe and struck his overseer with it, injuring but not killing his antagonist. Slaveowner Joel Cameron was not so lucky as Wesley's overseer. Three of his slaves clubbed him to death and dumped his body in a lake near the Yazoo River. But the lines of battle were not always so clearly defined as they were in these examples. The war between master and slave could be subtle, its influence more far-reaching than most people, black or white, understood. Violence that began with the master-slave relationship rarely ended there.[32]

Maddened by the breakup of his family, Henry Jones vented his anger by killing his wife, whose behavior confused him. That his master sold him could not have surprised him; masters separated slaves regularly. But Diana, by not running with him, had wrecked his efforts to keep his family together. Far from protecting her family and household against the power of the master, she had, from Jones's perspective, turned against them. Diana, of course, was only trying to spare herself the punishment inflicted on captured runaways, a punishment that her owner undoubtedly assured her would be both harsh and certain. She accepted the breakup of her marriage as an accomplished fact. She understood better than her husband that marriages existed when they suited masters' purposes, or at least when they did not conflict with them. Whereas Henry had deluded himself into thinking that his family

existed apart from or even despite slavery, Diana knew that it could survive only so long as it suited her master's convenience.

Henry Jones's murder of his wife was no isolated outburst of slave violence, but was rooted in the reality of the household within the household. Slaves like Jones, in the space masters granted them, married, built
homes, raised and provided for families, and found themselves lulled
into believing that their lives were their own only to discover suddenly
how much they had been fooled, that their lives actually belonged to
someone else, that they lived in another's household. Such awakenings
were enraging, not to mention confusing. On one hand, slaves wished to
remain loyal to their family and friends, of whom they expected the same
in return. On the other hand, they were forced to oblige their masters.
Aware of the tenuousness of their existence slaves like Diana tried to protect themselves and those they loved by compromising the integrity of
their households and families to meet the demands of the master. But in
so doing they admitted that their homes and families did not belong to
them after all. For that they risked the hatred and bitterness of the Henry
Joneses who had forgotten, or who could not bear to be reminded that,
despite the marriages, families, homes, and gardens, they were all slaves.

Confusion and the potential for violence were never greater than
when a master physically intruded into the domain of the slave family,
shattering the very illusion of the separate and secure household he had
helped foster, and in which he even seemed to believe. In December
1859, an overseer working for John D. Fondren of Hinds County, which
adjoins Warren County, forced a slave named Charlotte "to submit to
sexual intercourse with him." The woman reported the rape to her husband Alfred, who avenged the attack on his wife, and on himself as head
of his household, by killing the overseer. In court, Alfred's appointed
lawyers built their defense around the sanctity of marriage and family
and the man's obligation to protect it. "Our law," they contended, "re-
gards with as much tenderness the excesses of outraged conjugal affections in the negro as in the white man." Slavery "had not deprived him
of his social or moral instincts, and he is as much entitled to the protection of the laws, when acting under their influence, as if he were free."
These are words Alfred surely believed, had been taught to believe not
only by example of others, white and black, but by his own experience as
a husband and household head. But Alfred's life as he understood it existed only within the world of his master's plantation. The lawyers failed
to convince a jury and judge who knew what Alfred did not, that slaves
were chattel property first, and people second, and then only when it
suited the interests of their owners to treat them as such. Charlotte, too,
had been misled, believing that her husband could actually do something to help her. True, the overseer was dead, but there would always
be another. And Alfred was condemned to the gallows.[33]

Charlotte might have chosen not to tell Alfred of the overseer's assault. But her illusion of family sanctity would have been shattered just

the same. Moreover, Alfred might have blamed her. That is what seems to have happened to a slave woman on W. C. Green's plantation in Claiborne County, just across the Big Black River from Warren County. Her relationship with her master is not stated in the record, but circumstances certainly put them in close company: she was his house servant. All that is known is that she did something to anger her husband enough that he attempted to kill her in the kitchen adjoining the big house. When master Green arrived on the scene and attempted to intervene, the slave fired a gun at him, just missing, but in the ensuing struggle, which moved to the yard outside the kitchen, Green suffered a mortal stab wound. In the confusion the woman tried to flee, but was caught by her husband, who dispatched her with the same knife he had used on the master moments earlier. The cause of this violent affair might have come out in a trial, had there been one. Neighboring whites, however, hastily silenced the surviving party of this triangle with a rope and a tall tree, leaving us to draw conclusions based on circumstances. The slave's turning on his owner before he had killed his wife indicates that the master was no innocent who just happened upon a domestic quarrel.[34]

Of course, not all cases of miscegenation ended violently. Noah Rogers was born of a liaison between a Warren County house servant and her master. He recalled no feelings of bitterness on the part of either the black or white members of the household. The master's wife treated him like a son, while his white half-brother taught him to read, and eventually became a close friend. A planter named Carter fathered a child with his servant Fanny. He cared deeply for his light-skinned daughter, whom he hoped might actually pass as a white woman. According to the terms of his will, Harriet was to remain on the plantation where she would live "as a free white person, and in no way to be treated as a slave." She was to be "fed from his table, in his house; to sleep in his house, and be clothed from the store, both fine and common"; to "have the full benefit of her labor." Carter even instructed his executors to provide Harriet with a suitable dowry should she wed a white man. Of course, the probate court voided the will on the grounds that a mulatto treated in such a manner "would necessarily exert a most baleful influence upon the surrounding negro population."[35]

Affairs in Curtis Wood's household gave new meaning to the phrase "my family black and white." After three years of living as a tenant farmer Curtis Wood married his landlady, the twice-widowed Pyrena Grubbs, and moved to Warren County. For some time before the wedding Curtis had "been carrying on an adulterous intercourse with a certain negro woman slave named Melinda," with whom he fathered "several children." Pyrena, however, knew all about Curtis's affair; Melinda was her slave. She never objected. At one point several years after they married Curtis suggested that he and Pyrena separate so as to spare her the indignation of the "rumors and stories then in circulation." But Pyrena refused the offer. As an elderly widow Pyrena had married a man she believed would provide for her and protect her property. Whatever else Curtis did was of little concern to her. Evidently the marriage had fulfilled Pyrena's expectations. Indeed, her husband's affair had increased her estate. Moreover, she seems to have enjoyed having young children in her home. She sat them at her table. One neighbor recalled that she even "nursed" the youngest child. Only when Curtis proposed to take Melinda and the children to Ohio and free them did Pyrena finally file for divorce. She would not permit him to free *her* slaves, though they were his children.[36]

Pyrena was not so perverse as she appears. Without denying that Melinda and the children were people, she never forgot they were also property, her property in fact. Pyrena's open acceptance of her husband's affair was unusual. Nevertheless, her acquiescence only demonstrated the logic of a system that kept humans in bondage. Perhaps as a property owner she understood from experience what most Southern women, who tended to treat their slaves more personally, did not.[37] Slaves were people who might be loved; they were property and would be owned. Curtis Wood had forgotten this truth. The court, however, did not, and a divorce was granted. Pyrena reverted to the status of a single woman and received title to the children. Curtis Wood remained "at law a married man and subject to all the disabilities of such." He could never remarry.

Slaves were people and property at once. Masters permitted their slaves to live in homes, tend gardens and sell their produce, to marry and have children, to live like human beings because that was good for business. They could not destroy the human qualities of their slaves, but then they did not have to. That was the real tragedy of American slavery. The system did not dehumanize the slaves; it thrived off the very humanity of the people it kept in bonds. At no point was this truth more apparent than during moments of sexual confrontation, when masters approached slaves as their owners and assaulted them—and assaulted is really the only appropriate word—as people. Miscegenation thus came easily to the master; not, however, to the slave who failed to appreciate the logic of human bondage, who saw instead contradiction and deception. Few masters ever knew until too late the risks they took when they visited the quarters after dark.

Lafayette Jones learned a hard lesson in a most bizarre case of miscegenation and murder that occurred in Bolivar County, although the affair began on a plantation in Madison Parish, Louisiana, just across the Mississippi River from Warren County.[38] One evening in February, 1857, Jones sat down to dinner with his wife of two years, and their one-year-old daughter, Lelia Virginia. After the meal their cook, a slave named Josephine purchased recently in New Orleans, served them all some tea. Within minutes the family was retching and doubling over in pain, victims of what a doctor diagnosed as arsenic poisoning. The baby died during the night. Josephine, the obvious suspect, proclaimed her innocence and pointed a finger at another slave, a field hand named George. When questioned, several other slaves acknowledged having seen George with a small vial of rat poison, which the sheriff discovered shattered in a fireplace. Both slaves were arrested and tried for murder.

In court, neither defendant disputed the circumstantial evidence against them. Josephine had served the lethal tea, and George readily admitted that the poison had been his. The case thus hinged on the question of motive. George had belonged to Jones for over a decade, although for the last two or three years he had complained of rheumatism and begged off field work. Recently, however, a new overseer had convinced Jones that the slaves had been "indulged." Poor George soon found himself back in the field laying off rows of corn, his master "tighter on him than ever before." For her part, Josephine had been unhappy about being moved from New Orleans to a Mississippi plantation. When she complained to her master, she received a whipping. Her continued bad humor earned her another lashing from her mistress on the very day of the poisoning.

The principal suspects in the murder were not the only slaves with motives for trying to kill the master and his family. Jones's first wife had died mysteriously several years earlier on a plantation near Vicksburg. On that occasion Jones had two servants, Eliza and Elsey, arrested for murder, although he later dropped the charges and made no more of the incident. Other slaves later claimed that Eliza bragged about poisoning her owner's first wife, and of how she would do likewise to the new mistress. If there was an earlier poisoning, Jones apparently provoked it by his repeated raping of Eliza, and of Elsey's daughter Lethe. Fear of embarrassment should his lascivious activities be made public would certainly explain why he squelched any investigation. In any case, he did not change his ways. Only a few months after Jones remarried, Lethe gave birth to a mulatto child said to have been fathered by her master. Moreover, Jones had taken a fancy to his new slave Josephine, raping her in New Orleans before moving her into the kitchen of his big house in Mississippi.

Juries convicted George and Josephine. Whether they were actually the guilty parties will never be known, although George was probably a scapegoat whose only crime was keeping a bottle of rat poison that he had found washed ashore by the river. By all reports, Josephine was clearly unhappy, and received regular rounds of abuse from both her master and mistress. The real killer might well have been Eliza, or Elsey, possibly for a second time. Regardless of who actually performed the deed, the incident demonstrated how the relationship between master and slave, in this case between Jones and Josephine, could strain all relations within the household.

Problems began as soon as Jones brought the object of his passions into his home and made her his cook. Josephine's presence in the big house understandably strained her relationship with Mrs. Jones, who must have worried about the health of her young marriage. Moreover, Josephine often quarreled with the other slaves. She was a newcomer and it would take time before she would be welcomed by them. Already she had incurred the anger or resentment of Elsey, whom she replaced as cook. Elsey might have been expected to understand Josephine's situation, but she had problems of her own. An elderly slave who had worked for Jones for twenty years she suddenly found herself cast out of the big house and into the fields. But Elsey had family and friends to lean on. Josephine, a newcomer to the community, had to fend for herself the best she could, alone. Whether or not she administered the arsenic, once accused of murder she acted to save her life in the best possible way, by implicating someone else. George was the obvious choice. He had possessed the poison, and had been heard to grumble about the harsh treatment he had received of late. By fingering him, though, Josephine further alienated herself from the other slaves, who rallied to George's defense. Meanwhile, Eliza and Elsey kept quiet, for if they administered the poison they were content to let the accused take the blame.

The record says nothing of relations between Jones and his wife, but one can certainly imagine. Mrs. Jones, her daughter dead, her own life nearly lost, and hearing stories of her predecessor's murder, must have wondered if her husband's libido doomed her, too. For his part, Jones realized that he had erred gravely in bringing Josephine into his home. He wanted her gone for good, and assisted in the prosecution against her while hiring the attorneys who worked for George's defense. In the end, juries condemned both slaves, although Josephine received a second trial on grounds that questions of sexual relations had been improperly rejected as irrelevant. The appellate judge declared them relevant indeed, for they went straight to motive. Evidence that Jones "was in the habit of sexual intercourse with her" indicated that Josephine "was not discontented with her condition and could have had no malice to lead her to commit the crime." The paternalism reflected in this opinion probably terrified Jones. He surely wanted to believe it, had to believe it to justify his regular raping of the women he owned, and yet he knew well how far the statement was from accurately reflecting relations within his household. In the end, those relations probably did not change. With Josephine gone Elsey probably moved back into the big house. Eliza and Lethe were still present; their master tempted by them as before. And the mulatto baby served as a continuing reminder to Mrs. Jones of her husband's activities, and of the danger to her life and family that lurked in her home.

The Jones baby poisoning was an exceptional affair that nevertheless illustrated the inherent instability of the slaveholding household. In the early settlement period masters and slaves came together only when one required the labor of the other. The households and families of each had little or no place within this working relationship. With the rise of staple agriculture, however, masters demanded more of their laborers, and assumed for themselves a far greater role in the lives of their servants, integrating the black household and family into the productive enterprise of the slaveholding household. This new context personalized the master-slave association to a greater degree, giving it a more significant place in the lives of individual blacks and whites, and in the relationship of each person to the remaining members of the household.

At the same time, slave households and families did not disintegrate. Blacks took advantage of their increasing numbers to fashion a vital family life that would mitigate relations with their owners, and with whites generally. Masters did not oppose the efforts of their slaves to marry and raise children, for they contributed to the productivity of the slaveholding household. The same conditions that enabled the formation of black households and families also encouraged masters to interfere in the lives of their slaves, who felt their master's presence all the more because their families meant so much to them.[39]

Historians have argued that the slave family and community provided comfort and security in otherwise unbearable conditions. The slave household within the white household did precisely that. Yet, frequently forgotten is how family and community—the group—placed great responsibilities, even burdens, on individual slaves. When a slave was forced to turn children over to a slave trader, or to sleep with a master, or to implicate another slave in murder, neither love nor a sense of loyalty for children, spouses, comrades in bondage made such occasions any less painful. Neither did love make it easier for others to understand why sometimes one had no choice but to let loved ones down.

5

BROTHERS AND NEIGHBORS:
THE POLITICS OF PATRIARCHY

One warm but windy spring day Benjamin Wailes took a leisurely ride around his neighborhood. From his home at Fonsylvania plantation near the Big Black River he headed southward, over his pasture toward Ivanhoe, an old plantation built by John Stephens forty years earlier, but recently purchased by Wailes for his niece Susan Covington. Susan had lived in the neighborhood as a girl, although she had moved to Natchez when her father died, since then visiting her childhood home infrequently. From Ivanhoe Wailes rode westward to Old Mr. Harris's place, and then on to Doc Hunt's. Finding no one at the doctor's home Wailes ambled through the fields, examining the cluster of Indian mounds south of Hunt's house. Several, he noted "have been ploughed over for a long period and the smaller ones almost obliterated." Wailes continued his tour, heading north at Mrs. Cameron's farm toward the old Valentine plantation. The new owner, a former Vicksburg miller named Austin Mattingly, intercepted the passerby and offered to sell him a load of bricks. The two men settled on a price of eight dollars per thousand before Wailes rode on, passing Mattingly's quarters and barns, near the large artificial pond graced by magnolia trees, and traveling beyond the brick kiln to a shallow creek, which he followed for perhaps two miles to the church. Bethel Methodist, more commonly known simply as Redbone church, attracted a large congregation from the neighborhood on most Sundays. Wailes usually attended, although sometimes he visited Antioch Baptist or, on occasion, if the visiting preacher happened to be a favorite, the chapel at Asbury campground. None was particularly close to Fonsylvania, each requiring a journey of about eight or ten miles round trip. One Sunday Wailes arrived at Redbone after Mr. Drake had already begun his sermon. A large crowd filled the building. Unable to get inside Benjamin listened from a window near the pulpit. After a while he left his station and wandered through the graveyard, among the "large number of handsome monuments," many of which he thought "exhibit considerable taste." He recognized some of the names, including those of several who, like himself, had come to this Warren County neighborhood from Natchez. From Redbone Wailes followed the road back to home, where he found slaves Robert and Alex clipping cedar trees in the yard.[1]

If we take a step back from the individual households we see larger social units. In particular we notice rural neighborhoods like the one Benjamin Wailes lived in, spaces of twenty or thirty square miles containing perhaps two or three dozen households linked by friendship, family, or proximity. During the early years to be sure, but even as late as the start of the Civil War, the world for many people began at one's doorstep and ended at the edge of the small cluster of farms and plantations that encircled one's home. In time small villages and towns—urban places—supplanted rural neighborhoods as the spots where people did much of their socializing and conducted the majority of their business, although they never did so entirely. Expanses of wilderness tended to isolate the earliest settlements. Roads, steamboats, and railroads, however, eventually broke down geographical barriers between neighborhoods, linking households to distant urban centers. Nevertheless, a mesh of kinship ties formed during the early years connected households and the resources they controlled, and continued to give structure to the rural neighborhood.

When individuals and families first trickled into the Mississippi Valley they tended to settle in small clusters along rivers and streams, or upon old Indian fields, if there were any nearby, and at the junctions of wilderness pathways. Europeans and their descendants repeated this pattern over and over as they moved across North America. Along the Mississippi River, however, pioneers learned the dangers of situating themselves too close to the water's edge. In those days there were no levees to keep the river from overflowing its banks; it did so regularly. Much of the most fertile land in the country lay underwater from March through May, and was subjected to flash flooding at any time during the summer. Families built their homes, therefore, on high ground, but as close to the river, to the rich bottom land, as they dared.[2]

During the 1770s the first white residents of the region that became Warren County settled near the Nanachehaw hills on the Loosa Chitto River. Over the next twenty years the location selected by the original settlers remained popular. By 1800 newcomers had built homes to the north of the Loosa Chitto, along the crude roadway built by the Spanish atop the bluff that ran to the now abandoned Fort Nogales. During the following decade new neighborhoods appeared, where the ridge first approached the river, and at the Walnut Hills. Yet another cluster of farms materialized on a thin strip of high

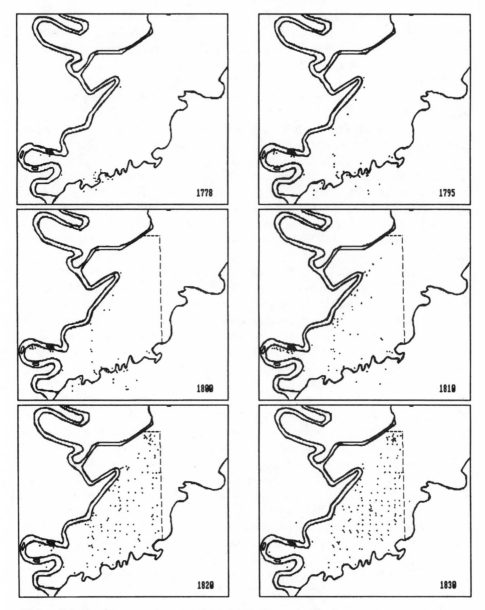

Figure 5.1 Settlement patterns 1778–1830. (*Source:* Study Data.)

ground bordering the Mississippi adjacent to the uppermost of the
Three Islands (Figure 5.1).

In 1809 the legislature for the Territory of Mississippi responded to
the growing white and black population between the Loosa Chitto River
and Choctaw Indian lands by organizing Warren County. Within ten

years farms could be found in the northernmost corner of the new county. By 1830 farms had become so numerous as to make neighborhoods almost indistinguishable. Moreover, the pattern of settlement had changed. The majority of families no longer lived along the edges of the rivers, or even along the bluffs, but chose instead to build their homes on land farther inland, among the cane hills. The extension of roads into the interior both reduced the premium placed on locations adjacent to major water- and roadways and enabled farmers to escape the flooding waters of the Mississippi.

Isolation and economic interdependence kept social relations within Warren County's earliest neighborhoods locally and inwardly oriented. Before 1810 only two or three clusters of households, separated by large expanses of uninhabited territory, specked the 400 or so square miles of countryside north of the Big Black River. Within these early settlements—the experience of the Rapalje family and their neighbors as discussed in Chapter 2 was typical—people exchanged labor, tools, and produce with one another. They depended on each other for information, for help in times of need, for company. In 1809 a group of farmers along the Bayou Pierre in Claiborne County tried to formalize their interdependence through a "society" organized to promote "the public good individual and public economy," to "bargain contract and purchase for their own use their annual supplies," and to purchase and hold land and slaves. But the objectives listed in the society's charter merely stated the obvious. There was no need for such formality, and the society lasted but briefly. Cooperative interdependence, however, continued.[3]

Of course, more than geography, a shared locale and economic interdependence linked neighboring households. Kinship and friendship also fastened people to one another. Westward migrants tended to travel and settle with associates from their former homes. The Vick and Cook families, for example, together moved to Jefferson County, Mississippi, from Virginia. When after a few years the Cooks moved upriver to Warren County the Vicks soon followed, again settling among their old friends in the Open Wood neighborhood. The Gibson family migrated in several waves from South Carolina, some settling near Natchez, others at Bayou Pierre, with descendants from both branches eventually resting in the same Warren County neighborhood.[4]

Warren County's rural neighborhoods were not, however, peaceable little kingdoms of family and friends happily and harmoniously working together in some cooperative eden. Isolation and need forced people into associations not always to their liking. Those who lived near family and friends, next door to people whom they both trusted and liked, were fortunate indeed. Those who did not, however, still had to live, work, and trade with people whom they did not know very well, or even disliked. No one had the luxury of associating only with friends. Rather, one either did or did not make friends of those with whom one regularly associated. When William Stephens killed a hog that wandered into his field his neighbor and owner of the hog, one Jonas Griffin, accused him of stealing it. In his defense Stephens freely admitted that he had thrown a hatchet at the animal intending merely to scare it away, but that his aim had been poor, and having killed it albeit quite by accident—the damage already done so to speak—he saw nothing wrong with helping himself to a delicious meal of pork. In another case of hog stealing James Beard, aided by his servants and several hounds, hunted down Thomas McElrath's hogs where they ran in the woods. While McElrath sued Beard in court for damages, another similarly angered neighbor took matters into his own hands, shooting several of Beard's dogs as they attacked his swine. Such bickering and feuding over property could quickly become personal, as happened in yet another case of alleged hog thievery. By one report David Pharr "had learned well his father's trade." This slight against character became the issue of dispute, provoking an assault and a suit for libel, although nothing came of that.[5]

Relations between neighbors could be harmonious; they could just as easily be antagonistic. Seldom were they detached. For each household's best interests depended on the mutual cooperation and support of all who lived nearby. It mattered a great deal that everyone lived up to neighborhood expectations. It is thus not surprising that failure to do so incited anger, and sometimes violence. Nevertheless, most surely made a conscious effort to keep relations friendly. Thus, newcomers found themselves warmly welcomed, sometimes even presented with gifts. Cabin-raisings were turned into social events. Camp meetings resembled fairs. The slaughtering of a steer, which no family could consume in its entirety before it began to spoil, offered an excuse for a neighborhood barbecue. Such events, in which everyone participated and those who received favors could expect to give next time, stood as reminders of the continued need for cooperation and reciprocity. But so long as people lived so close to one another their relationships would be marked by both amity and enmity, with the need for and expectations of friendship only increasing the likelihood and intensity of hostilities.[6]

With the continued growth of population, and the integration of local economies into a regional trading system, the character and definition of rural neighborhoods changed. The geographical isolation that had distinguished them, and the close cooperation between households that had characterized social relations within them, diminished or disappeared altogether. Where once they had enabled individuals to survive and improve their circumstances in frontier conditions of scarcity, neighborhoods increasingly functioned to serve the property-holding and wealth-accumulating interests of extended kin networks.

By 1830 the once visible clusters of homes disappeared, drowned in the mass of new farms and plantations that covered the county from top to bottom. Uninhabited terrain no longer separated one settlement from another, for they all ran together. No longer can we see merely by looking at a map of households where one neighborhood ended and another began. Our definition of a neighborhood as a visible cluster of homes will not do, unless we are to assume that they ceased to exist. However, such a conclusion would be misleading. Warren County residents continued to refer to the places where they lived as neighborhoods. If rural neighborhoods persisted as places, at least in the minds of the people who lived within them, how are we to find them, and how are we to know that the places we find were *their* neighborhoods? We cannot, exactly, but there is enough evidence to allow us to approximate the location and definition of Warren County's rural neighborhoods as their inhabitants saw them.

Evidence indicates that people associated the places where they lived with particular families. More than one document speaks of a Gibson neighborhood, for example, and when isolated on a map family groups do appear in clusters (Figure 5.2). A generation after arriving in Warren County, most members of the Vick family continued to live in the Open Wood neighborhood. The Gibsons gathered in the cane hills region, while the Evans family inhabited the vicinity of Redbone Creek. Of course, not all family members resided in their "home" neighborhoods. Kin networks typically spilled into precincts generally associated with

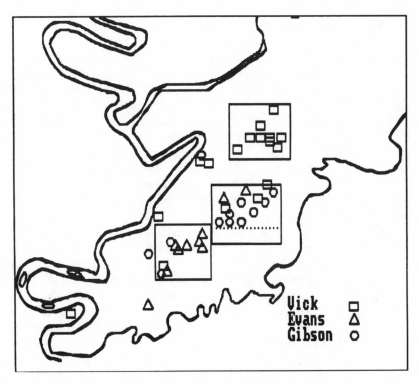

Figure 5.2 Family groupings. (*Source:* Study Data.)

other people. Moreover, throughout the period under study newcomers unconnected by blood or marriage to any other household built homes in Warren County's rural neighborhoods, around and between such established families as the Vicks, the Gibsons, and the Evans, whose relations did not even account for a majority of homes within their particular vicinities. Network densities, a measurement of interconnectedness, were surprisingly low in each of the three neighborhoods tested, the highest figure indicating that kinship linked a mere 20 percent of the households around the Vick family.[7] Of course, by reducing the size of each neighborhood we can obtain higher densities. However, doing so would be to assume what needs to be proven, that by associating neighborhoods with particular families Warren County residents had in their minds places where kinship connected nearly all nearby households. In fact, the Gibsons referred to a place that took their name but that extended well beyond the homes of their kin.[8] The dotted line in Figure 5-2 represents the border for the Gibson family as it might have been presumed had their own testimony not indicated that they understood their neighborhood to have included the territory within the solid line. Thus, while rural neighborhoods took on the identity of particular families, those families did not confine themselves to a particular place, nor did they exclude nonrelations from them.

The development of family connections between nearby households grew naturally out of the conditions in which the early settlers found themselves. Affiliation with anyone other than one's nearest neighbors was difficult. Roads were really no more than paths barely wide enough for a person on horseback, broken by sharp hills and steep ravines, and by unbridged streams and rivers. Lorenzo Dow, the Methodist preacher who built a crude home between the Big Black River and the Bayou Pierre, told how "once he met three animals, when going to a neighboring house, upon a by-way, which he hacked out through the cane; he told them to get out, and chinked his tins together; one took to the left and two to the right a few feet, and he passed between, then they closed behind." Upon reaching his neighbor's house Dow "enquired if Mr. Neal had been there, having seen his *bull dogs*. The family on hearing their description, replied that they were wolves!"[9] Faced with such conditions men and women, more often than not, found spouses close to home. The difficulties of traveling kept contact with outsiders to a minimum. Moreover, so long as there remained plenty of vacant land nearby, children tended to settle alongside parents. Within a few generations, nearby households became enmeshed in interlocking networks of kinship.

The conjunction of family with neighborhood, and the place of both within antebellum Southern society, can easily be misunderstood. Farm households settled as groups in western peripheries of the North as well as the South. Pioneers in both regions alleviated conditions of hardship and isolation by building homes nearby one another. With time, kinship connected households in Illinois just as surely as it did in Mississippi.

Thus, there was nothing inherently significant or special, and certainly nothing particularly "Southern," about Southern neighborhoods in either their pattern of settlement or in their development of family networks. But a single extended family could, and in Warren County frequently did, control most of the land and labor, slave labor in particular, for several miles around it, and this most assuredly gave a distinctly Southern structure and meaning to the South's rural neighborhoods. While Northern farmers had access to the labor of their wives and children, plus a few wards perhaps—minors left by deceased relations—and of course the occasional hired hand, that simply could not be compared to the Southern planters' access to slaves, those owned outright as well as those owned by kin. Moreover, the power and status that came with wealth made for a distinctly Southern politics of patriarchy for which rural neighborhoods were the main arenas. A particular family's property holdings, and the influence that gave them within their neighborhood, more than just the size of the clan or the fact that kinship connected several though never a majority of households, were responsible for the association of family with place. Property and power gave certain families notoriety beyond their numbers.[10]

Each neighborhood had its one or two leading families. At the center of each family stood one or two men who were, in effect, the leaders not only of their respective clans but also of their neighborhood. Personally wealthier than the average Warren County household head, clan patriarchs also had direct access to the considerable wealth held by the other members of their families. To begin with, they already owned, on average, 16 slaves and nearly 400 acres of land, four times the slave- and landholding average of all Warren County household heads. In addition, extended families, of which these men stood at the center, owned an average of 63 slaves and 1400 acres. The clustering of families within the space of small neighborhoods, moreover, meant that their combined property lay close at hand, and frequently adjoined, enabling several households to combine their resources into a single operation.[11]

Patriarchs, by virtue of their status as such, often acquired direct control over the property of other family members. Elijah and James Pace, for example, served as executors of their father's estate, which placed in their hands their own inheritances as well as those of their minor siblings. For four years Elijah supplemented his own labor force with three slaves that belonged to his younger brother Lorenzo. James Hyland personally owned a modest amount of property, five slaves and 200 acres, but also controlled 640 acres and seven slaves as administrator of his deceased brother Christopher's estate. In addition, he acquired upon the death of his wife's brother-in-law partial interest in another 350 acres and ten slaves. In another example, John Lane wrestled the executorship of the sizable legacy left by his father-in-law Newit Vick from two other heirs, and became the indomitable head of the largest and wealthiest family in the north end of Warren County. All of the Vick family, and all the families that married into it, waited over ten long years before Lane finally distributed what remained of the estate among its rightful heirs. Lane almost singlehandedly built Vicksburg, lining his own pockets in the meantime with profits that the deceased Vick had intended for his children.[12]

Patriarchal control of family property did not go unchallenged, although much of the time there was little the discontented could do. Catherine Chamberlain was furious when she discovered that the $4000 left to her by her deceased husband was to be managed by her brother-in-law, and that she would receive only the interest as an annual allowance until she remarried. Doubtless concerned about whether anyone would marry her with this arrangement and obviously frustrated by her lack of control over her own affairs Chamberlain at first complained to her guardian and then threatened to decline the interest forever if she could not have her way. "I will have nothing to do with the interest," she promised, "and I will be destitute indeed, and do God only knows what, in my present feeble health." The brother-in-law was not moved.[13] In another example, Benjamin Cook and his new bride Ann received a wedding gift of four slaves from her father just before they left Virginia for Mississippi. The father, however, did not give them direct control of their gift, but rather placed it in the hands of Foster Cook, Benjamin's older brother and leader of a large Warren County clan. The young couple were to receive an allowance raised from the hiring of the slaves. Moreover, Ann's father reserved the right to reclaim the property at any time, and if he should die intestate, Foster Cook was to continue as the slaves' keeper.[14]

The significance of patriarchal authority and the pattern of concentration of family property in the hands of male leaders of extended families raises questions about the egalitarian relations some historians claim prevailed in some Southern planter families. Surviving wills suggest that testators often intended to distribute their property more or less evenly among their children. But conditions conspired against them. Women rarely received absolute control of the property they inherited. Moreover, early parental death inevitably meant that the equal portions of property bequeathed to minors actually fell into the hands of elder men. Wills perhaps reflected egalitarian intentions. In reality property and the power that came with it were distributed unevenly.[15]

Rivals of similar status and power could mount serious challenges to patriarchal authority, although at risk of tearing their families apart. As leader of his family Stephen Gibson assumed the duties of administrator of the estate left by his deceased brother Nathaniel, and of the property left to his nephews and niece. Although he permitted his wards and their slaves to live with Nathaniel's widow even after she remarried, Gibson moved immediately upon the woman's death to bring all of the estate, especially the slaves, under his direct control. Seth Caston, the widowed second husband who had had tacit control over the property while his wife was alive, proved reluctant to turn it over, forcing Gibson to go to Caston's farm and seize his wards' property. The affairs of Caston and his brother Green were in "declining circumstances." They badly needed the slaves. So the pair stole them back and carried them to Texas, where they intended to sell them out of the country and, they hoped, out of the reach of Gibson influence. Stephen Gibson, and following his death brother James, pursued the Castons in court, impounding their Warren County farm until they received the slaves plus $1200 in damages.[16]

James Gibson had less success in winning court approval in his bid for control of brother Stephen's property, but he did not let a judge's decision stop him from trying. Martha, Stephen's widow, remarried one Patrick Sharkey, who successfully defeated James Gibson's challenges for possession of the estate. Courts preferred to keep children together with their mothers, whom they trusted with whatever property the children had coming to them. But stepfathers, having no familial stake in the welfare of the wife's children, jurors deemed less reliable. In this case, however, Sharkey, unlike Caston, commanded some respect and faith in his financial abilities and integrity. He came from an established family of prosperous farmers, and was well connected to some of the wealthiest and most politically powerful planter families in the county. There was no reason for the court to fear he would perform his duties as guardian in any way but responsibly. Nevertheless, James Gibson, who perhaps feared Sharkey as an increasingly influential rival within his neighborhood, rejected the court's ruling. He took matters into his own hands by removing six slaves from Sharkey's quarters. Sharkey had Gibson arrested on charges of slave stealing, a serious offense for which a jury found the defendant not guilty. Upon his release Gibson, still unwilling to let the matter go, sued Sharkey for libel, claiming that the suit for theft had tarnished his reputation. Perhaps sensing that the affair was getting out of control—Gibson was a hothead, which resulted in his demise in a duel several years later—Sharkey wisely made a lengthy excursion to Texas, whereupon the court placed the estate in the hands of a third party respected by both men. Gibson may not have won his battle entirely, but he did gain a partial victory when he forced his opponent to surrender control of the property in question despite the probate court's very clear decision in Sharkey's favor.[17]

Perhaps the greatest turmoil occurred when the deaths of family leaders led to succession crises. This was particularly so if the patriarchs died intestate. When the sheriff seized for debt a portion of James Hyland's land plus one of his slaves, Hyland turned to his older brother Jacob, leader of the family since the death of their father. When the land came up for public auction only Jacob showed up to bid. Prior to the sale he had publicly announced his intention to buy his brother's property and to hold it for him until he could afford to buy it back. As he had hoped, several neighbors who had expressed an interest in the property demonstrated their respect for Jacob and his motives by holding their tongues. Thus the auction was, as a member of the Hyland family observed, "not a bonafide but a sham sale," in which James Hyland's creditors received considerably less than the market value for the land and the slave that were supposed to compensate them for the bad debt. Moreover, the property remained in the hands of James Hyland, or at least he continued to work the slave and the acreage as before; Jacob held the deeds. James Hyland, in his efforts to convert his rich bottom land quickly into a productive cotton plantation, continued to borrow money, only to overextend himself at least once more. As before, his brother Jacob came to his aid, again saving another portion of property from public auction. Eventually, James transferred all his property to his brother.[18]

Suddenly, within a year of each other, both men died. Neither left a will. Further complicating matters, their earlier agreements had never been put in writing. Frances Hyland, James's widow, beseeched her in-laws to uphold the original understanding, for if Jacob had lived, she pleaded, he would certainly have acted "with good faith & integrity & would not have made use of the unbounded confidence" that James "reposed in him as a brother & *neighbor* for the purpose of defrauding & injuring" him. Initially Jacob's widow and brother-in-law, administrators of the estate, agreed, but then abruptly changed their minds, deciding instead to consolidate the Hyland plantations. They evicted Frances and her children, who presumably went to live with her brother, and tore apart James's house, pulling down the chimney, lifting up the floor, and removing bricks, boards, and all other fixtures to their own residence. While Frances implored them to respect the sacred trust between brothers, between kin, Jacob's heirs slaughtered the stock of hogs and much of the cattle that still ran in James Hyland's pastures. To Frances and her chief ally, William Knowland, her son from an previous marriage, the behavior of Jacob's administrators was nothing less than "sordid and selfish." And so it seems, except that there was more to this dispute than at first appears.

James Hyland had acquired some prime cotton land upon marrying Frances Knowland. When he transferred his land to his brother Jacob, William Knowland therefore lost what would have been his had his mother not remarried. William further entangled himself with the Hyland family when he married his stepsister, a daughter of James Hyland's from a previous marriage. Martha Ann, William's bride, died within a year of their marriage, but not before presenting him with a baby girl. William Knowland thus laid claim to part of his father-in-law's estate in the name of his daughter, who was, after all, a Hyland. But she was also a Knowland. Frances's protests to the contrary notwithstanding, she and her son perhaps showed more concern for Knowlands than Hylands. Their failure to procure the support of James's adult children in their cause—his minor heirs, whom Frances claimed to represent, could not legally speak for themselves—stood in marked contrast to their success in winning to their side several of his hungry creditors. Jacob's heirs, who sought only to keep Hyland property in Hyland hands, could claim to be the true guardians of the whole family.

Obviously, self-interest motivated both sides of this dispute, just as it had the original agreement between James and Jacob Hyland. Yet each side of the Hyland family acted on its own behalf and in the name of the whole family. No one openly challenged the sanctity of kinship, for without its bonds, and the trust individuals placed in them, James Hyland would have lost his land long before he died, and the whole family would have been the poorer for it. Once the dust settled the family was more united than before. Matilda, Jacob's widow, successfully warded off all claimants to the family plantation, preserving it for the Hylands.

The essence of neighborhood politics, both within and between extended family groups, was the struggle for control over resources. People strived to maintain and build upon their holdings of land and slaves, and used whatever influence they possessed to this end. In their endeavors family was crucial. Property and power went hand in hand. Families, by deferring to the leadership of certain individuals, and by granting them access to their land and slaves, enhanced the power of the patriarch. He, in return, used his influence to protect the interests of the entire clan. Years after the Civil War, Mississippi historian J. F. H. Claiborne remembered the Gibson clan as "numerous, intelligent, generally esteemed, wealthy and most of them members of the church." That they were numerous is certain. However, the very size of the clan would have prohibited him from knowing them all sufficiently well to attest accurately to their intelligence or the regularity of their attendance at church. He was wrong in thinking them all wealthy. But Claiborne based his impressions of the Gibsons on his encounters with its leaders. If family and name carried some special meaning in the Old South it was because the wealth, power, and respect given the patriarch extended in no small way to all who shared his name, for it was they who, collectively, made him what he was.[19]

One might have expected public officials, judges in particular, to have settled family disputes. By law responsibility for the appointment of guardians and administrators lay with the county probate court, which sought individuals who had a stake in the estate in question, and whose personal history and circumstances demonstrated a certain fiscal acumen and responsibility. Such individuals did not have to be family members. In practice, however, older sons, brothers, and uncles—the leading men—best fulfilled the court's criteria. But when such leading men challenged each other the courts were quite unable to arbitrate, for power ultimately rested not with them. Rather, it lay in the hands of the patriarchs within each family and neighborhood. This is not to say that the Hylands or James Gibson subverted or undermined the authority of the law and the court. Their behavior was in no way illegitimate. Law and the authority to enforce it came from within their neighborhoods, from themselves. If the formal authority of public office was not exactly illegitimate either, its influence was certainly secondary. Power, that is, the ability to make and execute decisions that affect others, rested first and foremost in the hands of Warren County's leading property holders. Public office, elected or otherwise, did not on its own provide officials with the authority to overrule decisions already hammered out in big-house parlors of ruling patriarchs scattered around the county. Probate judges, indeed, public officials in general, whether located in the county courthouse or state capital, tended to confirm, rather than establish, the social order that evolved within each family and neighborhood. They risked repudiation when they tried to do otherwise. The litigiousness of Warren County's residents attests to their willingness to try to settle disputes in court. But they were quick to ignore jurors' rulings whenever they did not meet neighborhood expectations. Politics started in the neighborhoods, informally, face-to-face, personally.

Just as kin competed and sometimes conflicted with each other over control of resources within the family, different clans competed for access to resources within the neighborhood. People debated and decided questions of local development, where to place churches, levees, or roads and fences, and while official authority for such neighborhood projects as road building came from the county government, in practice neighbors worked out arrangements before they petitioned officials for permission to carry out their plans. Only once during the 1830s, the earliest decade for which there remain records for county supervisors, did a group of household heads, deadlocked on a question of where to place a road, seek mediation from county officials. The board told the men to resolve the problem on their own, which they did.[20]

Unfortunately, the limited role of county government prevented the process of neighborhood decision-making from being set down in the official record. What seems clear, however, particularly for matters of local economic development, is that the family patriarchs who owned the largest land- and slaveholdings dominated neighborhood politics. They were more likely to own the land across which a road would be built, or to possess the most feasible spot on a river for a ferry. With their slaves, they provided the bulk of the labor needed to complete projects. Sometimes they donated their resources to the local community, as only they could afford to do. Gabriel Griffin and Moses Evans, for example, each set aside a portion of his plantation for a church. Newit Vick also built a church on his large estate, and then urged his neighbors to attend sermons that he preached. In 1810 Jacob Hyland allowed Warren County's first court to hold sessions in a building on his plantation until a permanent seat of justice could be selected.[21] Poorer families stood to benefit from churches and roads. Limited in resources needed to complete such undertakings, however, they depended on their wealthier kin and neighbors, and so naturally yielded to them on matters of local development.

Through their command of land and labor during these years of scarce capital wealthy planters won the deference of those who lived around them, especially of dependent relations, whose interests they claimed to represent. Of course, patriarchal authority did not always go unchallenged within neighborhoods any more than it did within families. But the structures of local society, the informality and closeness of life in a small place, almost guaranteed that such challenges would be taken personally, and settled violently if need be. Jimmy Tyler and Claudius Rawls settled the "ill feeling" between them, which came to a head during a debate over a school, first with words, then fisticuffs, and finally sword canes.[22] An argument between John Deminds and Lewis Pennel turned into a shoot-out when Deminds armed seven of his slaves, making of them a small militia, and surrounded Pennel's house. At first the slave army tried to lift up the cabin and overturn it, but when that failed they proceeded to blast it with firepower. Pennel, to his good fortune, had observed their approach and escaped out back without notice.[23] D. H. Baker killed his "near neighbor" Dr. William Monett in a duel fought for reasons not known.[24] Thomas Beall shot down Isaac Selser, and then knifed a third party who tried to break up the fight, in front of a crowd on the main street in Warrenton. Apparently Selser had insulted Beall in warning him to cease calling on his sister.[25] In all cases someone pressed charges, and thus the record of the incident exists, but nothing came of them, and the defendants found themselves quickly released, for the score had already been settled. Justice was done.

James Gibson and Anthony Durden squared off in one of Warren County's most famous battles. The cause of the fight is not known, exactly, but it probably began when Durden, who was married to Gibson's sister, assumed the duties of administrator of Jordan Gibson's estate. Almost immediately there arose a dispute over the ownership of a slave. Gibson's loss to one of Durden's kinsmen in a recent election for state senator probably did not help their relationship. Bad feelings came to a head one evening at Mr. Lindsey's supper room, at Clinton in Hinds County. According to witnesses the two were seated opposite each other at the table when Gibson declared that "one or the other would dye [*sic*] before they left this place." "They both rose from their seats & walked towards the upper end of the table," where "each one drew their swords from their canes and commenced thrusting at Each other." Several dinner guests tried to break up the fight by grabbing Durden and pinning him against the wall, but when Gibson continued jabbing at his helpless opponent they had to let him defend himself. "In a few moments Gibson fell," mortally wounded. Friends carried him home to Warren County where he slowly bled to death. (For the next eighty years or more descendants kept the carpet stained with Gibson's blood in the home where he died.) The state presented Durden for murder, but a jury acquitted him.[26]

The cause of the fight probably boiled down to a simple rivalry between two leading families, the Gibsons and the Vicks. It began when

Durden, the son of a Vick, married Mary Elizabeth Gibson. James Gibson, very much aware of the Vick family's standing, may have feared the influence Durden would have within the Gibson clan. In any case, this was no matter for the court to decide. James Gibson was himself a judge; indeed, he was the judge of probate who had awarded control of Jordan Gibson's estate to Anthony Durden, no doubt with the expectations that in doing so his wishes as patriarch of the Gibson clan would be respected. If he had trouble keeping his upstart son-in-law in line the gavel would be useless and he would have to use the sword, for power lay in the person, not the office. Durden would not be intimidated. The judge did what he had to do—fight the man or else surrender some of his authority as family leader to a man from a rival clan.[27]

The ineffectiveness, almost irrelevance, of official authority in neighborhood affairs did not make for lawlessness. Order came from the bottom up, from the material and social structures within the small places in which people lived. Patriarchal authority within rural neighborhoods and extended families made formal authority unnecessary, even impractical. Although patriarchal families developed in Northern farm communities, too, they never ordered local affairs in that part of the country to the extent they did in the slave South.[28] Thus, in the North a formal system of justice soon supplanted customary procedures based on patriarchal authority, while in the South customs evolved into a highly formalized though unwritten set of ideas of proper behavior—expectations, really—what historian Bertram Wyatt-Brown has identified as the code of honor. The duels, the violence, did not signify a lack of order; they attested to its existence. Notions of paternalism and honor delimited patriarchal power, as illustrated in an incident involving, again, the Gibson family.[29]

On an August day in 1836 Levi Gibson, two of his cousins, and several of their cronies rode up to Keziah Griffin's home. Their visit probably came as no surprise to Mrs. Griffin, not if she had heard that one of Levi's slaves had been found dead. The men demanded that she and her family leave the neighborhood. They warned the woman of the consequences should she refuse. Heeding her neighbors' threats, Keziah fled across the Mississippi River, her daughter with her, to join kin in Louisiana. Elijah, her son, stayed behind to take his chances with the Gibsons, who returned a few days later with a horsewhip and persuaded the boy that he, too, should leave.[30]

Trouble began two or three months earlier when Keziah's horse had wandered into Levi's fields. Legally, she was not responsible; Gibson should have erected fences. But the law, the written law in any case, had no business here. An owner of 23 slaves, which placed him in the richest 10 percent of Warren County taxpayers, and a member of the neighborhood's ruling family, Levi did as he pleased, and so he shot Keziah's horse. When next the woman's hogs strayed into his yard he had his overseer chase them away with hounds that relished the taste of bacon.

Neither Levi, his family, nor even his slaves, however, treated Keziah Griffin, a propertyless widow, with the paternalistic concern that people of her status had come to expect from male authorities. Men like Levi Gibson expected the deference and respect of women like Keziah Griffin, who looked to them for leadership and protection; he in return had to perform his duty by living up to her expectations. He had failed to do so. He and his kin had persisted in using a short-cut between their several plantations, over the woman's objections, until they had worn a road through her field. Much-maligned Keziah promised "that she would have satisfaction," and that Levi Gibson "need not be surprised if he found a thousand dollar negro dead in the road some time or other." Then the dead slave turned up in the lane.[31]

The Gibsons thoroughly dominated their neighborhood. Their farms and plantations completely surrounded Mrs. Griffin (Figure 5.3). Yet they overstepped their bounds. Levi Gibson seems to have sensed after the fact that patriarchal power had to be tempered with paternalistic concern for the weak, and that he had greatly abused his authority by

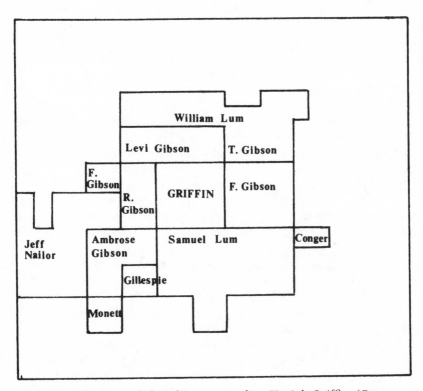

Figure 5.3 The Gibsons and their kin surrounding Keziah Griffin. (*Source:* Sectional Index, Township 15, Range 4 East, Chancery Clerk's Office, Warren County Courthouse, Vicksburg.)

treating Keziah Griffin so harshly. He and his family certainly worried about how their behavior looked to people outside their neighborhood when they justified their actions in an unusual but telling notice published in the Vicksburg newspaper. "To the Public," read the headline. "This publication is to show the cause of the expelling of Mrs. Griffin and family from the neighborhood." Their apology was in vain. Keziah and her son filed suits against their antagonists, just as Matilda Cotton had sought legal protection from her abusive husband. For five years they sought retribution in court while witnesses, subpoenaed on their behalf, habitually failed to appear, no doubt intimidated by the Gibsons. Eventually the Griffins gathered support from around the county until finally several of the Gibsons themselves, concerned about their family's tarnished reputation, turned against Levi and testified on behalf of the plaintiffs. Keziah Griffin and her son won their suit, and over $6000 in damages. They did not return to Warren County. It is significant that law and the court provided justice only when local male rulers came to the Griffins' aid, moved by a sense of paternalistic duty or honor.[32]

The change in relations between households within the county's rural neighborhoods is summarized in three models of exchange relations shown in Figure 5.4. The first model diagrams the early neighborhoods of pioneer households. Ideally, none had any particular advantage over the others in access to resources, but rather each depended upon the contributions of all. Isolation and cooperative exchange linked each household directly to all others in the group. In the terms of network analysis, each household was structurally equivalent. The second model shows the changes in exchange patterns that occurred after 1810 or so with the formation of clans and the pooling of resources by kin groups. The patriarch of the wealthiest family, however, continued to interact economically with other families. He could provide them with essential services, such as ginning or access to credit. In return, he won respect and deference as neighborhood leader. The third diagram portrays the breakdown of associations between and within families, after 1850 or so, as households acquired more of the wherewithal to free them of dependence upon others, but especially as they acquired contacts with outsiders such as urban merchants, who provided services formerly supplied by neighborhood leaders. Kinship ties remained, linking households as before, but their significance diminished somewhat when they no longer corresponded with economic associations. In particular, Vicksburg's rise as the county's economic, social, and political center signaled the demise of the rural neighborhood as the heart of Warren County.

The one constant through all phases of development was place, and as places, as pieces of common ground, the neighborhoods in which people spent most of their lives provided some continuity over time in the face of ongoing change. They smoothed transitions, linked households that otherwise had nothing joining them, and even connected the present with the past, the living with the dead. Benjamin Wailes had

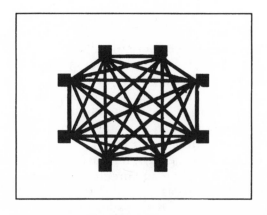

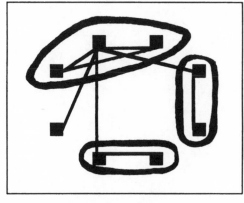

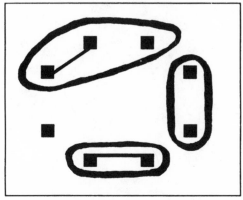

Figure 5.4 Three models of relations between households within rural neighborhoods. The top figure represents the earliest stage of development, with increasing complexity represented by the middle and, finally, the bottom figures.

lived at Fonsylvania only five years when he took his ride around his neighborhood. His business ties were mostly with merchants in Natchez where he still maintained a home. But he had had kin here for three decades, had married into a Warren County family, and had visited regularly before actually moving in. As he rode around the place in which he lived he felt a part of the community and its history. Among the Indian mounds, at plantations still known by the names of bygone owners, at the cemetery where he discovered the graves of former associates, he could sense the presence of the past, his past. "The memorials of perishing humanity speak to the living and proclaim the certainty of death," he wrote in his diary on the occasion of his wandering through Redbone cemetery. In a sense by 1857 when Wailes recorded his thoughts neighborhoods had become a collection of memorials speaking to all who cared to listen.[33]

6

HAMLETS AND TOWNS: THE URBAN PROCESS

By 1860 nearly half the population of Warren County, numbering 8000, lived in or nearby Warren County's only incorporated city.[1] Vicksburg: The public wharf crammed with steamboats, barges, and pirogues so that much of the city's business district actually floated upon the Mississippi; Levee Street clogged at certain times of the year with wagons, stacks of cotton bales, and discharged freight so "that a man could scarcely get about on horseback"; avenues ascending steep hills and lined with stores, restaurants, taverns, small manufacturing businesses, and law offices; hilltop mansions with names that betrayed the self-importance of their owners—the Castle, Belmont; an imposing new courthouse with massive columns on all sides, built by slaves but symbolic of the power of the masters, standing like the Parthenon with a whole civilization at its feet. Vicksburg was by the end of the antebellum era the center of Warren County society. But it was not the county's only urban place.[2]

Another two hundred or so people lived in the half-dozen villages that dotted the surrounding countryside. They stood as reminders of Vicksburg's humble beginnings. Warrenton, Redbone, Redwood, Bovina, Mt. Albon, Oak Ridge—such places consisted of little more than a church, one or two stores that doubled as taverns, perhaps a blacksmith shop, and maybe a post office. Some hamlets had a cotton gin and warehouse established by a local planter who made his facilities available to friends and neighbors. These hamlets might appear as little more than meeting places within rural neighborhoods, and thus perhaps were not truly urban at all. Yet as a public landing at the river, or a train station, or a simple fork in the road, such locales betrayed an urban function and process that set them apart from surrounding farms and plantations. Like the clearly identifiable cities, most especially Vicksburg, the country villages served as gathering places for rural people and produce,

as collectors of goods and information, as points in a chain that
stretched upward and outward from farm households to New Orleans,
to New York, and finally to the great cities of Europe.

As centers for the collection of agricultural products and the distribution of manufactured goods, Southern villages and towns grew out of
the countryside that surrounded them. They were as much a part of
Southern society as the farm and plantation. Nevertheless, as contemporary observers and modern historians have pointed out, the Old South
was not urban like the North. An economy rooted in agriculture, a low
population density, and an attachment to slavery that prevented the development of a consumer market and a manufacturing sector left the
South with fewer and smaller cities and towns than in the free states.
Still, Southern society had its urban dimension, although historians
looking for towns and cities of several thousand or more people, like
those more common in the North during the antebellum years, have not
appreciated this point as much as they might have had they looked for
Southern, not Northern, urban places.[3] Function more than geography
distinguished urban from rural in the Southern states, where urban
places consisted essentially of small clusters of households. Their inhabitants made a living in some way other than by farming, usually by offering marketing or manufacturing services to rural farm households.[4]

Staring into the wilderness, Warren County's first settlers envisioned a
capital city that would be the economic, political, and cultural center of
their colony. They never realized that dream. That they even had such a
dream, however, is significant. It demonstrates the equation in their
minds of civilization and urbanization. As the forests disappeared before
fields and furrows rather than blocks and buildings, the vision of an
urban civilization persisted nevertheless. At no time did Warren County's
rural residents express any antipathy toward the towns that did eventually appear, nor did they ever stop laying plans for more urban places.

Beginning in 1810 with the establishment of Warren County and its
seat of government, Warrenton, town building commenced. It proceeded in earnest during the 1830s with the rush of population into the
area and continued until the Civil War. Elias Hankinson offered for sale
lots in a town he laid out on his plantation on the south side of the Big
Black River. He found no buyers. After a fire consumed his gin and
warehouse, along with 150 bales of cotton, Hankinson sold his plantation, purchased some new acreage across the river in Warren County,
and tried again. There he established Mount Vernon. Although it made
its way onto several state maps, it, too, never amounted to much more
than a cluster of small farms and a post office. Meanwhile, at the opposite end of the county, Thomas Redwood laid off lots for the new village
of Carthage. This enterprise proved more successful. By 1850 Carthage,
or Redwood, as it came to be known, had two stores and a post office. In
addition, a cluster of nonagricultural workers—two carpenters and a

dozen raftsmen who plied the nearby Yazoo River—kept homes there. At Warren County's eastern extreme lay Bridgeport, while at the far western extreme, on the Louisiana side of the Mississippi, lay Tuscambia. Both places existed more in the minds of their founders than they ever did in reality. The same was true of DeSoto, across the river from Vicksburg. The streets lay most of the year under water, but such circumstances did not discourage its founders. In 1819 Warren County's most successful town founder, Newit Vick, marked off a grid in one of his cotton fields and sold a lot later that same year. Vicksburg very quickly became the largest urban place in the county, and second largest in the state behind Natchez (Figure 6.1.)[5]

Few of Warren County's towns developed much beyond the planning stage. All efforts to the contrary, Warren County society remained essentially rural, at least until late in the antebellum period. So long as material conditions—plantation economy and low population density in particular—precluded the rise of urban areas, the ambitions of town founders remained unfulfilled.[6] With the exception of Vicksburg, the most successful urban places in and around Warren County—successful in the sense that they achieved some measure of permanency—arose on their own. They evolved out of the countryside without any prior planning, appearing when a local agricultural population, in order to continue to increase its interaction with the national and international economy, needed a central place for processing, shipping, and receiving goods on their way to and from distant markets. Predicting when and where such a stage of development was about to occur required the talents of Cassandra.

Prior to the appearance of villages and small towns, planters, particularly those located on waterways, performed urban functions for their neighbors. They ginned cotton, milled corn, stored what was to be shipped to market, arranged for shipment to metropolitan merchant houses, and imported supplies and consumer goods for local distribution. Jacques and Isaac Rapalje provided mercantile services along the Big Black. Sinclair Gervais did likewise for his neighbors at the Walnut Hills. Large landowners could afford the equipment necessary to raise cotton for market. Moreover, in the absence of local merchants they developed ties with firms in New Orleans. In setting themselves up in the business of staples agriculture, however, early planters such as Gervais and the Rapaljes encouraged their poorer neighbors merely by extending to them processing and marketing services to increase production for sale. Where there were no plantations small farmers pooled resources and collectively began producing for market.[7]

At some point the flow of goods into and out of a new cotton region attracted the eye of distant merchants who shortly sent representatives to set up stores in the area. George Locker and Benjamin Temple, partners in a Kentucky firm, operated a store at Port Gibson, in Claiborne County, Mississippi. In 1811, believing the new seat of government in

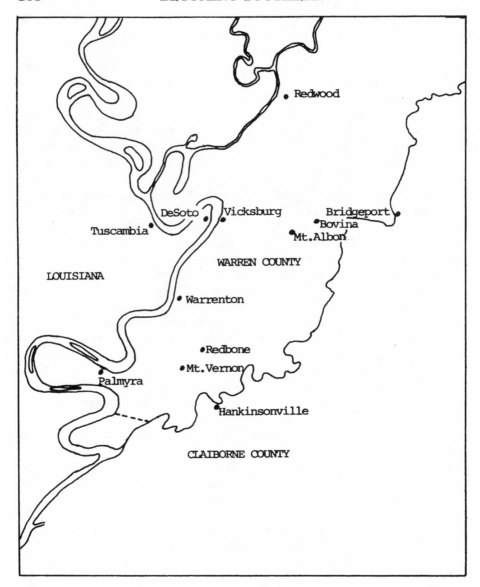

Figure 6.1 Villages and towns in and around Warren County, 1810–1860.

Warren County "promised to become a place of some considerable importance," they opened a branch store in Warrenton.[8] Similarly,
Eliphalet Frazier, also of Port Gibson but with ties to the Natchez firm
run by Abijah and David Hunt, opened a store on the Big Black River.
The Hunt brothers, whose mercantile connections stretched to Philadelphia, New York, and London, traded on the same river.[9] Edmund Reeves

and Thomas Grymes arrived about 1809. Their long-distance trading connections are not known. They opened a store at the Palmyra community on the Mississippi River among a cluster of small farmers, all of whom raised cotton for market.[10]

Warren County's earliest storekeepers were not all outsiders. Local residents reached outward as surely as distant merchants moved in. Hartwell Vick, the son of the planter who established Vicksburg, owned a mercantile, saw-milling, and planting business at the Walnut Hills, as did his cousins Willis B. Vick and Anthony Durden.[11] Anthony Glass, another Walnut Hills planter, arrived in the county during the Spanish period, and worked as a carpenter on Fort Nogales. He managed to obtain a patent for some land. After the Spanish left he remained and took up cotton planting. He also worked as a local producer and shipper of agricultural products. At various times he owned a mill and gin at a landing on the Big Black River and on the Mississippi River at Palmyra.[12] His son also combined cotton planting with a dry goods business.[13] Yet another Glass, Anthony's brother Andrew, engaged in mercantile activities more directly. With Edmund Reeves, who closed the books on his Palmyra business, and John Hyland, a planter's son, Andrew opened the doors of his trading company for business at Warrenton. At the same time he was a partner with Matthew Sellers in a second Warrenton store. By 1820 A. Glass and Company was one of the busiest firms in the county. In that year the enterprise sold over $18,000 in merchandise. Meantime the firm of Glass and Sellers transacted an additional $6000 in business. The next year this homegrown merchant bought out Locker and Company's Warrenton operation, including their three town lots, warehouses, and gin. As testimony to Glass's financial success, he was one of Warren County's first residents to pay a luxury tax.[14]

The facility with which planters took up store-keeping, and with which merchants took up cotton planting, suggests the close and easy relationship between the two enterprises. This is not surprising; planting and marketing were obviously interdependent. Farmers needed merchants to market their products and to bring them goods not produced locally. When no merchants were around, as was the case during the pioneer period, they took that task upon themselves. Merchants, of course, depended on farmers to produce marketable crops and to purchase consumer goods. From the time of the earliest settlers through the antebellum period production went hand in hand with distribution. In one sense, an 1830s planter-merchant such as Anthony Glass, Jr., was no different from the pioneer farmers of an earlier era who also served as merchants within their small and somewhat isolated neighborhoods.

In another sense, however, Glass was quite different from his predecessors; he separated his planting and trading businesses. His cotton plantation lay three or four miles south of Vicksburg, but he conducted his dry goods business in town. Close connections between planting and

trading did not interfere with the increase in specialization that occurred with the development of the local economy, as the volume of
trade grew to a point where one had to concentrate on one business or
the other, or at least keep the two separate, if either was to succeed. The
separation of collection and distribution activities from production operations within Warren County's local economy thus marked the beginning of urbanization.

With some variations, the urban process generally unfolded as follows:
Stores, warehouses, and mills first appeared on waterways, usually at favorite landings, and at well-traveled country crossroads, initially as part
of a local landowner's planting operation, but utilized by the neighborhood at large. Recognizing the advantages of such locations for collecting
and distributing goods, merchants with strong connections to distant
firms soon arrived and set up their own stores. They often leased or
bought an acre or two from a local landowner, perhaps even taking over
an original store from a planter who deferred to the merchant's expertise
and connections. As central locations for conducting business within
rural neighborhoods, river landings and crossroads also attracted artisans, blacksmiths and carpenters especially. They set up shops and added
to the growing cluster of nonfarm households that made up this small but
now urban place. At this point the local planter might attempt to capital-
ize on his situation adjoining a growing village by subdividing part of his
acreage into town lots and advertising their sale. Or he might sell a piece
of land to speculators and they would try to parcel it out as town lots. In
most cases few buyers appeared, and the town remained a village tied
closely to adjoining farms and plantations. But some villages blossomed
into towns and cities, offering services to an agricultural economy that extended for miles in all directions. In the process their relationship with
the rural neighborhood in the immediate vicinity, that which first gave
them life, reversed as farmers began to serve urban demands. All the villages and towns in and around Warren County conformed fairly closely to
this general pattern of urban development. Vicksburg was no exception.

Situated at the point where the ridge that follows the Yazoo River
from deep within the state converges with the Mississippi, the Walnut
Hills had long been a central meeting place. Before the arrival of European settlers the hunting and trading routes of local Native Americans
intersected at this spot. Here the Spanish built Fort Nogales and opened
the first store in the region. Following the departure of the Spanish, the
Walnut Hills continued as a local meeting place, although most of the
surrounding land was now privately owned.

As early as 1797 a passerby remarked that the Walnut Hills would be
"a beautiful situation for a town." A decade later another traveler made
the same observation: "These hills are the finest situation for a town I
have yet seen on the Mississippi. They are of an eligible height, the as-
cent easy, the soil luxuriant, and the climate the most temperate on the
river."[15] The owner of most of the land at that spot agreed. Years earlier

Elihu Hall Bay, a judge who lived in Charleston, South Carolina, began to acquire Mississippi acreage while working as an agent for the governor of British West Florida. By the turn of the century he had title to 3000 acres at the Walnut Hills.[16] Bay was the first actually to lay out town lots, although before he could sell any he transferred all his property to his kinsman and fellow Charlestonian Robert Turnbull. Turnbull chose not to proceed with the establishment of a town. Instead he turned this large tract of forest into a cotton plantation.[17] Nevertheless, the spot where the bluff met the river continued to attract people, and a small urban place appeared anyway. By 1814 the "numerous buildings, dwelling houses, gin-house, negro quarters" on and adjoining the Turnbull plantation looked to a passing river boatman "like a little village."[18] Honore P. Morancy kept a store at the Hills. Hartwell Vick, another local merchant, built a warehouse there. The blacksmith shop belonged to E. D. Walcott. James Center operated the saw mill. Then the owner of a cotton plantation adjoining Turnbull's laid off lots for the new town that was to bear his name. Newit Vick managed to sell only one lot before dying, leaving his heirs to complete the plan.[19]

Lots in the new town of Vicksburg sold quickly.[20] The spread of cotton plantations into the interior of the county, and into the interior of the state after the Choctaw Indian land cession in 1820, had created an urgent need for a commercial entrepôt on the Mississippi River. The Walnut Hills were the obvious place for a river port, as Vick and others before him had foreseen. The bluff would save a town from the springtime floods that inundated other places. More important, that location was the closest accessible point on the river for the inhabitants of newly settled regions to the northeast. It is not surprising that Vicksburg flourished, quickly surpassing in size an older Warrenton, located a mere ten miles downriver. But timing was as important as location. Two decades earlier Elihu Bay had envisioned a town. The years between his aborted attempt to realize that vision and Vick's success on the same spot made all the difference. Until the 1820 Choctaw cession and the development of cotton agriculture in the interior of the state, the farm households around the Walnut Hills could support only a village, and Warrenton, with its more central location within the most settled regions of the county, was the larger and more important urban place.

On the strength of a large hinterland that reached far beyond the Warren County line, Vicksburg in the space of a decade rose from wilderness to commercial center second in the state only to Natchez.[21] In the mid-1830s farmers from along the Big Black and beyond, a hundred miles distant, sent 30,000 bales of cotton to river boats docked at Vicksburg's wharves, nearly four times the cotton marketed through Warrenton. Incredibly, the number of bales that found their way to Warrenton's levee actually declined nearly 50 percent between 1812 and 1833, even as the cotton economy around the town boomed.[22] As Vicksburg grew, offering more goods and services—and in turn a growing market for them—lawyers, merchants, and mechanics moved their shops from Warrenton to Vicksburg, so that farmers increasingly had to take their business to the bustling new town even if it entailed a longer trip over rough roads. Of course, roads, especially the best ones, now more often than not led to Vicksburg. Eventually a majority of county voters decided to move the courthouse to Vicksburg, thereby stripping Warrenton of its last claim to prominence within the county.[23] By the mid-1840s Vicksburg not only provided access to national and world markets, but had become a market in its own right, as R. Y. Rogers discovered. Rogers gave up cotton planting and began to raise corn and vegetables, especially tomatoes, for Vicksburg consumers. He also established a profitable dairy business in town.[24]

The growth of Vicksburg ultimately reoriented trading patterns within the county by rechanneling lines of communication between the county and the outside world. While the wealthiest planters, particularly those with river frontage, continued to deal directly with commission houses in New Orleans, inland farmers and planters sold their cotton and purchased manufactured goods and supplies through any one of the many forwarding merchants in town, most of whom worked as agents of such New Orleans firms as Miller and Gooch and J. B. Byrne and Company. They gave advances in cash or supplies for consignments of cotton. In this manner they replaced wealthy planters and country storekeepers who had previously worked as liaisons between rural communities and distant markets.[25] In addition, the lower prices and greater selection of Vicksburg stores undercut the business of village shopkeepers, particularly those close to town.

Figure 6.2 shows the location of country stores in 1820, before Newit Vick's town had materialized. All were located in the north end of the county, three of them at the Walnut Hills. South-end residents took their business to one of the six stores at Warrenton, which at that time was a thriving town with a promising future. The rise of Vicksburg, however, displaced by 1850 all but the most distant neighborhood stores in the vicinity of the Walnut Hills, while the concurrent decline of Warrenton created opportunities for country storekeepers in the county's southern end (Figure 6.3). The appearance of several peddlers, who carted wares around the county from home bases within the city, stretched Vicksburg's tentacles farther still.[26]

By 1850 Vicksburg's commercial orbit reached much farther than the above figures suggest, for the county's country storekeepers conducted a very localized trade. W. S. Hankinson's store at Yokena Plantation, south of Warrenton, provided all the usual services. The firm arranged for the shipment of small amounts of cotton to Vicksburg merchants; lent small amounts of money; acquired for customers such specialty items as books, sheet music, cigars, glassware, oysters; bought butter, apples, and turkeys from local farmers for resale in Vicksburg; and acted in general as a conduit between the surrounding rural neighborhood

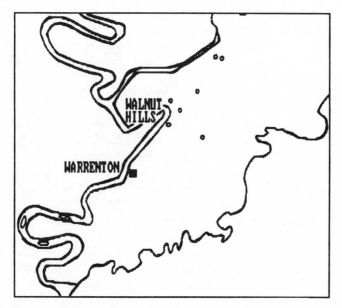

Figure 6.2 Country stores, 1820. (*Sources:* U.S. Census Population Schedules, Warren County, 1820. Warren County Sectional Indexes, WCC; and Study Data.)

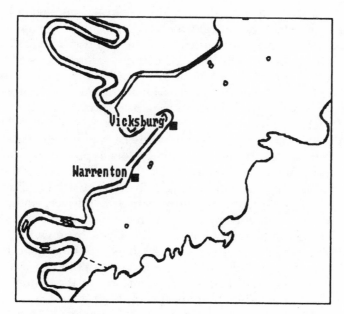

Figure 6.3 Country stores, 1850. (*Sources:* U.S. Census Population Schedules, Warren County, 1850. Warren County Sectional Indexes, WCC; and Study Data.)

and the urban market. However, not all the stock Hankinson purchased from local farmers went on to Vicksburg. Much of it, perhaps most of it, ended up in the pantries of his neighbors. The Yokena store, in other words, stood at the center of a small and surprisingly self-contained exchange network, collecting local products for distribution locally. The exact proportion of the business devoted to this trade is not known. The surviving account book is not precise on this point. But it appears to have been considerable, for the majority of his transactions consisted of local produce sold to neighbors.[27]

Country stores sometimes stood at the center of the small economic worlds of the slaves. A slave named Montgomery ran the store at Hurricane plantation, for example, facilitating trade among several hundred laborers as well as among the planter's family and neighbors. With his master Joseph E. Davis's permission and oversight, Montgomery even conducted business with suppliers in New Orleans. His store, with adjacent warehouses and a post office, provided the nucleus of what was in effect a plantation village.[28]

Warren County's country storekeepers had always engaged in local trade. Years earlier the Rapaljes had provided for their neighbors services similar to those provided by Hankinson. But the Rapaljes had also offered a connection to distant markets. As Vicksburg merchants started to direct trade between the county and the outside world, leaving the neighborhood trade to storekeepers such as Hankinson, they detached external from internal trade networks. This realignment of exchange patterns thus connected rural neighborhoods to Vicksburg but did so without undermining the integrity of each as a distinct place. Only the settlements close to town and along the rail line that ran eastward through the middle of the county had no country storekeepers, indicating that they had lost their local trade to Vicksburg's merchants.

Vicksburg's tentacles stretched into the interior of Mississippi and Louisiana, bringing the business of distant communities to the town wharf or the merchant houses along Washington Street, then connecting those places to national and international markets. A culling of place names from several Vicksburg newspapers provides the basis for a sketch of Vicksburg's supralocal business network, presented in Figure 6.4. Each number on the figure refers to the number of mentions each place received in the newspapers, with dots representing single mentions.[29] What emerges is the outline of a regional town system within west-central Mississippi, and spilling into Louisiana and Arkansas. The majority of places mentioned were situated upriver, indicating the influence of the river current on trade networks. Planters and farmers shipped their cotton to nearby towns and villages, from which it was sent downriver to a larger collection center such as Vicksburg, and from there to New Orleans, New York, and Europe. It is significant that no place above Memphis received mention. That city sat at the center of its own hinterland, and directed its trade past Vicksburg. Likewise, Natchez was

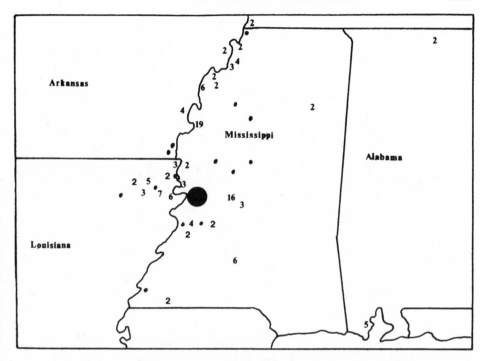

Figure 6.4 Places mentioned in an economic context in the *Vicksburg Whig*, February 29, March 7, June 6, and October 18, 1860.

situated at the center of the region downriver and Baton Rouge below it. Very clearly there was no interregional network.[30] None of the major river cities between Memphis and New Orleans received more than one or two mentions, with the exception of Greenville, a new town in the largely unsettled delta region north of Vicksburg. Greenville and Jackson to the east of Vicksburg probably served as local collection and distribution points within smaller subhinterlands. Newspapers named New Orleans 62 times, more than any other place. New York received the second most mentions with 33, while Cincinnati received 13. Thus Vicksburg sat on the downriver side of a hinterland which included two subregions around the smaller towns of Greenville and Jackson, and connected its hinterland directly to the major metropolises of New Orleans and New York. Connections to cities of similar size and importance were almost nonexistent.[31]

Founded by cotton planters, Vicksburg always remained closely connected to the countryside. Nevertheless, the city eventually outgrew its local origins and the influence of local planters, as its hinterland spread beyond the borders of Warren County. Moreover, urban society became more distinct from the rural neighborhoods that surrounded it. Economic ties to the countryside notwithstanding, by the 1850s Vicksburg residents lived in a place apart from the countryside.

7

A PLACE APART FROM THE COUNTRYSIDE: THE CITY OF VICKSBURG

The villages and towns in and around Warren County from their earliest existence were tied closely to the countryside. To the extent that they supported a predominantly rural economy they differed from larger cities, north and south, where the urban-rural relation was reversed, where the countryside functioned to support a predominantly urban and manufacturing economy. But the relationship between town and country in Warren County indicated only a stage of development and not some unique urban process peculiar to the Old South. While urban development in the South lagged behind the Northeast it nevertheless unfolded in a similar manner. By 1860 Vicksburg's relationship with the surrounding rural area had begun to change, as the town showed signs of leading the local economy while portions of the countryside settled into a more secondary and supportive role.

The urban process inched along in Warren County. Nevertheless, throughout much of the antebellum period the countryside set the tone for life in the county's urban areas. People familiar with agriculture populated them, people who had lived on a farm or plantation, or who perhaps still owned one, or who had close kin living in the countryside. In particular, cotton planters dominated urban society. They founded five towns and villages and kept them alive with their business. They built homes in them, and tried to bring urban residents into their patriarchal webs. They imported to town some aspects of their way of life, too. Warren County's most popular dueling grounds were located at Vicksburg, although on the Louisiana side of the river to avoid legal troubles. But planters were not the only people who took the country to town. Slaves drove wagons of cotton down streets and lanes to the public wharf. They usually stayed long enough to visit the store and purchase some tobacco or a piece of fancy cloth. Some lingered long enough to get drunk. All the elements of rural society from masters to slaves brought to town their business and their way of life.

The strong influence of the countryside on urban life, however, did not prevent the larger towns and cities from developing into worlds apart. While still young and quite small, Vicksburg became noticeably distinct from the surrounding plantation districts. In particular, its people were different. They came from a greater variety of places, worked at a greater variety of occupations. They created a heterogeneous and fluid society that contrasted sharply with rural neighborhoods. Strong ties of kinship and patriarchy so vital in the plantation districts were never as strong in the city, creating problems of social control. As in urban places throughout antebellum America the formation of voluntary associations helped to alleviate problems of order. The influence of the countryside continued, yet townfolk still developed their own ideas of politics, of making money, of how one ought to live.

The ongoing development of Vicksburg society forced its citizens to readjust their ways of life. Sometimes they made those adjustments reluctantly. To people imbued with the values of rural life, living in a village that grew in to a city of 8000, Vicksburg could seem orderless, chaotic.[1] Life in the countryside appeared permanent, even if it in fact was not, but by comparison life in town sometimes seemed to race out of control, even if in fact there was always an order to urban society. Certainly, Vicksburg was different. In particular, next to the rural neighborhood its society was more dynamic, more complex, its population more heterogeneous in terms of where people came from and what they did once they got there. Town residents had trouble comprehending their growing urban environment. On more than one occasion they tried with violence to enforce their vision of social order. By 1850 or so, however, they reformed their vision, though not their society, mentally adjusting themselves to their urban surroundings and letting go of the countryside, if only a little bit.

By 1860 Vicksburg had become a remarkably cosmopolitan town. Persons of foreign birth constituted a quarter of the total free population. By comparison, immigrants accounted for only 6 percent of the population living outside the city limits. Although the majority, over 80 percent, came from Ireland, England, or Germany, the city's foreign-born population represented over seventeen countries in Europe and the Americas. Signs that hung over the shops along Washington Street reflected the ethnic mix of Vicksburg's population: J. F. Baum, fruit stand; Bazsinsky and Simmons, dry goods and clothing; Botto and Spengler, coffee house; Antonio Genella, general variety store; Francis Hernandez, Havana cigars; Henry Volker, shoemaker; Patrick Burns, blacksmith; A. J. Carnahan, merchant tailor.[2] Houses of worship scattered around town reflected the variety of cultural and ethnic groups too.

Episcopalians, Presbyterians, Baptists, and Methodists had churches in town as they did in several rural neighborhoods. But only Vicksburg included a Roman Catholic church and a synagogue.[3]

Vicksburg's ethnically mixed residents earned their living in a greater variety of ways than did the county's rural inhabitants. In 1860 the census reported 193 different occupations among urban working people, two and a half times the number of occupations among rural folk. Of course the census enumerator frequently gave different names to what amounted to the same job, but the point stands nonetheless, especially considering that at the very least 62 percent of free workers living outside Vicksburg shared the same occupation: farming.[4] In contrast, the majority of urban workers can be distinguished according to several occupational categories.

Table 7–1 groups Vicksburg's free working population for the years 1850 and 1860 into six categories. It reflects some changes in the local economy during the last decade before the Civil War. Since the 1830s the city had had a strong contingent of skilled artisans and mechanics. Early fears of competition from manufacturers upriver in the Ohio Valley had not materialized owing to the spread of Vicksburg's hinterland which eventually provided a sufficient market for their wares. By the end of the antebellum era artisans were gaining in numbers.[5] However, over the same period opportunities diminished for unskilled workers, most of whom supplied the city with menial labor—ditch digging, levee building, road work. With the city's and the surrounding area's surge of growth over by the mid-1840s they began to leave, perhaps for new towns in Texas or California. Similarly, business for local shopkeepers and proprietors remained steady, but the earlier years of rapid growth were clearly over.

TABLE 7–1. Occupation by Percentage of All
Employed Free Persons, 1850 and 1860

	1850	1860
Professional	5	6
Merchant-Service	17	18
Clerical	16	20
Skilled	25	34
Semi-skilled	4	5
Unskilled	34	17
n	808	1076

Source: U.S. Census, Population Schedules, Warren County 1850 and 1860. For a listing of the occupations assigned to each classification, see Appendix F.

Matilda Cotton. This victim of an abusive husband appealed to the honor of male authorities and successfully won a divorce. (Old Court House Museum Collection, Vicksburg, Mississippi.)

Edward Cotton. His testimony against his father helped his mother win her divorce. (Old Court House Museum Collection, Vicksburg, Mississippi.)

Sarah Pierce Vick and a slave, Nitta Yuma Plantation, north of Vicksburg. (The Historic New Orleans Collection.)

This portrait of a slave nurse and her charge suggests the close, and sometimes explosive, living and working relations between white families and their African-American servants. (Old Court House Museum Collection, Vicksburg, Mississippi.)

The African–American community at Hurricane Plantation, gathered before the guest house, 1863. (Old Court House Museum Collection, Vicksburg, Mississippi.)

Vicksburg riverfront, 1828, when the village consisted of little more than riverside cotton warehouses, probably owned by the Vick family. This drawing was made by an unknown artist, who copied it from a French original. (Old Court House Museum Collection, Vicksburg, Mississippi.)

Vicksburg riverfront, 1848. The hamlet had become a small town. The boats be-longed to some of the floating merchants, mostly from the upper Mississippi and Ohio rivers, who crowded the levee every winter, frustrating Vicksburg's established shopkeepers. (Old Court House Museum Collection, Vicksburg, Mississippi.)

Vicksburg riverfront, 1860, showing a very busy waterfront. The city's new court-house sits prominently on a hill. (Mississippi Department of Archives and History, Jackson, Mississippi)

Vicksburg, looking up China Street from Washington Street, circa 1865. Even at this late date the town's streets remained unpaved. (Old Court House Museum Collection, Vicksburg, Mississippi.)

Jefferson Davis's home at Brierfield Plantation during Union Army occupation. Though large—the people standing on the veranda indicate how high the ceilings were—the plain, single-story design was typical of antebellum homes among even the wealthiest planters in Warren County. (Old Court House Museum Collection, Vicksburg, Mississippi.)

Jacob Hyland, patriarch of the clan that dominated the Warrenton neighborhood during the early decades of the nineteenth century. (Courtesy of the Hyland Family, Yokena Plantation, Warren County.)

Workers born in the United States dominated the professional and clerical occupations, while foreigners held more than their representative share of the skilled, semi-skilled, and unskilled occupations. Some 72 percent of all free unskilled laborers in 1860 were not native to the United States, a conservative figure that does not include migrant workers. Immigrants also accounted for a disproportionate number of merchant-service workers. Between 1850 and 1860 the representation of foreigners in the unskilled and skilled jobs increased relative to their proportion in the total group of employed free males. Their relative share in all other categories decreased. The pattern for native-born Americans was exactly opposite, as they accounted for an increasing percentage of the professional, merchant-service, clerical, and semi-skilled occupations. Ranked according to average wealth-holding per worker, the two job categories at the bottom—skilled and unskilled— were the ones that became increasingly filled with foreigners.

Immigrant workers within occupational groups may be divided further by their place of origin (Table 7–2). Those from Ireland predominated among unskilled laborers, providing much of the back-breaking menial labor around town and serving as a pool from which local planters could draw as they needed. For example, during the spring of 1860, his slaves presumably occupied with planting cotton, Aleck Gwin hired three or four hundred migrant Irishmen to construct a levee around his riverfront plantation at Brunswick Landing.[6] In 1850 Irish men and women accounted for 44 percent of all foreign-born workers in the city, but they accounted for 64 percent of those without a skill, and their representation in that category increased over the decade. German immigrants were more likely to arrive with a skill, and eventually to open their own shops. They formed the heart of the local storekeeper

TABLE 7–2. Occupation by Place of Birth (percentage of all foreign-born)

	England or Scotland		Ireland		Germany	
	1850	*1860*	*1850*	*1860*	*1850*	*1860*
Professional	20	20	20	0	20	20
Merchant-Service	7	1	18	28	38	32
Clerical	13	10	43	16	27	49
Skilled	12	24	42	21	36	34
Semi-skilled	20	24	40	14	20	38
Unskilled	7	4	64	74	17	11
All occupations	10	13	44	36	27	29
Total number	29	53	125	147	77	121

Source: U.S. Census, Population Schedules, Warren County 1850 and 1860.

and business community. When they did not work for themselves they could be found keeping the books or managing stores owned by others. A minority worked at menial tasks, as did George Mindrop, a red-headed boy recently arrived from Baden-Baden. J. M. Gibson found him digging in a ditch alongside slaves on Cherry Street.[7] However, in contrast to the Irish, the Germans largely avoided such work. Indeed, by 1860 they were overrepresented in every category except unskilled. Max Kuner's experiences were perhaps more typical than were young Mindrop's. Born in Bavaria, on Lake Constance across from Switzerland, Kuner arrived in New Orleans at the age of twenty-three. Though he spoke no English he found work upriver repairing watches for a Vicksburg jeweller. Within seven years he owned the store. By 1860, thirteen years after his arrival in Mississippi, his business had $56,000 on the books, and he owned a $5000 home on Grove Street.[8] English and Scottish immigrants took up the same occupations as native laborers, spreading themselves throughout several categories but generally avoiding unskilled and merchant-service jobs, the same type of work least attractive to the American-born.

For every three white laborers in Vicksburg there were four slaves. What kind of work they did can only be surmised, however, because the census did not record slave occupations. Nevertheless, their employment presumably was connected to their owners' business. That few free skilled laborers—23 percent in 1850 and 12 percent in 1860—owned or hired slave assistants suggests that few slaves worked in the small shops of local artisans, especially by the end of the decade. The largest slaveholding in Vicksburg—28 men, 2 women, 10 children—worked in manufacturing at Abraham Reading's foundry. But the majority of Vicksburg slaves probably served in the homes and offices of professionals, merchants, and storekeepers, for the whites most able to afford them.[9] The absence in the historical record of complaints from local artisans about competition from slaves further indicates that most of the city's unfree population worked as domestic servants.[10] In addition to those who lived and worked in town, slaves from the countryside crowded the streets along the riverfront during late autumn and winter, unloading bales of cotton from wagons, reloading them with supplies. Typically unsupervised, they stayed in town as long as a week, spending what cash they had before returning to their masters.[11]

Slaves were not the only people to venture to town during the winter. Its streets empty and quiet during the hot summers, particularly when yellow fever threatened, Vicksburg was filled with strangers in December and January. Boatmen, gamblers, entertainers, businessmen, people looking for work, drifters—if their travels took them south at all they arranged to go when the weather up north turned cold.[12] In addition to this seasonal flow of population there were always people for whom river towns like Vicksburg were merely way-stations along extended journeys. Indeed, the majority of Vicksburg's inhabitants simply passed through. Vicksburg was over forty years old by the start of the Civil War, but at that moment, incredibly, slightly more than one in four household heads could say they had lived there for even a decade. The town was full of newcomers. For every stranger who wandered up the hill from the levee, unpacked a carpet bag at a hotel or rented a room in a boarding house someone else loaded a wagon or placed a trunk on a river boat and moved on. By 1860 only 39 percent of Vicksburg's 1850 household heads remained. The typical migrant was a man in his twenties who found work as an unskilled laborer. Usually foreign-born, or at least foreign to Mississippi, bound for Texas maybe, or California, he settled in Vicksburg for a couple of years, worked, saved some money, sometimes married, then moved on.[13]

Not all of those who passed through Vicksburg were aimless wanderers. Of course some did simply drift. Others, however, moved with purpose. Unskilled workers often experienced rapid upward mobility. Half of those present in 1850 and 1860 had moved into new types of work by the later date, a third of them into retailing and shopkeeping businesses. A large minority of clerical workers also experienced some mobility, both upward into mercantile and service occupations and downward into unskilled jobs. Workers in other categories, however, tended to remain where they were. Thus the most geographically mobile people were also the most occupationally mobile, patterns that suggest how the fluidity of urban society could prove advantageous to poor white workers and ultimately may have given many of them a stake in the cotton economy and plantation society.[14]

Propertyless and unskilled migrants from the North, from older plantation districts, from Europe landed in cities like Vicksburg, found work and a steady income that enabled them to accumulate savings, which they applied toward the purchase of a plot in the countryside. For the upwardly mobile who started without the advantage of an inheritance, the goal of settling on a farm or plantation was reachable. Towns and cities provided them with work and an income. Admittedly, evidence on this point remains impressionistic. On average people with little money or property flowed into Vicksburg while people with some accumulated savings moved out. In the countryside the trend was reversed: incoming migrants had considerably more property than out-migrants. In the absence of a full study of migration these patterns of wealth-holding and population flow nevertheless hint that Michael Brady's experience may have been shared by others. Born in Ireland, the thirty-year-old Brady migrated to Vicksburg where in 1850 he worked as a clerk. He owned no slaves and no real estate. Before the end of the decade he had accumulated enough money to purchase a slave and a piece of land in the Warren County countryside valued at $1000.[15]

Michael Brady's experience indicates that some Vicksburg residents maintained the town's close ties to the countryside. However, Brady was exceptional in that he remained in Warren County. Most of the people who left Vicksburg moved out of the area entirely, presumably for places less settled, where farmland could be had for a cheaper price. In stark contrast to Brady, most of the city folk who did eventually settle in the immediately surrounding countryside tended to be wealthy members of the town establishment, such as Abraham Reading, owner of the town foundry, lawyer William C. Smedes, a former partner with Seargent S. Prentiss, and Austin Mattingly, a prosperous miller. All started in Vicksburg business and eventually purchased plantations locally, thereby strengthening urban-rural ties.[16] In contrast to these quite visible success stories, however, were the masses who flowed in and out of Vicksburg. As purposeful as these migrants may in fact have been, to the town's more permanent residents—always a minority of the total population—they were rootless, aimless transients, appearing out of nowhere, staying but a brief while, then leaving for who knows where without forming any lasting ties to the community.

Vicksburg had been built by local people with purposes clear enough for any to see: to provide marketing services for the surrounding countryside, and to profit by so doing. The town never lost its original purpose, although in time it also developed into the county's social and political center. Locals built it to serve local ends. For this reason they saw outsiders as potentially threatening, even dangerous, simply for being outsiders with no apparent desire to join with the local population, but also because there were so many of them. Controlling the masses of newcomers, however, was a problem. Urban society, contrary to the plantation districts, was not structured by strong ties of kinship and friendship. Vicksburg elites, most of whom had once held sway in the countryside and perhaps still did, had difficulty extending their influence over the strangers who wandered through their town.

In September 1831 a notice appeared in the local newspaper addressed "to the citizens of Vicksburg, particularly the young men." The author called for the formation of a militia company, the first in the county since Mississippi's territorial period. "There is a prospect of a great many visitors the coming winter," the notice warned, "and in all probability a number of which will need regulating, and such a company may be found beneficial to the protection and harmony of our Town." In a separate item the newspaper's editor also called for a patrol to enforce the law, and at the same time warned readers of the rising frequency of thefts in Vicksburg. It is amazing that the bodies left in the wake of Nat Turner's bloody uprising were barely two months in the Virginia ground, yet the cry for a militia in Warren County first came from the town, not from the surrounding plantation district. More frightening than the county's enslaved blacks, apparently, though they outnumbered whites by a thousand, were the numerous strangers who would wander into Vicksburg that winter. That fear never dissipated. In 1860 three militia companies patrolled city streets, regulating in particular "all itinerants and persons being in this community without any visible means of support, and who are unknown in this community."[17]

Vicksburg's celebrated gambling riots soon confirmed the dangers posed by the town's temporary citizenry. The affair began when a professional gambler disrupted a Fourth of July picnic. It ended with a shoot-out and a mass hanging. In all six people died. The card players and faro dealers, at least those who knew what was good for them—and most of them did—heeded the warnings of the hastily organized Anti-Gambling Society to flee the town or face severe consequences.[18]

That the people of Vicksburg would come to blows with the gamesters who plied the boats and wharves of the Mississippi River is not surprising. The very nature of their profession kept gamblers rootless and disrespectful of local authority. "Unconnected with society by any of its ordinary ties, and intent only on the gratification of their avarice," wrote the local editor, they were the most threatening species of migrant to wander into Vicksburg, all the more so because their disease was so contagious: "Every species of transgression followed in their train. They supported a large number of tippling houses to which they would decoy the youthful and unsuspecting, and after stripping them of their possession, send them forth into the world the ready and desperate instruments of vice."[19]

The people of Vicksburg lashed out at more than the gamblers, however, using the opportunity to purge their city of all kinds of undesirable sorts. The militia took the lead, suspending the law for twenty days while they tarred and feathered suspected thieves. "If a man says aught against the Company proceedings he is either whipped or hung," observed one townsman whose misgivings about the handling of the crisis superseded his concern for the "many stragglers about."[20]

The leaders of Vicksburg attacked the gamblers in part because they were a particularly visible target collected as they were in their own section of town. Very quickly after its founding Vicksburg divided into three neighborhoods. A business district developed along the water front and back a few blocks toward the courthouse. Beyond the public square along the hills were the constantly expanding residential sections. A third neighborhood, the favorite haunt of Vicksburg's gamblers, boatmen, and stragglers, appeared in the swamp land north of the business district. This section of town, known as the Kangaroo after its most illustrious bawdy house, with its soggy streets and crude shanties, squatted in stark contrast to the fine brick homes in the neighborhood atop the bluff. Its card dealers, prostitutes, and bar-room brawlers were notorious throughout the lower Mississippi. Only Natchez Under-the-Hill was more famous. The Kangaroo was a constant source of embarrassment and fear for Vicksburg's established residents.

A year and a half before the riots the Kangaroo burned to the ground. In all likelihood a drunken rowdy simply kicked over a lantern. But if concerned local residents were not so zealous as actually to set the fire themselves, they applauded it nonetheless. A hundred or so gathered to mourn the death, as one local wit put it, of their "friend," the "celebrated

KANGAROO." "Its ashy remains were interred upon the spot which its
deeds have immortalized, and a splendid oblation of sundry time-hon-
ored and antiquated rats was offered up as a propitiation, for whatso-
ever misdeeds it might have committed in the flesh." Pushing his tongue
further into his cheek the author of the obituary continued: "It is with
regret that I state, that some of the by-standers were so injudicious and
unseemly withal, as to make the whole a subject of jeering and mockery;
but not one of them will close his mortal career with so much of light
and lustre as did my lamented friend." In Vicksburg, however, kanga-
roos have several lives; the district was resurrected almost as quickly as
it burned down. Nevertheless, the excitement generated by the fire illustrated the antipathy elicited from the rest of the townfolk by that neighborhood's raucous inhabitants.[21] Residents found other targets for those
same feelings. The theater burned down more than once, to the delight
of Mr. Patterson, who "thought morality would be benefitted by the
burning." Others apparently shared his views.[22]

Vicksburgers did not reserve their fear of outsiders for such shady
characters as gamblers and entertainers. Every fall flatboats loaded
with wares descended the Ohio and Mississippi rivers. Crowding the
wharves of the lower towns, their captains dispensed goods, and eventually the boats themselves, to local buyers before returning in the
spring to their homes up north. These boatmen, who were by and large
businessmen not unlike Vicksburg's shopkeepers, became objects of the
town's xenophobia.

While local storekeepers depended on the wholesale supplies of the
boatmen to keep their shelves stocked, they naturally resented competition from floating retailers. "Nearly every produce house has been
closed," wrote one disgruntled Vicksburger to the town council, "and
that business usurped by a few strangers, who, I am told, lie here all
winter, trade in all things, and to a large amount, without paying *one
cent tax*, either to the State or corporation."[23] The writer worried about
more than the competition the flatboaters presented to local merchants,
however. In language that could have been applied to the gamblers, he
feared for the moral influence the visitors would have on the city. Their
liquor "seduces the poor, and particularly our slaves to buy, and the constitution is injured by its drink, whilst the morals are corrupted."[24] Furthermore, these strangers came "from a country whose people entertain
deep rooted prejudices against our institutions, who have for us a secret
hatred."[25] The appearance in the North of abolitionism did nothing to
ease tensions between the townfolk and the boatmen.

In the winter of 1838 riots nearly erupted in Vicksburg once again. In
an attempt to chase away some of the several hundred flatboats docked
at the public landing the city government began to charge a daily wharf
fee. Their efforts had no effect, so officials kept raising the wharfage
rate. When it reached fifty dollars a day per boat, the flatboatmen suddenly rebelled. A mob of perhaps a thousand angry people armed with

guns, clubs, and at least one cannon crowded the waterfront opposite the local militia, which took up positions behind a wall of cotton bales. Lines were thus drawn for a very bloody fight. Perhaps those prospects brought all parties to their senses. Before a shot was fired all laid down their arms and agreed to let the court settle the dispute.[26]

At bottom of the gambling riots, the flatboat war, and possibly the fires that erupted in certain sections of town, lay a nagging sense among Vicksburg residents that they were losing control of their city to strangers. Of course the threat posed by drunken knife- and gun-wielding gamblers was to an extent quite real, as was abolitionism. More alarming than either, however, was the helplessness of town leaders to do anything about them. Vicksburg's permanent residents, businessmen and workers alike, found themselves torn between on one hand their desire for the river trade and on the other hand their fear that the swarms of people who came with that trade would eventually seize the town. Thus, in their minds all strangers were gamblers, abolitionists, drunkards, or troublemakers out to destroy their "respectable" society.

As happened in towns and cities throughout antebellum America, Vicksburg's household heads responded to rapid population growth and high rate of mobility, and to their sense of social disorder created by demographic patterns, by forming voluntary associations. In 1831 a group of young men started Vicksburg's first voluntary militia. That same year the Temperance Association met for the first time. The next year the Clerks' Debating Society and the Vicksburg and Warren County Colonization Society started meeting. Succeeding years saw the organization of the Carpenters' Society, the Anti-Duelling Society, the Mechanics' Mutual Benefit Society, the Sons of Temperance, the Hibernian Society, at least two more militia companies, half a dozen chapters of Masons, Odd Fellows, and Sons of Malta, the Chess Club, several volunteer fire companies, the Agricultural and Mechanical Association, and the boosterish Magnolia Club.[27]

Voluntary associations performed two almost contradictory functions that managed to give some much-needed structure to Vicksburg's dynamic society. First, they provided a means of integrating newcomers into the town establishment, thereby easing the worries caused by the large transient population. Prior to the formation of voluntary associations the best claims to membership among the town establishment rested on a long-standing position within the local community. Newcomers without some connection to a local resident who could introduce them and vouch for their character were thus shut out. Voluntary associations gave newcomers an easier way to become a part of established society; they could join a club, a process that was particularly easy for new arrivals who had joined a chapter of a national organization elsewhere, Odd Fellows and Masons, for example.

Second, associations nevertheless maintained the division between the established citizenry and newcomers by sharply contrasting both groups. Voluntary societies, their leaders especially, in effect defined by example what it meant to be a part of the established citizenry: hard-working, responsible, prosperous. Older and wealthier men of long time residency in the community, most of them professionals, storekeepers, or artisans who owned their shops, filled the leadership posts of Vicks-burg's voluntary associations. Typically, they owned two and a half times as much real estate and five times as many slaves as the average household head, sufficient property to place them among the wealthiest 10 percent of the city's household heads. They were native-born, with most coming from Southern states but not in numbers disproportionate to the representation of Southerners among the total population. Not only did officers share similar backgrounds and lifestyles, they were so well connected to each other that they must have presented a solid front, a consensus image of town leadership. Several served on the boards of more than one club at a time and could have introduced each of the re-maining officers to half the people in the group. The clubs, however, if not the leadership positions within them, were open to any male resi-dents. To refuse to belong was to reject the order of Vicksburg society, at least the order as defined by club leaders. Indeed, the word voluntary may not accurately describe the societies.[28]

Of course, some organizations did more than simply present an image of consensus and order. The militias, for example, went about their business with little subtlety or tact. However, they were effective at easing social tension only in part by providing overt social control. Like the more benign organizations such as the Chess Club, they also helped relieve the sense of disorder by simply bringing residents together, by defining one's position within the community, and by giving the town a more visible social structure.

Despite the militias the gamblers returned, flatboats crowded the wharf, and masses of strangers came and went. Gun clubs did not clean up the town. Temperance organizations did not stop the liquor from flowing. A glance at a single newspaper issue from December 1860 con-veys a picture of a society as raucous as ever: At Molly Bunch's "house of ill-fame" several boatmen got into a fight. One was killed. A city consta-ble tried to break up the struggle and was shot at but not hurt. Another fight broke out, this time at Coppersmith's "whiskey mill" on Levee Street. The same day a local magistrate dismissed charges on two drunks found asleep on a sidewalk, but did order the offenders to leave town. And authorities incarcerated another drunk, a woman, also found asleep on a sidewalk. Meanwhile, concerned citizens organized another police society. Yet this new society did little more than elect officers and debate rules concerning purpose and membership.[29] Little had changed over the preceding thirty years except in the perception of the problem posed by drunken and troublesome strangers. There was until just be-fore the Civil War a noticeable waning of the sense of urgency. Mobs no longer purged the city of undesirables perhaps because voluntary societies gave to their members, to the permanent residents as a whole, a sense of being in control. Thus they were able live in a society that was really no more or less "disorderly," that is, prone to drunkenness and brawling, than it had been in the days of the gambling riots.

The people of Vicksburg responded to the dislocations caused by rapid urbanization and high population turnover by organizing clubs to strengthen ties among established residents, to mitigate tensions with newcomers, and to organize a leadership that could give some direction to local development. In so doing they repeated a common pattern.[30] In two important ways, however, the voluntary societies of this town were different from Eastern cities, north and south, though they were typical of newer, Western towns. Vicksburg men completely dominated the voluntary societies. Furthermore, local churches did not actively participate in the town's reform associations.

Women were absent even from the reform societies that they were so actively involved in elsewhere, most specifically, temperance organizations and orphan asylums.[31] The task of dispensing "noble charities" fell entirely to the Masons, Odd Fellows, and various male organizations. So, for example, while her husband and brother-in-law went out to Sons of Temperance, Odd Fellows, Singing Club, and Fire Company meetings, often until late in the evening, Mahala Roach stayed home and sewed and looked after her children. "Husband enjoys his society so much," wrote Mahala. As they did in rural neighborhoods, men dominated life in the city, too, largely because they owned the property and the businesses that depended on a stable social climate. Moreover, their control of money gave them power over their women. "Mr. Roach made me a present of *50 dollars*—to my great gratification," Mahala Roach wrote in her journal, with more than a touch of sarcasm.[32]

Yet there were real differences between the lives of city women and their country counterparts. The urban household was much more of a woman's domain. Of course, it could be a lonely place, lonelier than the most isolated plantation, where at least husbands typically were present. Mahala Roach agonized over her husband's absences.[33] He was hardly ever home, spending his days at the office and evenings with cronies at his society meetings. On a rare occasion, he "came home to tea very early, in time to see Nora & Soph undressing and bathing, quite new for him as he usually comes after they are asleep." Men inhabited what Mahala called the "outer world"; they left the "inner world" to women. Such a distinction between worlds would have made little sense to country women and men.[34]

Unlike in Eastern cities, local churches did not actively participate in Vicksburg's reform associations.[35] Such an active reformer as James Roach did not take communion for the first time until he was 38 years old, some time after he joined the Sons of Temperance.[36] On occasion a preacher would make special efforts to reach the transient population. The pastor of the Presbyterian church, for example, spent some Sunday afternoons preaching before the flatboatmen at the landing, although he may have been exceptional. For not all ministers tried so hard to tame the town's more rough-and-tumble elements. In his history of Presbyterians in Mississippi, C. W. Grafton told of how several drunken rowdies interrupted the Reverend George Moore of Vicksburg one Sunday as he delivered his sermon to his congregation. The troublemakers demanded an end to "such silly doings as preaching." According to Grafton, Moore removed his jacket, stepped from his pulpit, marched down the aisle, and like a bar-room bouncer slammed his adversaries with several good punches and threw them out the door. The pastor then "went calmly back to the pulpit and put on his coat and began again to preach the glad gospel."[37] No doubt Grafton exaggerated to tell a good story. Nevertheless, there were no bible or tract societies organized, no revivals like those that occurred in Rochester, New York, that would bring the masses of outsiders into Vicksburg congregations.[38] On the whole evangelical attitudes did not have the influence on Vicksburg's associations they had elsewhere, as was apparent in the style of the town's reformers. Instead of appealing to individual conscience, they threatened community wrath. A local newspaper reflected this attitude in a warning to all "loafers, rowdies and gamblers. If you cannot get high wages work for low ones; if you cannot get low ones work for your victuals and clothes. It is much more respectable than lounging about and doing nothing." The writer did not, however, hold up the positive rewards of hard work and a job well done. He pointed out the negative rewards for idlers: "There is a feeling rapidly gaining strength in this community which says in tones not to be mistaken or misunderstood, that idleness and profligacy must be put down. It rests with you to choose whether you will do it yourselves *or have the citizens do it for you.*"[39] Such threats were real, backed up by several enthusiastic militias charged with the responsibility of removing "all itinerants and persons being in this community without any visible means of support, and who are unknown in this community."[40]

The explanation for the peculiar character of Vicksburg's voluntary associations lies in the town's close association with the countryside, and in the fact that the town's founders and early leaders were either former planters or else were closely associated with rural slaveholders. In seeking to bring some order to a dynamic urban environment Vicksburg's leaders tried to recreate the structure they had known in the countryside. They built organizations that worked like extended patriarchal families, marshaling the power of a few on behalf of the many who pledged loyalty in return. It is thus not surprising that they preferred the authoritative style of the militias and the Anti-Gambling Society to the softer, more persuasive approach of the temperance societies, which they left to townsmen born outside the South.[41]

Leaders perceived the town as a close-knit community, not as a mass of individuals, an image they reflected through the weaving and overlapping of their societies. Vicksburg's voluntary associations tended to be inclusive, rather than exclusive, a trait of societies in other Southern, though not Northern, cities.[42] Members encouraged, if not expected, any and all resident men, regardless of wealth, occupation, or ethnicity, to join a club. Indeed, the associational web constructed by the officers of the town's voluntary societies was more interconnected than the kin networks of rural neighborhoods. The odds that any two officers were linked directly or by one intermediary were 40 percent, double the chances of kinship connecting two household heads in the most densely connected rural neighborhoods.[43] Of course leadership in Vicksburg depended not on kinship and the control of large estates, but on reputation for prominence in town affairs, maintained by frequent public display. Edward Welles, a Yankee newcomer, described the funeral of "an old resident," in which the Volunteer Southern Military Company, the Vicksburg Military Association, the Masons, and a band all joined the procession. "Secret societies and public associations," he observed, "are more generally cultivated here than at the North. The public displays of the Masonic Lodges in this town are more frequent, more gorgeous in their arrangements and more universally appreciated than in Northern towns."[44] More demonstrative of their power, but occurring less frequently, were the public displays of authority during moments of crisis. When called to act Vicksburg's rulers did so quickly and decisively, as during the gambling riots, in the manner of any planter patriarch defending his clan.

A rural style could not last long in an urban place, however. By the late 1840s and through the next decade the character of Vicksburg's associations had begun to change. New types of societies appeared. Edward Welles, who was so taken with the Masons and militias, complained about the lack of a scientific or literary association, but his comments came almost too late.[45] Within a few years a chapter of the State Historical Society, a Chess Club and Reading Room, and for the more scientific-minded the Agricultural and Mechanical Association were meeting regularly, improving the city not by forcefully removing unwanted sorts but by bringing to it an air of civility and refinement.[46] Vicksburg and its citizens were coming of age as a city apart from the countryside.

Eventually, even women became more active in Vicksburg societies. The separate worlds noted by Mahala Roach left room for women to extend their special concerns and talents beyond the confines of their homes. In the summer of 1853, for example, while yellow fever raged in Vicksburg, Mahala attended to the sick, nurturing them as though they were part of her family. "I visited the sick, gave them medicine, etc— sent food to *three* families—(one of my families are well)—four times today."[47] In 1850 several Vicksburg women established the Ladies' Benevolent Association, though it may have been short-lived.[48] By the end of the decade there was a Ladies' Church Association, with which

Mahala Roach worked. Thus, male domination of voluntary associations and charitable groups in Vicksburg, a vestige of a rural and "western" past, appears to have been waning in the years just before the Civil War.[49]

By late twentieth-century standards, American cities before the Civil War were crude and dirty. Vicksburg was no exception. Most buildings were constructed of wood and unpainted. Hogs roamed freely in the town's dirt streets, which looked "almost like one vast hog-pen." They frequently ripped open feed sacks piled along storefronts. Packs of scavenger dogs also wandered the streets. And "nearly every house in the city" was infested with roaches. Still, Vicksburg's residents began to think of their city, however it may appear to modern scholars, as a "civilized" and "cultured" place in contrast to what they perceived as a more "backward" countryside. By the late antebellum years residents attempted to clean their city. They paved several streets and built a new courthouse, which brought some architectural style to Vicksburg. Officials restricted livestock and in 1860 began a campaign to reduce the canine population. By October they had captured and drowned in the river 129 dogs. Newspapers advertised remedies for cockroaches. But the most important reforms were those aimed at the people themselves. If Vicksburg was to be a civilized place its inhabitants would have to behave in a civilized manner.[50]

The new urban sensibility arose from Vicksburg's development as an urban place. It was particularly evident during the debate over dueling and in the efforts of several Vicksburg leaders to cease such affairs once and for all. The duel is nearly synonymous with the Old South. Warren County certainly had its share, usually stemming from disputes between rival planter patriarchs. But the duel evolved into an accepted means by which gentlemen, including urban elites, could settle their disputes. Indeed, these affairs of honor became more important in the city among nonplanters because their authority rested so much on prestige and public display rather than on real power held through control of family property. Seargent S. Prentiss, Vicksburg's famous Whig lawyer and orator, fought more than one duel. For a time the Black Knight, Alexander K. McClung, perhaps the South's most feared duelist, made his home in Vicksburg. The city's editors were notorious. Between 1841 and 1860 four of them died in gunfights. Another killed a man, received a wound in another duel from which he recovered, only to meet his end in yet another conflict, this time in Texas. Vicksburg more than the surrounding countryside served as the main arena for duels, as urban residents adapted the planters' culture to a dynamic urban environment.[51]

In the years following the gambling riots there emerged in some quarters of the city a sense that the lynchings and duels were wrong. Perhaps they were even immoral, or at least not proper behavior for civilized people, gentlemen especially. Vicksburg took a beating in the national press following the hanging and banishment of the gamblers. The city acquired a national reputation that took years to live down, much to the dismay of its boosters. The frequency with which some residents shot at one another did not help the city's image. For example, in 1837 an alleged abolitionist named Grace received twenty or thirty lashes for encouraging slaves to escape by writing false passes for them. The Northern press voiced shock and dismay at yet another lynching in Vicksburg. They expressed particular outrage that the whipping had taken place within earshot of the victim's wife and children. Clearly, town life had not visibly changed much since the gamblers' riot two years earlier. But the attitudes of some residents had indeed changed. In the town's defense the editor of the *Advocate and Register* pointed out that critics had exaggerated the event. Grace had not been "'whipped within hearing of the shrieks and lamentations of his wife and children,'" as Northern papers reported. "It was at a considerable distance, we cannot state it exactly, but entirely out of hearing of his house."[52] That town residents cared at all about the opinions of outsiders, especially Northerners, attested to the continually developing position of Vicksburg within a national urban system, which was effectively pulling the city away from the countryside, away from the South. The town's national stature began to matter to local boosters, who sounded defensive tones when reminded of its reputation for violence. Wrote a local editor, "There is not now another place of the size in the United States where there is generally less crime or so resolute and determined hostility to lynching is manifested as in Vicksburg."[53] Perhaps. In any case, Northerners were sometimes relieved to find that the town did not live up to its "unenviable reputation," and that in Vicksburg "it is by no means necessary to peel your apples with a Bowie Knife."[54]

The event that actually precipitated the organization of the Anti-Duelling Society was the murder of James Hagan, an editor of the Democratic *Vicksburg Sentinel*. Ever the irascible old man, Hagan had let his vituperative pen get him into dangerous scrapes before but had always managed to survive. In this instance he turned his poison on a Whiggish judge and ruffled the feathers of the juror's son. The young man came from Jackson armed and ready to fight. He met Hagan on the street around the corner from the editor's office, and there they quarreled and wrestled to the ground before the young man fired his pistol, sending a ball between Hagan's shoulders, up through his neck, and into his brain.[55]

Horrified by this bloody affair, and fearful that it would resurrect the city's reputation for violence, a group of men led by John Bodley pledged to eradicate Vicksburg streets of all gun battles. Nine years earlier Bodley's kinsman had sought to clean up the town when he helped to blast the gamblers out of a coffee shop in the Kangaroo district. He died trying. How times had changed since then. The solution had become the problem. No less than card-sharking and drunkenness, dueling and violence in general, no matter who its perpetrators, and regardless of motives, was "subversive of the peace and happiness of society." Members of the new society resolved to withdraw their business from

newspapers that published slanderous remarks, or challenges and responses. They promised to "sustain any person, by all means in our
power, who will refuse to challenge, or to accept a challenge." They
would press the state legislature to forbid public officials from fighting,
and urge officers of the law in Louisiana, where Vicksburg's dueling
grounds were located, to arrest promptly "all parties engaged or about to
engage in such practices."[56]

Bodley's resolutions did not go unopposed. Country elites led by
Joseph and Jefferson Davis argued for moderation. Hagan had not died
in a duel, they pointed out, but in a crude and unnecessary brawl, a
"puppy fight." Efforts to stop such violence were to be encouraged, but
they should not impinge upon the right of gentlemen to settle their affairs
honorably. Borrowing an argument from proslavery theorists, Jefferson
Davis insisted that dueling "can only be suppressed by the progress of intelligence, morality and good breeding." For this reason an effort should
be made to resolve only those conflicts that arise "unnecessarily."

Jefferson's older brother Joseph was more to the point. Directing his
comments to Judge Bodley, he argued that "when men had become so
just and enlightened to do away with the necessity for personal account-
ability, . . . his Honor would be required no longer to sit upon the
bench." "Let us correct the abuses," he urged, "but, sir, let us, for all
gross insults not properly atoned for, make it imperative upon the
agressed to stand on equal terms and fight; make it so, sir, that he must
fight, atone, or leave the country." For the Davises and their followers
the duel was a privilege, indeed a mark, of their standing in society. But
urban elites were shedding the notions of honor that still guided rural
folk. Bodley and his followers no longer distinguished between crude
and genteel violence. "The duel was against the laws of God and man,"
the staunch anti-duelers cried, to which Seargent Prentiss responded
with the suggestion that they reread the scriptures and note the "splendid duel" between David and Goliath. In the end Bodley carried the day,
shutting the Davises and their followers out of the association leadership.[57]

That Jefferson and Joseph Davis would not oppose dueling in instances when a gentleman's honor had to be defended is not at all surprising. And one would expect they would be joined by the likes of Seargent S. Prentiss, a practiced duelist, and by Colonel Thomas E. Robins, a
son-in-law to Joe Davis and owner of the "Castle," perhaps Vicksburg's
most renowned mansion. Such men were gentlemen of the highest
standing. What is surprising, however, is how much they had in common with the self-styled "whole-hog anti-fighting men." The backgrounds of seven in the group that opposed dueling are known. All were
Southern-born. They were as wealthy as their opposition, owning on average enough real estate to place them among the top 4 percent of the
county's household heads. At least two were planters, including Henry
W. Vick, nephew of Vicksburg's founder, owner of a large plantation on

Deer Creek in the Yazoo Delta, developer of Vick's Hundred Seed, one of the South's most popular strains of cotton. Yet these gentlemen stood opposed to the duel, the most famous mark of their breed.

The two groups differed, however, in the size of their slaveholdings, in their place of residence, and along party lines. Only three of the "whole hog" anti-fighters owned more than seven slaves. Joe Davis, alone, owned nearly 250 slaves. All but one opponent of the duel was a Whig. The Davises and Colonel Robins were Democrats. All but one of the seven anti-duelers lived in Vicksburg. The Davises, of course, lived on large plantations. The lines of division were not perfectly clear. Prentiss, as a Whig and a long-time resident of Vicksburg, was an exception among the Davis group, just as Nicholas Coleman, a Democrat, a rural resident, and an owner of 27 slaves was an anomaly among the anti-duelists. Nevertheless, the pattern is apparent enough to suggest the emergence of an alternative, more modern definition of gentleman.

Owning on average fewer slaves, living in a city of several thousand people, making their living off the cotton trade to be sure, but as investors, merchants, and lawyers and not by overseeing its production directly—even Henry Vick lived fifty miles from his delta plantation—the urban anti-duelers would have been more cosmopolitan than many planters, more conscious of how gentlemen in other regions of the country were expected to behave. Thus, a step removed from the plantation elite, and a step closer to a national elite joined by an expanding urban and economic system, they began to reflect new sensibilities, alien perhaps to those predominant in the countryside, but very much in line with elites in New York or London. Henry Vick, amateur botanist, astute businessman with investments in Texas, perhaps in Cuba, symbol of Vicksburg's emerging urban elite, represented a different kind of gentleman. Next to him a Seargent S. Prentiss whose lifestyle of dueling, high-stakes gambling, and heavy drinking, which ultimately brought him financial ruin and an early death, seemed anachronistic.[58]

Vicksburg society continued to be much more heterogeneous than rural society. But urban residents ultimately came to accept diversity as a kind of order. They stopped trying to force consensus and instead accepted the inevitability of difference, which town residents expressed in a vigorous political party competition that simply did not exist in the countryside. Henry Vick and others like him developed a brand of Whiggery that reflected their urban and urbane sensibilities, and which was quite unlike the Whiggery of rural planters, or of older urban elites such as Prentiss.

8

ORGANIZING A COUNTY COMMUNITY: NEIGHBORHOODS, PARTIES, AND THE POLITICS OF DEVELOPMENT

In 1810 the state legislature established Warren County and asked a commission of local taxpayers to find a suitable location for the courthouse. After surveying the more settled southern region of the new county, and consulting with their neighbors, the four commissioners decided on a spot near where the old Spanish road to the Walnut Hills passed close by the river, a location convenient to most people living in the county at that time. Here they established Warrenton, the seat of justice. Fifteen years later another commission moved the courthouse ten miles north to the new town of Vicksburg. Warrenton area residents were furious. Led by the Gibson and Hyland families, they determined not to let Vicksburg's founders, who had already captured much of Warrenton's trade, steal their courthouse too. When the question was put to a vote, however, Warrenton's leaders simply could not muster enough support from around the county to place even one of their own on the commission of three that finally settled the matter.[1]

The debate over the location of the courthouse left some feeling bitter. The written record of the event is spare, but locals more than a hundred and seventy years later tell how officials transferred deed books, probate files, county court minutes, all the official documents of life in Warren County, quietly, after dark, so as not to provoke angry outbursts from the losers. Some descendants of south-end families still speak, jokingly now, of how north-end residents stole *their* courthouse.

Warrenton's leaders had good reasons to be angry. With the courthouse gone their town lost its only chance to become something more than the small village it was to remain. But the event had a greater significance. It marked a shift in the direction of Warren County's development as a social entity. Hitherto people had lived their lives primarily in the face-to-face, horizontally and inwardly organized worlds of family and neighborhood. The outside world seemed distant and of little importance. In time, however, as people began to turn their attention outward, they sought access to the vertical ties that linked them to the larger society, forming supralocal organizations to coordinate affairs and protect their interests over long distances. They also looked, with a new enthusiasm visible at election time, to the one organization that had been there all along but which had never really been relevant until now: government. The location of the county seat thus became a matter of special interest.[2]

The outward turn and the fusion of Warren County's various rural neighborhoods and urban places into a larger, more complex organization is most visible in the growth of roads over the period from 1814 to 1860 (Figures 8.1 to 8.3). At the earlier date only one road traversed the county from south to north, allowing a minimum of communication between settlements. By 1835 several new roads snaked their way through hilly countryside toward the county's two main river ports, at Warrenton in the county's south end and Vicksburg in the north end. By 1860 a dense network of roads created the image of a single unit, with all the many small settlements connected to the central hub of Vicksburg. Neighborhoods continued to function as the primary arena for the mixing of family and friends, but they also became part of a larger economic, social, and political entity comprising the whole county.

The driving force behind the county's transformation was the unfailing energy of its residents. However self-contained rural neighborhoods seemed, their inhabitants never ceased pushing the peripheries of their worlds outward. They steadily improved the roads, bridges, and ferries that linked them with people and places beyond the immediate vicinity, pouring time, money, and sweat into improving transportation and communication with the same determination they showed when clearing fields and mending fences. In the process they broke down neighborhood isolation, extended their interests farther afield, and forged a larger economic, social, and political unit roughly contained within the county lines.

Such a transformation was not necessarily the conscious objective of the people responsible for it. But farmers would have attested to the difficulty of travel, whether to market or to a friend's house. They would also have said that they made such journeys nevertheless, even if they tried to keep them as short and infrequent as possible. Any improvement in the roads, by widening, or by building bridges, they welcomed because they made their lives easier. The better the roads, however, the farther and the more often they would be willing to travel, and the more willing they would be to produce a crop for market. Thus the improvement cycle

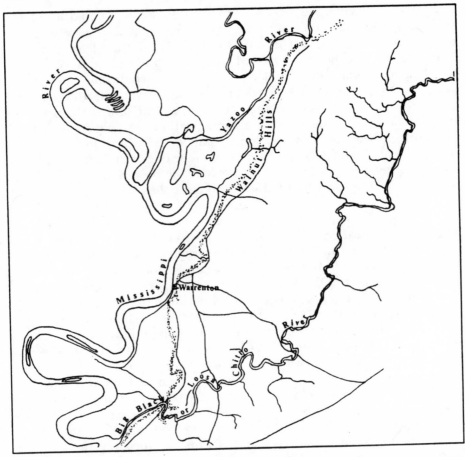

Figure 8.1 Warren County roads, 1814. (*Source:* A list of the overseers of roads in Warren County for the year 1814, OCHM.)

began. An interest in improving transportation and communication connections and a commitment to production for distant markets grew together. Farmers' economic and social worlds consequently expanded to
include people who once seemed distant and unimportant, people in other
neighborhoods, town dwellers. At first a rider on horseback needed a day
to travel from one side of the county to the other. With the improved road
finished in 1823, he could travel as far as Jackson in the same amount of
time, and by stage coach if he so desired. By 1838 a railroad cut that same
journey to a mere two and a half hours, while another, completed twenty
years later, put the once distant city of New Orleans within just one day's
reach. Intended or not, steady development of the material links with the
outside world transformed Warren County society.[3]

Early settlers undertook the county's first improvements within the
neighborhoods where they lived. In small groups they surveyed routes

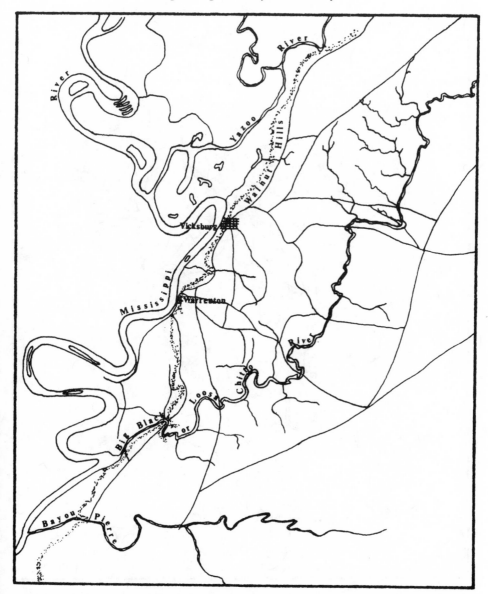

Figure 8.2 Warren County roads, 1835. (*Source:* Police Court Minutes, 1833–34, OCHM.)

through the woods, designed bridges, constructed ferries. They pooled their labor to see the job through to the finish just as they did barn-raisings. Joseph Davis and his neighbors built a series of levees around their homes to protect them all from flooding.[4] In the opposite corner of the county six planters along the border of Warren and Hinds counties took advantage of their location, plus their combined resources in land and

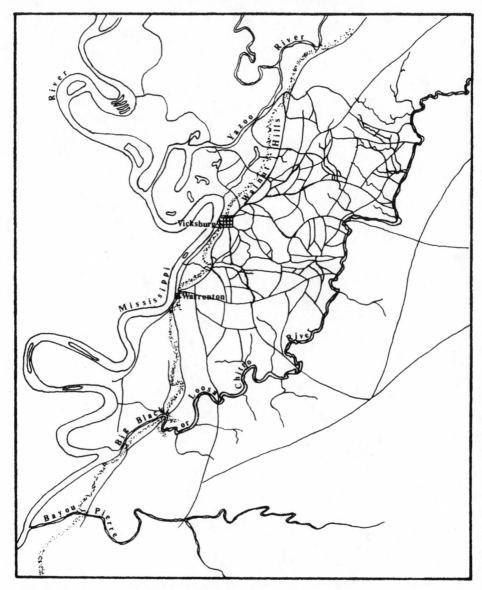

Figure 8.3 Warren County roads, 1860. (*Source:* Map of the county between
Vicksburg and Meridian, Miss. Showing the route followed by the Seventeenth
Army Corps under the command of Major General J. B. McPherson in February
1864. Surveyed by Lieutenant H. M. Bush.)

labor, to join in building a bridge across the Big Black River and collecting a toll from all travelers between Vicksburg and Jackson.[5] Only on occasion did individuals or neighborhoods seek direct government assistance, and these tended to be for undertakings too large for one

neighborhood. A group of planters from the vicinity of the Open Wood petitioned the legislature for assistance in building a road between their homes and the state capital at Jackson. With the support of a similarly interested group in Hinds County they won the legislature's consent, plus $300 to help cut costs.[6]

By the mid-1820s people looked beyond their own farms and neighborhoods for improvement opportunities elsewhere. Their successes at home encouraged them to repeat the process of land development and cotton production in other places. To do so they organized on a grander scale. In 1825 four planters from around the county, plus two lawyers and a doctor from Vicksburg, met to discuss the possibility of procuring a bank charter.[7] Two years later a branch of the state bank opened in Warren County, and shortly after that a second, the Planter's Bank, with capital of $100,000, "exclusive of the stock that may be subscribed there," opened it doors in Vicksburg.[8] Banks were an essential means of pooling capital for the purchase and improvement of land.

Warren County's residents were not alone in their interest in developing new lands. These were the famous "flush times," when speculators and cotton planters with insatiable appetites for land, emboldened by the demonstrated success of cotton planting in the Southwest—the magnificent mansions at Natchez, the overnight transformation of places such as Warren County from pioneer settlement to thriving plantation belt—left their tired lands in South Carolina and Virginia and headed in great hordes for Alabama and Mississippi. A speculative whirlwind that few had ever seen before, or would see again, seemed to sweep up all before it, newcomers and old-timers alike, anyone and everyone with access to a little credit.[9]

Alexander McNutt purchased, then resold, 7000 acres in the Mississippi delta north of Vicksburg.[10] Job Baker purchased a large tract, "more land than he can cultivate," in the hills above Vicksburg. Over the next year he built a grist mill, cleared and planted 200 acres, then sold his improvement for profit.[11] Henry Vick, his cousin John Wesley Vick, William Miles, and William Pescod borrowed money to form a land company in Texas.[12] The shareholders of the Planters' Bank purchased in the bank's name land all over the state for quick resale.[13] Vicksburg's greatest speculator, clothing merchant J. J. Chewning, borrowed and invested madly until by 1840, when he tallied his holdings, he owned: 815 acres and 39 slaves near Lake Providence, Louisiana; 1,360 acres in Carroll County, Mississippi; 1,526 acres and 31 slaves in Bolivar County, Mississippi; 1,570 acres near the Sunflower River, in Washington County, Mississippi; 600 acres in Yazoo County Mississippi; 1,000 acres in Crawford County, Arkansas; a lot with a house in Clinton, Mississippi; interest in the town of Pine Bluff, Arkansas; several lots in Vicksburg, plus acreage near the railroad and cotton press; and a home and five slaves in Warren County.[14]

Land was not the only opportunity that attracted speculators during these heady years. In 1834 a group of Warren County investors, "in the name of the planting and commercial interests of the State," organized the Commercial and Railroad Bank of Vicksburg and announced the sale of $4 million of stock, to enhance the availability of credit, to increase the circulating medium, and to promote internal improvements, in particular a railroad they planned to build between Vicksburg and Jackson.[15] Of the twenty organizers whose backgrounds can be determined, all but four lived in Vicksburg. Among them were ten merchants, including one from Warrenton, three lawyers, three planters, and one manufacturer. Several of the merchants had close ties to local planters. William Pescod, for example, was a close friend of the Vicks, one of whom was a commissioner. Erasmus Downs belonged to another of the county's oldest planter families. William R. Campbell had recently taken up planting himself, having acquired 1700 acres on the chosen route. Lawyer and land speculator Alexander McNutt was a close friend of cotton planter Joel Cameron and Cameron's wife, whom he married shortly after her husband's death.[16]

Vicksburg's merchants may have been the driving force behind the railroad venture, but they could not do it alone. Their success depended on their ability to unite much of the county behind them. Nor could the small plantation neighborhoods along the proposed line have managed such a project on their own. They had required government assistance just to build a dirt road. Thus, Vicksburg merchants whose businesses depended on selling supplies and manufactures to residents in the interior of the county and state and interior planters whose livelihood depended on getting their cotton to market organized to pool capital, purchase land, and construct a railroad that would benefit all parties.[17]

The role of government in matters of economic development had always been minimal. Neighborhoods built their own roads and bridges, chose their own supervisors, conducted their own surveys, supplied their own labor and materials. County officials simply approved what neighborhoods had already decided. Occasionally a large project required governmental funding and supervision. The Spanish colonial government had constructed the road from the Big Black to the Walnut Hills. Thirty years later the state legislature appropriated funds for a road from the Hills to Jackson. Small-scale improvements, however, were handled locally, until locals began to expand their horizons. When they did, they sought government protection of their increasingly far-flung interests. The role and authority of public officials in Warren County consequently expanded, superseding the political order of small neighborhoods.

Authorized by an interested electorate to direct county affairs, officials lost their earlier reluctance to interfere with neighborhood affairs. Neighborhood business became county business. Elias Hankinson lost to the board of police the right to set rates for the ferry that ran between his property on both sides of the Big Black. In earlier days he operated his ferry for the income it provided, but also as a service to his friends and kinfolk who lived nearby. Fees acceptable to both parties had always been worked out on a personal basis. This informal mode of operation no longer worked once the growing number of travelers to and from Vicksburg formed the bulk of the ferry's passengers. Hankinson had no interest in whether or not someone he had never seen before got across the river. What business was it of his? Why should he or one of his slaves leave more pressing concerns to assist every wayfarer? Helping a friend was a duty and a pleasure, but he would charge strangers for their inconvenience. Travelers, and the county in general, saw Hankinson as providing an essential service, not a neighborly favor. His informal and whimsical way of conducting business was too unpredictable. On behalf of the county the board of police saw to it that the ferry operated all the time, that no one was refused service except during high water when travel was dangerous, and that rates were fair and reliable. Operators who found such regulations objectionable had only one alternative: They could turn their ferry over to a keeper hired by the county, and receive no compensation.[18]

The board did not always oppose the interests of ferry keepers. In regulating their number and location they sometimes protected them. John Miller received monopoly privileges when the board prohibited all other persons from conveying people, animals, or carriages across the Mississippi River within three miles of his ferry. Competition, board members reasoned, brought frequent changes in ownership and shifts in location that added an element of unpredictability to county trade and travel. When Henry Lewis petitioned for approval to begin a ferry service across the Mississippi the board made no decision without first consulting Miller to make sure that he thought there was sufficient demand to warrant a second service. In return for such protection the county reserved the right to set Miller's rates.[19]

Officials tried to accommodate any individuals they crossed, and even compensated them, sometimes, as when they sequestered private property for public projects. However, they exercised final authority. For example, when the county board of police decided to widen a road on the outskirts of Vicksburg in 1839 they appointed a commission to do the surveying and ordered the razing of all structures, buildings, and fences that stood in the way. In another case, the board ordered commissioners to "obtain if possible the consent of the owners of the land through which said road may be laid out," and thereby minimize the "charge or damage to the county." But while county officials were prepared to bargain on the amount of compensation paid those whose land would be taken for the new road, the actual location of the road was not negotiable.[20]

Wrangling over county roads created conflict between neighborhood and county interests. It also strained relations between private and public interests. Neighborhoods had managed to accommodate both. Now the county struggled to do the same. Farmers had to fence their fields to

prevent open-ranged livestock from damaging crops. If a road ran
through a field, then they also had to build gates. This was an added expense, but, worse still, it left crops vulnerable to the careless traveler
who might leave a gate unlatched.[21] As a rule, surveyors tried to plot
roads around privately owned fields. This became difficult to do, however, as farmers cultivated more and more acreage. Landowners found
the other alternative, to run fences along roadsides, prohibitively expensive. In a series of incidents beginning in the late 1830s, several people
simply strung fences across roads, without providing gates. Officials
fined the offenders two dollars for every twenty-four hours that the
fences remained standing, putting an end to that, although in some
cases at great expense to offenders. A particularly stubborn Alexander
Magruder left his illegal fences standing for a year, forcing travelers to
detour or climb over. His fines totaled over $700. Wiser men quickly
conceded the board's authority to protect the interests of the county
even at the expense of certain individuals.[22]

That authority continued to expand. Before landowners could even
enclose a field that had a road running through it they had to receive
permission from the board. By the late 1840s the board required publication in a Vicksburg newspaper of all petitions for gates, to inform distant people who might have reason to oppose the plans so that they
might come forward and express their views.[23] Where to place a road
was no longer a neighborhood decision. The very wording of the law
that granted authority over roads to county boards of police expressed
the change in local decision-making. All roads were to be laid out by a
commission of *disinterested* citizens selected by the board.[24] Of course
commissioners were only disinterested in the individual and neighborhood considerations that had determined where roads would or would
not go in earlier days. They were very much interested in the county as a
whole. Distance from individual neighborhoods enabled the county government to ignore the personal relationships that were central to more
local affairs. When a group of neighbors petitioned the board to replace
a road overseer with whom they disagreed, board members refused, ar-
guing that it was "not in the power of the board to remove [overseers]
except for neglect of duty." Personal squabbles mattered not at all.[25]

The county government's largest development project was the construction of a system of levees to protect the fertile bottom lands along
the Mississippi from inundation. Residents along the river for a stretch
of fifty miles would have to be organized so that land could be acquired,
taxes assessed and collected, building completed to a common standard,
and maintenance provided for. Success would not be achieved if the
project proceeded on a smaller scale, piecemeal fashion. A single hole in
the wall jeopardized the lands and levees of neighborhoods miles downriver. To work properly a levee system had to seal off protected land
completely. All segments had to be interconnected, uniformly built, and

incorporated into a larger system. There could be no missing links in the chain or the river would find an opening.

As early as 1811, a year after the state legislature established Warren County, residents in and near the county seat sought government assistance in constructing a levee in front of the town of Warrenton. The cost of the project was, as it would remain for some time, an insurmountable obstacle. In 1812 the state legislature authorized a lottery to raise the $3000 needed for the levee, but tickets were never sold, and construction never began. Officials deemed it "impracticable" to try to raise money during the cash-scarce years that Americans fought the British. Flooding continued, "leaving waste and desolate a vast body of most excellent Bottom Lands filling them with marshes and stagnant pools of water." Two decades later found Warrenton residents still trying to raise the funds for a levee, but the cost always proved greater than the taxes which property-holders were willing to spend on the project. Moreover, the people who actually wanted the embankment were always too few to pay for such an expensive project on their own, and too powerless to persuade others of its need. Eventually Warrenton got its levee, a low and short one that never worked properly. Water regularly flowed over or behind it and onto the town's streets.[26]

During the early decades of the nineteenth century few of the county's rural residents had any interest in levee building. Most lived above the bluff, beyond the river's reach. Moreover, the regularly inundated marshes served as excellent grazing areas for early cattle herds. Once the county seat moved to the bluffs of Vicksburg the urgency of a good levee at Warrenton diminished. Only the cotton planters near the river's edge needed levees, and they usually built their own. The fertile floodplain, superior in quality to interior farmland, was the best cotton land in the South, but required substantial inputs in capital and labor to realize its advantages. In particular, it had to be drained and protected from flooding. As a consequence, all but the wealthiest farmers settled elsewhere. Joseph Davis built one of the first plantations on Warren County's rich bottom land, at a bend in the river below Warrenton. Arriving from Natchez with over fifty slaves he immediately set his hands to work on the construction of a levee. Until safe from high water there was no point in clearing, planting, or erecting buildings. In the late antebellum years, however, farmers with few slaves, if any, began to settle in lower regions despite the great risk of being washed away. The best land on high ground was taken. Moreover, they wanted to plant cotton, and on soil so rich the risks seemed worth taking.[27]

As the unprotected flood plain filled up with voters the county and state governments came under new pressure to organize the construction of a levee system. But government was slow to act. A consensus on this internal improvement project remained elusive. Petitioners circulated, levee boards planned, engineers surveyed, tax collectors assessed,

but the county continually backed down before it collected money or initiated construction. The state authorized the sale of public lands in low-
lying areas as a way to raise funds and thereby keep taxes low, and further to encourage the settlement on the flood plain of people willing to
pay taxes for levees. Objections to the project persisted. A single em-
bankment following the river from the bluff above Warrenton to the
southern county line would, argued one group of petitioners, "add materially to the taxable property of the county and greatly promote the interests of all parties directly concerned." Other groups whose lands were
subjected to floods less frequently, or who had levees of their own that
worked well enough, objected to the plan, believing that they stood to
lose more in taxes than gain by a county levee system. When Warrenton
residents had first tried to gather support for a levee project, Royal Pace,
a nearby planter, complained that a levee would raise the level of the
river and flood lands that under normal conditions were safe from inundation. Years later Joseph Davis made the same argument. For the moment he sat safe and dry behind a slave-made wall of earth that surrounded him and three neighbors, but he feared the construction of
more levees would raise the water level above existing embankments. He
therefore wanted no part of the project, certainly was not about to help
pay for it, and urged his neighbors to join him in resisting. Obviously
this was no ordinary plantation neighborhood, for it included, besides
Joe Davis, Warren County's wealthiest resident, his brother Jefferson,
the future president of the Confederacy, and one Henry Turner, brother-
in-law to wealthy Natchez planter and state governor John A. Quitman
(Quitman himself owned several hundred acres adjoining Turner). The
residents of Davis Bend were rich enough to construct a successful series of dikes without government assistance. Their desire and more especially their ability to remain aloof from public projects blocked the
schemes of county developers. Davis and his neighbors owned nearly
one-third of the most valuable bottom land in the county below Vicksburg. Their share of the tax burden, over $2000, over 10 percent of the
cost of the whole project, was absolutely essential to the county's plans
for developing its prime cotton region.[28]

By the start of the Civil War Warren County residents were still debating the merits and expense of a county levee system. The problem
was that the project was simply too monumental an undertaking for
local government, let alone private citizens, the small fiefdom of Davis
Bend notwithstanding. The task was particularly difficult in Warren
County. Not everyone needed protection from flooding. Most county residents did not live on the flood plain. Thus, the whole county never organized for the project; only a portion did, and their combined resources
were insufficient, particularly when the richest planters refused to participate. But interest in the bottom land remained so long as cotton
ruled that part of the South. To take advantage of the rich alluvial soil
developers would have to step forth from their small neighborhoods,

their counties, their states even, and organize on a grand scale. The great earthworks that eventually lined the Mississippi would have to await the fantastic resources of the early twentieth-century federal government.[29]

In their efforts to manage development projects too large for single neighborhoods to undertake Warren County residents turned to their county government, investing it with more authority than it had had earlier. In the process they transferred the scepter of leadership from family patriarch to elected official. Of course that transfer remained incomplete. Neighborhoods and patriarchs persisted as part of the county's social structure, as part of the experience of living in a slave plantation society. That experience, moreover, had an effect on the development of electoral politics because it shaped the way people looked at government. To planters, their kin, and neighbors, the county appeared as a big neighborhood, its leaders as patriarchs who would apply their resources in land, slaves, and money to the benefit of the whole community, just as they continued to do in each neighborhood.[30]

Thus the county promoted development for the benefit of the community. It continued to do so throughout the antebellum period, both positively by raising funds and granting charters and negatively by regulating and policing. Officials restrained competition by granting monopolies to ferry operators and bridge builders, by fining developers whose reckless pursuit of profits endangered the community. Farmers unable to afford the cost of fencing pastures along the railroad line lost stock to the trains. Within a two- or three-month period one Mr. Miller "lost seven mules valued at fifteen hundred dollars, and he had to compromise with the road at half price."[31] But the directors of a railroad company were not likely to take seriously the complaints of scattered individuals. They did pay heed to government, however. On occasion excavations and piles of dirt from track line construction and repairs obstructed adjacent roads. Travelers complained to county officials who then fined company directors. Similarly, when the railroad company allowed its bridges to fall into a dangerous state of disrepair the board of police chastised directors with threats of prosecution. Following a yellow-fever epidemic the board of police appointed flour and pork inspectors "to protect the community against unwholesome provisions being vended among them." It had inspected and licensed liquor peddlers long before that. In 1832 just as county government was assuming responsibilities in organizing economic development it also took over the responsibility of caring for the poor.[32]

County elections reflected the gradual amalgamation of rural neighborhoods into a county community, although tendencies toward localism persisted. Wide variation in voting patterns among the county's towns and rural neighborhoods continually characterized local elections. The election of sheriff could be hotly contested in some places, and won by a landslide in others. In 1835 the winning candidate for sheriff polled 60 percent of the total vote, but received only 26 percent of the ballots cast at one precinct while garnering 85 percent at another. Such neighborhood variation remained the salient feature of local elections throughout the antebellum years. In the 1858 election for sheriff the leader of a pack of five candidates carried only 38 percent of the total votes cast in the first heat, but won as many as 60 percent in one place, and as few as 3 percent elsewhere. Three of the contenders each carried at least one precinct.[33]

Localism proved difficult for politicians to overcome. Adam Gordon sought a seat in the state senate in 1823 for the district comprised of Claiborne County, where he lived, and Warren County. Gordon lost the election badly, polling only half the votes of winner Thomas Freeland. He ran a much closer race in his home county than he did in Warren, where he received only 13 votes.[34] After the election Gordon claimed that his campaign had been sabotaged by the publication of a defamatory hand-bill, or "lie-bill" as he called it, fully intending the pun. Gordon believed that the assault on his character would have had little impact had the bill "been confined in its circulation to the limits of Claiborne county, wherein my course of conduct through life has been known to be consistent and honorable." But, he claimed, the bill's circulation in Warren County, where he was a stranger to many folks, had destroyed his chances.[35] Gordon may have lost the election in Warren County anyway, "lie-bill" or not. As he was well aware, Warren County residents were unacquainted with him. Voters simply preferred known quantities over unknown, and they knew few people beyond the vicinity of their homes. Jacob Hyland, a third candidate in this election, easily defeated Gordon at the polls in his home county of Warren. Gordon just as easily routed Hyland in Claiborne County. At the precinct level in Claiborne County—precinct data for Warren County is not available— Hyland won the neighborhood of Rocky Springs, located just across the Big Black River from Warren County, but fared poorly in more distant neighborhoods. Only the winner, Thomas Freeland, acquired a following in both counties, perhaps because he had gained some notoriety as a delegate to the state constitutional convention six years earlier, or perhaps because he owned some land in Warren County, although he had never lived there.[36]

Localism never disappeared from electoral politics, although during the 1840s neighborhood idiosyncrasies diminished somewhat in county sheriff's elections. Neighborhoods, slowly, began to agree politically. However, local variation actually increased for state gubernatorial elections when voters began to take state elections more seriously and to vote in greater numbers. When state government became more important, and elections for governor became more contested, neighborhoods extended their idiosyncratic patterns to state elections.[37]

The persistence of localism in Warren County politics was consistent with the structure of its rural neighborhoods. Within a context of close interpersonal association, often between kin and characterized by dependency and patriarchy, the heads of extended families would have exerted their influence to rally neighbors on behalf of favorite candidates. There was no party system. Lopsided contests were an inevitable result of local social and power structures.[38] In sheriff's elections between 1835 and 1851 Warrenton voters gave winning candidates on average a landslide 84 percent of their ballots. In some elections the winner at the Warrenton precinct claimed over 90 percent of the vote. In state elections Warrenton voters gave an average of over 70 percent of their ballots to their favorite candidate for governor. Elections at Milldale were just as lopsided, although voters in that precinct tended to oppose the candidate favored by the majority of voters at Warrenton. At Bovina the vote usually split somewhat more evenly than in other rural precincts, although elections with winning candidates taking over 60 percent of the vote occurred more often than not. In contrast to most rural areas, elections in the town of Vicksburg tended to be quite close, with winners in state and local contests receiving on average only 60 percent of the vote. Gubernatorial elections were particularly close in town. No families dominated and directed the voting patterns of Vicksburg's heterogeneous population, with its various ethnic and occupational groups, and its large number of newcomers to Mississippi.

At first glance the cleavages of local elections do not appear to have been duplicated in state elections. However, closer inspection reveals some important continuities. Over the whole period for which precinct level data exist a split between the southern and northern halves of the county marked every election for sheriff. Typically, whenever the voters at Warrenton cast the majority of their ballots for the eventual winner the voters at Milldale voted for someone else, and vice versa. The reason for the division cannot be known for certain, but in all probability it dated back to the hard feelings stirred by the long debate over the moving of the courthouse. Voters near Warrenton and Milldale cast their ballots overwhelmingly for the candidate from or nearest to their own district, and flatly refused to support the man from the other precinct. Bovina's location between Milldale and Warrenton helps explain the more closely contested elections in that precinct. Voters at Bovina owed no more allegiance to the people to the north than to the south (Figure 8.4).

In gubernatorial contests after 1840 a large majority of Warrenton's voters always favored the Whig party candidate. Milldale residents, continuing the county's north-south split, were more inclined toward the Democratic candidates, giving them a majority of their votes on two occasions. In the 1840 presidential election only Milldale gave less than 70 percent of its votes to Harrison.[39] Milldale's leanings toward the Democracy may have begun when one of their own, Alexander G. McNutt, ran

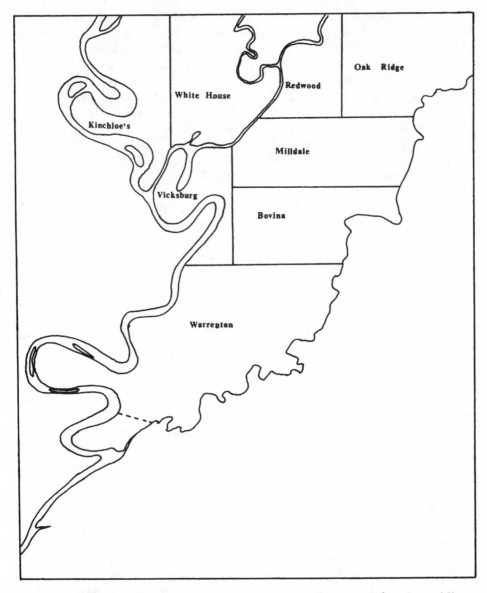

Figure 8.4 Warren County election precincts, 1852. (*Sources:* Police Court Minutes, 1834, pp. 95–97; 1849, p. 200; 1851, p. 597; 1852, p. 617; *Vicksburg Weekly Whig,* November 12, 1851; and Anderson Hutchinson, *Code of Mississippi* [Jackson, 1848].)

as a Democrat for two terms as governor, winning both times. Of course, that raises the question of why McNutt, a planter, speculator, and bank board member, was a Democrat. Perhaps his party preference stemmed in part from his antipathy for the Whigs from the south end of the county who regularly dominated local affairs. In any case, by running for governor McNutt made it easy for his neighbors to continue their opposition to Warrenton's residents.

Evidence will not permit any demonstration of family and local loyalties influencing individuals at the polls. Nevertheless, political events were social events. Not just voters, but women and children, too, attended the frequent debates held at local campgrounds or springs. Usually someone donated a side of beef for a barbecue. Others brought their fiddles. Soon more people were up threading "the mazes of the cotillion" than listening to the speakers stumping under the trees but a short distance away. In this setting little wonder voting patterns were consistent with neighborhood structures of society and authority, and with a history of alliances and disputes older than Whigs and Democrats.[40]

Local history persisted in local elections, and apparently in state contests as well, much to the dismay of national party organizers. On one occasion the leaders of the county Whigs called a meeting to discuss the prospects for nominating party candidates for local offices, sheriff in particular. Worried at first about maintaining party unity, leaders left the meeting secure in their belief that "all jealousy about the selection of candidates" had been quelled, that "every portion of the county [was] to be represented." But before a second meeting could be held to nominate party candidates men from around the county stepped forward on their own and announced their intentions to run for office. The local Whig convention never happened. Party leaders reluctantly concluded that "the people seem disposed to let matters take their own course, without the aid of nominations." Candidates for county offices ran without party affiliation. Overall, for reasons discussed below, Warren County voters found the pull of the Whigs strong enough to give the party their continued collective support. But Warrenton and Milldale voters took with them to the polls the additional considerations of family and neighborhood.[41]

Rural neighborhoods endured through the period of party competition as discrete social and political entities, with their unique structures of patriarchal authority embedded in the slave plantation economy. Deference came naturally to Warren County's small- and nonslaveholders; leadership came just as naturally to planters. Both parties respected the priority of this arrangement because it was in their material interests to do so. Nonslaveholders depended on neighboring planters who controlled valuable productive resources for both access to and protection from markets. Planters in turn relied on the support of dependents in struggles with competing elites for access to the privileges of government. Within this context democracy and electoral politics acquired a unique meaning: dependents and clients were free to support their local patrons in contests with elites from elsewhere, from the other side of the county, from Natchez, from the North.[42]

The framers of the new state constitution endeavored to remove some of the effects of patriarchy and deference on electoral politics.

Until 1832 the territorial governor, and then the state legislature, appointed all county judges. In that year the new constitution, hailed by historians as typical of the democratic reforms that marked the Age of Andrew Jackson, allowed an electorate of adult free men to choose their local officials. Moreover, it split the authority of the old county court, in which legislative, executive, and judicial power had been combined, between an administrative and legislative board of police and a civil court of probate. Government by planter nabobs was to be no more.[43]

The new constitution did alter county politics. In earlier days local government mirrored informal structures of authority. That is to say, they acknowledged the importance of kinship and neighborhood leadership. In 1820 the state legislature confirmed Jacob Hyland's unofficial position of prominence as head of one of the wealthiest and best-connected families in the county by appointing him justice of the quorum. The next year Hyland's brother-in-law took a place on the bench as judge of probate. Andrew Glass, for several years a partner in business with Hyland's brother, and also connected to the Hyland family by marriage, won the most powerful local elected office, that of sheriff. The three men thus stood atop family, neighborhood, and county. Of course, other neighborhoods had their leaders, and not all could hold public office. But at that time public office meant little, particularly to those who lived at a distance from the county seat. It was no coincidence that Jacob Hyland's plantation abutted the seat of justice. But his position as justice of the quorum gave him little authority in neighborhoods other than in his own, where he was already leader even before he took his place on the bench.[44]

By 1835, the situation had changed. Government wielded authority, and local leaders actively sought public office. Three years following the constitutional convention, William Mills, a Vicksburg attorney with no apparent connections to prominent local families, was elected judge of probate. E. W. Morris, another Vicksburg resident with no connections to leading families, won election to sheriff. Only the new board of police maintained some connection to rural neighborhoods and prominent slaveholding families. John Cowan was closely associated with the Vick family, as was E. G. Cook, whose family had enjoyed power and prestige in the north end of the county since its arrival two decades earlier. Jesse Evans, another elected member of the board of police, belonged to a large family in the Redbone neighborhood near Warrenton. Kinship and neighborhood, however, did not connect board members to each other, or any of them to the judge, or to the sheriff.[45]

Nevertheless, the newly elected officeholders were connected to each other. They all shared the privileges of the county's economic elite. Indeed, from 1810 to 1860 the members of Warren County's government owned considerably more land and in particular more slaves than household heads did on average. Individually, some nonslaveholders did win elections. In a given year about one in five county officials owned no

Organizing a County Community

Organizing a County Community 149

slaves. Similarly, the county's great planters, the Joseph Davises and Henry Turners, men who possessed hundreds of slaves, rarely held elected office. They campaigned only on occasion; voters tended to reject them when they did, perhaps because they appeared as simply too aristocratic for a supposedly democratic society. Nevertheless, most officeholders were slaveholders, and large slaveholders at that. In 1850, for example, masters elected to a position in county government sometime during the preceding decade owned on average twenty slaves, a figure that nearly placed them among the richest 10 percent of the county's household heads. Throughout the antebellum years, Warren County's public officials, elected and appointed, consistently came from at least the richest 20 percent of the county's household heads.[46]

Thus the new constitution and the opening of electoral politics did not really remove the slaveholding elite as a group from public office. Indeed, as late as 1850 the difference in property-holding between officeholders and nonofficeholders was greater than in the years preceding the reforms. Moreover, the new constitution did not stop patriarchs from rallying their kin and neighbors on behalf of particular candidates, as the returns at Warrenton and Milldale indicate. Variation in precinct election returns continued despite constitutional reforms.[47]

The continued selection of leaders from the wealthiest strata of the local population is particularly remarkable, for it contradicts the usual picture of the expansion of democracy during the Age of Jackson. What it indicates, however, is the persistence of hierarchical social structures and corresponding ideas of deferential government. Change did not occur overnight. In his study of political transformation in early nineteenth-century Massachusetts historian Ronald P. Formisano described a deferential-participant politics resulting from "the existence of clear social distinctions which continued to shape behavior even as formal and outward displays of deference weakened."[48] Nowhere did social distinctions persist as they did in rural neighborhoods in the South's plantation districts. A yeoman's or small slaveowner's deference to the local planter was more than just an old habit. It reflected the continuation of patriarchal structures of authority within the face-to-face world of the rural neighborhood even as democracy expanded in electoral politics.

Warren County voters expressed a readiness to reject eighteenth-century notions of deference during the election of delegates to the constitutional convention in 1832. County resident Eugene Magee, a "whole hog" democrat who advocated the end of property qualifications and the election of all state and county offices, won the election for the state senatorial district. At the convention he distinguished himself by writing the majority opinion on the question of judiciary reform. Joseph Davis also ran for election to the constitutional convention as representative of Warren County. He lost badly. In 1817 a member of Mississippi's first constitutional convention, a one-time Natchez lawyer, and a well-known "aristocrat," Davis won only 39 votes out of 758 votes cast. Judge Alex

Covington, whose background was similar to Davis's, received a paltry 17 votes. The "whole hog" candidates, in contrast, each won over 200 votes.[49]

Democracy, however, was never really the issue. This was no uprising of Andrew Jackson's "common man." Rather, the new constitution represented the successful efforts of wealthy slaveholders in newer regions of the state to crack the monopoly on important public offices, the judiciary in particular, held by Natchez elites since the enactment of the first state constitution. As early as 1824 one local resident had complained of the "most odious feature in our code," referring to "that system of partial legislation which has obtained in relation to the city of Natchez," and which instituted a line of distinction between the "powder-headed gentry" of Adams County and the rabble elsewhere in the state. Before long "we must doff the hat, and bow the suppliant knee, to the lords and the dukes and the princes of Natchez." Not for eight years would the people finally have their day, led by "democrats" like Eugene Magee of Warren County, owner of a plantation and 67 slaves. Only three men in Warren County owned more. "Aristocrat" Joseph Davis was one.[50]

The absence of ideological conflict within Warren County enabled voters collectively to rebel against the nabobs of Natchez. A true democratic uprising of farmers against a planter aristocracy would necessarily have split the county along class lines. The bonds of family and dependency within each neighborhood, however, precluded divisions between slaveholders and nonslaveholders. But while the county's horizontal social ties remained firm within each settlement, its vertical ties linking neighborhoods together had not yet hardened. In this context two-party politics, when it arrived during Jackson's presidency, no more divided the county along ideological or class lines than had the debate over the state constitution. In Warren County party competition between Whigs and Democrats for the most part expressed neighborhood and family loyalties, rivalries between local insiders and outsiders, and not profound differences in ideology or interest.[51]

President Andrew Jackson's removal in 1833 of federal revenues from the Bank of the United States provided the occasion for the formation of a Whig opposition in Mississippi the following year. Jackson, once unshakably popular in the Southwest, had lost some supporters with his continuing partnership with the hated Martin Van Buren. Nevertheless, in 1832 the President ran unopposed in the South, although he appeared on the ballot with another vice-presidential candidate, Philip P. Barbour, a slaveholder from Virginia. Jackson's handling of public lands continued to erode his support in Mississippi, where investors and speculators such as Warren County's William L. Sharkey and John I. Guion believed the federal government was keeping the price of land high to appease Eastern manufacturers who worried about losing laborers and consumers to the West. But the bank war, and the subsequent brief panic in Mississippi, led finally to the organization of an opposition.[52]

In Warren County the Whig party found its support among those who gazed outward beyond their neighborhood or town, beyond their county, even beyond their region. Commercial interests in Vicksburg and in the countryside formed the backbone of the party locally. These were the very people who stood to lose the most from Jackson's war with the bank, but who could also see the possibilities of Henry Clay's expansive American System. Merchants and lawyers made up half of the group of active Whigs in town. Planters dominated the countryside Whigs, each of whom owned an average of thirty slaves. Both groups speculated in new lands in the northern half of the state, in Arkansas, in Texas. They also invested in internal improvements, railroads especially, to guarantee that cotton coming from and manufactures headed into the interior of the state would all pass over Vicksburg's wharves, through the stores, warehouses, and account books of the town's merchants. In all their ventures the support of government was crucial, particularly in maintaining a stable currency and sound banking system. Behind the county's commercial elite stood smaller businessmen—urban artisans, country storekeepers, ferrymen, dairy farmers—who while not in a position to speculate in railroads and land nevertheless were part of a commercial network that linked them to Vicksburg and beyond.

Of course, not everyone was a Whig. Most were, but a large minority voted for Democratic candidates in every election. Indeed, some staunch Warren County Democrats were virtually indistinguishable from the Whigs. Men such as Alexander McNutt, for example, lawyer, land speculator, railroad builder, frustrate efforts to differentiate party supporters on the basis of economic standing or personal attitudes. On average Democrats owned fewer slaves than did Whigs, but the presence within the group of individual slaveholders such as McNutt, who owned forty slaves, skewed the relationship between party and slaveholding enough to make it statistically insignificant. And while artisans were more likely to be found among Democrats, and merchants among Whigs, these differences were quite small, a matter of a few percentage points. The greatest difference between the active members of both parties was their place of origin. Southerners dominated the Whigs, while Northern and foreign-born elements, Irish especially, had a greater presence in the local Democratic party.[53]

Political cleavages seemed to have hardened in Vicksburg in part around the presence of immigrants. In 1839 the Irish Catholics created something of a stir in Vicksburg when Father O'Reily arrived to establish a church. Leading Whig Thomas Anderson in a public exchange with O'Reily proclaimed his "astonishment" that anyone would "submit his neck to the yoke of priestly domination." Democrats appealed for calm. In later years Democratic editors, their party by then the choice of immigrant voters nationwide, poked fun at Whig party efforts to shed its Americanist colors and woo the foreign-born. But in Warren County politics ethno-cultural issues remained confined to Vicksburg.

Even there they seem not to have been as salient as in some Northern cities where immigrants were more numerous, although this may be a reflection of biases in the historical record. Masses of people, many of them immigrants, stayed but briefly in Vicksburg, too briefly to have added their names to party lists. However, foreign elements drew attacks from militias and mobs. Surely they drew attacks at the polls, too. Notwithstanding the influence of immigrants on Vicksburg voting patterns, differences between active members of both parties were minimal.[54]

Alexander McNutt's efforts at bank reform during his two consecutive terms as governor demonstrate how he and his Whig opponents were in important ways cut from the same cloth. Driven by recalcitrant directors McNutt moved from a moderate position of bank reform to embrace the radical step of repudiation of bank bonds floated by the state. But he was not opposed to banks on principle. After all, he had been one of the founders of Vicksburg's Rail Road Bank, an institution which Democrats distinguished as "useful" because it fostered internal improvements, unlike so many other banks that were nothing more than the tools of "driveling picayune swindlers."[55] By law, however, that bank's profits were restricted to 7 percent. Moreover, the legislature had reserved the right of "visitation." McNutt understood the necessity of banks but believed that the state had to keep a watchful eye over the directors of such institutions to ensure that greed did not get the better of them to the detriment of the community they were supposed to serve. As governor he tried to enforce the terms of the banks' charters. When they refused to seat government representatives at their directors' meetings and failed to issue specie payments as required, McNutt threatened repudiation as a way of chastising directors for their irresponsible and incorrigible behavior.[56]

Democrats, at least those like McNutt from plantation districts, shared with Whigs a belief in a hierarchical society in which the deference of the lower orders balanced the patriarchal responsibilities of elites. Moreover, neither group was ready to unleash the creative energies of individuals freed of community restraint. In conflicts of interests between the individual and the group, the group took precedence. Where they differed was over how the balance between higher and lower orders and between individuals and the group was best preserved. Whigs tended to trust that society's property-holding leaders would collectively live up to their responsibilities to the community, although certain individuals might go astray. Democrats were not as confident. They worried more about the individuals who in their pursuit of material rewards sometimes abandoned community interests. Thus, both Whigs and Democrats saw government as an extension of patriarchal authority, as a means of both assisting individual property-holders in their development schemes, which would benefit the community, and restraining irresponsible and excessive individualism, which would hurt the community.

The basis of bipartisan ideological consensus was the slave plantation economy and rural neighborhoods of planters and their kinfolk. Through their expectations as voters and perceived responsibilities as representatives, Warren County residents extended the patriarchal ideal—a legacy of family and neighborhood politics in a slave society— to elected government. This was the same ideal that guided the judges who granted Matilda Cotton her divorce and recognized Keziah Griffin's claims against the Gibsons. At the same time the plantation economy, based on the production of a staple for export, gave both parties a similar orientation toward money, markets, the world in general beyond their neighborhoods. It created the desire for banks, railroads, levees, not to mention the desire for profits, that had caused people to turn to government in the first place. The slave plantation economy, therefore, pushed Southern communities such as Warren County forward even as it held them back. The resulting culture was a peculiar creature indeed, with one foot striding into the nineteenth-century world of liberal capitalism but with the other stuck in the eighteenth-century world of republican deference, hierarchy, and privilege.

Politics cannot be reduced to mere ideological expression, as some historians are wont to do.[57] Within Warren County the two political parties, each headed by wealthy planters and urban merchants, differed more in emphasis than in ideology. Locally, opposing parties often had more in common with each other than either had with their own parties in the nonplantation regions of the state. During a debate over a legislative bill to prohibit the circulation of notes printed out of state, one astute editor noted a split within the ranks of the Democratic party: "The Democrats who oppose it are mostly from the towns and trading points, representing, we suspect, those who have interest with the paper-financiers against the people." The editor added that "some of these gentry affect (in their speeches) to consider the bill 'an infringement of the people's rights.'" In other words, symbols and words that might seem to express ideologies—"gentry" versus "the people's rights"—were no certain indicators of political behavior.[58]

The traditional explanation for the Whig party's appeal in the South's plantation districts and the Democratic party's appeal in the small farming areas in the region's pine barrens and hill country links party preference to regional variations in wealth-holding, commitment to slavery, and relationship to markets.[59] Within regions, and particularly within single counties, however, both parties drew their support from the same society, from similar people. Within a local context both parties operated within a common political culture, and were therefore probably not separated by fundamental ideological differences, that is to say, by ideas of how politics ought to be conducted and of the role of government in society. For the most part, family and neighborhood loyalties divided them.

The process of organizing a county community began with the moving of the courthouse to Vicksburg, and continued through the subsequent rise of that town to the apex of an economic and political structure that connected each rural settlement and village in every corner of the county. The salience of neighborhood loyalties in electoral politics demonstrated how incomplete the organizing process remained throughout much of the antebellum period even as the turn to government and elected politicians indicated its occurrence nonetheless. By about 1850, however, the county community emerged. Neighborhoods lost their political distinction. Political realignment reflected a new community order.

In 1851 political leaders suspended old partisan differences in a gubernatorial contest over one issue—secession. The preceding year saw the furor over Wilmot's Proviso come to a head at Nashville, where a bipartisan convention discussed the expedience of a concerted Southern response to what they deemed as Northern aggression. They decided little except to meet again in a second session. By that time, however, Congress had already worked out a compromise. The flames of disunion had been quenched in the hearts of all but the most passionate fire-eaters—at least for the time being. State elections served as a final plebiscite on the matter.[60]

In Mississippi both candidates for governor were closely tied to Warren County. Henry Stuart Foote, U.S. senator, resident of Jackson, former resident of Vicksburg, ran as a unionist in favor of accepting the Compromise of 1850. Jefferson Davis, Mississippi's other U.S. senator, owner of a plantation in Warren County, campaigned against the compromise and for the states' right to secede, although he granted that at the moment disunion was not "practical." Both men had been Democrats. Foote had even been one of the instigators in Congress of the Nashville Convention, but had obviously changed his views in light of the compromise.[61]

The seriousness of both the North's attacks on slavery and the South's attacks on the Union were enough to shatter old party lines. As a unionist editor stated: "Regarding the old party issues which have heretofore divided the country as wholly swept by, and merged in, the momentous question of 'Union or Disunion,' a question whose elements are treason, civil war and blood shed, we shall sever all our former political ties."[62] In the countryside contests were still lopsided. Individual voters still followed the lead of family and neighborhood leaders. But Milldale voters did not oppose Warrenton voters as they had in the past. Instead, the rural areas of the county voted uniformly and overwhelmingly for Foote and the compromise. They presented no appearance of neighborhoods as discrete political units. Only in the most urban areas of the county, in Vicksburg and its suburbs in adjoining White House and Bovina precincts, where there had been a history of bipartisan competition, did Davis and the secessionists find any support, perhaps among immigrant and Catholic workers who would not vote with their native-born and Protestant neighbors.[63]

Old partisan lines disappeared for good. Even after the politics of union and slavery died down, and the Whigs and Democrats made their return, politics in Warren County were never the same. Neighborhoods continued to oppose one another in local elections, but no longer in state and national elections.[64] Sectional politics had disrupted the local order beyond repair. Yet the forces of change were not all external. Warren County had been undergoing a long process of restructuring. The debate over disunion and compromise found a county reaching out to a larger world, and thus more concerned with national politics and larger issues like slavery. Moreover, the county was no longer so divided into separate spheres of kin groups and rural neighborhoods as it once was. Warren County confronted the political issues of the 1850s as an integrated social and economic unit, rather than just a collection of families and neighborhoods.

9

A COTTON COUNTY COMES OF AGE

"Come out for 'Old' Warren!" The cry was heard frequently during elections when campaigning politicians and their followers tried to touch the hearts of the county's faithful. Odd that a county officially established only forty years before the breakup of the Union could be considered old. Long-time residents could have recalled the days before Vicksburg was founded, when the only settlement consisted of a cluster of farm houses along the Big Black River at the county's extreme south end, when the greater portion of the county was wilderness, some of it Choctaw territory. As late as 1860 most of Vicksburg's streets remained unpaved. Storekeepers were only beginning to replace wooden fronts with brick. In the surrounding countryside there were as yet no magnificent mansions to rival those clustered about the much older town of Natchez in Adams County. Warren County was still too new, too close to its western beginnings to have blossomed into the flower of affluence and gentility that set the South's oldest plantation districts apart from those more recently settled. How strange that residents would cheer and huzzah for "Old" Warren.

Age, of course, is relative, and compared with most of Mississippi, Warren County was indeed old. As late as 1830 the north half of the state belonged to the Choctaw and Chickasaw peoples, and so was unsettled by white farmers and planters. Except for strips of land along the larger rivers and creeks, the Mississippi-Yazoo delta region between Vicksburg and Memphis, Tennessee, remained a vast wilderness into the twentieth century.[1] But one did not have to leave Warren County to comprehend its old age. The toll of passing years left signs visible within the county's borders, upon worn and eroded soil still worked by farmers and slaves who strained to dig up the very last of its richness. Moreover, by 1860 out-migration, intensification of agriculture, tremendous disparities in wealth-holding, and sharply delineated lines in the social strata all signaled the maturing of Warren County as a slave plantation economy and society.

Half a century of planting had left its mark on the soil of Warren County. "It used to be celebrated as one of the best cotton-growing counties in the state," wrote visiting agriculturalist Solon Robinson, "but a continued cropping of the land, without manure, or even returning the cotton seed as manure to the soil, has so worn out much of the land that it hardly pays for cultivating."[2] On another occasion Robinson found farms "gone past all redemption, and worthless for every purpose except Bermuda-grass pastures." He suggested farmers stop planting cotton and commence raising sheep.[3]

The rains washed away what good soil remained. Travelers noted "those great ulcers" of land literally "gullied to death" and abandoned by their owners.[4] The powdery dirt was particularly vulnerable on the many hills that pebbled the countryside. In its natural state the land had been protected by trees and plants. Cane breaks, with their extensive root systems near the surface, had been particularly vital. But even before clearing and planting the cane had begun to succumb to grazing cattle. The plant simply could not recover quickly enough to survive steady consumption by the invading beasts that found it so tasty.[5] By the end of the antebellum era some local farmers introduced to the area such plants as willow trees, which they hoped would save some of their topsoil. But many found such projects too costly.[6]

Not all Warren County farmers suffered a shortage of good land. Between 1850 and 1860 the county's total number of acres under cultivation increased by 32,000, as planters continued to slash and burn stores of timberland, as James Allen did at his 3000-acre Nanechehaw Plantation, just as the plantation's founders, the Rapaljes, had done over half a century before. Allen was not alone. Planters along the Mississippi River busily cleared new land and left stacks of wood at the river's edge for sale to steamboat captains, who as a consequence were never at a loss for fuel. By the end of the decade the county still had more land in reserve than many other cotton counties. However, most of this new acreage was located in the delta region between the Yazoo and Mississippi rivers northwest of Vicksburg, and in the bottoms near the mouth of the Big Black in the southern part of the county. These swampy lands had to be drained, cleared, and leveed before they could be planted with cotton, and that required a tremendous amount of labor. Allen assigned five hands to full-time duty clearing timber from swamps. In any case, the stores of rich bottom land did nothing to help landowners in the older interior sections of the county, especially those in the hills east and southeast of Vicksburg, where erosion and continuous cropping had ruined some farms. Thus the county was split geographically and economically between its declining interior neighborhoods and its thriving delta and flood-plain regions.[7]

Regardless of region or condition of soil, cotton was still widely planted. Over the last decade before the Civil War production doubled, from seven to 14 million pounds. Acres brought into production for the first time were responsible for much of the increased cotton output, although landowners farmed older acreage more intensively. Little of the new land was devoted to corn, the production of which increased only 25 percent. Harvests of oats, potatoes, and nearly every other crop for food or fodder actually declined as farmers concentrated on raising ever more cotton. Only peas and beans, important more for their fertilizing effect on the soil than for food, and orchard products—a few planters had discovered that peach and pear trees could make eroded hillsides useful once again—continued to attract attention from agriculturalists. Some planters virtually ceased all efforts to provide more than a small portion of their own subsistence needs. For example, Basil Kiger had his slaves plant vegetables, but purchased the bulk of their food supplies, including 1,140 barrels of corn and 59 barrels of pork, most of it from Northern farmers. William L. Sharkey purchased pork and corn from Northern flatboat men who stopped at Warrenton. Benjamin Wailes supplied Fonsylvania plantation with pork purchased from Ohio and Missouri. It was more common for planters to maintain a basic self-sufficiency in corn at least even as they expanded cotton production. Thus James Allen put his slaves to work clearing new fields yet reserved about 200 acres of his total for corn.[8]

High cotton prices during the last half of the 1850s partly explain the surge in cotton production, although farmers had more on their minds than prices. They did not constantly adjust their planting to the market's cycles.[9] Indeed, the general tendency among slaveholders was to plant more and more of the staple regardless of the price expected at the next winter's market. At any price, more cotton meant greater income, and in any case there was no available substitute that brought similar returns, though, to be sure, prices higher than they had been in nearly a decade were powerfully persuasive. For small farmers the lengthy period of a depressed market may have been as important as its sudden recovery. Some may have fallen into debt, caught off-guard when prices fell several years earlier. They would have welcomed renewed market growth as a way out of debt. In any case, after three years of good prices, even those so cautious as never to have risked planting cotton might have mustered the courage to do so.

Thus, by 1860 Warren County farmers were planting more cotton than they had before, enough to double the county's output. Some did so because they were trapped in a downward cycle of debt, others because they pursued an upward cycle of increased production and consumption encouraged by high expectations brought by a stable market. However, as the soil steadily deteriorated, as outputs in older fields diminished, as stores of new land shrank on smaller farms, wealthy planters were much better poised than their poorer neighbors to take advantage of the cotton market. If they had abundant reserves of good land, as some planters in the river bottoms apparently did, they could continue to maintain a level of self-sufficiency in corn production while expanding cotton production. Moreover, they could afford the capital outlays necessary to restore old and worn fields, intensify production, and continue to increase output. For example, planters began to experiment with fertilizers. In one year Basil Kiger spread 100 barrels of lime on the soil of Buena Vista plantation. James Allen dropped guano on his fields at Nanechehaw. Steam-powered gins became popular among those who could afford them. A man named Blake purchased one for $20,000. Kiger probably spent a similar amount for his. But manufacturers found no mass market for these high-priced products. One mechanic bragged he had made twenty steam-powered gins for Mississippi and Louisiana planters. Such means of increasing production proved far too costly for all but the most wealthy.[10]

It is not surprising that over time the gap between richest and poorest widened from ditch to canyon. In 1810 a slaveholder whose wealth-holding placed him among the county's richest 10 percent had perhaps 11 more slaves than his poorest neighbor. By 1860 the difference between two similar county residents was at least 40 slaves, and in some instances as many as 300. The distance between the richest and poorest elements had also increased when measured in terms of real estate holdings.[11]

During the county's early years, when the land was still sparsely settled, patterns of wealth distribution fluctuated wildly, tilting one way with the arrival of only a few wealthy planters, the other way with the incoming flocks of propertyless farmers. Between 1830 and 1850 patterns stabilized. The rich added to their wealth, but so did everyone else. Then during the last decade before the Civil War a new trend emerged. The wealthiest third of household heads continued to expand their slaveholdings, apparently at the expense of everyone else. The percentage of household heads who owned no slaves began to rise for the first time in forty years, approaching 50 percent by the decade's end. A similar trend occurred in landholding patterns, although they are somewhat more difficult to ascertain fully. Over the decade of the 1850s the number of farms in Warren County diminished, even while the total amount of cultivated land increased. Thus, by the end of the decade fewer people owned much larger farms. Meanwhile, the number of farm families that did not own the land they worked more than doubled.[12]

Cotton planting and ecological damage, the latter particularly troubling for smaller farmers in the county's interior, slowly divided the society in the countryside into two groups, one firmly in possession of the means of production, the other dispossessed of land and slave labor, though by 1860 this process was hardly complete. The average rural slaveholding was 24, enough to place one among the top 20 percent of rural household heads, yet only enough for one gang of field hands and two or three house servants. And the bulk of farms were under 500 acres in size. The trend, however, was clear, and had war and emancipation not intervened it would have continued as in older regions. Adams County, for exmaple, was similar environmentally and economically to Warren County but its process of development was more advanced, having begun earlier. In that county 46 percent of the farms were larger than 500 acres. Only 18 percent of the farms were smaller than 100 acres.[13]

A new or heightened awareness on the part of Warren County residents of economic and social distinctions appears to have followed from growing disparities in wealth-holding. Of course, some had always had a keen sense of their standing. Joseph Davis, one of Warren County's wealthiest planters, had distinguished elites from commoners since territorial days when he helped author Mississippi's first constitution. His opponents, self-styled democrats though many of them were quite wealthy, were just as prepared to make such distinctions when they rewrote the constitution to restrict the influence of "aristocrats" such as Davis.

The Sharkeys, one of the oldest families in Warren County, also acquired a strong sense of social superiority. Clay Sharkey, who actually grew up just across the Big Black River in Hinds County, recalled how his parents taught him not to look down upon the poorer boys in the neighborhood. To do so was unbecoming of a young gentleman. Sharkey could not have been more aware of social distinctions and of his place within the strata. He divided the boys of his neighborhood into three groups: planters' sons, overseers' sons, and the sons who worked in fields with other members of their families. Planters' sons, whenever they got together with their less fortunate friends, brought extra foods, ponies, guns, and fishing equipment for all to share. They even brought slaves, which their parents "sent along to wait on all alike." No doubt the other boys and their families appreciated such gestures of generosity from the up-and-coming gentry, but they, like Sharkey, could hardly have failed to recognize the social distinctions they demarcated.[14]

Until the 1850s few aside from Davis and Sharkey could have been so aware of social distinctions. As late as 1830 perhaps several dozen people owned enough slaves to free them of work in the fields.[15] However, many of these planters lived in log cabins not unlike those inhabited by their poorer neighbors, though some such as William Hyland at Bogue Desha plantation and Benjamin Wailes at Fonsylvania closed in the dogtrot and added half a story. Basil Kiger's two-story frame and clapboard house at Buena Vista plantation was more elaborate than most. Still, by the end of the antebellum era few besides Joe Davis lived in a big house comparable to those that were the pride of the Natchez nabobs. As late as 1839 a visitor described Hurricane plantation as "a wild & tangled forest of heavy timber—to all appearances untrodden by man or beast." Twenty years later a three-storied brick mansion with galleries on all sides, a Greek revival guest house and library nearby, all surrounded not by wilderness but by grand lawns and gardens, represented a level of affluence and gentility only just emerging in Warren County. Social distinctions, in other words, while they had always been present in the minds of some, had not been so readily apparent in earlier years. Moreover, economic and social mobility formerly had blurred the relatively small differences between the richer and poorer elements. In the 1790s Don Rapalje, for all his pretentions to the contrary, lived like a simple farmer. By 1860 there could be no mistaking a gentleman planter, owner of a grand home and several hundred slaves, for a simple man who actually dirtied his own hands in the soil. The *Natchez Weekly Courier* estimated that a 2000-acre plantation capable of producing 1000 bales of cotton annually required a capital investment of nearly $200,000, a sum well out of reach of any small farmer in Warren County.[16]

As the social strata hardened more individuals seem to have become aware of their place within it. Basil Kiger was horrified upon learning that his sister-in-law Bettie, a young widow with a small child, intended to marry a poor boy she met while vacationing in Tennessee. He was convinced such a marriage could only end in disaster. "In a few years she would find the little property left her Daughter and herself gone and she with a Family of children left dependent upon the cold charity of Friends and relatives for support." With sarcasm Kiger greeted assurances that the boy was a partner in a country store: A store "with a stock no doubt that might be carried in a mans coat Packet consisting of a Bag of shot 10 lbs of sugar as much coffee and a Bbl. of sweet cider flanked by a home mad[e] ginger cake." The concerned patriarch worried about more than the lad's present financial circumstances, however. He questioned his ambition, his education, even his people, "these inert, slow motioned know nothing Tennesseans." Kiger likened him to the poor whites of his own neighborhood, whom he thought were so mired in a culture of poverty that they would rather starve than work. He compared him unfavorably to a slave: "He does not write as well as old Racheal." Perhaps worst of all, the boy was a Baptist. Furious, Kiger promised his wife Carrie that he would never forgive her "for leaving Bettie among such a people." "*I do not dislike him*," he protested, unconvincingly. "I only dislike him as a Husband for Bettie." After a six-month battle Bettie succumbed to her brother-in-law's will and let go of the boy from Tennessee.[17]

People interpreted the process of social stratification in various ways. Elites were especially willing to associate wealth with individual character. In their mind economic success matched gentlemanly comportment; the condition of their poorer neighbors only demonstrated that they were common to begin with. Whites in the middling and lower ranks were not so quick to equate property with a person's character. They resented those who thought themselves superior solely by virtue of success

in business. On occasion resentment and frustration led to violent outbursts. For example, three overseers, all recently discharged for mis-
management, vented their anger by getting drunk and destroying some
outhouses and other property of their former employers.[18] They recognized, perhaps, that they were somehow being left behind by their more
prosperous employers and neighbors, in whose eyes, and perhaps in
their own too, they were no longer their equals. But patriarchal societies
provide men with more vulnerable targets for the anger they feel but
cannot understand—dependent women. Lafayette Lee, having lost his
farm and "being in a rather destitute condition," moved into the home of
a more successful kinsman. Each day he became more "low spirited,
and threatened on several occasions to kill himself and wife." Then he
actually did it. One evening as his wife sat on the porch playing chess
with their host Lee calmly drew a pistol and shot her twice. His slow action seemed to ask for his own death, which came from his kinsman's
pistol.[19] But Lee was an exception. Few were so inclined toward melo-
drama. More men took to drinking and wife-beating. By 1860 domestic
violence seemed to be on the rise. Newspapers reported a sharp increase
in the incidence of wife-beating. They noted with alarm more men such
as Isaac Kizer, who spent ten days in the workhouse breaking rock as
punishment for pommelling his wife. Kizer's wife persuaded the mayor
to release him, pleading that her three children depended on their father. Within days Kizer was back in jail.[20]

Increasingly, men responded to diminishing opportunities by moving
away. Three-quarters of all nonproperty-holders present in Warren
County in 1850 were gone by the end of the decade. But poor farmers
were not the only people to consider the costs and benefits of moving
elsewhere. Some 56 percent of rural slaveholders present in 1850 were
gone by the end of the decade. Nevertheless, those at the lower end of
the economic ladder, including some with a few slaves and a little land,
had the least to gain by staying and the least to lose by leaving. They
surely felt the strongest urge to move on, especially if still young. Persistence rates were lowest for men in their twenties.[21]

Where Warren County's out-migrants went after they disappeared
from local records can only be surmised. Most probably headed for
newly settled regions to the west, or else upriver to the delta region of
Mississippi. Darling McGraw, a Warren County resident for over twenty
years, moved to Arkansas. His economic circumstances could not have
been good, for he left behind a destitute and elderly slave woman to live
as best she could off charity. Perhaps he meant to send for her. More
likely he no longer had use for or means of supporting her.[22] Charles
Harlan moved to California, where he hoped to make enough money to
return and marry his beloved Nell. His heartbreaking letters told a hard-
luck tale that ended when he stopped writing and disappeared altogether.[23] Asabel Gaylord and his friend Irvine did not venture so far.

They found work as loggers in the Yazoo swamps north of Vicksburg. Life among the snakes and alligators was lonely, not to mention dangerous, but in Warren County "There is no business here of any kind that a Man can get to make enough to pay his board. Irvine and I, has tried, until we are tired, and we shall try no longer."[24]

For people with family and friends in Warren County, leaving could be emotionally painful. Still, if they could not make a living at home then they had no choice but to leave. Howard Morris was an Ohio native who in 1845 followed his sister to Vicksburg, where he entered the publishing business with one of his in-laws. "Howard," wrote his new partner, "this is just as good a country as any, and this town is improving, not very fast but *permanently*—it is bound to be the great metropolis of the state of Mississippi." That was in 1845. After six years of trying, without success, Howard Morris moved again, this time to Keosauqua, Iowa. He hated to leave his friends and family in Vicksburg, but took heart when he met two other former Warren County residents in his new state. Together they arranged to have the *Vicksburg Whig* sent to them so they could keep abreast of news back home. Often in his letters Morris talked of returning, "provided I could get employment," but he never did. Prospects for a young man were few in "old" Warren County. By comparison, "Iowa is certainly one of the most fertile, and one of the handsomest States in the Union—but it is so *bominable cold*." As hard as it was to leave, Morris had no alternative. As he slowly realized this fact he began, mentally, to cut ties to his old home. "I may see you next winter," Morris wrote his sister and brother-in-law from Iowa after he had been there for nearly two years. "Should I not, it is doubtful whether we [will] ever meet on earth again."[25]

Out-migration did not drain Warren County of its population. For every four people who left three others arrived. Newcomers, however, tended to be younger and poorer than those who left the county, two-thirds owning neither land nor slaves. For some Warren County still seemed to offer opportunities, if only the chance to rent a farm or earn a living as an overseer. Out-migrants measured Warren County unfavorably against its own recent past as a prosperous cotton district with plenty of unexploited land, and against expected opportunities in newer places further west. Newcomers from the East, from regions that were more depressed, had lower expectations and thus still saw promise in Warren County.[26]

Intensification of cotton production and the hardening of lines separating the social strata must have affected the slaves, although scarce evidence only hints at how their lives changed as the county's plantation society matured. Masters and overseers, determined to maximize the cotton output of each acre, probably worked slaves harder than ever. There is demographic evidence to support this hypothesis. The slave population increased during the 1850s, after declining over the previous decade. Moreover, 91 percent of Warren County's rural slaves lived in holdings larger than ten. Most significant, in 1860 male slaves outnumbered female slaves for the first time since the boom years nearly thirty years before, and by the substantial margin of 140 men per 100 women. Planters prized men over women as field laborers because they could be driven to produce more cotton per acre.[27]

By 1860 Warren County's rural society was maturing, becoming more noticeably affluent if one looked at the large plantations and fine homes just then appearing, or more noticeably poorer if one looked instead at abandoned and eroded lands, and at the growing number of tenant farmers. Vicksburg's urban society was also maturing, though in ways not immediately apparent. During the 1850s the city's population increased 25 percent, three times the increase in the surrounding countryside. Despite this growth, however, the distribution of wealth remained unchanged. A large proportion of the population, about two-thirds of all household heads, owned no real estate or slaves, but that had always been the case. The members of the city's elite were not becoming disproportionately wealthier either. The consolidation of large plantations in the countryside apparently did nothing to enrich urban merchants and alter urban patterns of wealth-holding. Indeed, the formation of great plantations may have hurt business in Vicksburg, which had been built to service more middling cotton farmers. Wealthy planters could bypass Vicksburg factors and deal directly with New Orleans firms. But if the rich were not getting richer, nor the poor poorer, nevertheless, urban economy and society were changing. Elites were beginning to take an interest in manufacturing. The propertyless, who would work in the new factories, while not growing in number, were changing in character.[28]

As a growing marketplace for the surrounding plantation district Vicksburg seems to have peaked with the completion in 1858 of the railroad that linked Jackson to New Orleans.[29] Rail, which compared with steamboat proved a faster and cheaper way of shipping cotton to market, diverted trade from river ports to such inland cities as Jackson. The previous year brought a downturn in the national economy, which ruined several Vicksburg firms, including that of W. C. Smedes, the town's business leader. Smedes owned a large plantation on the edge of town, a symbol of his success, but had to sell it to pay creditors. Mr. Robb also went bankrupt. He "resolved never to go into business again." Instead, he would go to California and try his hand at planting grapes. The inability of several merchants to pay depositors upon demand sparked incidents of violence. A fight erupted when someone named Whaley demanded his deposit from Mr. Cockburn of Oakey Hawkins & Company. Fearing for his life Cockburn "left town in a hurry." Mr. Carellier threatened to kill J. H. Johnston because Johnston had refused to pay Mrs. Carellier her "large deposits."[30]

Not until the very end of the decade did Vicksburg's future begin to look a little brighter. Editors glimpsed certain "Evidences of Prosperity": "We think we can perceive a small stir in the line of improvements—if not in the erection of new buildings, at any rate, in the renovating and alteration of old ones."[31] Vicksburg's resurgence would rest, in part, on the renewed expansion of its hinterland, northward into the Mississippi-Yazoo delta, and westward into northern Louisiana and Texas. Merchants talked of investing in a railroad north to Memphis to bring delta cotton to Vicksburg warehouses. A rail line extending toward Texas, funded in part with $100,000 in municipal funds, brought more cotton every year to the wharf across the river from Vicksburg. Emblematic of the city's optimism, in 1859 Vicksburg hosted the Southern Commercial Convention.[32]

The promise of economic revitalization in Vicksburg, according to the town's merchants, would require more than the development of the city's potential as a transportation hub. The sorts of investments businessmen were prepared to make indicated that Vicksburg was shifting into a new phase of development. In 1859 the Agricultural and Mechanical Association, an organization of merchants and planters, spearheaded an effort to raise the $60,000 needed to found a cotton factory. Boosters made their pitch to investors with the two-tined fork of profit and patriotism. They claimed stockholders would be paid 25 percent annually in a venture that would help end Southern dependence on Northern manufactures. Although they never made the point in their public appeals it surely occurred to them that such a factory would draw cotton from wealthy planters who otherwise shipped directly to New Orleans. Their appeal worked. The money was raised. War, however, halted the project before construction of the factory could begin.[33]

The model for the projected Vicksburg cotton mill was very likely the Mississippi Manufacturing Company of Bankston, in Choctaw County. The company's success, as well as the business philosophy of its founder, James M. Wesson, received regular notice in the Mississippi press.[34] In 1847 Wesson and a group of partners, all experienced textile manufacturers from Columbus, Georgia, opened the Mississippi business with a capital investment of $25,000. Over the next ten years capital stock quadrupled. By the end of the antebellum period nearly two hundred men and women made linseys and jeans for retailers in New Orleans, Vicksburg, and Jackson. The business continued to grow through the war years until destroyed by federal soldiers only three months before Lee's surrender at Appomattox. At that time, according to the colonel who ordered the mill's destruction, the company employed 500 people.[35]

Conceivably, had war and Reconstruction not intervened textile manufacturing may have taken hold in Vicksburg just as it did in Bankston and in other towns across the South. Although the heyday of Southern milltowns came after the war, the industry's significance in antebellum times, particularly in its relationship to the plantation economy, is not fully appreciated.[36] In Warren County as elsewhere the founding of a mill by local planters and business leaders represented a high level of capital accumulation. More important, it signified a new approach toward investment. Capital formed in the agricultural sector of the economy was to be invested in manufacturing, rather than returned in its entirety to planting and supporting services. Mills like the one planned for Vicksburg also indicated a new approach to labor.

Mississippi's first textile mills opened in Natchez. All relied on slave labor. None lasted more than a few years. Wesson's Bankston operation employed white wage workers. It proved to be one of the South's most successful businesses. The combination of success and white wage labor was no matter of luck or coincidence. Wesson knew what he was doing. As historians have long known, the continued expansion of the plantation economy into new regions, as well as the intensification of production in older areas, created a great demand for slaves. During the 1850s the price of a prime field hand soared. So frustrated were planters with the apparent shortage of slaves that they talked seriously of reopening the trans-Atlantic slave trade. Incidents of smuggling captive Africans into the Deep South increased. Some Africans even landed at Vicksburg's auction house.[37] However, the same process that created such a demand for slaves also pushed whites off the land and into towns and cities where they formed a pool of cheap labor. But so long as the unemployed caroused through city streets, refusing to seek or accept the patronage and authority of established leaders, neglecting their responsibilities as caretakers of their own families, fraternizing with slaves and free blacks, they flaunted, and hence weakened, the patriarchal order that was the basis of slave society.

Wesson's success lay in his use of free labor. Slaves were simply too expensive. "We use white labour," he explained, "because white is cheapest and really more efficient." But before he could begin hiring wage workers he had to explain to the planters whose cotton he would buy why they should not view his enterprise as a threat to slavery. He rested his case on his conviction that cotton manufacturing would bind poor whites to the slave plantation economy and bring them once again under patriarchal control. "It is a debatable question whether they [poor whites] are benefitted by the peculiar institution, or not." However, a "general system of Manufactoring would raise them above the manual labour performed by the Negro, and identify them with the institution, and make them the connecting link between the producer and the consumer." Wesson provided his workers and their families with regular preaching and Sunday schools to instruct them on the values of "industrious sobriety" and the "economy of time as well as money." Ultimately, "the very dregs of society," that unwanted and worrisome side-effect of slavery and plantation agriculture, would blossom into "a large and prosperous class of population." Wesson's financial success was undeniable. His arguments regarding white workers were just what Warren County planters and businessmen wanted to hear.[38]

By 1860 vagrants had again become a problem in Vicksburg, despite signs of an imminent return to prosperity. Since the 1830s they had been a presence, although the city's established citizens had managed to make peace with them after some initial clashes. In 1851 the poor house, established years earlier to help remedy the vagrancy problem, closed its doors.[39] Vagrants, although they continued to wander Vicksburg's streets, brawling in the shanties near the river, no longer posed a general threat to society. The actual number of unemployed and homeless people is not known, and it may well have dwindled somewhat. In any case, Vicksburg residents by 1851 certainly felt less threatened by the rootless elements of the town population than they once did. This apparently had less to do with the actual number of vagrants than with new attitudes toward urban life that developed as residents reared in the country adapted to the city, as they ceased trying to impose a rural order in an urban context.[40] Instead, they came to view vagrants as a normal if regrettable part of any urban population. By the end of the decade, however, town residents once again worried about vagrants, and reopened the poor house.[41]

"Our city at present is full of suspicious characters with no visible means of support," observed the editor of the *Whig*, "and we are informed that Vicksburg is also blessed with an organized gang of Burglars who have already commenced their depredations." In other editorials the same editor warned vagrants to clear out or face a "repetition of the scenes enacted in 1832 and 1835," an allusion to earlier times when vigilantes purged the town of its unwanted elements.[42] Citizens responded to the perceived threat in the traditional manner. They formed volunteer police clubs in both the town and the countryside.[43]

There is no sure way of knowing whether the number of vagrants was on the rise. In appearance, however, if not in numbers, they certainly differed from vagrants of earlier times. During the 1830s Vicksburg's floating population of gamblers and roughnecks was typical of Western river towns in the throes of rapid, even booming, growth. Two decades later another sort of people wandered into town. As opportunities contracted for small farmers throughout the Mississippi Valley many collected in the region's urban areas. Seeking work but finding none they simply drifted, scavenged, took odd jobs, and in some cases turned to crime. This is an oft-repeated pattern in the history of cities and countryside. Unlike their predecessors, who were in a sense career vagrants, many of the new scavengers had until recently lived more settled and respected lives. Many had families, or at least did at one time. Many were women, and they attracted much attention to the new character of the vagrant problem, though male observers could not always comprehend them. Descriptions of homeless women as a "horde of worthless, abandoned females" reflected patriarchal assumptions about relations between the sexes.⁴⁴ As dependents, "worthless" women might be left by their husbands; that women might be so worthy as to take matters into their own hands and flee their men was almost unimaginable. But in desperate circumstances economic ties of dependency snapped. Men with no property or means lost authority over their wives, and women no less than men could strike out on their own.

The changes afoot in Warren County during the last decade before the Civil War, in the countryside and in town, were interconnected and represented the maturing of the local economy and society. In the countryside successful planters purchased more slaves and more land from less successful farmers who gave up their struggle against deteriorating soil and rising prices. In an effort to escape inevitable demise, middling and poorer farmers began to leave the Warren County countryside in greater numbers. Some farmers, if they had managed to avoid falling into debt, received a large sum for their land from neighboring planters, which they probably took west where they began farming anew. Other farmers, caught in a downward cycle of debt, wound up with little or nothing. They either stayed on the land as tenants and overseers, or else left for wherever they thought they could find employment. For many that meant moving to the city. Changes in the countryside had their effects on life in Vicksburg. Business slowed. Several firms folded. Poor whites wandered in from rural areas in search of work; finding none they joined the ranks of the town's vagrants. However, the solution to the city's problems, as always, came from the countryside. Planters provided capital for railroads that would give new life to urban commerce, and for factories that would transform vagrants into producers. In 1860, from the perspective of Warren County's propertied elite, the future seemed bright.

10

AN END AND A BEGINNING

On November 6, 1860, Warren County voters went to the polls. By the end of the day a clear majority had cast its ballots for John Bell, the Constitutional Union candidate from Tennessee. The election in Warren placed the county at odds with most of the state, which Southern Democrat John C. Breckinridge carried easily. Emboldened by victory in Mississippi and across the South, and faced with Lincoln's sweep of the North, Breckinridge's more radical followers began to agitate for disunion. Warren County voters held firm. Six weeks later they sent two cooperationist delegates to a state convention. Both men spoke passionately on behalf of the Union, but their voices fell on deaf ears. On January 9 the convention passed an ordinance in favor of secession. With that Mississippi left the Union, the second state to do so.[1]

Civil war brought national attention to Warren County. Favorite son Jefferson Davis became president of the new Confederacy. The siege and fall of Vicksburg was arguably the most critical Union victory. Certainly the war was the most important event in the lives of the people who lived in Warren County at that time. How ironic that most of them had sought to avoid the conflict in the first place. Indeed, Warren County's resistance to the secessionist impulse that seized most of Mississippi provides a rather anticlimactic ending to the story of its evolution as a Southern place. A much more dramatic conclusion would trace the closing of ranks within the county behind Breckinridge and Southern rights, the capture of the state convention by local leaders whose fiery oratory roused the passions of their fellows and carried Mississippi out of the Union, the rush of young men to form regiments and join the fight for the way of life they and their parents had created. But that is not what happened. The community did not want secession or war.

Warren County's stand for the Union was more than ironic, however. It was an appropriate conclusion to the community's growth from isolated frontier settlement to mature society. During the early years what

happened nearby mattered most. Events as great as the American Revolution unfolded far away, touching this place only lightly and for the
most part indirectly. Between 1776 and 1861, however, Warren County
moved from the periphery toward the center of the United States—thus
the community's strong desire to see the Union hold together. But with
the county's integration into the nation came a certain loss of control
over local life. Increasingly the outside world impinged on the world between county lines, and there was little that even the community's might-
iest patriarchs could do about that. In the grand scheme of events that
ripped apart the country, Warren County's resistance to the South's cause
was largely irrelevant. But that very irrelevance heralded the completion
of a process that had been unfolding since the community's birth.[2]

At first the outside forces that pushed Warren County toward a destiny
its citizens had tried to avoid were imperceptible. War crept up behind
people as they busied themselves with the harvest, proposed marriage,
awaited the birth of a child, gathered in taverns to share the latest word
from the Liverpool cotton market, or sat around the dinner table planning moves to Texas or California. They neither ignored nor failed to appreciate the significance of national politics, yet they placed national
events within their local context and thus sustained an illusion of control over their lives. Events so outstanding in hindsight seemed remote
at that time. They were subjects for conversation, perhaps concern, yet
they did not disrupt daily life. Despite the transportation and communication revolutions of the day, the country remained vast, its centers of
power and action distant. Washington was still a one-week trip away.
Most Warren County residents had never been there or seen it outside of
a few drawings in magazines. How could they have comprehended how
close to the nation's center they had become over the previous three-
quarters of a century? Of course, war, when it arrived, shattered all illu-
sions that Warren County remained largely outside the nation's concerns. But in the fall of 1860 people went about their regular routines
with no foreboding.[3]

Thus James Allen, though no proponent of secession, cast his vote for
Breckinridge, yet took the election lightly; it presented an occasion for a
friendly wager with a neighbor. Meanwhile, he concerned himself with
the daily business of his plantation. It was cotton picking and hog killing
time. He also looked into purchasing an adjoining piece of land, visited
with neighbors, worried about a killing frost, arranged to have a large
shipment of wine insured. Allen was a reticent diarist, perhaps. Moreover, his journal was primarily, though not exclusively, a record of plantation activities and so the scant entries of political events is to be expected. Still, his brief comments indicate the continuing hold of local
affairs over his daily life. Whatever he thought of the chances of secession and war, he remained confident that his regular routines would not

change much. Anyone who stocked his cellar with 77 cases of wine expected the future would bring plenty of good times.[4]

Benjamin Wailes was more expressive. During the election, which he expected Lincoln to win, he wrote in his diary that he felt "much exasperated" and "feared that Gov. Pettus will by some hasty and intemperate action seek to precipitate the state into secession." Wailes did not hesitate to declare his thoughts on secessionists. They were all "very violent and intemperate—and insane." But Wailes's diary, too, records the continued routines of daily life. Such outbursts on politics notwithstanding, his entries are no different in the long secession winter than in other years.[5]

Allen, Wailes, and their neighbors were no fools. They knew their interests were tied to a country that flirted with self-destruction. Their unionism indicated this much. Still, they did not, could not, fully comprehend the tremendous implications of those events for life within their community. As they expanded the size of their plantations, sold more cotton at prices higher than they had been in a long time, invested in railroads and textile factories, they gained too much confidence in the future and in their ability to control it to believe that their way of life was seriously endangered by distant politicians. Stephen Duncan of Adams County, one of the South's richest planters, surely expressed the thoughts of many in Warren County in a letter published in the *Vicksburg Whig*. "Any man of sense and reflection," Duncan proclaimed, "cannot fail to see that, after disunion, we should be in no better condition *in any one respect*, and in almost all respects infinitely worse." He especially feared higher taxes would necessarily follow the loss of national income derived from import duties collected mostly in the North. Clearly, Duncan recognized the benefits of a national, rather than a sectional, economy. He even penned his letter while traveling in New York. The people of the North, Warren County's William L. Sharkey reminded voters, owned and controlled "the Great Father of Waters," a lifeline that firmly bound South to North. The *Vicksburg Whig* was more pointed. "What way," the newspaper asked secessionists, did "they intend dividing the river?"[6]

The unionism of Warren County's planters raises the old question of Southern distinctiveness on the eve of the Civil War. Historians, it would appear, have created a false dichotomy. Within their neighborhoods planters were conservative patriarchs, paternalistic husbands, neighbors, masters. When they pursued interests outside their neighborhoods, however, they became energetic capitalists, as willing and able to operate in the liberal marketplace as any Yankee. This dual personality, as it were, was no paradox, however. Their success as patriarchal planters and slaveholders within their community was the basis of their success as capitalists within the nation. Historians intent on characterizing wealthy planters as either capitalists in pursuit of financial interests or as pre-bourgeois masters in pursuit of social interests fail to appreciate how much they were both at once. By voting to remain in the Union Warren County's planters demonstrated their commitment to liberal capitalism but also their confidence in their power as local patriarchs.[7]

This sense of confidence pervaded the county's plantation neighborhoods, bridging partisan rivalries. At the long-time Whig stronghold of Warrenton, voters overwhelming supported John Bell, an old Whig himself. However, voters at Milldale and Oak Ridge, who had supported Democrats on past occasions, also gave a large majority of their ballots to Bell. A small group of older and somewhat wealthier long-time Democrats could not bring themselves to support a former Whig, though they were hardly the "violent" and "insane" radicals castigated by Benjamin Wailes. They, too, wished to preserve the Union. Warren County's leading Democrat, Jefferson Davis, hesitated when finally confronted with secession. His reputation as a proponent of disunion, earned in the 1851 gubernatorial campaign, was greatly exaggerated, and radicals did not hide their disappointment in him. Davis's brother Joseph, for years a leader among state Democrats, wrote after the war, "My opinion of the right of a state to secede was the same as that of most democrats, that it might be done peaceably, but [I] had been always opposed to a dissolution of the union from the belief that it would destroy the *grandure* and *power* of the *Great Republic*." James Allen was probably typical of those who voted for Breckinridge. He opposed secession yet expected Breckinridge to carry every Southern state but Maryland and Tennessee. He apparently calculated that if Northern Democrat Stephen Douglas could hold his own against Lincoln in the contest for electoral votes above the Mason and Dixon line Douglas would compromise with Breckinridge on the South's terms, put a Democrat in the White House, reunite the party, and preserve the Union.[8]

As had been the case in the 1840s, during the heyday of competition between Whigs and Democrats, Warren County's two major parties agreed on the fundamental issues. Southern Democrats and Constitutional Unionists alike opposed secession and supported the Union, even in the event of Lincoln's election. After Lincoln's election they joined forces and handed the cooperationist candidates for the state convention a greater percentage of the total vote than Bell had won in the presidential race. The cooperationists advocated secession only after all other constitutional means of obstructing the Republicans had been tried, and then only if the whole South, including the border states, seceded in unison. If the candidates who stood for immediate and independent secession expected support from all who had earlier voted for Breckinridge, they were disappointed.

Confidence in the future and in the Union extended from the planters to their dependents, bridging not only political but social boundaries, too. That so many voters followed the planters' lead by supporting unionist and cooperationist candidates, when their futures were not as bright, is a testimony to the strength of patriarchal influence, which could only have added to the planters' assuredness. Property, homes, way of life increasingly separated Warren County's planters from the small- and non-slaveholders, tenant farmers, and overseers who lived among them. However, planters, no matter how wealthy, remained heads of families and neighborhoods. To be sure they summoned patriarchal authority to serve their individual interests as owners of large tracts of land and tens or hundreds of slaves. Still, family and neighborhood ties forged in earlier years blurred distinctions in wealth and standing. Poorer farmers, perhaps because they were kin, or neighbors, or former Whigs, or men, or white, or all at once, still identified with local planter patriarchs, and expressed that identification when they voted for the same candidate. After all, who understood better the seriousness of the Republican party's threat to slavery than wealthy slaveholders? The *Vicksburg Whig* guffawed when Breckinridge supporters claimed nonslaveholders knew best how to protect slavery against Northern abolition. Such a notion was "maintained by these men, most of whom do not own the toe-nail of a negro, and who would not know what to do with one, except to sell him, if they had one, for the purpose of justifying their impertinent intermeddling in the affairs of slave owners."[9]

Pressure and intimidation from neighborhood leaders had long kept the party faithful within the ranks. Had James Allen voted at Warrenton, his home precinct, he might well have had to run a gauntlet of taunting friends and kinsmen, among them his brother Court, his brother-in-law James Glass, Glass's cousin William Steele Hyland, and the stepson of Hyland's uncle, all prominent former Whigs and current Unionists. Though he, too, supported the Union, Allen was a Democrat. In his case party loyalty mattered more than squabbles over slavery in far-off halls of Congress. So he voted at Vicksburg. Bob Harris was not so wise. He confronted the Warrenton gang from the wrong end of a gun, though he escaped unharmed.[10]

Patriarchal authority in Vicksburg had always been more uncertain than in the surrounding countryside. By 1860 it seemed about to unravel completely. Thus, the confidence that allowed planters to put the growing political crisis in the back of their minds did not permeate Vicksburg, where Bell captured just twelve more votes than Breckinridge. Indeed, townfolk greeted Lincoln's election and the events of the preceding year with a sense of urgency not present in the countryside.[11]

In the autumn of 1858, with Vicksburg largely deserted, many of its citizens having fled a yellow-fever epidemic, a series of fires destroyed seven or more buildings. Break-ins, including one in which thieves made off with $500 worth of pistols and knives, accompanied some of the burnings. Clearly, the fires and burglaries were neither imagined nor accidental. Initially, if slaves were suspected no one admitted as much, at least not publicly. Hidden concerns occasionally surfaced, however.

After one fire James Roach "Pitched into his honor"—the mayor—"for neglect of his duty in regard to selling grog to slaves." The mayor "made but a weak defence."[12]

The following October came news of John Brown's raid on the federal arsenal at Harpers Ferry, Virginia. It barely stirred the countryside despite the fact that there slaves outnumbered whites. Its effect on Vicksburg, however, was quite different. Economic uncertainty and large numbers of strange whites had already mixed to make a volatile brew. The threat of slave insurrection increased the heat and risked combustion.[13] A party of town citizens searched the swamps for arms and "suspicious characters." When they found nothing, fears dissipated, but only temporarily. Another rumor circulated a few months later, although no evidence of its authenticity materialized.[14] Still concerns mounted as the presidential election approached. In August a mob of Vicksburg citizens tarred and feathered a stranger, thought to be an "abolitionist," and sent him down the river in a skiff. Another man narrowly escaped a similar fate. In yet another incident of mob action vigilantes charged a man named Way with "tampering with slaves," but meekly banished him from town upon learning the suspect was a Southern-born son of a slaveholder.[15] City authorities clamped down on all people who conducted illicit business with slaves. They gave a flatboatman tied to the wharf across the river ten hours to move on or face stern consequences for selling liquor to slaves. They charged Joseph Bilgery, a beer-hall keeper, with allowing slaves to gamble in his establishment, and Mrs. Maguire, a grocer, with selling liquor to slaves.[16] Nervous officials warned free blacks to leave town or risk being sold into slavery. Annie Lindsey, a "free woman of very light complexion," refused to leave. At the last minute, before the auctioneer could raise his voice, someone produced evidence that proved Lindsey's Spanish, not African, ancestry.[17]

Unionists "smelt disunion & fire eating" in all the talk of insurrection and secret abolitionism.[18] Undoubtedly there was a lot of truth to their accusations. "The reports of negro insurrections, which always occur previous to a Presidential election, gotten up for party purposes, in nine cases out of ten" amounted to nothing, claimed a local Unionist newspaper.[19] But, as secessionists liked to point out, behind all the rumors lay an element of truth. Thus, slave resistance became politicized in Vicksburg. And as the slaves came to understand the political significance of resistance, they became more daring.[20] Eleven slaves fled a plantation in Hinds County and hid along the Big Black River for two weeks. When discovered they fended off dogs with clubs and pulled out the eyes of one of their human pursuers. Six escaped with a gun. In Quitman County whites caught a slave placing obstructions on the railroad tracks, "endangering the lives of hundreds of passengers." In Panola County runaways daringly yelled "huzzahs" for Lincoln as they fled. Officials in Leake County jailed five whites and forty slaves for plotting insurrection. One hundred bottles of morphine allegedly given to slaves by abolitionists were discovered in Helena, Arkansas. In Yalobusha County a slave killed his master and narrowly escaped a lynching.[21]

Closer to home, in the three months of October, November, and December, 1860, no less than fifteen acts of arson committed in and around Warren County destroyed gins and warehouses stuffed with thousands of dollars' worth of cotton.[22] "All up and down the river we hear of fires," reported a Delta newspaper in a story reprinted in the *Vicksburg Whig*. "There appears to be a system about these burnings, and we are inclined to believe they are set on fire by abolitionists. The country is flooded by Northern carpenters, and so soon as a gin is burned down they apply for the job of rebuilding it, and if they get the job, they then have a fine opportunity of communicating with the slaves."[23] Some of the stories and suspicions were exaggerated. Many were totally unfounded. Others were completely true. Regardless, many in Vicksburg perceived they were losing control of the slaves.[24]

Planters and their rural neighbors were hardly oblivious to slave resistance, yet they did not politicize it to the extent that Vicksburg's residents did. For example, just one week before the 1860 presidential election Benjamin Wailes witnessed in Natchez "the smoldering remains of a block of houses on Main St., opposite the Masonic Hall, burned down" about 12 midnight. He noted this was "the third or forth fire which has occurred in the city in a short time," that "they had created considerable excitement in consequence in the city," and that "a committee of vigilance has been formed." Wailes, however, remained unmoved. He did not participate in any mob activity. He did not restrict the movement of his slaves between his plantations or between his plantation and town, or even understand the efforts of officials to do so. James Allen complained of losing seven bales of cotton "from stealage by the negroes." His overseer "caught them stealing twice—once from the wagon at noon as it was going to the Gin." Such bold acts sent shivers down the spines of Vicksburg whites, although Allen took them in stride.[25]

By 1860 state law forbade slaves from engaging in any sort of trade. The Warren County board of police added a few new restrictions of their own. Slaves found without passes were to receive 39 lashes. All dogs owned by slaves were to be killed. All firearms were to be confiscated. All places of unlawful assembly were to be investigated. Between 1856 and 1860 the state brought 70 cases before the court, charging whites with selling liquor to slaves, trading with slaves, allowing slaves to go at large, allowing slaves to assemble and preach. At the same time officials cracked down on free blacks, revoking all licenses that granted them permission to reside in the county. Only thirty years earlier Mississippi land speculators advertising for settlers in the Eastern press had made special appeals to free blacks, provided they were of "good character." During the last decade before the Civil War fewer than three dozen free blacks lived in Warren County, nearly all in Vicksburg, and all with special permission from the legislature.[26]

Still, planters trusted their slaves, or at least their ability to control them. Even though they frequently agreed in principle with efforts to restrict the movement of slaves and free blacks, they did not believe those new restrictions needed to be applied to *their* dependents. Thus, county officials charged Anthony Durden and John Vick, both wealthy planters, with permitting slaves to preach on their premises in blatant violation of local ordinance.[27] While nervous citizens of Vicksburg busied themselves with rounding up free blacks for expulsion or sale into slavery, planters worked to protect trusted dependents from such threats. For example, when state officials tried to expel a free black named Green, local planters objected. "Green is a very superior ginwright," "a *very useful* man to the *planters* of this county," who "would find it very difficult to get anyone else who could supply his place." Some 33 rural residents signed another petition to prevent the expulsion of Jordan Cheiwes, a sixty-year-old free black and former soldier in the War of 1812. It would be, petitioners argued, "cruel and unjust" to banish an old man from his home of "many years." Efforts to expel William and Candis Newman aroused a similar response. The Newmans, the petition stated, had been the "faithful and favorite family servants" of a local planter who had freed them upon his death, though heirs and creditors, specifically a certain Mr. Hazard, had so far managed to delay manumission. Nevertheless, through Hazard's "kindness and indulgence," the Newmans "have lived for many years under his protection in a manner free, yet without enjoying any of the rights pertaining to the State of freedom." Furthermore, the petitioners assured the legislature, "their intercourse and dealing have been entirely with white people and have carefully avoided commingling with or having transactions with slaves." In other words, the Newmans were not typical free blacks; they could be trusted. The legislature did not agree and ordered their expulsion. Typical or not, the Newmans were technically free, and therefore potentially dangerous.[28]

The case of the Newmans was full of revealing contradictions. On one hand they were legally free blacks, treated accordingly by the legislature. On the other hand, they lived as slaves, or so the petitioners claimed. But the petitioners exposed their lie when they assured the legislature that the couple voluntarily avoided interaction with slaves, as if they were free. William and Candis Newman were indeed free. Mr. Hazard had not successfully overturned the will. But to prevent their expulsion and to keep their services as laborers Hazard and the petitioners pretended otherwise. The Newmans might well have been partners in the charade. With full recognition of their freedom came expulsion from Mississippi and separation from loved ones. They may have had good personal reasons for wanting to remain enslaved just enough to convince the legislature to permit them to stay.

When lawmakers enacted their restrictive codes they treated individual slaves and free blacks as members of groups that could not be trusted. They did not recognize the extenuating circumstances in a case as complex as the Newmans'. Fear of certain people—slaves, free blacks, vagrants—also lay behind the concerns of many Vicksburg residents, who were not certain that even slaveholders could be trusted with their responsibilities. Planters, however, because they were more familiar with individual slaves, were not so fearful of them as a group. They believed they could be trusted and controlled, that stealing, running away, even arson indicated problems with particular slaves, not the secret designs of distant politicians and abolitionists, or of suspicious characters lurking nearby. Of course, the many and apparently mounting acts of resistance demonstrate how much the planters in fact did not know their slaves, and how illusory was their sense of control.

The young, single, Mississippi-born men of Vicksburg who supported the Southern Democrats, who spoke out against compromise with the North and for secession if Lincoln were elected, apparently did not share the confidence of the planters. By directing attention to the "horde" of vagrant women who "infested" the city, to the "Darkies of 'questionable reputation'" who roamed the streets and lived by stealing from respectable citizens and trading for liquor from low-class whites, they explained the social ills they perceived in terms of weak white male authority. Moreover, they saw the Republican party, particularly its abolitionist threat, as a serious challenge to an urban order that had never been particularly solid. Rural planters, confident of their status and authority within their neighborhoods, took the threats posed by distant politicians more lightly than did urban residents who felt besieged at home.[29]

Of course, even in Vicksburg secessionists were a minority, though a larger one than in the countryside. Older men with families, established merchants with personal and business connections around the country, spoke out on behalf of the Union.[30] They planned railroads to bring new business to Vicksburg stores, and a cotton factory that would eliminate vagrancy, stabilize society, and, of course, increase profits. Why would they jeopardize future prosperity with secession? Moreover, perhaps because they were older businessmen with families, unionists were more fearful of war. "Surely," urged Vicksburg's J. W. H. Harris, compromise "is worth the trial when peace, harmony and prosperity upon the one side, and civil war, bloodshed and ruin upon the other side, stand dependant upon the result."[31] Unlike in the countryside, however, extensive networks of kinship, friendship, and dependency had never emerged to spread the confidence or coercive power of urban elites throughout the city. They could do little to stem the hysteria that arose within certain quarters of Vicksburg.

Sensing an erosion of their authority, some Vicksburg residents responded by asserting their power ever more forcefully. The mayor and council imposed tighter restrictions on the movement of slaves. They warned that masters "who send their negroes to town to peddle pigs or anything else, should be careful about the date of the 'permit' and the amount of such article or articles they may send to be disposed of, as the law in regard to negroes vending without authority is very stringent." After Lincoln's election several avowed secessionists formed a vigilance committee, dubbed the Police Association, to help the mayor's enforcing "especially the law regulating the sale of liquor to slaves." Also, they encouraged masters "to end the practice of allowing their slaves to hire themselves out." At the initial meeting someone suggested that vigilantes refrain from extralegal punishment of acquitted but "known" violators of restrictions against trade with slaves. A majority rejected the idea. The law tied the hands of city magistrates, who were obliged to presume innocence until presented with sufficient evidence to the contrary; law did not apply to a group of concerned citizens, however. Several of these same people also formed a "minuteman" association, to assert, among other things, "the respect which we owe to ourselves as men." The organization resolved to withdraw peacefully from the Union, but also to resist any acts of aggression designed to keep them from achieving that end. Accordingly, each member was required to own and know how to use firearms.[32]

Secessionist activities in Vicksburg, however, only roused the unionist majority. In town the November presidential election had been close. The December convention election was not; secessionists lost badly. Thus the hysteria that descended on Vicksburg following John Brown's raid was something of a red herring. Once the majority was moved to action the radicals could not win. Only in Vicksburg, however, where in November every vote counted and a handful could make the difference, was there a large voter turnout in December. In contrast, half the county's rural voters did not bother with the latter election. In November 1860, as had been the case in every presidential election for twenty years, partisan loyalties fired up the electorate and sent voters to the polls in large numbers. But traditional rivalries between families, neighborhoods, Whigs, and Democrats played no part in the next month's contest. Instead, voters fell into a deep sleep from which they could not be wakened by either the admittedly few but certainly zealous secessionists or the unionists who warned of the horrors of war. The "minuteman" chapter that met at the village of Bovina, for example, did nothing to persuade rural folk that the fate of the Union, the South, or life in Warren County was at stake. In that neighborhood, as elsewhere around the county, the electorate remained unmoved and unconcerned. Though cooperationist candidates won, apathy carried the day.[33]

Warren County voters were not alone in their willingness to withdraw from politics and simply let events take their course. Around Mississippi and across the Lower South turnouts for convention elections were low. In Mississippi, of the 41,000 votes cast in December—only two-thirds of the November turnout—secessionists captured just 16,800. Cooperationists and undeclared candidates split the remaining votes. In a state in which secessionists seemed to have the upper hand, if only because they attracted much attention to themselves, held the most rallies, and published the most inflammatory editorials, it is unlikely that undeclared candidates were secret radicals. They had no need to hide their true opinions. Undeclared candidates, therefore, were either unionists intimidated into silence, or else were unable or unwilling to commit themselves one way or the other. Similarly, voters worked into a frenzy by fire-eaters, convinced that abolitionists lurked in dark alleyways and taverns with slaves who sharpened knives for white throats, certain that the security of their families demanded immediate disunion, were not the sort to stay home on election day. A better-organized and more vocal core of unionists might have brought candidates off the fence and more voters to the polls. Instead, an active secessionist minority carried the day because a silent majority, hearing no calls from the parties and local leaders that normally commanded them, and in any case confident that their lives would not change significantly, disunion or no, let them. The consequences were war and emancipation, and they changed everyone's lives.[34]

Historians used to debate the extent to which the Civil War was a conflict that could have been avoided. One side emphasized the inevitable clash of two fundamentally different economies, societies, even cultures, one based on slavery, the other on free wage labor. The other side stressed the history, government, and culture that linked white Americans, North and South, in a union broken needlessly by careless, ignorant, self-serving politicians. Of course, there was much to recommend both points of view. Slavery certainly made some sort of showdown inevitable, though not necessarily a violent one. But events perhaps might have turned out quite differently had the people involved chosen different courses of action. It was an endless debate that no longer seems to matter. Both views missed the real issue. The extent to which the South as a society was fundamentally different from the North only matters because both regions were being brought together in a process that created a nation out of discrete communities and regions. The United States in 1860 was neither a single nation divided nor two nations trapped within a single government waiting to explode like steam trapped in a pressure cooker. It was a country in the making. Secession, Civil War, and emancipation were byproducts of that process.[35]

The Civil War signaled the integration of thousands of communities into a nation that linked the destinies of all Americans, though the war itself neither began nor ended that process. However, years of relative isolation had rendered most people myopic. Whether they supported the Union or secession or—the most popular choice—decided just to let events take their course, they placed national politics within local contexts and thus could not see the calamity that awaited. In retrospect such shortsightedness and apathy seems foolish, in view of the repercussions. But such inactivity was a natural inclination for people accus-

tomed to defining their world narrowly. But even those with keen fore-
sight, whose field of vision reached beyond county lines, who could see
how their community was tied to the Union, could not comprehend how
much a national conflict would affect them, safe and sound within their
little fiefdoms. And even if they had they were powerless; existing mecha-
nisms of control and influence—family, ties of dependency, personal respect, intimidation—stopped at local borders. In this respect the nation-
building process was still far from complete. The Civil War thus ripped
apart a country that few knew existed until armies or federal marshals
appeared in their neighborhood. By then there was no escaping it.

Warren County's stand against secession was appropriate for a mature society. The community was too well integrated with the rest of the
country to support disunion. But while a part of the United States, the
county was also a part of Mississippi, which was part of the South.
When Mississippi seceded, Warren County's unionism became irrelevant. And so it was across the South. Whatever their stand on the issue
of secession, the actions of individuals in small places on their own
made no difference. What mattered was what happened everywhere and
no place in particular: a slow and barely visible process that created a
nation out of communities. Then in April 1861, the earth shook, the sky
fell, a world came to an end, all of a sudden, or so it seemed.

In fact, the war came on cat's paws, silently stalking Warren County
residents such as James Allen. On a clear November Monday in 1860
Allen oversaw his hands as they picked cotton in the 270-acre "big field"
at Nanachehaw plantation. Then, just after the midday meal Allen, his
son Charles, and the man who tutored the Allen children, Mr. Henzler,
hitched a team of horses to a wagon, climbed in, and headed for Vicksburg. After two hours of bumping along the road they reached Warrenton, where they rested for half an hour before pushing on, arriving at
their destination just before suppertime. The three men spent the night in
Vicksburg. The next day father and, presumably, teacher voted for president; son Charles, being just seventeen, could only watch. Having completed their business, they climbed back onto their wagon and drove
home. Back at Nanachehaw picking continued in the "big field" despite
the rains that set in mid-week. Allen started two teams of slaves to gathering corn in "lake field." He checked his supply of bagging and rope used
for baling and, finding stores low, ordered more. He wrote his agent to
make sure that the shipment of wine he had purchased, 77 cases, was
properly insured. On Thursday word arrived that Abraham Lincoln had
carried New York. "Bad news," Allen allowed, and said no more.[36]

In early December Allen was in New Orleans to meet his mother,
who was arriving from New York on a steamer. "Found hard times in
N.O.," he wrote, "on ac[count] of Mr. Lincoln's election & the Secession
movement, nothing else talked of." Politics replaced the weather as the
subject of conversation. Meanwhile, he and the people he met went
about their lives as usual. On his way downriver he stopped at Natchez

to investigate the authenticity of a neighbor's Spanish-era title to a piece of land that adjoined his plantation, and which he coveted. While away Allen missed the election of delegates to the state convention. When the state seceded from the Union, Allen left no comment in his journal. He was more concerned with an outbreak of measles among members of his family. Regular routines continued on the plantation into the spring planting season. Allen recorded no political news until April 20: "Clear, pleasant & cool—Dr. Glass, Mr. Henzler & C.B.A. off for New Orleans; balance family to V'burg & back—hear of secession of Virginia & a fight at Baltimore. Plantation: finished planting all but Hill field—corn wants working—trash gang in it, but want plows; Alex has a float [of timber]; he has five hands, & ran out today 20 tier." Events in the East loomed, though on a still-distant horizon.

Following the shots at Fort Sumter, South Carolina, James Allen received the first indications of how war was going to affect him. "Ret[urned] from V'burg," he recorded in his journal, "went up yesterday to meet Dr. Glass, Mr. H. & Charly—they came home yesterday [from New Orleans]—been gone a week; war fever on them." Five days later two overseers employed by Allen's brother Court joined the Warren County Rifles, a local militia company. Allen's son, Charly, paid a visit to Joseph Davis, brother of the president of the new Confederacy, "to solicit his influence for a staff appointment in the army." Then came word of the "glorious battles" at Manassas, Virginia.

Regular work continued at Nanachehaw. Slaves replanted several fields of cotton ruined by cold weather and rain. But news of war kept coming, and one by one friends and neighbors departed. William Glass, a nephew, left first, "off for the war." Mr. Henzler, the tutor, returned to his home in New York. Neighbor Tom Bedford headed "off for war with his brother Mat." Meanwhile, Charly continued to search for a suitable regiment and finally succeeded. On July 2 he left for Virginia to join the "Southrons" at Manassas. The war had now touched the Allen family intimately.

If James Allen had thought he could escape the war he now knew that was impossible. All he could do was hope it did not bring personal tragedy. He accompanied his son to Virginia and saw him off to his regiment. "Packed extra clothing for Charly." Allen also "bought $25 worth of liquor for Capts Moody and Peck," to see that they looked out for the young man. Then he caught the train home. On board were three of the Cowan brothers of Vicksburg "bringing on their brother's body—he belonged to [the] Southrons & died at Richmond." Next day came word of another battle at Manassas, in which Charly surely participated. He "would have been in the fight on Sunday—our loss abt 500 killed, 1000 wounded, the enemy 5 times that number." Life for the Allens of Nanachehaw, and for everyone in Warren County, would never be the same.

EPILOGUE

Charly Allen survived his first battle in Virginia. At his mother's urging he left his militia unit and returned to Warren County the following November, to run the plantation after his father had taken ill. But his father, James, soon recovered and Charly went back to the war, only this time he stayed a little closer to home. Along with a number of Warren County boys, he joined Wirt Adams's cavalry regiment in Earl Van Dorn's army then assembling at Corinth, Mississippi.[1] By the time Charly returned to the army there were few young men left in Warren County. Some of the older planters took it upon themselves to recruit, and they circulated around their neighborhoods, urging boys to join the fray.[2]

Jefferson Davis, of course, was the first to leave Warren County on account of disunion. He got on his train for Montgomery that February afternoon in 1861, and returned to his home county only once during the war, nearly two years later. He stopped in Vicksburg but briefly and did not visit his plantation, which by then was in Union hands. Although he eventually regained possession of Brierfield after his release from prison following the South's defeat, he never lived in Warren County again.

While Charly Allen, Jefferson Davis, and so many other men left to fight for the Confederacy, others returned, slowly at first but in growing numbers with each month. The fortunate returned alive. On April 11, 1862, for example, the train arrived at Vicksburg with about fifty men, all wounded at the Battle of Shiloh. And while some left and others returned, those who spent the war in Warren County tried to carry on their usual routines, and to contribute to the South's cause in whatever ways they could. They paid war taxes, for example, which though not unduly burdensome, pinched pockets all the same. Allen sold corn to raise cash to pay his taxes. Wailes paid taxes with gold.[3]

Much more difficult to bear than added taxes were the shortages that came with the disruption of the national and international market. In July 1862, Mississippi High Court Justice William Sharkey had "no crop in except on overflowed ground, no meat, no money, no credit." James Allen was able to supplement his plantation food stores by hunting, for several weeks almost daily. Allen and Sharkey were among the county's most affluent residents, and were much better off than one of their neighbors who died in part from hunger. A man named Middleton and his family, all squatters, had taken sick, could not fend for themselves, had nothing in store, and began to starve. "From all accounts," Allen predicted, "the whole family are likely to die; sent some meat and meal." There were those who found devious ways of overcoming food shortages. Allen's overseer stole 1300 pounds of meat from the smokehouse, which he probably sold to hungry farmers, or sold to folks in town, where shortages of food were more acute than in the countryside. Very quickly after the war began provisions ran out in Vicksburg. Speculators made matters worse by hoarding supplies and demanding outrageous prices.[4]

Farmers met shortages as their ancestors had done during previous periods of scarcity, and in some ways rural folk resurrected a frontier-style economy. They provided as best they could their own subsistence needs. In 1861, when James Allen expected to purchase corn from suppliers in such Northern states as Illinois and Iowa, and did not expect such arrangements to change, he planted two acres in cotton for every acre of corn. The next year he doubled his corn acreage and planted one and a half acres of corn for every acre of cotton.[5] Neighbors helped one another when they could with loans of small amounts of food.[6] Farm households also began to manufacture cloth, something most had not done for some time, though some had trouble locating the necessary equipment. When they did locate a loom or a spinning wheel they had to remember how to work them. Neither Allen nor his wife knew how much wool was required per yard of cloth, so he turned to a neighbor who recalled: one pound wool for two yards linsey. By January 1863, Allen had four hands operating looms. Benjamin Wailes "Collected together the parts of an old loom which was in service in Adams County in the family of Judge Covingtons during the War of 1812—Fifty years since!!! Put it together and find that with some slight repairs to the slays, harness, shuttle etc. it may be made as efficient as ever, and should the present unnatural and barbarous war continue we shall require its service to clothe our negroes and ourselves the ensuing year." Wailes hired Mrs. Ferguson to show his slave Ann how to operate the machine. The overseer at Ivanhoe plantation also tried to get a loom, but had no luck locating one. A man named Floyd began making them for sale, and sold one to the James Gibson household. Mrs. Humphreys, who lived across the Big Black River in Claiborne County, started up a small factory. She supervised slaves who ran twelve looms with flying shuttles, as well as spinning wheels and spring machines with six spindles each. Together Mrs. Humphreys and her workers produced 250 yards of cloth a day.[7]

Union soldiers first arrived in Warren County in May 1862. A small skirmish occurred near Warrenton. In June came orders from the army command to burn all cotton within danger of falling into enemy hands, and that included the harvest of plantations along the Mississippi River and its tributaries. Landowners objected, of course, but to no avail. Appeals made to Jefferson Davis himself proved fruitless. His cotton was the first to be lighted, as an example to others. Joe Davis, the Confederate president's brother, hid 200 bales in a swamp along the Big Black River. He was not alone. But it was all discovered. Neighbors did not like to see their crop burn knowing that others' would be spared, so they reported hidden stashes. James Allen's former overseer, still angry about being fired for stealing meat, turned in his one-time employer. Then came the orders for evacuation. General Van Dorn could not guarantee the safety of neighborhoods within eight miles of the Mississippi, and urged people to leave.[8]

Joe Davis was one of the first to leave. In June a Union raiding party set fire to Hurricane mansion and Warren County's most spectacular country house was gone. Inexplicably, they spared Jefferson Davis's place. The Davises moved farther inland; meanwhile, General Grant made plans to turn the plantations into a "home farm" for African-American refugees collected from Mississippi and Louisiana. By war's end over 4000 former slaves lived and worked for the U.S. government on the plantations of the Confederate president and his brother.[9]

Only the riverside planters fled. Most people decided to stay on, at least for the time being. Even the people of Vicksburg remained, fleeing to the countryside only when Federal gunboats shelled the city, returning when the shelling stopped. They were determined to stay put and fight. In April, New Orleans had fallen to David Farragut and his fleet of Union gunboats. Farragut pushed upriver, taking Baton Route and Natchez, but not Vicksburg, though he bombarded the city intermittently for nearly eight weeks. Vicksburg would be conquered by land, not by water.[10]

In November Vicksburg residents readied themselves for battle. General Martin Luther Smith, in charge of defending the city, continued the construction of batteries and requisitioned local slaves to provide necessary labor. Despite the war, it was cotton-picking time, and slaveholders resented Smith's demands. "The planters," wrote James Allen, "very much dislike to bear the overbearing & insulting manner in which Genl Smith in his assumed authority is pl[eased] to enforce his order." Nevertheless, the planters obliged the general, and none too soon. Union soldiers returned in December, moving up the Yazoo River, burning plantations along the way.[11]

With Federal troops in the area, slaves took advantage of the opportunity to run to freedom. But many had begun to give their masters trouble not long after the war started. When food got scarce, they began to steal meat. Some ran off, not far at first, and usually returned within a few weeks. But once Union soldiers arrived they had someplace to go, and so many fled for good.[12]

On April 30, 1863, General Grant's army landed south of Vicksburg and marched north. Those in his path who had someplace to go made plans to leave. Union officials later counted 136 abandoned plantations around Vicksburg. The Allen family packed up what they could in several wagons, and then with 65 slaves moved to a plantation they rented in the interior of the state. In addition, Allen shipped a number of his slaves to work in Confederate Army iron mines in Alabama. Those who remained faced the trials of occupation by an enemy army. "There are *four* families of us here now," wrote Tryphena Fox from Woodburne plantation near Vicksburg. "Dr. Raymond is staying with me & Fanny, merely to help Pa as much as he can—for there are no negro men left to do anything now. Daniel's wife & three children were with Mrs. M[essenger]—She 'has been burned out of house & home' & Angelina was forced to come here." "Many of the negros have left," she continued, "the corn & meat were taken the 1st week the Yankees came in here & they are driving off cattle & sheep & killing hogs every day. The garden is a perfect waste & nothing is left but a few green apples & the flowers & weeds. We are not allowed to pass outside the pickets to gather berries. The cows are yet left us, but may be taken any day." When Federal troops arrived at Fonsylvania plantation they found the slaves working in the fields. "The yankees came and set the Negroes All Free and the Work All Stoped [sic]," recorded the overseer. The soldiers left with two wagons loaded with corn, two teams of oxen, and four freedmen drivers. Over the next several days they returned for the livestock. Most of the former slaves began to leave. Those who chose to stay planted potatoes for themselves. The cotton remained untended for the rest of the season.[13]

On May 19, Grant began his attack on Vicksburg. On July 4, forty-seven days later, the city surrendered. The story of life in the besieged city, of life in the caves, the shelters people dug under the bluff and which they made their homes until the shelling finally stopped, has been well told. There is no need to repeat it here. It is another example of how much people can endure when they believe their cause is right. The white citizens of Vicksburg did not forget their stand, nor their surrender, and they let many years pass before they celebrated the Glorious Fourth again. The city's black residents did not forget the surrender either. They lined the streets and cheered as Grant's army marched in.[14]

With the fall of Vicksburg the Old South in Warren County died. James Allen's moment of realization of that fact came upon his return to his plantation. Few of his former slaves remained. "Wife sick," he recorded in his final journey entry, "no one to wait on her." Everyone else, black and white, would have similar moments when they became aware that one world had ended and another begun. Of course, no one knew what that new world would look like. As people worked out social arrangements post-emancipation, the years that followed were to be filled with pain and violence and hope, legacies of war but also of the community's previous life.

ABBREVIATIONS USED IN THE APPENDICES AND NOTES

LSU   Hill and Shreve Memorial Libraries, Louisiana State University, Baton Rouge

MDAH   Mississippi Department of Archives and History, Jackson

NTC   Natchez Trace Collection in the George W. Littlefield Southern History Collections, Center for American History, University of Texas at Austin

OCHM   Old Court House Museum, Vicksburg

WCC   Warren County Courthouse, Vicksburg

APPENDICES

Appendix A: The Study Data

This study of Warren County rests on a large body of evidence, referred to in the end notes and in the sources for tables and figures as the Study Data. I compiled this database largely though not exclusively from the public records of Warren County, which I broke down or stripped of pertinent information—name, date of birth, date of marriage, name of mother, and so forth—and then reassembled in the form of some 6000 machine-readable personal biographies. The process is tedious and time-consuming. At the moment the database is complete from the arrival of the first settlers in the 1770s to 1835. Every person who managed to get his or her name on the public record during those years should be in the Study Data, although in some cases individual files consist of nothing more than a name. Moreover, I continued to strip records from the period after 1835 in order to complete the files of individuals who lived in Warren County prior to that date. Thus, for example, I searched cemetery records through the end of the century to find dates of death for people in the Study Data. The Study Data for years after 1835 I compiled from the manuscript census schedules for 1850 and 1860.

To further illustrate the method of record stripping, I offer an example: Jacob Hyland. I first came across his name in the 1810 census (Census of Claiborne and Warren Counties, 1810, RG 28, microfilm roll 546, MDAH). (This census has been published by Madel Jacobs Morgan, ed., "Census of Claiborne and Warren Counties, Mississippi Territory, 1810," *Journal of Mississippi History* 13 (January 1951): 50–63. However, only the original manuscript distinguishes Warren County from Claiborne County residents.) Court records listed him as a landholder in 1797 (May Wilson McBee, comp., *The Natchez Court Records, 1767–1805: Abstracts of Early Records* (Baltimore, 1979), 363), but a year earlier a neighbor mentioned the Hyland family in an account book (George Rapalje note book, typescript, MDAH). Thus, in 1796 Jacob Hyland first appeared in Warren County, although at that time he probably lived with his father. Land records enabled me to locate his place of residence, and to track his moves over the years. (Private Claims and Field Notes in Mississippi, microfilm roll 14, case 31476, MDAH. McBee, *Natchez Court Records,* 363. Orphans' Court Book B, p. 408, WCC. Deed Book C, pp. 159–61, WCC. Sectional Indexes, townships 14 and 15 north, range 3 east, WCC.) At the time of his arrival in Warren County Jacob was seven-'teen. Cemetery records, plus a family bible, give his date of birth. (Marlene Rutland Brooks and Lisa Yarbrough Grant, comp., "Words in Stone," 3 volumes of cemetery records for Warren County, in OCHM. Jacob Hyland Bible record also in OCHM.) The bible, court records, the neighbor's account book, plus a will all helped identify Jacob's parents and siblings. (Rapalje Note Book, MDAH. Will Book A, pp. 17–18, WCC.) For the years 1810, 1820, and 1830 census records indicate the size of his household, plus the gender and age distribution of its members. (For 1810 see above. U.S. Census, Population Schedules for Warren County, 1820 and 1830, available on microfilm.) Census plus tax records give his wealth-holding in land and slaves. (Personal Tax Rolls, Warren County, 1810, 1818, 1820, 1825, 1830, 1835, MDAH.) Cemetery records tell me that Jacob Hyland died in 1830.

While scanning records for such vital information as date of birth, I also noted every occasion that the record mentioned Jacob Hyland's name. This allowed me to flush out more of Hyland's life history by supplementing his machine-readable file with qualitative information. I noted, for example, the details of the occasions when the court appointed him guardian, or made him the administrator of an estate, when he served as a witness to a legal transaction, when he put up security for someone else. I noted that at his death he owned one-quarter interest in the press used by the *Vicksburg Register.* This enabled me to get a more intuitive sense of Hyland's life history, his place and stature in his family and community, than I could have had I collected only the easily quantifiable data. But where I have made use of this more qualitative evidence I have given the full citations. Study Data refers only to the machine-readable database.

Appendix B: Local Exchange Patterns

Table B–1. Mean Prices of Commodities Bought and Sold, 1789–1797

	Mean	Minimum	Maximum	n
Sugar				
Market purchase price	.32	.21	.50	4
Local sale price	.38	.38	.38	3
Coffee				
Market purchase price	.44	.38	.63	5
Local sale price	.50	.50	.50	3

Source: Rapalje Notebook, typescript, MDAH.

Table B–2. Participation in Local Exchange, by Sex

	Females	Males
Borrowing and lending	78	23
Buying and selling	22	77
	100%	100%
	n = 9	n = 60

$X^2 = 8.53$; d.f. = 1; significance = .0035; lambda = .24

Source: Rapalje Notebook, typescript, MDAH.

Appendix C: Cattle, Slaves, and Cotton

Table C-1 gives the standardized regression coefficients for several variables that might be expected to influence variations in the amount of cotton reported in probate inventories. Nonproductive wealth, for example, could be sold during a financial crisis, and thus might have been a safety against the risk of planting cotton. This hypothesis is not supported, however. Similarly, cotton production did not vary with the number of adult white males (over age 21 as reported by the census) and free blacks living in the household. Of course, women and children also worked in fields, and so family size might also have influenced cotton production; this hypothesis is not supported either. Only the value of slave property, a proxy for the number and productivity of slaves, indicates a relationship with cotton inventories. The partial correlation coefficient indicates that slave value accounts for 44 percent of the variation in cotton inventories.

TABLE C–1. Multiple Regression and Partial Correlation Coefficients for Cotton Production (dependent variable is pounds of cotton)

	Standardized Coefficient	t-value	r^2
Value of nonproductive wealth	−.26	−1.42	.04
Number of adult white males and free blacks	−.24	−1.19	.00
Household size, including slaves	−.59	−2.00	.22
Number of whites	.31	1.50	.00
Value of slave property	1.14*	3.47	.44†
r^2 = .36			
n = 32			

*Significance at the .01 level.
†Significance at the .005 level.
Source: See Table C–2.

Table C-2 indicates a strong positive relationship between cattle and slaves. There would appear to be no relationship between corn and cotton, although this may be a product of seasonal variations in inventory accounts of crops. Also, there is only a weak, negative association between hogs and slaves.

As a source of agricultural data, probate inventories pose serious problems. Often, appraisers simply ignored the value of crops, particularly if they were still in the field. The appearance of crops in inventories also varied according to the season. No inventories reported cotton

TABLE C–2. Multiple Regression and Partial Correlation Coefficients for Slaveholding (dependent variable is size of slaveholding)

	Standardized Coefficient	t-value	r^2
Bushels of corn	.05	.43	.06
Number of cattle	.72*	4.59	.29†
Number of hogs	−.21	−1.37	.10
r^2 = .39			
n = 119			

*Significance at the .0001 level.
†Significance at the .001 level.

Source: Claiborne County Records, Estates, Appraisements and Inventories of, Microfilm roll 70, MDAH; inventories from probate file boxes, WCC; Orphans Court Minute Book A, OCHM; Orphans Court Minute Book B, WCC; Probate Court Account Book D, WCC; 1820 and 1830 Census, Population Schedules; Madel Jacobs Morgan, "Census of Claiborne and Warren Counties, Mississippi Territory, 1810," *Journal of Mississippi History* 13 (January 1951) : 50–63.

during the summer months of June, July, and August, while corn reported for the same season averaged only five or six bushels. Spring inventories had the most cotton on hand, while winter accounts reported the greatest number of bushels of corn. In addition, coming as they do, generally, at the end of the life cycle, inventories give a biased account of wealth-holding, which usually peaked late in life before declining somewhat during old age. Inventories also do not account for property given away as bequests just prior to death. They also misrepresent household size, which could be either reduced if children have grown and are living elsewhere, or expanded if the decedent at time of death lived in a grown child's household. Nevertheless, as a source of agricultural data, they are all that is available before the agricultural schedules of the 1850 census. On the necessary precautions of using probate inventories, see: Gloria L. Main, "Probate Records as a Source for Early American History," *William and Mary Quarterly*, 3d ser., 32 (1975): 89–99; Lois Green Carr and Lorena S. Walsh, "Inventories and the Analysis of Wealth and Consumption Patterns in St. Mary's County, Maryland, 1658–1777," *Historical Methods* 13 (Spring 1980): 81–82.

Appendix D: Households

TABLE D–1. White Households

	1792	1796	1810	1820	1830	1850
Percent stem-family households	20		60	53	47	42
Percent nonstem-family households	20		28	30	43	49
Percent single-person households	60	13	12	17	10	9
Average number of whites per household	3	5	5	5	5	5
Average number of children per household	1		3	3	2	2
Percentage of white population living in stem-family households	54		50	45	37	39
N	10	23	127	279	672	696

Source: Spanish Census of Natchez District, District of Big Black, 1792, MDAH; Rapalje Notebook, MDAH; Abstract of Census, Mississippi Territory, 1801, Pickering County, microfilm roll 546, MDAH; U.S. Census, manuscript population schedules, Warren County, 1810, 1820, 1830, 1850.

To make the comparison more valid with earlier years when there was no large urban place in Warren County, the figures for 1850 do not include households located within Vicksburg. In the city the proportion of stem-family households was smaller, and the proportion of single-person and nonstem-family households was greater than in the countryside.

The 1796 Households

The number of whites per household for 1796 was estimated by using the census made by Jacques Rapalje in 1796, which gives number of households and size (including slaves), and the aggregate census for 1800, which gives the number of whites and slaves. In 1796 there were 132 people in 23 households on the Big Black River. How many were slaves is not known. In 1800, however, there were 29 slaves. If there were the same number of slaves for the earlier date, then that would leave 103 whites, or 4.5 whites per household. Twenty-nine is surely too many slaves, thus the estimate of the number of whites is lower-bound. Alternatively, if the number of whites in 1800 is divided by the number of households for 1796, then the average number of whites per household was 5.6, a figure that is upper-bound because there were surely more households by the later date. Thus, five whites per household is the estimate for both 1796 and 1800. The latter source was published in 1801 as "The Second Census, 1800," but contains typographical errors that need to be corrected with the handwritten abstract in the MDAH.

Method for Estimating the Number of Stem-Family Households

Before 1850 the decennial census did not list household members other than the head. The relationship between other members to the head of the household can thus only very roughly be estimated. I counted any household with an adult male and female with or without children, and any with a male or female with children (children being residents under 21 but young enough to plausibly be a child) as a stem-family household. All remaining households were nonstem. These rules were applied intuitively, however. Obviously, an adult couple in their twenties could not be parents to a child between 16 and 21 years of age. Likewise, a woman aged 18 living with a very young child was considered a stem family.

When this method was applied to the 1850 census, for which household composition is known, the count proved to be 4 to 12 percent too low, depending on whether I counted adults as age 21 and older or 16 and older. In other words, the method of counting stem-family households in the 1810 census (people aged 21 and older were considered adults) undercounted by perhaps 5 percent, while in the 1820 and 1830 censuses (people aged 16 and older were considered adults) undercounted by as much as 10 or 12 percent. The corrected estimates appear in the above tables.

The method for estimating the percentage of stem-family households could have biased the results in the above tables. As the population aged over time, a greater percentage of actual stem families would have been dropped from the estimate, which by including primarily adults with children is biased toward young families. As Table D-2 shows, the

TABLE D–2. Age of Household Heads

	Mean Age	Minimum Age	Maximum Age	Standard Deviation	N
1810	33.17	20	41	8.08	6
1820	34.70	20	53	11.04	23
1830	36.01	20	75	11.14	87

Source: U.S. Census, Population Schedules, 1810, 1820, 1830.

average age of household heads did increase with each census. But if this biased the results, it did so unnoticeably. I would expect a correlation between the age of the household head and the type of household (stem/nonstem). No statistically significant correlation existed.

This ratio of men per 100 women was higher than was typical of frontier areas. From 1800 to 1840, the ratio in Southern frontier areas hovered around 120/100. Northern frontier areas fluctuated more, ranging from 108/100 in 1800 to 143/100 in 1840, but were nevertheless comparable to the ratio in Southern frontier areas. See James E. Davis, *Frontier America 1800–1840: A Comparative Demographic Analysis of the Frontier Process* (Glendale, Calif., 1977), 75, Table 16.

TABLE D–3. Men per 100 Women, 1800 (age 16 or older)

	Men	Women	Ratio
Walnut Hills	14	8	175
Big Black River	37	24	154
Bayou Pierre	162	106	153
Combined region	213	138	154

Source: Second Census, 1800, "Schedule of the Whole Number of Persons in the Mississippi Territory." See also, "Abstract of Census, Mississippi Territory, 1801, Pickering County [later Jefferson, Claiborne, and Warren Counties]", microfilm roll 546, MDAH.

TABLE D–4. Wealth-Holding of Warren County Household Heads with Highest Degrees

	Average Slaveholding	Average Acreage
Personal wealth of extended family heads	16	379
Combined wealth of the whole extended family	63	1,427
All household heads	4	83

Source: Study Data. Household heads with what network analysts term the highest degree are those who have connections to the highest number of other members of the network. See David Knoke and James H. Kuklinski, *Quantitative Applications in the Social Sciences,* vol. 28: *Network Analysis* (Beverly Hills, 1982), 45.

Appendix E: Mortality and Fertility

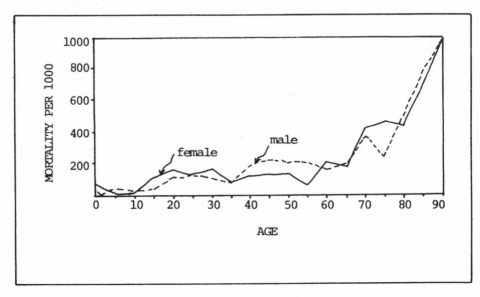

Figure E.1 Mortality for men and women born before 1860. (*Source:* Study Data).

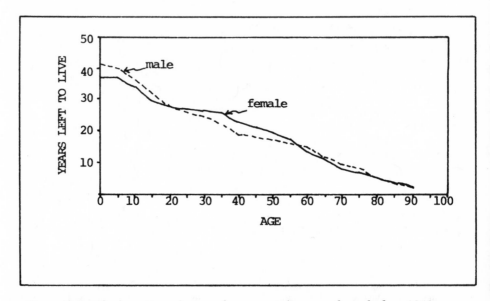

Figure E.2 Life expectancy by age, for men and women born before 1860. (*Source:* Study Data).

TABLE E–1. Crude Fertility Ratios (children under age 10 per 1000 women ages 16 to 45)

1800	1830	1850
2,273	1,552*	1,204

*For 1830 the ratio was calculated using women of age 15 through 49, thus is low relative to ratios for the other years. If the calculation is made using only women of age 15 through 40 the ratio increases to 1,760, but nevertheless indicating a steady decline in fertility over time.

Source: U.S. Census, 1810, 1830, 1850. For a comparison with other places in the nineteenth-century U.S., see: Davis, *Frontier America, 1800–1840: A Comparative Demographic Analysis of the Frontier Process* (Glendale, Calif., 1977), 169; John Mack Faragher, *Sugar Creek: Life on the Illinois Prairie* (New Haven and London, 1986), 253, n. 3.

Appendix F: Slave Hiring

The historical literature on slavery pays scant attention to the incidence of slave hiring in the antebellum South. Although historians differ slightly in their estimates of the number of slaves in rural areas who were hired out, placing the figure between 5 and 10 percent, they do agree that with the possible exception of the urban areas of the Upper South the subject warrants little attention. Eugene D. Genovese, for example, devotes two pages in his more than 600-page book on slavery to the question of hiring. I suggest, however, that the subject of slave hiring seems unimportant only because we know so little about it, and that more imaginative research will show that hiring was more widespread, and that it was integral to the slaves' experience.

The number of slaves leased by their owners is difficult to establish. Censuses did not report whether household heads owned or rented the slaves who lived on their farms. Contracts, which might have been, and sometimes were, recorded in county deed books, or in probate records when guardians rented out the slave property of wards, are an obvious source. Yet they, too, are scarce, thus creating the impression of a low incidence of slave hiring. Qualitative evidence suggests otherwise, however. Clearly, we need better estimates of the incidence of hiring.

The 1860 census free and slave population schedules provides both the number of slaves and the personal property (including slaves) in dollars for all slaveholders. This is enough information to permit an estimation of the extent of slave hiring. If we assume that, on average, slaveholders had approximately x in nonslave personal property, and that slaves cost, on average, y, then we would expect a household head with S slaves to have personal property worth $(S \times y) + x$. Personal property equal to or greater than this amount would indicate that the slaveholder most likely owned all the slaves enumerated under his name by the census taker. Personal property less than the expected amount would indicate that the household head was probably renting slaves.

In 1860 the mean personal property of rural Warren County slaveholders with more than one slave was $1200. Roger L. Ransom offers the most recent estimate of average slave price, which he places at about $800. This figure might be high, in that the least valuable slaves, the old and the young, were under-represented in the slave market from which average prices are calculated. Probate inventory estimates of average slave value, which tended to be $300 or $400 lower than average sale prices, support this point. Although appraisers might have been tempted to undervalue property somewhat in order to minimize tax assessments, they would not have deliberately miscalculated to this extent. Furthermore, average slave value of $800 would leave an average nonslave personal property of $400, which might be low. Lee Soltow estimated average nonslave personal property of $600 for slaveholders with more than three slaves. Thus, we assume average nonslave personal property (x) was $500, and average slave value (y) was $700.

The number of household heads most likely to have rented slaves can be calculated: If $TP < (S \times 700) + 500$ then the slaveholder is a renter, where TP is total personal property, and S is the number of slaves. The calculation suggests that 20 percent of Warren County's rural slaveholders rented at least one slave.

The number of slaves rented by each slaveholder can also be calculated with the following equation: $(TP - 500)/700$. In rural Warren County, in 1860, renters rented on average 10 slaves, for a total of 911, or 9 percent of the slave population.

If the actual value of slaves was higher than the estimate of $700 used here, then the estimated incidence of slave renting increases. For example, if slaves were actually worth on average $1000, then the estimated number of renters increases to 45 percent. Although such a high incidence of slave hiring seems unlikely, nevertheless, the estimate of 20 percent could well be low. Although it is possible that differences in the value of slaves owned by small and large holders might mean that the estimate is too high, this is unlikely. If poorer slaveholders owned slaves of less value than the average, then the figure of 20 percent would be high. But this was not the case. Holders of five or fewer slaves tended to have greater personal property per slave than holders with more than five slaves, probably because small holders were less likely than large holders to own lower-priced infant or aged slaves. Thus, the estimate of 20 percent should be considered low rather than high.

Estimating the incidence of slave hiring for years before the 1860 census requires a different method because personal property is not known. Instead, we must compare the slaveholdings reported by the census with those recorded on county tax rolls. There are three approaches, illustrated with data for 1810. First: A substantial number of slaveholders appeared on the census but not on the tax roll, presumably because they did not own the slaves who lived in their household. The presumption may be incorrect, but accepting it for the moment, we find that 23 percent of the slaveholders recorded by the census did not pay taxes on any slaves. Most of these slaveholders, however, did not appear on the 1810 tax roll at all, although we would expect all adult males present in Warren County to have been assessed at least a poll tax. Perhaps they owned their slaves, but the tax collector overlooked them, or maybe they were absent from the county at tax time but present when the census enumerator arrived. If we assume that the slaveholders listed on the census paid taxes on all their slaves even though they did not appear on the tax roll, then the estimate of the incidence of slave hiring drops considerably, to 13 percent of slaveholding heads of household. We are left with two estimates, which can be considered high and low boundaries with the actual figure somewhere in between.

Of course, we have not taken into account slaveholders who owned and rented at once. Again, using the data for 1810, several slaveholders listed as such on both lists were found to have more slaves under their names in the census than in the tax roll, suggesting that perhaps they rented the extra slaves. Adding their number to the estimate raises the high and low estimates to 35 and 25 percent of slaveholding heads of household.

The problem may be approached a second way. The assumption that slaveholders who rented slaves did not pay the taxes on them may be incorrect. Perhaps the renters paid the taxes, but the actual owners had the slave counted by their name in the census. Using the same approach discribed above, but starting with slaveholders who paid taxes on slaves, but who were not listed as slaveholders in the census, we get two new high and low estimates, 10 and 5 percent of taxpaying slaveholders.

The estimate varies considerably, depending on whether one assumes that the renters or the owners paid the taxes on the slaves. Most likely, both occurred. Long-term contracts of a year probably required the renter to pay the tax, while the owners who hired their slaves out to different people every few weeks or months must have paid the taxes. The problem might best be approached in a third way. In 1810, 76 percent of all slaveholding heads of household appeared on both lists with exactly the same number of slaves. Presumably, they did not hire out any slaves, nor use hired labor. And presumably, the remaining 24 percent did. If there was one buyer for every seller of hired slave labor, then 12 percent of the slaveholding heads of household rented at least one slave. This estimate falls between those given above, and is thus the most acceptable. Table F-1 summarizes the results for 1810, 1820, 1830, and 1860, and also includes counts of the slaves involved.

TABLE F–1. Estimates of the Incidence of Slave Hiring

	1810	1820	1830	1860
Percentage of slaveholders who rent				20
First method	25–35	42–54	45–59	
Second method	5–10	20–39	12–31	
Third method	12	34	34	
Percentage of slaves involved				9
First method	26	18	24	
Second method	7	19	15	
Third method	10	9	17	

Source: Study Data. For estimates of the extent of slave hiring, see: Claudia Dale Goldin, *Urban Slavery in the American South 1820–1860: A Quantitative History* (Chicago and London, 1976), 36, Table 8, which gives a figure of 5% for females and 6% for males in rural Virginia, 1860; Robert William Fogel and Stanley L. Engerman, *Time on the Cross: The Economics of American Negro Slavery* (Boston and Toronto, 1974), 56, which uses Goldin's figure; Eugene D. Genovese, *Roll, Jordan, Roll: The World the Slaves Made* (New York, 1976), 390, which gives a rate of 5 to 10% of all slaves, although how he arrived at the figure is not clear. On slave prices, see Roger L. Ransom, *Conflict and Compromise: The Political Economy of Slavery, Emancipation, and the American Civil War* (Cambridge, Eng., 1989), 75, Table A.3.3. See also Robert Evans, Jr., "The Economics of American Negro Slavery," in Universities National Bureau Committee for Economic Research, *Aspects of Labor Economics* (Princeton, 1962), 185–243; and Goldin, *Urban Slavery*, 72–73, Table 24. For an estimate of the amount of personal property accounted for by slaves versus other property, see Lee Soltow, *Men and Wealth in the United States 1850–1870* (New Haven, 1974), 137.

Appendix G: Classification of Occupations

Below is a list of the occupations reported in the 1860 manuscript census for Vicksburg, and the classifications into which they were placed:

Professional

Attorney, dentist, justice of the peace, lawyer, magistrate, music teacher, physician, preacher, priest, probate judge, school teacher, teacher

Merchant-Service

Barkeeper, beerhouse, beer saloon, billiard hall keeper, boarding house, book merchant, book store, brewery, china merchant, clothing merchant, coffee house, commercial merchant, dry goods merchant, eating house, feed store, fruit store, furniture dealer, grocer, grocery, hide merchant, ice merchant, hotel keeper, merchant, music store, negro trader, produce merchant, restaurant, saloon keeper, shoe store, tin merchant, tin store, trader

Clerical

Agent, auctioneer, banker, book agent, bookkeeper, brakes clerk, city collector, city hospital superintendent, city marshal, clerk, constable, county ranger, deputy sheriff, druggist, editor, express agent, express clerk, gin agent, insurance agent, jail guard, jailor, mail guard, mayor, petitioner, policeman, rail road superintendent, sheriff

Skilled Labor

Artist, baker, blacksmith, boilermaker, bookbinder, boot maker, brick layer, cabinet maker, carpenter, coachmaker, confectioner, contractor, dress maker, founder, gunsmith, harness maker, jeweller, machinist, mechanic, milliner, pattern maker, piano tuner, plasterer, printer, saddle maker, sawyer, sewing, shoe maker, silversmith, stone cutter, stone mason, tailor, telegraph operator, tinsmith, upholsterer, wagon maker, watch maker

Semi-Skilled Laborer

Apprentice saddler, apprentice watchmaker, barber, butcher, cook, crack painter, finisher, gas fitter, gin wright, layer, levying, midwife, mill man, painter, pilot, saw mill, shingle maker

Unskilled Laborer

Boatman, steamboatman, city watch, dirt digger, drying cloth, drayman, fishing, gardener, gas work, house mover, laborer, livery stable, marble yard, miner, peddler, raftsman, railroad, servant, soapmaker, steward, washing, watchman, working

Appendix H: Elections and Office-holding

Not until 1860 did Warren County's wealthier slave- and landowners begin to lose their grip on public office. In that year elected officials, while still wealthier than household heads in general, did not possess as many slaves or as valuable land as other property owners.

TABLE H–1. Office-Holding and Nonoffice-holding Property Owners

	1850	1860
Size of slaveholding		
Office-holding slaveowner	20	15
Nonoffice-holding slaveowner	16	18
Value of landholding		
Office-holding landowner	8557	9889
Nonoffice-holding landowner	4991	12096

Source: United States Census, Warren County, Mississippi, 1850 and 1860, Population Schedules.

TABLE H–2. Wealth in Slaves of Officeholders, 1810–1860

	1810	1820	1830	1850	1860
Average size of slaveholding	10	8	9	20	15
Slaveholding percentile	90	86	80	89	87
Percentage owning no slaves	18	22	3	24	20
Number of officeholders	11	36	32	29	35

Source: Register of Appointments, County Officers, Series A, vol. N, roll 2108, MDAH. Elections Returns, Warren County, RG 28, MDAH. Vicksburg *Daily Whig,* November 8, 1841; November 5, 1847; November 11, 1843; November 7, 1845. Vicksburg *Weekly Whig,* November 14, 1849; November 12, 1851; November 12, 1853; October 13, 1858; October 12, 1859. Tax Rolls, Warren County, 1810, 1820, 1830, RG 29, MDAH. United States Census, Warren and Claiborne Counties, RG 28, microfilm 546, MDAH. United States Census, Mississippi, 1820, 1830, 1850, 1860, population schedules, microfilm.

TABLE H–3. Election Results by Precinct, Governor's Election, 1851

	Foote	Davis	Percentage of Vote for Foote
Vicksburg	431	334	56
Bovina	58	58	50
White House	6	21	22
Warrenton	152	52	75
Milldale	49	14	78
Oak Ridge	40	15	73
Thornley's	7	2	78

Source: County Election Results, Vicksburg *Whig,* November 12, 1851.

Appendix I: Wealth

Two patterns emerge from the long-term trends in wealth-holding in Warren County. First, the actual distribution of wealth and the share of total wealth held by the wealthiest 10 percent of household heads was remarkably stable. Second, despite the overall stability in wealth distribution, the difference between the poorest and richest household heads increased tremendously over time.

Table I-1 shows the Gini coefficients and the size share of the top 10 percent (SSTT) for property in slaves. The Gini coefficient is a statistical measurement of wealth distribution where 0 represents perfect equality (all members of the sample have the same wealth) and 1.00 represents perfect inequality (one member of the sample has all the wealth). In

TABLE I–1. Distribution of Wealth in Slaves

	1810	1820	1830	1850	1860
Gini	.74	.80	.74	.74	.77
SSTT (%)	54	68	57	57	60

Source: Study Data.

Note: Figures for 1850 and 1860 do not include Vicksburg, but are for the rural areas of Warren County only, for better comparison with years before Vicksburg grew to be a substantial urban place.

1820 inequality increased somewhat, apparently reflecting the arrival in the county of a lot of nonslaveholders. But except for that year distribution of slaves remained virtually unchanged, and only in the last decade was there a modest trend toward greater inequality.

Figure I-1 shows the minimum number of slaves owned by household heads among the richest 10 percent. In 1810, for example, the difference between the poorest household heads or those with no property and those in the wealthiest decile stood at only 10 slaves. By 1860 the difference between rich and poor had increased to 40 slaves. Bear in mind that the figure presents only minimum slaveholdings of members of the wealthiest decile. Some owned much more.

Table I-2 shows the Gini coefficients and SSTTs for real estate. The first three dates give the distribution of taxable acres, while the last two

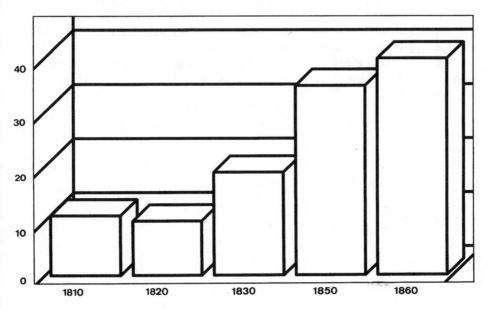

Figure I.1 Minimum number of slaves owned by household heads among the wealthiest 10 percent.

TABLE I–2. Distribution of Wealth in Real Estate

	1810	1820	1830	1850	1860
Gini	.81	.96	.83	.80	.80
SSTT (%)	66	100	71	72	71

Source: Study Data.

Note: Figures for 1850 and 1860 do not include Vicksburg, but are for the rural areas of Warren County only for better comparison with years before Vicksburg grew to be a substantial urban place.

TABLE I–3. Distribution of Property in Vicksburg

	1850	1860
Wealth in slaves		
Gini	.84	.85
SSTT (%)	75	76
Wealth in real land		
Gini	.85	.83
SSTT	81	77

Source: Study Data.

dates give the distribution for land value. While acres and land values were not necessarily equivalent, the table nevertheless demonstrates a trend of stability. As with distribution patterns for property in slaves, only in 1820 was there marked increase in inequality, again probably owing to an influx of nonproperty-holders.

Wealth in Vicksburg, as Table I-3 presents, tended to be more unequally distributed than in rural areas, but there too patterns were stable.

NOTES

Introduction

1. Eugene D. Genovese, *The Political Economy and Slavery: Studies in the Economy and Society of the Slave South* (New York, 1965); *The World the Slaveholders Made* (New York, 1969); *Roll, Jordan, Roll: The World the Slaves Made* (New York, 1974). Elizabeth Fox-Genovese and Eugene D. Genovese, *Fruits of Merchant Capital: Slavery and Bourgeois Property in the Rise and Expansion of Capitalism* (New York, 1983). James Oakes, *The Ruling Race: A History of American Slaveholders* (New York, 1982); *Slavery and Freedom: An Interpretation of the Old South* (New York, 1989). Steven Hahn, *The Roots of Southern Populism: Yeoman Farmers and the Transformation of the Georgia Upcountry, 1850–1890 (New York, 1983).*

2. William Freehling *The Road to Disunion,* vol. 1: *Secessionists at Bay, 1776–1854* (New York, 1990).

3. Allan Kulikoff, *Tobacco and Slaves: The Development of Southern Cultures in the Chesapeake, 1680–1800* (Chapel Hill, 1986), and Richard Beeman, *The Evolution of the Southern Backcountry: A Case Study of Lunenburg County, Virginia, 1746–1832* (Philadelphia, 1984).

4. For a full discussion of abstractionists and substantialists, see Christopher Morris, "The Southern White Community in Life and Mind: A Critical Review," *Canadian Review of American Studies* 21 (Fall 1990): 203–22.

5. Marvin Harris, *The Rise of Anthropological Theory: A History of Theories of Culture* (New York, 1968), 568–604; Harris, *Cultural Materialism: The Struggle for a Science of Culture* (New York, 1980), 31–45; Thomas N. Headland, Kenneth L. Pike, and Marvin Harris, *Emics and Etics: The Insider/Outsider Debate* (Newbury Park, Calif. 1990).

6. Harris, *Cultural Materialism,* ix. Curiously, Jane Censer, "Planters and the Southern Community: A Review Essay," *Virginia Magazine of History and Biography* 94 (October 1986): 387–408, detects a "fashionable" discontent with the examination of small places. Yet Southern historians are only beginning to comprehend how such studies can contribute to an understanding of the whole section, as Censer's own article demonstrates. Historians of early America have reaped tremendous benefits from local studies. See Darrett B. Rutman, "Assessing the Little Communities of Early America," *William and Mary Quarterly* 43 (April 1986):163–78, and Jack P. Greene, *Pursuits of Happiness: The Social Development of Early Modern British Colonies and the Formation of American Culture* (Chapel Hill, 1988).

7. My definition of community is based on: Conrad M. Arensburg and Solon T. Kimball, *Culture and Community* (New York, 1965), 7–27, and Colin Bell and Howard Newby, *Community Studies: An Introduction to the Sociology of the Local Community* (New York, 1972), 19. Darrett B. Rutman: "The Social Web: A Prospectus for the Study of the Early American Community," in William L. O'Neill, ed., *Insights and Parallels: Problems and Issues of American Social History* (Minneapolis, 1973), 57–89; "Community Study," *Historical Methods* 13 (1980); 29–41. Also, Darrett B. Rutman and Anita H. Rutman, *A Place in Time*, vol. 1: *Middlesex County, Virginia, 1640–1740*, vol. 2: *Explicatus* (New York, 1984). Rutman offers an etic and substantialist perspective of community as observed behavior. An emic and abstractionist view of community as a mental image or emotion based on experience is provided by Thomas Bender, *Community and Social Change in America* (New Brunswick, N.J., 1978).

8. On the environment and social/cultural evolution, see William Cronon, *Changes in the Land* (New York, 1983).

9. Two who have decried the "new social history," quite correctly, for its tendency to avoid discussion of the politics of human interaction are Eugene D. Genovese and Elizabeth Fox-Genovese, *Fruits of Merchant Capital*, 179–212. Politics and power, formal and informal, exist to some degree in all human interaction, and thus are at the heart of community.

10. This model is an elaboration on the stimulus-organism-response model used frequently by social scientists. The model's use of mental "feedback" is based on Marvin Harris's model of the socio-cultural system. See Harris, *Cultural Materialism*, 70–75. On tracking observable patterns of human interaction, see Rutman, "Community Study."

11. John Schlotterbeck's study of Orange and Greene counties, Virginia, discusses the process of agricultural and social "devolution" that occurred as these counties switched their staple crop from tobacco to wheat. See: John Thomas Schlotterbeck, "Plantation and Farm: Social and Economic Change in Orange and Greene Counties, Virginia, 1716 to 1860" (Ph.D. dissertation, Johns Hopkins University, 1980), and Schlotterbeck "The 'Social Economy' of an Upper South Community: Orange and Greene Counties, Virginia, 1815–1860," in Orville Vernon Burton and Robert C. McMath, eds., *Class, Conflict, and Consensus: Antebellum Southern Community Studies* (Westport, Conn., 1982).

12. For a discussion of the study data, see Appendix A.

13. *The Evening Citizen* (Vicksburg), February 11, 1861.

Chapter 1

1. Hugh Hammond Bennett, *The Soils and Agriculture of the Southern States* (New York, 1921), 213–15, 225.

2. Verdadiera Relacam, *Narratives of the Career of Hernando de Soto in the Conquest of Florida, as Told by a Knight of Elvas, and in a Relation by Luys Hernandez de Biedma, Factor of the Expedition.* Buckingham Smith, trans. (New York, 1866).

3. Alfred W. Crosby, *Ecological Imperialism: The Biological Expansion of Europe, 900–1900* (Cambridge, Eng., 1986), 215. Henry F. Dobyns, *Their Number Become Thinned: Native American Population Dynamics in Eastern North America* (Knoxville, 1983).

4. Gary B. Nash, *Red, White, and Black: The Peoples of Early America* (Englewood Cliffs, N.J., 1974), 108–9. Daniel H. Usner, Jr., *Indians, Settlers, and Slaves in a Frontier Exchange Economy: The Lower Mississippi Valley before 1783* (Chapel Hill, 1992), 65–76.

5. Usner, *Indians, Settlers, and Slaves*, 268–75. John Mack Faragher, *Sugar Creek: Life on the Illinois Prairie* (New Haven, 1986), 18–24.

6. Usner, *Indians, Settlers, and Slaves*, 50, 108, 112–13.

7. This argument may strike readers as somewhat Turnerian, as indeed it is. After suffering death by revisionism, Turner has recently been reconsidered by scholars who have turned our attention westward once again. See for example, William Cronon, George Miles, and Jay Gitlan, *Under an Open Sky: Rethinking America's Western Past* (New York, 1992), especially the introductory essay.

8. Cecil Johnson, *British West Florida: 1763–1783* (New Haven, 1943), 115–31. Bernard Bailyn, *The Peopling of British North America: An Introduction* (New York, 1986), 74. In February 1774, the Crown, fearful of the effects of heavy emigration on wages and rents in England, ceased granting land and began selling it in plots at set prices.

9. Marcus L. Hansen, "The Population of the American Outlying Regions in 1790," American Historical Association *Annual Reports* 1 (1931): 405. Lewis C. Gray, *History of Agriculture in the Southern United States to 1860*, 2 vols. (Washington, D.C., 1933), 2:897. Usner, *Indians, Settlers, and Slaves*, 114. In 1774, Lt. Governor Elias Durnford estimated that 2500 whites and 600 blacks lived on or near the Mississippi. His figures, however, include the more densely populated territory below Natchez, around Baton Rouge, Manchac, and along the Amite River. Johnson, *British West Florida: 1763–1783* (New Haven, 1943), 155.

10. Carondelet to Don Luis de las Casas, November 24, 1794, Mississippi Provincial Archives, Spanish Dominion, RG 26, vol. 22, letter no. 129, MDAH; Marshall (Maria Chotard and family) Papers, Hill Memorial Library, LSU; Dorothy Williams Potter, *Passports of Southeastern Pioneers 1770–1823* (Baltimore, 1982), 25, 26. Bernard Bailyn, *Voyagers to the West: A Passage in the Peopling of America on the Eve of the Revolution* (New York, 1986), 483.

11. Bailyn, *Voyagers*, 482.

12. Johnson, *British West Florida*, 144–49. Wilbur H. Seibert, "Loyalists in West Florida and the Natchez District," *Mississippi Valley Historical Review* 2 (March 1916): 465–83.

13. Petitions of Patrick Doyle, John Felt, Benjamin Barber, and Henry Dwight, 111-E, microfilm reel 4, U.S. General Land Office, Records, Division D, RG 49, West Florida Claims 1760–1800, British Collection, P. K. Yonge Library of Florida History, University of Florida, Gainesville. Robin F. A. Fabel, *Economy of British West Florida, 1763–1783* (Tuscaloosa, 1988), 193–95.

14. Fabel, *Economy of British West Florida*, 153–97. Bailyn, *Voyagers*, 475–94.

15. Matthew Phelps, *Memoirs and Adventures of Captain Matthew Phelps, Formerly of Harwington in Connecticut, Now Resident in New Haven in Vermont, Particularly in Two Voyages from Connecticut to the River Mississippi, from December 1773 to October 1780 . . .*, Anthony Haswell, comp. (Bennington, Vt., 1802), 8–11, 13–14, 50–54.

16. Chester quoted in Bailyn, *Voyagers*, 483.

17. Johnson, *British West Florida*, 137–38; Chester quoted in Bailyn, *Voyagers*, 482.

18. Johnson, *British West Florida*, 127, 130–31.

19. In 1773 the Crown suspended the granting of large tracts. Johnson, *British West Florida*, 141–42. Fabel, *Economy of British West Florida*, 168, 175. May Wilson McBee, comp., *Natchez Court Records 1767–1805: Abstracts of Early Records* (Baltimore, 1979), 96. Cecil Johnson, "Expansion in West Florida, 1770–1779," *Mississippi Valley Historical Review* 20 (1934): 488.

20. Bailyn, *Peopling of British North America*, 65–85.

21. See note 23.

22. Phelps, *Memoirs*, 103.

23. Claims, surveys, and petitions, 111-E, microfilm reels 3 and 4, U.S. General Land Office, Records, Division D, RG 49, West Florida Claims 1760–1800, British Collection, P.K. Yonge Library; Great Britain, PRO, Colonial Office, CO 5/607, pp. 216,217, CO 5/608, pp. 269, 447, British Collection, P. K. Yonge Library. Fabel, *Economy of British West Florida*, 183–87. Marion B. Bragg, "British Land Grants in Warren County, Mississippi," *Journal of Mississippi History* 26 (1964): 231–33. McBee, *Natchez Court Records*, 232, 483.

The number of people in this community circa 1778 can be roughly estimated. Nineteen household heads have been identified. Women, both daughters of Phineus Lyman, headed two of them, while single men headed at least seven. For several, the record indicates the size of the household, and if the remaining received land based on family right, that is, 100 acres for the head of the household, and 50 acres for spouse, each child, and each slave, then the total population would have been about a hundred. This total includes 14 known slaves, although there might well have been more. Thompson Lyman, for example, had 600 acres, suggesting that his household consisted of himself plus 10 other people, some of whom may have been slaves. The estimate of total population, on one hand, may be high. Some grants, particularly those given to the Lyman women, may not have been based on family size, but may instead have been given as bounty for loyalty to the Crown. On the other hand, the total cannot account for unknown squatters who lived in the area. At least one, Peter Doyle, squatted on land that belonged to George Grant, an absentee landowner, and several others had squatted before petitioning for title.

In 1792 there were 10 households and a total of 26 whites and 12 blacks. Single men headed 7 households. Only two households had slaves. Spanish Census of Natchez District, 1792, MDAH. In 1796 Jacques Rapalje counted 132 "souls" in 23 households. Rapalje Notebook, typescript, pp. 5–6, MDAH.

24. The British established a court at Natchez in 1774. Johnson, *British West Florida*, 143. Lyman administered an oath and signed John Felt's petition for land in 1777. West Florida Claims, reel 4, British Collection, P. K. Yonge Library.

25. Margaret Fisher Dalrymple, ed., *Merchant of Manchac: The Letterbooks of John Fitzpatrick, 1768–1790* (Baton Rouge, 1978), 162.

26. Quoted in Robert V. Haynes, *The Natchez District and the American Revolution* (Jackson, 1976), 19. See also Johnson, *British West Florida*, 145, 212. A table of distances between various points along the Mississippi River is in Thomas Hutchins, *An Historical Narrative and Topographical Description of Louisiana, and West-Florida*, with an introduction and index by Joseph G. Tregle, Jr. (1784; rpt., Gainesville, Fla., 1968).

27. The Spanish census for 1792 reports crops and livestock. In that year, among Big Black households, the largest holding of cattle was 20. The largest

holding of hogs was 140. Only half the households had a horse. Of the four crops reported by the census—indigo, tobacco, cotton, corn—Big Black farmers raised only the last. Spanish Census of Natchez District, 1792, MDAH.

On the advantages of hogs over cattle in a forest environment, see Marvin Harris, *The Sacred Cow and the Abominable Pig: Riddles of Food and Culture* (New York, 1987: previously published as *Good to Eat,* New York, 1985), 113–14.

28. As he passed by the Walnut Hills in February 1797, Andrew Ellicott noted "A number of peach trees which had been planted on the hills were now in full bloom." Andrew Ellicott, *The Journal of Andrew Ellicott* (Chicago, 1962), 39. On the introduction of the peach to North America, see Crosby, *Ecological Imperialism,* 156–57.

29. McBee *Natchez Court Records,* 512, 579. Walter Lowrie, ed., *American State Papers. Documents, Legislative and Executive, of the Congress of the United States, in Relation to the Public Lands, from the First Session of the First Congress to the First Session of the Twenty-third Congress: March 4, 1789, to June 15, 1834,* 8 vols. (Washington, D.C., 1834), 1:570. Phelps, *Memoirs and Adventures,* 31, 105–6.

30. Martyn (Michael), letter, August 17, 1774. MDAH. Fabel, *Economy of British West Florida,* 119–24. John G. Clark, *New Orleans, 1718–1812: An Economic History* (Baton Rouge, 1970), 184, 189–92. Gray, *History of Agriculture,* 1:159. Haynes, *Natchez District,* 41.

31. Martyn letter, MDAH.

32. Fabel, *Economy of British West Florida,* 120, 124.

33. McBee, *Natchez Court Records,* 123.

34. Ibid., 246. *William Brocas v. Benjamin Day* (1781), vol. F, p. 5, and *John Stowers et al. v. John and Samuel Watkins* (1781), vol. F, p. 20, and *Eleanor Price v. John Stowers* (1783), vol. G, p. 74, Mississippi Provincial Archives, Spanish Dominion, RG26, microfilm, MDAH. Rapalje Notebook, typescript, pp. 8–15, 23, 25; Dalrymple, *Merchant of Manchac,* 162, 347–52.

35. William S. Coker and Thomas C. Watson, *Indian Traders of the Southeastern Spanish Borderlands: Panton, Leslie & Company and John Forbes & Company, 1783–1847* (Pensacola, 1986), 168–69, 172, 175.

36. *Eleanor Price v. John Stowers* (1783), vol. G, p. 74, Mississippi Provincial Archives, Spanish Dominion, RG26, microfilm, MDAH. Dalrymple, *Merchant of Manchac,* 162, 347–52.

37. Rapalje's notebook mentions one transaction in Baton Rouge, and none at Natchez or New Orleans. On Turnbull, see Coker and Watson, *Indian Traders,* 175.

38. Dayton (Smith J., Joseph, Ebenezer) Papers, NTC. McBee, 217, 278–79, 281.

39. Rapalje Notebook, typescript, p. 2, 20.

40. Ibid., 31.

41. Ibid., 20, quotation from p. 18.

42. Ibid., 17.

43. See Appendix B, Table B-1.

44. See Appendix B, Table B-2.

45. Allan Kulikoff, *The Agrarian Origins of American Capitalism* (Charlottesville, 1992), 13–33.

46. McBee, *Natchez Court Records,* 303.

47. By 1777, a year after streets were laid off in Natchez, four merchants made the town their place of business. Haynes, *Natchez District,* 19.

48. *William Brocas v. Benjamin Day* (1781), vol. F, p. 5, and *John Stowers et al. v. John and Samuel Watkins* (1781), vol. F, p. 20, Mississippi Provincial Archives, Spanish Dominion, RG 26, microfilm, MDAH.

49. Some of these ideas are treated, although somewhat differently, in Bruce H. Mann, *Neighbors and Strangers: Law and Community in Early Connecticut* (Chapel Hill, 1987), 9–27.

50. Phelps, *Memoirs*, 30, 102. Emphasis is added.

51. McBee, *Natchez Court Records*, 232.

52. E. H. Bay to George Poindexter, June 19, 1805, Claiborne (J. F. H.) Collection, Book E, Group 4, microfilm roll 7, MDAH. "Extracts from Mr. Turner's Letters to E. H. Bay," Natchez, July 1822, Bay (William and E. H.) Papers, NTC. See also: E. H. Bay to Anthony Hutchins, August 2, 1800, August 9, 1801, December 17, 1802, Claiborne Collection, Book E, Group 4, microfilm roll 7, MDAH.

53. Phelps, *Memoirs*, 107.

54. Haynes, *Natchez District*.

55. McBee, *Natchez Court Records*, 189, 303, 304, 579. Lowrie, ed., *American State Papers*, 1:570.

56. McBee, *Natchez Court Records*, 9, 23, 93, 104, 577. Lowrie, ed., *American State Papers*, 1:566. Fabel, *Economy of British West Florida*.

Chapter 2

1. John G. Clark, *New Orleans, 1718–1812: An Economic History*, (Baton Rouge, 1970), 210–14. According to Clark, trade between Spanish New Orleans and U.S. farmers was greater than Arthur P. Whitaker suggested in his book *The Spanish-American Frontier: 1783–1795: The Westward Movement and the Spanish Retreat in the Mississippi Valley* (Boston and New York, 1927), although it was considerably less than it became after the Spanish evacuated the Natchez District. In 1798, the year the U.S. actually assumed control of the Natchez District, although still six years before acquiring New Orleans and Louisiana, American inland farmers sent one million dollars' worth of products to New Orleans. R. W. Towne and E. Wentworth, *Pigs: From Cave to Corn Belt* (Norman, 1950), 183.

Cut off by the Appalachian Mountains from Eastern Seaboard markets, Ohio and Kentucky farmers looked to New Orleans as the best outlet for their produce. Indeed, during the 1780s, restricted navigation of the Lower Mississippi became, according to Thomas P. Slaughter, "the greatest single grievance" of farmers from western Pennsylvania south to western North Carolina, heating the frustrations that boiled over in the Whiskey Rebellion. Slaughter, *The Whiskey Rebellion: Frontier Epilogue to the American Revolution* (New York, 1986), 35.

2. Carondelet to Gayoso, January 17, 1792, Despatches of the Spanish Governors, Book 7, pp. 296–99, quotation from p. 299, John C. Pace Library, University of West Florida, Pensacola. Note: This letter reads as if it were written by Gayoso to Carondelet. Mississippi Provincial Archives, Spanish Dominion, vol. IV, January 1792–June 1793, RG26, MF33, p. 5, MDAH. Abraham P. Nastir, *Spanish War Vessels on the Mississippi 1792–1796* (New Haven and London, 1968), 157–58n. Coker and Watson, *Indian Traders*, 166, 167.

3. Estevan Miro to Gayoso, January 29, 1791, Despatches of the Spanish

Governors, Book 7, p. 164, Pace Library. William Hartley, for example, delivered *carne fresca*, fresh beef, which may mean on the hoof, to Nogales in February 1794. For other examples of beef sales to the Spanish by Loosa Chitto herders, see Certificaciones de credito, Los Nogales, 1794, No. 30, Archivo General de Indias, Papales Procendentes de Cuba, legajo 534, microfilm roll 71, Hill Memorial Library, LSU.

4. Jack D. L. Holmes, "Livestock in Spanish Natchez," *Journal of Mississippi History* 23 (January 1961): 15, 26–35, and *Gayoso: The Life of a Spanish Governor in the Mississippi Valley, 1789–1799* (Gloucester, Mass., 1968), 101–2, 113. Guice, "Cattle Raisers of the Old Southwest: A Reinterpretation," *Western Historical Quarterly* 8 (April 1977): 177–78.

Government, in the form of regulations, dogged frontier settlers wherever they went. See Malcolm J. Rohrbough, *The Trans-Appalachian Frontier: People, Societies, and Institutions 1775–1850* (New York, 1978), 105, and William B. Hamilton, "The Southwestern Frontier, 1795–1817: An Essay in Social History," *Journal of Southern History* 10 (1944): 402.

5. McBee, *Natchez Court Records*, 264–65.

6. During the first sixth months of 1801, according to one report, 450 flat-boats, 26 keelboats, 2 schooners, 1 brigantine, and 7 pirogues, all from up river, checked in at customs at the Spanish border, then at Loftus Heights below Natchez. Total cargo included: 93,000 bls. flour; 882 hhds. tobacco; 57,900 lbs. pig lead; 22,800 lbs. hemp; 57,600 lbs. bacon; 43 bls. beef; 196,000 lbs. cordage; 565 bls. whiskey. See John W. Monette, "Progress of Navigation and Commerce on the Waters of the Mississippi River and the Great Lakes, A.D. 1700 to 1846," Mississippi Historical Society *Publications* 7 (1903): 487. For other examples of Kentucky flatboats and their cargoes see: Potter, *Passports*, 23–24, and McBee, *Natchez Court Records*, 149, 258. Richard C. Arena, "Philadelphia-Spanish New Orleans Trade in the 1790s," *Louisiana History* 2 (Fall 1961): 429–45.

While some farmers near the Bayou Pierre planted tobacco, the local economy of the Big Black had yet to develop to the point where staple agriculture was viable. In 1789, the Bayou Pierre region produced 97,000 lbs of tobacco, less than a third produced by the Cole's Creek region near Natchez. Individual producers are listed, but none of the Big Black families appears. Laurence Kinnaird, ed., *Spain in the Mississippi Valley, 1765–1794, Post War Decade, 1782–1791*, Annual Report of the American Historical Association for the Year 1945, vol. 3 (Washington, D.C., 1946, 1949), 310. Tobacco was also one of the crops reported by the Spanish Census of 1792, but by that time few Bayou Pierre households planted any at all, the total crop amounting to only a few thousand pounds. Apparently by then competition from Kentucky producers had taken its toll.

7. P. C. Henlein, *Cattle Kingdom in the Ohio Valley 1783–1860* (Lexington, Ky., 1959), 154–57.

8. Grady McWhiney and Forrest McDonald, "Celtic Origins of Southern Herding Practices," *Journal of Southern History* 51 (May 1985), 165–82, and McDonald and McWhiney, "The South from Self-Sufficiency to Peonage: An Interpretation," *American Historical Review* 85 (December 1980): 1095–118. While few historians accept entirely the thesis of Celtic origins as put forward by McDonald and McWhiney, most see the spread of Southern herding practices as a process of cultural diffusion from Scotland to the backcounty of Pennsylvania and Virginia and across the South as plain folk followed the frontier. See, for ex-

ample: Frank L. Owsley, *Plain Folk of the Old South* (Chicago, 1965), 23–50; David Hackett Fischer, *Albion's Seed: Four British Folkways* (New York, 1990), 741–43; John Solomon Otto, "The Migration of the Southern Plain Folk: An Interdisciplinary Synthesis," *Journal of Southern History* 51 (1985), 183–200. Otto, however, does stress the importance of local conditions, to which cattle herding practices were adaptations, over cultural heritage. See J. S. Otto and N. E. Anderson, "Cattle Ranching in the Venezuelan Llanos and the Florida Flatwoods: A Problem in Comparative History," *Comparative Studies in Society and History* 28 (October 1986): 672–83.

9. A partial tax roll for 1803, listing the property of 28 taxpayers residing from the Big Black to the Walnut Hills, shows one person with a herd of 100 head of cattle, and two people with herds of 200 head. In 1805 the largest herd assessed for taxes numbered 250 head. Claiborne County Tax Roll, 1803, Delinquents, and Claiborne County Tax Roll, 1805, Claiborne County Records (microfilm), MDAH.

Nineteen probate inventories made between 1794 and 1810 showed herds ranging in size from 5 to 150 head, with the mean numbering 42 head. By comparison, when the Spanish took a census in 1792 (see "Spanish Census of the Natchez District, 1792," MDAH) just as the building of Fort Nogales had begun, the largest herd on the Big Black numbered only 20 head. When the households of nearby Bayou Pierre are included, one of which contained 100 steers, the mean herd size numbered only 14 head, a third the size of the mean herd a decade or so later.

In contrast, the largest drove of hogs counted by the 1792 census numbered 150, and another contained only 10 fewer, while the inventories taken during the next decade show none with as many as 100 hogs. The mean size of hog droves for the later period, however, was nearly 20 hogs larger, reflecting the growth of slavery and the need for larger droves to meet household requirements.

10. Livestock raising is typical of sparsely settled frontier regions, but generally gives way to agriculture as population increases. For a discussion of this process as it occurred in the nineteenth-century South see John Solomon Otto, "Southern 'Plain Folk' Agriculture: A Reconsideration," *Plantation Societies in the Americas* 2 (1983): 29–36. For places outside the United States where the same relationship between land, labor, and livestock has occurred, see Arnold Strickon, "The Euro-American Ranching Complex," in Anthony Leeds and Andrew P. Vayda, eds., *Man, Culture, and Animals: The Role of Animals in Human Ecological Adjustments,* American Association for the Advancement of Science, publication no. 78 (Washington, D.C., 1965), 229–58; Otto and Anderson, "Cattle Ranching," 672–83.

11. Henlein, *Cattle Kingdom,* 43.

12. Hilliard conservatively estimates the annual yield for cattle herds in the antebellum South at 20 percent, that is, 20 marketable steers every year from a herd of 100. Sam B. Hilliard, *Hog Meat and Hoecake: Food Supply in the Old South* (Carbondale, Ill., 1972), 128–29.

13. Inventory of Gabriel Griffin, 1796, Natchez Court Records, vol. C, p. 395, Mississippi Provincial Archives, Spanish Dominion, MDAH. Deed Book A, pp. 42–44, WCC. Five dollars per head is a low estimate. In 1796, an inventory reported a price of six Spanish dollars. In 1811 a deed of sale reported the same price, only in U.S. dollars.

14. French immigrant to the Hudson River Valley of New York, J. Hector St.

John de Crèvecoeur, *Letters from an American Farmer and Sketches of Eighteenth-Century America* (New York, 1986), 227, described "frolics," when neighbors joined to help a member of the community to complete an arduous task. Compare the Big Black community with the Sugar Creek community in Illinois a few decades later. Despite the presence of slavery in one and its almost total absence in the other, the two were very much alike in their cooperative use of scarce resources. Faragher, *Sugar Creek*, 130–36.

It is worth noting that the Northwest Ordinance, Article VI, which prohibited slavery from the territory north of the Ohio River, did not shape early economic development so much as reflect certain realities—that settlers came from New England, Pennsylvania, and western Virginia, rather than from slave plantation regions, that the territory was removed from slave markets, that the environment was best suited to the production of grain, which was grown easily without slave labor. Thus the ban on slavery passed into law with little objection from slaveholding members of Congress. However, in later years as those material realities began to change and make slavery seem more feasible, the ordinance's ban became more important and more contested than it had been initially. See Peter S. Onuf, *Statehood and Union: A History of the Northwest Ordinance* (Bloomington and Indianapolis, 1987), 109–32.

15. James A. Padgett, "A Decree for Louisiana Issued by the Baron of Carondelet, June 1, 1795," *Louisiana Historical Quarterly* 20 (July 1937): 590–605.

16. Rapalje Notebook, original copy, p. 78, typescript copy, pp. 7, 29, 31, 32, MDAH.

17. In the cattle-ranching regions in the peripheries of another slaveholding society, colonial Brazil, much like in early Mississippi, slaves and free blacks were left largely unsupervised to tend herds. Moreover, they were often permitted to keep a portion of the yearly increase. James Lockhart and Stuart B. Schwartz, *Latin America: A History of Colonial Spanish America and Brazil* (Cambridge, 1983), 381–82.

18. Otto, "Southern 'Plain Folk' Agriculture," 29–36; J. S. Otto and N. E. Anderson, "Slash-and-Burn Cultivation in the Highlands South: A Problem in Comparative Agricultural History," *Comparative Studies in Social History* 24 (January 1982): 131–47; Durwood Dunn, *Cades Cove: The Life and Death of a Southern Appalachian Community, 1818–1937* (Knoxville, 1988), 23–45.

19. McBee, *Natchez Court Records*, 286. Holmes, *Gayoso*, 100.

20. Rapalje Account Book, typescript, MDAH. American State Papers, 1:775–824. Plat Book of original landholders, Chancery Clerk's Office, WCC. McBee, *Natchez Court Records*, 438.

21. Thomas Ashe, *Travels in America Performed in 1806, for the Purpose of Exploring the Rivers Alleghany, Monongahela, Ohio, and Mississippi, and Ascertaining the Produce and Condition of Their Banks and Vicinity* (London, 1808), 315.

22. Simon Gratz, "Thomas Rodney," *Pennsylvania Magazine of History and Biography* 45 (1921):51. Francis Baily, *Journal of a Tour in Unsettled Parts of North America, in 1796 & 1797* (London, 1856), 147. Zadock Cramer, *The Navigator*, 8th edition (1814; Ann Arbor, 1966), 312.

23. J. H. Ingraham, *The South-West by a Yankee*, 2 vols. (1835; New York, 1968), 2:169. *Besançon's Annual Register of the State of Mississippi for the Year 1838* (Natchez, 1838), 207. United States Census Office, *Compendium of the Sixth Census* (Washington, D.C., 1841), 228. The census figure was calculated by

assuming the average bale weighed 500 pounds, as the census only reported total pounds. In 1840, Adams County (Natchez) produced over 40,000 bales of cotton.

24. John Q. Anderson, "The Narrative of John Hutchins," *Journal of Mississippi History* 20 (January 1858): 5.

25. On one acre of new land a good farmer could have raised perhaps as much as 50 bushels. At 50 cents per bushel his crop would have brought him $25. The same farmer could have worked 0.59 acres of cotton (cotton required 70% more labor per acre than did corn), which at 20 cents per pound would have brought him $47.20.

On the labor requirements of cotton versus corn, see Robert William Fogel, *Without Consent or Contract: The Rise and Fall of American Slavery* (New York, 1989), 71.

26. Nicholas P. Hardeman, *Shucks, Shocks, and Hominy Blocks: Corn as a Way of Life in Pioneer America* (Baton Rouge, 1981), 51–58. Martin L. Primack, "Land Clearing Under Nineteenth-Century Techniques: Some Preliminary Calculations," *Journal of Economic History* 22 (December 1962): 484–97, estimates that five acres per year was the extent of forest cleared by one family. Primack, however, bases his estimates on the time and labor required to clear a field completely, including stumps, which pioneer farmers did not do because such a task was not only demanding, but unnecessary. The first fields were established in forests that had been slashed and burned. Stephen Hymer and Stephen Resnick, "A Model of an Agrarian Economy with Non-Agricultural Activities," *American Economic Review* 49 (September 1969): 500. Otto and Anderson, "Slash-and-Burn Cultivation," 131–47. Otto and Anderson explain slash-and-burn agriculture in the South as a product of the Celtic origins of many of it practitioners. But this explanation underestimates how widespread slash-and-burn agriculture was not only in the southern U.S. but in any place where population density is low and forests are abundant. Marvin Harris, *Cannibals and Kings: The Origins of Cultures* (New York, 1978), 135–36.

27. John Q. Anderson, "Narrative of John Hutchins," 4.

28. Gray, *History of Agriculture*, 2:708, 816. Otto, "Migration of the Southern Plain Folk," 194. Hardeman, *Shucks, Shocks, and Hominy Blocks*, 64, 71, 73. William Drowne, *Compendium of Agriculture, or the Farmer's Guide, in the Most Essential Parts of Husbandry and Gardening* (Providence, 1824), 262. John T. Schlebecker, *Whereby We Thrive: A History of American Farming, 1607–1972* (Ames, Iowa, 1975), 30. Paul Gates, *The Farmer's Age: Agriculture, 1815–1860* (White Plains, N.Y., 1960), 170; Robert E. Gallman, "Self-Sufficiency in the Cotton Economy of the Antebellum South," *Agricultural History* 44 (January 1970): 10, 13.

According to Gray, one hand could work six acres of corn and ten of cotton. Otto claims that one man could tend 25 to 30 acres of corn, an estimate that seems rather high. Hardeman offers a more conservative estimate: Two bushels of seed planted ten pounds to the acre provided a crop ample for a large family. At 60 pounds per bushel a large family would require 12 acres. However, with a yield of 25 bushels per acre, six or seven acres would have fed a small family, if they consumed corn at a rate of one bushel per person per month, as Gallman has estimated. On new soil yields were, of course, much higher, and sometimes reached 100 bushels. Thirty bushels were raised easily without even ploughing. Moreover, corn planted in newly cleared land required little attention because weeds did not invade until at least the second season. Once corn stood knee-high in the fields it required almost no attention until harvest.

29. Cattle herds yielded 20 percent per year, while hog droves yielded 43 percent: Hilliard, *Hog Meat and Hoecake*, 104, 128–29. Hilliard's estimates are rough, but if anything they are too low. For example, he intentionally allows sows only one litter per year, while on established, well-run farms, two litters were normal. Moreover, he estimates litter sizes at five, which was half the norm on intensively operated farms in England at about the same time. See John Lawrence, *A General Treatise on Cattle, the Ox, the Sheep, and the Swine: Comprehending Their Breeding, Management, Improvement and Diseases* (London, 1809), 429, 448. By contrast, the pig common on trans-Appalachian farms took longer to mature, yet was hardier, free of disease, and very prolific. For a description of the frontier pigs, see H. G. Dawson, *The Pig Book* (Chicago, 1911), 34. Henlein estimates one hand per 30 head of cattle: Henlein, *Cattle Kingdom*, 43.

Prices of farm products and of consumer items are taken from the Rapalje Notebook, typescript, MDAH.

30. I do not mean to suggest that pioneering and backcountry farming was easy. But the worst difficulties came from forces beyond anyone's control: disease, bad weather, Indian attacks. Moreover, much of the ruggedness of frontier living came from the lack of material comforts, not from any difficulty in meeting subsistence requirements. The ease with which wilderness land could be turned into something productive and valuable is precisely why it was settled so quickly. Indeed, Thomas Jefferson and his followers noted the ease with which farmers could achieve subsistence and worried that idleness and intemperance would result: Drew R. McCoy, *The Elusive Republic: Political Economy in Jeffersonian America* (New York, 1980), 82–83.

31. Loosa Chitto farmers traded for a variety of consumer goods. See for example the items listed in the Rapalje Account book. On consumerism in another late eighteenth-century American backcountry settlement see Elizabeth A. Perkins: "The Consumer Frontier: Household Consumption in Early Kentucky," *Journal of American History* 78 (September 1991): 486–510.

32. Gavin Wright, *The Political Economy of the Cotton South: Households, Markets, and Wealth in the Nineteenth Century* (New York, 1978), 62–74; Wright and Howard Kunreuther, "Cotton, Corn and Risk in the Nineteenth Century," *Journal of Economic History* 35 (September 1975): 526–51. Robert McGuire and Robert Higgs, "Cotton, Corn, and Risk in the Nineteenth Century: Another View," *Explorations in Economic History* 14 (April 1977): 167–82, and the reply by Wright and Kunreuther, pp. 183–95 of the same issue. McGuire, "A Portfolio Analysis of Crop Diversification and Risk in the Cotton South," *Explorations in Economic History* 17 (October 1980): 342–71. David Freeman Weiman, "Petty Commodity Production in the Cotton South: Upcountry Farmers in the Georgia Cotton Economy, 1840 to 1880" (Ph.D. dissertation, Stanford University, 1983), 25–51.

33. McBee, *Natchez Court Records*, 286. According to Benjamin L. C. Wailes, virtually all households grew some cotton for home use. Benjamin Leonard Covington Wailes, *Report on Agriculture and Geology of Mississippi* (Philadelphia, 1854), 131.

34. Farmers regularly experimented with different crops. Near Natchez, for example, farmers tried indigo, tobacco, hemp, and cotton with varying degrees of success. For similar experimentation among Georgia and South Carolina

farmers see Joyce E. Chaplin, "Creating a Cotton South in Georgia and South Carolina, 1760–1815," *Journal of Southern History* 57 (May 1991): 175–77.

35. When Wright tested his model he found that his independent variables (available acreage, population per improved acre, value of the farm operator's personal property) accounted for only 10 percent of the variance in the fraction of tilled acreage planted in cotton. While his regression coefficients were significant, the low r^2 indicated that even in older settled areas much more than risk accounted for the variation in crop choice. Wright, *Political Economy of the Cotton South,* 67–68.

36. Wright, *Political Economy,* 60–61. Ralph V. Anderson and Robert E. Gallman, "Slaves as Fixed Capital: Slave Labor and Southern Economic Development," *Journal of American History* 64 (June 1977): 24–46, quotation from 37. Weiman, "Petty Commodity Production," 31–32. Gray, *History of Agriculture,* 2:707. It seems unlikely that there could have been much necessary conflict between the demands of corn and cotton. Except during the spring and early summer, when both required hoeing, there was little overlap. They were not planted at the same time; farmers planted cotton earlier. Once corn was knee-high it could be left alone until harvest, which occurred at the farmer's leisure, even into the cold months of winter, allowing all attention to be devoted to the cotton crop. Only when intensively cultivated on poor or exhausted soils that required manuring and maximum control of weeds would labor demands have overlapped. These conditions did not exist in recently settled areas. See Gates, *Farmer's Age,* 170.

37. Gray, *History of Agriculture,* 2:708.

38. See Appendix C, Tables C-1 and C-2.

39. The notion of "drudgery" as a disincentive to surplus production that increases proportionately as production levels exceed subsistence needs was first suggested by A. V. Chayanov upon his observations of early twentieth-century Russian peasant households: Chayanov, *The Theory of Peasant Economics,* Daniel Thorner, Basile Kerblay, and R. E. F. Smith, eds., Introduction by Teodor Shanin (Madison, Wis., 1986), 6.

40. One of the greatest problems landowners faced following the Civil War was getting freedmen to work. Where public lands and wild areas enabled blacks to hunt and gather a livelihood, they showed no willingness to go back to picking cotton for their former masters. See: Eric Foner, *Nothing but Freedom: Emancipation and Its Legacy* (Baton Rouge, 1983), 88, 108; Michael Wayne, *The Reshaping of Plantation Society: The Natchez District* (Baton Rouge, 1983), 116.

41. "Capitalism came in the first ships," is how Carl Degler succinctly expressed this view. See Degler, *Out of Our Past: The Forces that Shaped Modern America,* 3d ed. (New York, 1984), 2–9. On the southern yeomanry and small slaveholders as upwardly mobile capitalists, see James Oakes, *The Ruling Race: A History of American Slaveholders* (New York, 1982).

42. This view builds on the work of Eugene D. Genovese, in particular, *The Political Economy of Slavery.* Genovese, however, formulated many of his ideas after carefully reading the work of U. B. Phillips, in particular, *American Negro Slavery: A Survey of the Supply, Employment and Control of Negro Labor as Determined by the Plantation Regime* (Baton Rouge, 1966). Most recently some historians have suggested that the South was at once capitalist and not capitalist. "In but not of the capitalist world" is how Elizabeth Fox-Genovese and Eugene D. Genovese now describe slavery in the Old South: *Fruits of Merchant Capital,* 16.

Morton Rothstein suggested that the South might best be understood as a dual economy: a capitalist plantation economy, and an underdeveloped, precapitalist backcountry economy. Rothstein, "The Antebellum South as a Dual Economy: A Tentative Hypothesis," *Agricultural History* 41 (October 1967): 373–82. Steven Hahn, *Roots of Southern Populism*, is the first important study of the nonplantation South since Frank L. Owsley, *Plain Folk of the Old South* (1949; Chicago, 1965). Interestingly, both James Oakes, who in *The Ruling Race* emphasized the capitalist nature of Southern society, and Hahn, who emphasized its precapitalist character, owe a great deal to Owsley's study of the plain folk. While Oakes developed Owsley's argument of the numerical preponderance of plain folk, as well as their high rate of mobility, Hahn focused on their distinction from planters and black-belt culture. Thus they came up with two interpretations very much at odds. See Hahn's review of Oakes: "Capitalists All!," *Reviews in American History* 11 (June 1983): 219–25.

Recent inquiries into the economic and social transformation of the Northern countryside, over whether the impetus for the transition to capitalism came from within or from outside rural communities, promise to reinvigorate discussion of cultural evolution in the South. A bibliography of this literature begins with two articles almost always cited together, both of which stress the precapitalist nature of eighteenth-century America: Michael Merrill, "Cash Is Good to Eat: Self-Sufficiency and Exchange in the Rural Economy of the United States," *Radical History Review* no. 3 (1977): 42–71, and James A. Henretta, "Families and Farms: *Mentalité* in Pre-Industrial America," *William and Mary Quarterly*, 3d ser., 35 (1978): 3–32. For recent summaries of the debate over the transition to capitalism see Allan Kulikoff, *The Agrarian Origins of American Capitalism* (Charlottesville, 1992), and Winifred B. Rothenberg, *From Market-places to a Market Economy: The Transformation of Rural Massachusetts, 1750–1850* (Chicago, 1992).

43. "Invaded" is Charles Sellers's word: *The Market Revolution, 1815–1846* (New York, 1991), 19. Anthropologists have found that the spread of capitalism in the third world depends very much on the ability of noncapitalist modes of production to generate capital. Thus, during the period of transition to capitalism, precapitalist and capitalist economies live off each other, or in the parlance of economic anthropology, they articulate. See, for example, Rodriguez O. Rodriguez, "Original Accumulation, Capitalism, and Precapitalistic Agriculture in Bolivia," Lillian Manzor Coats and Dianne Tritica Robman, trans., *Latin American Perspectives* 7 (Fall 1980), 50–66. Historians of early Latin America are reaching similar conclusions. See, for example, Steve Stern, "Feudalism, Capitalism, and the World-System in the Perspective of Latin America and the Caribbean," *American Historical Review* 93 (October 1988): 829–72.

44. The ease with which farmers produced their subsistence, particularly in pioneer areas and within the context of the warm Southern climate, explains the abundance of leisure or nonproductive time enjoyed by Southern small farmers and herders, and noted so frequently by contemporaries and historians. Otto, "The Migration of the Southern Plain Folk," and McDonald and McWhiney, "The South from Self-Sufficiency to Peonage." Grady McWhiney, *Cracker Culture: Celtic Ways in the Old South* (Tuscaloosa, 1988), 38–50. David Bertelson, *The Lazy South* (New York, 1967). Foreign observers, impressed by the high yield of corn, and by the fact that it could be cultivated by women and children, often associated that crop with idleness. See Hardeman, *Shucks, Shocks, and Hominy Blocks*, 35, 36.

With good reason, farmers were reluctant for exploit themselves. However, they were not so reluctant to exploit slaves. Robert Fogel argues slavery was exceptionally brutal because it forced people to work not only for someone else, but also against their traditional notions of time, work, and leisure. Slavery, particularly the gang system, like machines in Northern factories, violently disciplined workers who struggled against the demands of masters and bosses to work constantly. See Fogel, *Without Consent of Contract*, 34–35. On pre-industrial work rhythms and concepts of time, see E. P. Thompson, "Time, Work Discipline, and Industrial Capitalism," *Past and Present* no. 38 (December 1967): 56–97.

45. Fabel, *Economy of British North America*, 158.

46. Lorenzo Dow, *Vicissitudes in the Wilderness; Exemplified, in the Journal of Peggy Dow* (Norwich, Conn., 1833), 33–52.

47. Phelps, *Memoirs*, 29–30.

48. McBee, *Natchez Court Records*, 88, 96, 198, 324, 346, 388, 426. Lowrie, ed., *American State Papers*, 1:562–63. Spanish Census, 1792, MDAH. Claiborne County Tax Roll, 1805, Claiborne County Records, MDAH; Pope, "A Tour," 28.

49. Inventory of the Property of the Late Jacques Rapalje, 1797, vol. G, p. 289, Mississippi Provincial Archives, Spanish Dominion, MDAH.

50. English goods, wrote J. Hector St. John de Crèvecoeur, "present irresistible temptations. It is so much easier to buy than it is to spin. The allurement of fineries is so powerful with our young girls that they must be philosophers indeed to abstain from them." Crèvecoeur need not have limited his remarks to "young girls." Crèvecoeur, *American Farmer*, 275.

In his study of the capitalist transformation of the Panamanian countryside Stephen Gudeman emphasizes the importance of "market pull" on subsistence-oriented peasant communities. "Rural dwellers, defining themselves as Panamanians of low social and economic position, are," according to Gudeman, "receptive to those elements and symbols of modern life which characterize the metropolitans." "Peasants want very much to partake of consumer goods—'civilization'—but do not want to sell their subsistence crops for cash." Staple agriculture, however, "provided the long-awaited opportunity for participating in civilization." Agricultural transformation from subsistence to staple production, as Gudeman sees it, "is both a radical and a non-radical shift." Gudeman, *The Demise of a Rural Economy: From Subsistence to Capitalism in a Latin American Village* (Boston, 1978), quotation from 21, 31, 131.

51. Cattle herders were not necessarily upwardly mobile slaveholding cotton planters, as James Oakes describes them. For Oakes the actions of backwoods farmers manifested a particular mindset. He argues in circular fashion that Southern herders bought slaves and planted cotton because they were materialistic, grasping, upwardly mobile capitalists motivated by an ideology of liberalism, for proof of which he offers the fact thay they purchased slaves whenever they could. James Oakes, *The Ruling Race*, 19. But the same behavior could have been the manifestation of very different attitudes. Small farmers and herders might well have bought slaves to maintain their small-farm lifestyle. Lacy K. Ford, Jr., argues that because upcountry South Carolina farmers did not have to neglect foodstuffs when they took up cotton planting, cotton became for many farmers a way of maintaining self-sufficiency and independence from the market and from creditors. See Ford, "Self-Sufficiency, Cotton, and Economic Development in the South Carolina Upcountry, 1800–1860," *Journal of Economic History*

45 (1985): 260–67, and *Origins of Southern Radicalism: The South Carolina Up-country, 1800–1860* (New York, 1988), 44–84. Oakes and Ford observe similar behavior patterns and attribute them to different attitudes or ideologies; neither scholar considers the material reasons why small farmers and herders sometimes purchased slaves and planted cotton.

52. Kinnaird, ed., *Spain in the Mississippi Valley*, 3:xvi–xvii, 280–82, 285, 310.

53. Mississippi Provincial Archives, Spanish Dominion, vol. IV, Jan. 1792–June 1793, pp. 225–27, RG 26, MF33, MDAH. Despatches of the Spanish Governors of Louisiana, Messages of Francisco Luis Hector, El Baron de Carondelet, Sixth Spanish Governor of Louisiana, Book II, Gayoso to Carondelet, Nov. 10, 1792, pp. 168–71, Special Collections, Pace Library. Dunbar Rowland, ed., *The Mississippi Territorial Archives, 1798–1803*, vol. 1: *Executive Journals of Governor Winthrop Sargent and Governor William Charles Cole Claiborne* (Nashville, 1905), 1:226, 458. Arthur De Rosier, *Removal of the Choctaw Indians* (Knoxville, 1983). Richard White, *The Roots of Dependency: Subsistence, Environment, and Social Change among the Choctaws, Pawnees, and Navajos* (Lincoln, Nebr. 1983).

54. As early as 1813 visitors reported exhausted and eroded soil in the vicinity of Natchez. W. B. Hamilton, "Mississippi 1817: A Sociological and Economic Analysis," *Journal of Mississippi History* 29 (November 1967): 286.

Chapter 3

1. Rev. William Winans, *Funeral Sermons of Rev. Randal Gibson and Mrs. Harriet Gibson* (Lexington, Ky., n.d.), 3, 13, 14, 15, 34. Winans expanded his views of Christian womanhood the next year, over the grave of Mrs. Gibson. I am grateful to Elizabeth Monroe for bringing this document to my attention.

2. On the changing historical interpretation of women, primarily though not exclusively Northern white women, see Linda K. Kerber, "Separate Spheres, Female Worlds, Woman's Place: The Rhetoric of Women's History," *Journal of American History* 75 (June 1988): 9–39. On the "hidden" production of women within Northern households see Jeanne Boydston, *Home and Work: Housework, Wages, and the Ideology of Labor in the Early Republic* (New York, 1990).

3. Elizabeth Fox-Genovese draws a distinction between Northern and Southern households in *Within the Plantation Household: Black and White Women of the Old South* (Chapel Hill, 1988). Others have also made such a distinction, although their explanation for it differs from Fox-Genovese's. See: Catherine Clinton, *The Plantation Mistress: Woman's World in the Old South* (New York, 1982); Jean E. Friedman, *The Enclosed Garden: Women and Community in the Evangelical South, 1830–1900* (Chapel Hill, 1985). For a more systematic look at the composition of Southern households, see Orville Vernon Burton, *In My Father's House Are Many Mansions: Family and Community in Edgefield, South Carolina* (Chapel Hill, 1985), 104–47. For an overview of the historical literature on the experiences of Southern women see Jacquelyn Dowd Hall and Anne Firor Scott, "Women in the South," in John B. Boles and Evelyn Thomas Nolen, eds., *Interpreting Southern History: Historiographical Essays in Honor of Sanford W. Higginbotham* (Baton Rouge, 1987), 454–509.

4. Suzanne Lebsock, *The Free Women of Petersburg: Status and Culture in a Southern Town, 1784–1860* (New York, 1984), 244, suggests that "for the major-

ity of free women, North and South may not have been so very different after all." On Western women, whose experiences differed greatly from those of Eastern women, North and South, see Faragher, *Sugar Creek*, 96–118, and Joan E. Cashin, *A Family Venture: Men and Women on the Southern Frontier* (New York, 1991). Cashin's descriptions of Southwestern women's experiences are not unlike those offered by Faragher for Northwestern women.

5. On farms in the Northwest, which remained the homes of simple families through the antebellum years, see Faragher, *Sugar Creek*, 253 n. 10. Households in the Southeast, however, varied much more in composition, with slaveholders very likely to have extended family and nonfamily members. See Burton, *In My Father's House*, 109–14. Cashin, *A Family Venture*, distinguishes Southwestern nuclear-family households from extended-family households more prominent in the Southeast. But she does not examine the evolution of household patterns within the Southwest, in part because she examines families that settled in the West after 1830, that is to say, families that had not been settled for a long enough period of time to have changed significantly.

The term "household" is open to different definitions, but for purposes here it is applied to the people who lived and worked together in single productive and reproductive units. It is not the same as "family," which implies a biological or conjugal connection between its members. Of course, the two frequently overlapped. Some households may have been primarily a productive rather than reproductive unit, as in single-person homes for example. Usually, however, they provided both functions. Such was the case in the antebellum South. Lastly, households of Warren County operated as single enterprises. Thus, a slave plantation was one household, while a plantation worked by tenants who after paying rent to the landowner ran their operations separately and individually was a collection of households. On the definitional problems of the household, see Robert McC. Netting, Richard R. Wilk, and Eric J. Arnould, eds., *Households: Comparative and Historical Studies of the Domestic Group* (Berkeley, Los Angeles, and London, 1984), in particular, the first essay by the editors. They suggest that households are distinguished by five functions or activities that occur within them: production, distribution, transmission of resources, reproduction, and coresidence.

6. See Appendix D, Tables D-1 and D-2.

7. See Appendix D, Table D-4.

8. The average age at first marriage for men was twenty-six, while the average age for women was nineteen. Some 30 percent of Warren County residents married two years after they first appeared in the public record, which is the earliest indication of their presence. Over half married within four years. The source for these figures is the Study Data.

9. In later years men actually married at a younger age, while women married later. This pattern, however, reflected a balancing out of the sex ratio, and not necessarily a new desire on the part of men to marry earlier. They doubtless would have married much younger than they did in the early years had there been more women available.

10. Rapalje Notebook, typescript, p. 5, MDAH. McBee, *Natchez Court Records*, 194–96. Dow, *Vicissitudes*, 33–52. "What a useful acquisition a good wife is to an American farmer," wrote Crèveceour, "and how small is his chance of prosperity if he draws a blank in that lottery!" *American Farmer*, 299.

11. Anderson, "The Narrative of John Hutchins," 4.

12. For good descriptions of farm women and work, see: Ulrich, *Goodwives,* 13–34; Jensen, *Loosening the Bonds,* 36–56; Faragher, *Sugar Creek,* 96–105. The best descriptive study of Southern women's lives remains Julia Cherry Spruill, *Women's Life and Work in the Southern Colonies,* 2d ed., Introduction by Anne Firor Scott (New York, 1972).

13. Inventory of the estate of John Hartley (1794), vol. C, pp. 90–91; inventory of the estate of Jacques Rapalje, (1795), vol. G, p. 289; inventory of the estate of Gabriel Griffing (1796), vol. C, pp. 395–96, Mississippi Provincial Archives, Spanish Dominion, RG 26, microfilm, MDAH. Tench Coxe, ed., *A Statement of the Arts and Manufactures of the United States of America for the Year 1810* (Philadelphia, 1814), sec. 3, p. 159. "Abstract from the Census of Manufacturing Establishment," Territorial Governor Records, Mississippi Territorial Census Returns, RG 2 microfilm 2, MDAH. Warren County Orphans' Court, Minutes Book A, 1818–24, OCHM.

In a study of farm women in the Brandywine Valley of Pennsylvania, historian Joan Jensen also found textile-producing equipment located in the wealthier households. (Of course, in Pennsylvania slaves did not work the looms and the spinning wheels.) Jensen claims the wealthiest households used the greatest amount of linen, and thus had the greatest need to manufacture it. However, the reverse seems more likely, that wealthy households could afford the equipment necessary for home manufacture of linen, which in turn freed a larger portion of the household income for the purchase of other consumer goods. Households that did not manufacture their own cloth, in contrast, would have spent a larger portion of their income on textiles and less on other items. Household production, in other words, did not necessarily limit consumption of goods, factory-made or otherwise, imported from other regions of the country or world. During the initial phase of the slow transition toward commercial agriculture the relationship between household manufacturing and consumption of market products was not always direct. Rather, the items manufactured in the home could in part determine the types of goods purchased. Joan Jensen, *Loosening the Bonds: Mid-Atlantic Farm Women, 1750–1850* (New Haven, 1986), 49–50. Fox-Genovese, *Within the Plantation Household,* 121.

14. Ashe, *Travels in America,* 315. Christian Schultz, Jr., *Travels on an Inland Voyage Through the States of New-York, Pennsylvania, Virginia, Ohio, Kentucky and Tennessee, and Through the Territories of Indiana, Louisiana, Mississippi and New-Orleans; Performed in the Years 1807 and 1808; Including a Tour of Nearly Six Thousand Miles,* 2 vols. (1810; rpt., Ridgewood, N.J., 1968), 2:128. Lewis Gray noted a pattern of local manufacturing and distribution of cotton cloth in areas across the South that were taking up cotton cultivation: Gray, *History of Agriculture.*

15. Nancy Grey Osterud, " 'She Helped Me Hay It as Good as a Man': Relations among Women and Men in an Agricultural Community," in Carol Groneman and Mary Beth Norton, eds., *"To Toil the Livelong Day"; America's Women at Work, 1780–1980* (Ithaca, 1987), 92. Christopher Clark, *The Roots of Rural Capitalism: Western Massachusetts, 1780–1860* (Ithaca, 1990), 95–100, 132–34.

16. Laurel Thatcher Ulrich, "Housewife and Gadder: Themes of Self-Sufficiency and Community in Eighteenth-Century New England," in Groneman and Norton, eds., *"To Toil the Livelong Day",* 21–34, and Ulrich, *A Midwife's Tale: The Life of Martha Ballard, Based on Her Diary, 1785–1812* (New York, 1990), 84–87.

That women were motivated largely by a desire to reproduce the standard of living and way of life of the members of the farm household is the general thrust of Jensen's *Loosening the Bonds,* an argument that finds support here.

17. See Appendix E.

18. Study Data.

19. The examples of Elizabeth Clark and Vianna Smithheart are drawn from the family reconstitutions in the Study Data.

20. Death from childbirth was much more likely in the South than in the North for several possible reasons. The climate was more conducive to endemic diseases. Higher fertility rates placed Southern women at risk more frequently. The Southern medical profession may have been inferior, although professional medical attention frequently proved fatal in the North. See Sally G. McMillen, *Motherhood in the Old South: Pregnancy, Childbirth, and Infant Rearing* (Baton Rouge, 1990), 81.

21. For example, the number of children under the age of 10 per 1000 women aged 16 to 45 was: 2,273 (in 1800), 1,552 (1840), 1,337 (in 1850, rural areas only). See Appendix E, Table E-1. For comparison, ratios for the same years in six Connecticut towns declined from a high of 2,140 (in 1800) to 1,270 (in 1840). In Oneida County, New York, rates were 942 (1830), 822 (1840), and 809 (1850). Rates were always higher in Sugar Creek, Illinois, than in Warren County: 2,452 (1830), 2,228 (1840), 2,082 (1850), and 1,939 (1860). See: Clark, *Roots of Rural Capitalism,* 137; Mary P. Ryan, *Cradle of the Middle Class: The Family in Oneida County, New York, 1790–1865* (Cambridge, Eng. 1981), 249; Faragher, *Sugar Creek,* 253–254n.

22. Richard A. Easterlin, "Population Change and Farm Settlement in the Northern United States," *Journal of Economic History* 36 (1976): 45–83. Nancy Osterud and John Fulton, "Family Limitation and Age at Marriage: Fertility Decline in Sturbridge, Massachusetts, 1730–1850," *Population Studies* 30 (1976): 481–93, and Clark, *Roots of Rural Capitalism,* 134–39.

23. McMillen, *Motherhood,* 165–79.

24. Study Data.

25. *Vicksburg Advocate and Register,* November 1, 1832. Frederick F. Cartwright, *Disease and History* (New York, 1972). For a description of malarial fevers see Phelps, *Memoirs,* 50–54. On yellow-fever epidemics during the antebellum years see B.J. Hicks, "On the Yellow Fever of Vicksburg, Miss., in the Year 1847," in E. D. Fenner, ed., *The Epidemic of 1847: or Brief Accounts of the Yellow Fever, That Prevailed at New Orleans, Vicksburg, Rodney, Natchez, Houston and Covington* (New Orleans, 1848), 220–25. According to Hicks, in 1841, 1843, and 1847 serious epidemics struck Vicksburg and Warren County. In 1841 some 200 Warren County residents died. In 1853 occurred the most severe outburst. Susan Dabney Smedes, a resident of adjoining Hinds County, described the death of her brother, a victim of the 1853 epidemic, in Smedes, *Memorials of a Southern Planter,* edited and with an introduction and notes by Fletcher M. Green (New York, 1965), 154–58.

26. Study Data.

27. Ibid.

28. In the colonial Chesapeake an even higher death rate forced people to rely on still more extended relations or even nonkin than was the case in Warren County. Nevertheless, the effect of mortality on family formation in the nineteenth-century Lower Mississippi Valley somewhat repeated patterns of early

Virginia and Maryland. See: Darrett B. and Anita H. Rutman, " 'Now-Wives and Sons-in-Law': Parental Death in a Seventeenth-Century Virginia County," in Thad W. Tate and David L. Ammerman, eds., *The Chesapeake in the Seventeenth Century: Essays on Anglo-American Society and Politics* (New York, 1979), 153–82; Rutman and Rutman, *A Place in Time*, 1:113–20, 2:79–81.

29. Study Data. Robert Kenzer, in his study of kinship in Orange County, North Carolina, argues that family ties mitigated conflict. Yet he draws his conclusion from the mere existence of family ties and never explores the relationships between family members. As the Gibson-Sharkey dispute demonstrates, kinship often bred conflict. See Kenzer, *Kinship and Neighborhood in a Southern Community: Orange County, North Carolina, 1849–1881* (Knoxville, 1987). Joan Cashin has discussed the importance of extended family ties, and in particular the ties between cousins, but she, like Kenzer, emphasizes emotionally warm relationships and does not explore the often bitter rivalries. Cashin, "The Structure of Antebellum Planter Families: 'The Ties That Bound Us Was Strong,' " *Journal of Southern History* 56 (February 1990): 55–70. Moreover, Cashin locates extended families in the Southeast and does not appreciate the extent to which conditions in the Southwest also encouraged extended family arrangements. Cashin, *A Family Venture*.

30. Frank Edgar Everett, Jr., *Brierfield: Plantation Home of Jefferson Davis* (Jackson, 1971), 17, 20–28. James A. Ramage, "Jefferson Davis: Family Influences in the Making of a Great Statesman," *Journal of Mississippi History* (November 1989): 346, 348. Janet Hermann, *Joseph E. Davis: Pioneer Patriarch* (Jackson, 1990), 70–71.

31. Coxe, ed., *A Statement of the Arts and Manufactures*, 159; *Compendium of the Sixth Census*, 229. United States Census Office, *Agriculture of the United States in 1860; Compiled from the Original Returns of the Eighth Census* (Washington, D.C., 1864), 87, 206. The 1860 census gives the number of farms. The numbers for the other two dates were calculated from the tax rolls for 1810 and 1835. Robert E. Gallman, "Self-Sufficiency in the Cotton Economy of the Antebellum South," *Agricultural History* 44 (January 1970): 5–23. On the return of spinning and weaving in Warren County during the Civil War years see the Epilogue.

32. Stephanie McCurry, "The Politics of Yeoman Households in South Carolina," in Catherine Clinton and Nina Silber, eds., *Divided Houses: Gender and the Civil War* (New York, 1992), 30–33.

33. Ellen Hyland to Rev. Dr. Chamberlain, May 2, 1848; Ellen Hyland to Mary [sister], August 5, 1859; also two other letters from Ellen to her sister, neither showing a date, in box 2E508, Hyland-Chamberlain-Gould Family Papers, NTC. Carrie Kiger to husband Basil Kiger, March 31, 1854, box 2E516, folder 2, Kiger Family Papers, NTC.

A survey of Tennessee Civil War veterans revealed that 9 in 10 small-farm women did their own chores, while only 1 in 3 slaveholding women did their own chores. On the largest plantations only 8 in 100 mistresses worked in their homes. James Oakes, *Slavery and Freedom: An Interpretation of the Old South* (New York, 1990), 95. According to Elizabeth Fox-Genovese, plantation mistresses held a supervisory position within plantation households where slaves did the bulk of the work, and the master was supreme authority. See Fox-Genovese, *Within the Plantation Household*, 135–45.

34. Smedes, *Memorials*, 66, 68, 72, 179–80. Roach, Mahala Perkins Harding (Eggleston), diary, June 4, 1851, Virginia Historical Society, Richmond.

35. The effect of slavery on relations between husbands and wives is explored in Elizabeth Fox-Genovese, *Within the Plantation Household.*

36. Anne Firor Scott, *The Southern Lady: From Pedestal to Politics, 1830–1930* (Chicago, 1970), 3–44.

37. On the forced dependency of women on men see Wyatt-Brown, *Southern Honor,* 229–31.

38. Jane Turner Censer, " 'Smiling Through Her Tears': Ante-bellum Southern Women and Divorce," *American Journal of Legal History* 25 (Spring 1981): 24–47. According to Bertram Wyatt-Brown, "divorce for any cause was seldom granted, either by state legislatures or by equity or chancery courts." Wyatt-Brown, *Southern Honor,* 301. Catherine Clinton explored a small sample of divorce cases, but was able to draw "no broad conclusions" except that they were few, and that most seem to have come from the planter class. See Clinton, *Plantation Mistress,* 80–85.

39. Censer, " 'Smiling Through Her Tears' "; Wyatt-Brown, *Southern Honor,* 284.

40. Anderson Hutchinson, *Code of Mississippi: Being an Analytical Compilation of the Public and General Statutes of the Territory and State, with Tabular References to the Local and Private Acts, from 1798 to 1848* (Jackson, Miss., 1848), 495–97.

41. My analysis of divorce and abandonment in early Warren County corresponds to patterns in relations between men and women in similar circumstances but in a different time and place. For example, demographic patterns also gave women in the early Chesapeake greater control over their lives. See Lois Green Carr and Lorena S. Walsh, "From Indentured Servant to Planter's Wife: White Women in Seventeenth-Century Maryland," *William and Mary Quarterly* 34 (1977): 542–71. The evidence from Warren County and from the early Chesapeake does not support Joan Cashin's conclusion that women in Southern frontier households were utterly dependent on their husbands and quite unable to defend themselves against male authority. Cashin, *A Family Venture,* 108–12. Cashin does not examine divorce or abandonment.

42. Territorial Legislature, RG 5, vol. 126, Petitions to the General Assembly 1804–9, MDAH. Lorenzo Dow, *Vicissitudes,* 33–52.

43. *Simpkins v. Simpkins* (September 1818), *Barkley v. Barkley* (September 1819), *Williams v. Williams* (September 1819), Superior Court Record, Warren County, September 1818–March 1821, OCHM. See also *Sea v. Sea* (September 1819) in the same volume.

44. *Blackman vs. Blackman* (September 1818), *Lewis v. Lewis* (September 1818), both in the Superior Court Record, Warren County, September 1818–March 1821, OCHM.

45. Chancery Minutes, book 1, WCC. Censer " 'Smiling Through Her Tears,' " 26–27, 34.

46. *Vicksburg Whig,* May 22, 25, September 21, 1860.

47. *Cotton v. Cotton* (1856), Superior Court of Chancery, RG 32, SG 1, case 5307, MDAH. Study Data.

48. See the petition of Ann J. Singleton, Petitions to the General Assembly, 1804–9, Territorial Legislature, RG 5, vol. 26, MDAH.

49. Hutchinson, *Code of Mississippi,* 495–97.

50. *Bradley v. State,* 1 Morris (Miss.), 20 (1824).

51. My explanation for the dependence of Southern women on men and the

implications of dependence for marital relations differs from that given by Bertram Wyatt-Brown in his book *Southern Honor*. Nevertheless, his description of male honor and the family ideal corresponds to conditions and behavior patterns of Warren County husbands and wives by the 1850s, although not for the early 1800s. Moreover, as Wyatt-Brown explains, the community at large, not just the courts, could enforce the ethics and thus preserve society from itself. See Wyatt-Brown, *Southern Honor*, 281–85, and especially 462–93.

52. Faragher, *Sugar Creek*, 115–18.

53. Shared gender identities provided a basis for a republican proslavery ideology shared by yeomen and planters, as Stephanie McCurry has argued. McCurry, "Politics of Yeoman Households," 22–38.

Chapter 4

1. McBee, *Natchez Court Records*, 101, 104, 222–24.

2. Peter Kolchin, "American Historians and Antebellum Southern Slavery, 1959–1984," in William L. Cooper, Michael F. Holt, and John McCardell, eds., *A Master's Due: Essays in Honor of David Herbert Donald* (Baton Rouge, 1985), 87–111, and Charles B. Dew, "The Slavery Experience," in Boles and Nolen, eds., *Interpreting Southern History*, 120–61.

3. Data on Natchez slaves, hereafter cited as Natchez Slave Data, is derived from records of slave sales recorded at Natchez for the period 1782–97, and abstracted in McBee, *Natchez Court Records*.

4. Natchez Slave Data. At least half of the slaves imported from Africa came from Guinea, the region comprising the Windward Coast, Sierra Leone, the Gold Coast, and the Bight of Benin. The place of origin of 44 percent was given as Africa, with no further specification, but were probably from Guinea as well. Only 3 percent came from Angola or the Bight of Biafra, the two regions that supplied so many slaves to Virginia and South Carolina. Philip D. Curtin, *The Atlantic Slave Trade: A Census* (Madison, 1969), 150, 157, 159–61. Allan Kulikoff, *Tobacco and Slaves: The Development of Southern Cultures in the Chesapeake, 1680–1800* (Chapel Hill, 1986), 321–22. Herbert S. Klein, *The Middle Passage: Comparative Studies in the Atlantic Slave Trade* (Princeton, 1978), 152–55. George Peter Murdock, *Africa, Its Peoples and Their Culture History* (New York, 1959), 242–51. Basil Davidson, *Black Mother: The Years of the African Slave Trade* (Boston, 1961), 197–269.

5. Fear of insurrection led the Baron de Carondelet, governor of Spanish Louisiana, to order an end to the importation of slaves. Jack D. L. Holmes, "Some Economic Problems of Spanish Governors of Louisiana," *Hispanic American Historical Review* (November 1962): 521–43.

6. Sterling Stuckey, *Slave Culture: Nationalist Theory and the Foundations of Black America* (New York, 1987), 3–97.

7. Spanish Census of Natchez District, 1792, MDAH. Abstract of Census, Mississippi Territory, 1801, roll 546, Pickering County, MDAH. Because of the small number of households along the Loosa Chitto in 1792, I included Bayou Pierre in my calculations of slave-to-white ratio and slaves per household. See also Chapter 2, n. 21.

8. Natchez Slave Data.

9. David Hunt to Henry D. Downs, February 8, 1812, David Hunt Papers, NTC.

10. Daniel Burnet to William McAlpine, August 1815, Daniel Burnet Papers, NTC.

11. I have assumed that a slaveholding of ten or more included at least some variation of a family. According to the 1830 census 20 percent of all households and 34 percent of slaveholding households had ten or more slaves. MS Population Schedules for Warren County, Mississippi, 1830.

12. For a survey of scholarly treatment of slave families see Kolchin: "American Historians and Antebellum Southern Slavery," and Dew, "The Slavery Experience."

13. According to the 1860 census, Warren County slaveholders provided one cabin for every three or four slaves. Charles Sackett Sydnor, *Slavery in Mississippi* (New York and London, 1933), 39. Robert William Fogel, *Without Consent or Contract: The Rise and Fall of American Slavery* (New York, 1989), 153.

14. Kiger to wife, October 29, 1852, Basil Kiger to wife, January 1, 1852 (Kiger meant 1853), Kiger Family Papers, box 2E516, folder 1, NTC.

15. *Roberts v. Wailes*, (1839) Probate Court Minutes Book F, p. 69, Chancery Clerk's Office, WCC.

16. Ibid., 66, 67, 74.

17. Estate of E. H. Covington, Probate File 301, WCC. Probate Minutes Book F, WCC. The crude birth rate for slaves for the period 1820–50 was slightly more than 6 percent, that is, six births per hundred people. See Fogel, *Without Consent or Contract*, 126, fig. 20.

18. Fogel, *Without Consent or Contract*, 153. Fogel and Engerman, *Time on the Cross*, 78–86. Genovese, *Roll, Jordan, Roll*, 453–54. Gutman, 158–59. Richard Sutch, "The Breeding of Slaves for Sale and the Westward Expansion of Slavery, 1850–1860," in Stanley L. Engermand and Eugene D. Genovese, eds., *Race and Slavery in the Western Hemisphere: Quantitative Studies* (Princton, 1975), 173–210. Michael Tadman, *Speculators and Slaves: Masters, Traders, and Slaves in the Old South* (Madison, 1989), 121–29.

19. The rounded figure of $2000 was calculated in the following manner, using values given in the Covington estate papers: According to several witness, the plantation should have raised at least 5 bales of cotton—some said 7—per hand per year, plus a subsistence of corn. The figures are low, but reflect the broken terrain which would have slowed picking. In any case, if a woman picked only 2.5 bales per year over 15 years, at 1830s prices she would have picked $2100 in cotton ($56 per bale). If over that same fifteen-year period she raised 7 children to adulthood, she would have brought her master an additional $6650 ($950 per slave being the average. Men cost somewhat more, women somewhat less). The children, however, would have cost the plantation for food and clothing until they reached age 9, the break-even age (Fogel, *Without Consent or Contract*, 56, fig. 8). At $30 per year per child for their first nine years, the net income from the children was actually $6650 − (7 × 9 × $30) = $4760. This figure is of course low, for children did not suddenly become net earners on their ninth birthday, but gradually became so over their childhood. Thus, the woman earned her master a total of $4760 + $2100 = $6860.

If that same woman had picked twice as much cotton over the same fifteen-year period, but raised only four children, she would have brought her master $6920, a slightly higher return.

The key is that the master, to maximize his returns, had to keep the children for several picking seasons before selling them, if selling was his intention. If the

7 children in the first example picked only half a load over 5 years, they would have brought an additional $4900 into their master's coffer, for a total of $11,760. The 4 children in the second example, if they picked at the same rate, would have earned only $2800, for a total of $9720. Thus, the master in the first example, other things being equal, such as cost of feeding and clothing the mother and the productivity of the land, would have earned an extra $2040 per childbearing female slave.

20. *Crowder v. Shackleford* (1858) in Helen Tunnicliff Catterall, ed. *Judicial Cases Concerning American Slavery and the Negro* 5 vols. (Washington, D.C., 1926–37), 3:356. George P. Rawick, ed., *The American Slave: A Composite Autobiography,* 19 vols. (Westport, Conn., 1972–79), vol. 8, part 2:44–45. George P. Rawick, ed., *The American Slave: A Composite Autobiography: Supplement, Series 1,* 12 vols. (Westport, Conn., 1977), vol. 8, part 3:1243.

21. This can be tested statistically, for example, by comparing the variance in birth rate for individual farms of varying soil quality and cotton output. The Warren County data is not yet ready f ⸱ such a test, however.

22. Eugene D. Genovese, *Roll, Jordan, Roll,* argues that masters were forced by the slaves to recognize the humanity of the people they kept in bonds, and thus to treat them paternalistically even if it meant protecting slave families often at significant financial cost. Genovese has, it seems to me, underestimated the extent to which material conditions supported, not contradicted, paternalistic attitudes.

23. Kenneth M. Stampp, *The Peculiar Institution: Slavery in the Ante-bellum South* (New York, 1956), 34–60. Sydnor, *Slavery in Mississippi* (New York, 1933), 3–22. John Hebron Moore, *The Emergence of the Cotton Kingdom in the Old Southwest: Mississippi, 1770–1860* (Baton Rouge, 1988), 77–82.

24. Rawick, ed., *The American Slave: Supplement,* vol. 10, part 5:280.

25. Allen (James) Plantation Book, pp. 2–4, MDAH.

26. Rawick, *The American Slave: Supplement,* vol. 6, part 1:172–73; vol. 9, part 4: 1538. On plantation work routines in Warren County, see: Allen plantation book and the Shugart (Henry Frederick) Account Book/Diary, both in the MDAH, and the Buena Vista Plantation Record and Account Book, Kiger Family Papers, NTC.

27. Sydnor, *A Gentleman of the Old Natchez Region, Benjamin L. C. Wailes* (Durham, N.C., 1938), 101–4. Allen Plantation Book, MDAH, pp. 1–2, 62, 93. Buena Vista Plantation Record and Account Book, Kiger Family Papers, Box 2E22, folder 4, NTC. The slaves on John A. Quitman's Warren County plantation kept chickens, and sold eggs to their master at 20 cents per dozen: John A. Quitman Papers, NTC. Joseph E. Davis permitted his slave Ben Montgomery to operate a store, which did business with the plantation's several hundred slaves, plus the blacks and whites of neighboring farms. Moreover, Montgomery kept his own accounts with New Orleans merchants. See Janet Sharp Hermann, *The Pursuit of a Dream* (New York, 1981). See also Susan Dabney Smedes, *Memorials of a Southern Planter,* edited, and with an introduction and notes, by Fletcher M. Green (New York, 1965), 56–57.

28. *Roberts v. Wailes* (1839), Probate Court Minutes Book F, p. 73, Chancery Clerk's Office, WCC. Accounts of slaves Abram, Charles, Isaac, and several unnamed "boys" with the merchants who did business with E. H. Covington of Fonsylvania Plantation, all dated December, can be found in the Covington estate papers, Probate Files 301, 531, Chancery Clerk's Office, WCC.

In December 1857, Benjamin Wailes noted "an Immense throng of negroes in Natchez making their Christmas purchases." No doubt the same could have been said of Warrenton and Vicksburg in Warren County. Sydnor, *Gentleman from the Natchez District*, 103. A French traveler noted that in the Lower Mississippi near New Orleans slaves "raise poultry and hogs but seldom eat either," and instead "prefer selling them, and purchasing from their profits, cloathing and brandy." See Berquin-Duvallon, *Travels in Louisiana and the Floridas in the Year, 1802, Giving Correct Picture of Those Countries*, John Davis, trans. (New York, 1806), 90.

Masters were more likely to allow slave men than women the privilege of marketing products or to make purchases off the plantation. At the same time, however, care of the gardens, of producing marketable products, fell primarily to the women. Thus, masters appear to have extended the gender division that existed within the white household into the slave household in ways that historians have not considereded. Jacqueline Jones, *Labor of Love, Labor of Sorrow: Black Women, Work, and the Family from Slavery to the Present* (New York, 1985), for example, argues that masters tended not to ascribe gender identities to their field hands.

29. Several Warren County planters testified in a suit between rival administrators of E. H. Covington's estate that the Covington slaves could be fed and clothed for $35 to $40 per head, by one reckoning, $65 to $70 by another. If a slave made $12 to $20 from the sale of garden products, then that slave's income equaled 17 to 57 percent of what his master spent on him. See the Covington estate papers, Probate File 301, WCC.

"Proto-peasantry" is the term used by Sidney W. Mintz to describe the Jamaican slaves who were allowed essentially small farms to raise their own subsistence, thus underwriting the plantation operation. See "Slavery and the Rise of Peasantries," in *Historical Reflection/Reflexions Historique: Directions*, vol. 1: *Roots and Branches: Current Directions in Slave Studies*, Michael Craton, ed. (Toronto, 1979), 213–42.

The importance of the gardens for the slaves, especially by comparison with the Jamaican experience, should not be exaggerated, as both Genovese and Fogel warn. Fogel, *Without Consent or Contract*, 192. Genovese, *Roll, Jordan, Roll*, 535–40. Recent investigations into slave gardens and the internal economy suggest they were more important than historians have appreciated. Loren Schweninger, "The Underside of Slavery: Internal Economy, Self-Hire, and Quasi-Freedom in Virginia, 1750–1865," *Slavery and Abolition* 12 (September 1991): 4–9; Lawrence T. McDonnell, "Money Knows No Master: Market Relations and the American Slave Community," in Winfred B. Moore, Jr., and Lyon G. Tyler, Jr., eds., *Developing Dixie: Modernization in a Traditional Society* (Westport, Conn., 1988), 31–44; and the essays in Ira Berlin and Philip D. Morgan, eds., *Cultivation and Culture: Labor and the Shaping of Slave Life in the Americas* (Charlottesville, 1993), 203–99.

30. James A. Padgett, "A Decree for Louisiana Issued by the Baron of Carondelet, June 1, 1795," *Louisiana Historical Quarterly* 20 (July 1937): 601.

31. Rawick, *The American Slave, Supplement*, Series 1, vol. 8, part 3:45. For examples of poisonings, alleged or real, see *Sarah (a slave) v. State* (1854) in Catterall, ed., *Judicial Cases*, 3:337. For a fascinating case in Bolivar County, see *George (a slave) v. State* (1860) and *Josephine (a slave) v. State* (1861), Catterall, ed., *Judicial Cases*, 3:372–76. For barn and gin-house fires that may or may not have been started by Warren County slaves, see: *Port Gibson Correspondent*, January 10,

1823; *Vicksburg Weekly Southern Sun,* January 10 and 24, 1859. *Jesse (a slave) v. State* (1854), and *Sam (a slave) v. State* (1857), Catterall, ed., *Judicial Cases,* 3:336, 347. Estate Accounts and Inventories, April 1848–July 1850, p. 31, WCC.

32. Estate Accounts and Inventories, April 1848–July 1850, p. 31, WCC. *State v. Wesley, a slave* (1859), Warren County Court Files, OCM. *State v. Job and Edmund,* Board of Police Minutes Book 1831–38, pp. 30–38, OCM. *Vicksburg Register,* May 10, 1832.

33. *Alfred (a slave) v. State* (1859), 37 Miss. 296. See also Catterall, ed., *Judicial Cases,* 3:362. Alfred's lawyers won a retrial in a new venue on the basis of an impartial jury, but it is not likely that a different jury would have acquitted him, though his fate is not known.

34. *Vicksburg Register,* July 14, 1836.

35. Rawick, ed., *The American Slave,* vol. 6, part 1:1877. Catterall, ed., *Judicial Cases,* 3:342.

36. *Pyrena Wood v. Curtis Wood,* Chancery Court Minute, Book 1, WCC, pp. 358–60, and file 121.

37. Suzanne Lebsock has suggested that the relationship between white women and slaves was more personal than it was between white men and slaves. *Free Women of Petersburg,* 137–41.

38. *George (a slave) v. State* (1860), 39 Mississippi 570, and *Josephine (a slave) v. State* (1861), 39 Mississippi 613. See also Catterall, ed., *Judicial Cases,* 3:372–76. On the tensions between male and female slaves that resulted when masters raped slave women, see Melton Alonza McLaurin, *Celia, a Slave* (Athens, Ga., 1991).

39. For an enlightening investigation into personality and individual male responses to slavery, see Bertram Wyatt-Brown, "The Mask of Obedience: Male Slave Psychology in the Old South," *American Historical Review* 93 (December 1988): 1228–52.

Chapter 5

1. Wailes (B. L. C.) Diary Typescripts, March 7, 1860, February 22, 1857, MDAH. Study Data.

2. Robert C. Kenzer, *Kinship and Neighborhood in a Southern Community: Orange County, North Carolina, 1849–1881* (Knoxville, 1987), 10–11; Rutman and Rutman, *A Place in Time* 1:53–59. Milton B. Newton, Jr., "Mapping the Foundations of the Old Natchez District: The Wilton Map of 1774," in Noel Polk, ed., *Natchez before 1830* (Jackson and London, 1989), 84–87.

3. Hamilton, "Planters' 'Society,' " 69–70.

4. Study Data.

5. *Territory v. Stephens* (1810), Warren County Court Files, OCHM. *Thomas K. McElrath v. James Beard* (1820), *James Beard v. William Jordan* (1820), *David Pharr v. Royal Pace* (1820), *Royal Pace v. David Pharr* (1820), Superior Court Record Book, Warren County, September 1818–March 1821, OCHM.

6. George C. Osborn, "Plantation Life in Central Mississippi as Revealed in the Clay Sharkey Papers," *Journal of Mississippi History* 3 (October 1941): 281–82. Frances and James Allen Cabaniss, "Religion in Antebellum Mississippi," *Journal of Mississippi History* 6 (January–October 1944): 212.

7. Study Data. The network densities for the Gibson and Evans neighbor-

hoods were considerably lower, 6 and 5 percent, respectively. David Knoke and James H. Kuklinski, *Quantitative Applications in the Social Sciences*, vol. 28: *Network Analysis* (Beverly Hills, 1982); Darrett B. Rutman, "Community Study," *Historical Methods* 13 (1980): 29–41.

8. *Vicksburg Advocate and Register*, September 1, 1836.

9. Lorenzo Dow, *History of Cosmopolite: The Four Volumes of Lorenzo Dow's Journal. . .* (Cincinnati, 1848), 310.

10. Patriarchy has long been associated with the Old South. While scholars may agree that men dominated Southern homes and communities they frequently differ on the causes and effects of patriarchy. A few scholars, however, have challenged the existence of Southern patriarchy and have argued instead for more egalitarian household arrangements. Jane Turner Censer, *North Carolina Planters and Their Children, 1800–1860* (Baton Rouge, 1984), and Oakes, *The Ruling Race.*

In her recent study of families in the Old Southwest Joan Cashin argues that "In contrast to seaboard families who lived surrounded by kinfolk, Southwestern families lived near a few relatives or none at all. The planter family was reduced to its nuclear core." Cashin, however, looks at newly settled families and does not explore the process of extended family formation, which proceeded rapidly and immediately upon settlement. Indeed, the evidence from Warren County demonstrates that kin neighborhoods soon appeared to resemble those of older regions of the Southeast. Cashin, *A Family Venture*, 80. Robert Kenzer's descriptions of rural kin neighborhoods in North Carolina would be just as appropriate to rural Warren County. Differences between Western and Eastern neighborhoods in the significance of kinship, therefore, may be accounted for by their age. Kin networks took time to develop, but inevitably they did develop. Kenzer, *Kinship and Neighborhood*, especially chap. 1. Kenzer, however, is guilty of the type of circular argument that plagues most efforts to identify the distinguishing traits of Southern culture: The settlers of Orange County, North Carolina, built tightly knit family neighborhoods because that was the way Southerners lived; that they lived in such neighborhoods distinguished them as Southerners. But according to John Mack Faragher, in the community of Sugar Creek, Illinois, "kinship provided an organizing force which brought farmers together." See Faragher, *Sugar Creek*, 151. Moreover, Faragher also points out how "intermarriage facilitated the retention and concentration of family property" (p. 145). Differences between Northern and Southern neighborhoods, therefore, lay not in the significance of kinship nor even in the tendency of certain kin groups to pool local resources, but rather in the type of property involved. As the following discussion will make clear, slavery made all the difference.

11. The household heads with what network analysts term the highest degree, that is, having connections to the highest number of other members of the network, were considered, for the purposes at hand, to have been extended family heads. For a discussion of *degree of point*, a simple descriptive statistic used by network analysts, see Knoke and Kuklinski, *Network Analysis*, 45. See Appendix D, Table D-5, for a summary of wealth-holding of household heads with highest degrees relative to other Warren County heads of household.

12. Warren County Tax Rolls, 1830, Warren County Records, MDAH. Orphans' Court Record Book A, pp. 216, 354, 412, 419, 425–26, 523, OCHM. Orphans' Court Record Book B, p. 223, and Book C, p. 67, WCC. *John W. Vick et al. v. Mayor and Aldermen of Vicksburg* (1838), High Court of Errors and Appeals, RG 32, vol. 92, pp. 417–557. MDAH.

13. C. M. Chamberlain to D. Maynadier & Co., March 25, 1853, Sharkey (William Lewis) Papers, box 2E509, folder 3, NTC.

14. Deed book C, pp. 141–43, WCC.

15. Censer, *North Carolina Planters*, 104–18. Evidence in Censer's book on the regular practice of granting life estates to women suggests the author may have overstated her case about equal distribution of family property.

16. Claiborne County Orphans Court, minutes (January 1804), Claiborne County Courthouse, Port Gibson, Mississippi. Probate Docket (1810), WCC. *Green Caston v. Stephen Gibson* (March 1819), *James Gibson et al. v. Seth Caston and Green Caston* (September 1819), Superior Court Record Book, Warren County, September 1818–March 1821, OCHM. Study Data.

17. *Patrick Sharkey v. James Gibson and P. Knowland* (March 1819), *James Gibson v. Patrick Sharkey* (September 1820), Superior Court Record Book, Warren County, September 1818–21, OCHM. Orphans' Court, Book A, pp. 143, 153, 221, OCHM. Study Data.

18. The example of the Hyland family comes from papers filed in the following lawsuit: *Hyland v. Hyland* (1832), Superior Court of Chancery, RG 32, SG 1, Case 210, MDAH; Study Data.

19. "Letter from General J. F. H. Claiborne of the Confederate Army to General Randall Lee Gibson of the Confederate Army, Natchez, May 15, 1878," in Winans, *Funeral Sermons*, 45.

20. County Board of Police Minutes, 1831–38, pp. 102–3, OCHM.

21. John G. Jones, *A Complete History of Methodism as Connected with the Mississippi Conference of the Methodist Episcopal Church, South*, 2 vols. (1887 and 1908; Baton Rouge, 1966), 1:57, 59, 346–47. *Statutes of the Mississippi Territory* (Natchez, 1816), 99.

22. Ellen Hyland to sister, n.d., Chamberlain-Hyland-Gould Family Papers, box 2E508, NTC.

23. *State v. Deminds and Chambers* (1839), Warren County Court Records, OCHM.

24. *Vicksburg Register*, April 3, 1834.

25. Allen (James) Plantation Book, typescript, May 29, 1860, and note 11, p. 130, MDAH. B. J. Mathers to Col. James Allen, Warrenton, May 31, 1860, Allen (James) Collection, MDAH. State Docket, June 1860, OCHM. Beall's murder case ended in a mistrial.

26. Orphans' Court Book B, p. 230. *Daniel Whitaker, admin., v. Anthony Durden* (1830?), County Court Papers, box 53, in the attic of the WCC. Anthony Durden Murder Trial (1829) Papers, NTC. Cynthia Warriner, comp., "Gibson Families of Western Mississippi," unpublished genealogy, OCHM.

27. James Gibson served as a justice of the peace in Warren County from 1821 to 1826 when he was appointed judge of probate. Register of Appointments, County Officers, Series A, Volume N, roll 2180, MDAH. On rivalries between brothers-in-law, see Wyatt-Brown, *Southern Honor*, 382–87.

28. Faragher, *Sugar Creek*, 16–18, for example, describes patriarchal families in Illinois. But the influence of male family leaders seems not to have extended beyond the household and into the neighborhood to the extent it did in Warren County neighborhoods.

29. Wyatt-Brown, *Southern Honor*, 350–61; Steven M. Stowe, *Intimacy and Power in the Old South: Ritual in the Lives of the Planters* (Baltimore, 1987), chap. 1; Kenneth S. Greenberg, "The Nose, the Lie, and the Duel in the Antebellum South," *American Historical Review* 95 (February 1990): 57–74.

30. *Griffin v. Gibson*, County Court Papers, box 94, in the attic of the WCC. *Vicksburg Advocate and Register*, September 1, 1836.

31. *Vicksburg Advocate and Register,* September 1, 1836. Tax Rolls, 1835, Warren County Records, MDAH.

32. *Vicksburg Advocate and Register,* September 1, 1836. *Griffin v. Gibson. Vicksburg Daily Whig,* October 24, 1845, reported that E. D. Griffin was awarded $6000 damages plus costs of $497.60.

33. Wailes Diary, February 27, 1857, p. 15.

Chapter 6

1. The population figure of 8000, reported in H. C. Clarke, comp., *General Directory for the City of Vicksburg* (Vicksburg, 1860), 73, includes Vicksburg's suburbs, which extended well beyond the corporation boundaries. The census reported a population of 4,580 for Vicksburg proper.

2. *John W. Vick et al., v. Mayor and Aldermen of Vicksburg* (1838), High Court of Errors and Appeals, RG 32, vol. 92, pp. 468–523, MDAH. Seargent S. Prentiss, *A Memoir of S. S. Prentiss,* 2 vols., William Prentiss, ed. (New York, 1858), 1:184. Harriet Martineau, *Retrospect of Western Travel,* 2 vols. (London, 1838), 2:17. *Harper's Weekly* 6 (1862): 482.

3. Travelers often commented on the absence of towns and cities in the Southern countryside. For example, Frederick Law Olmstead on Mississippi towns: "I found that many a high-sounding name (figuring on the same maps in which towns of five thousand inhabitants in New England, New York, and Pennsylvania, are omitted), indicated the locality of merely a grocery or two, a blacksmith shop, and two or three log cabins. I passed through two of these map towns without knowing that I had reached them. . . ." *A Journey in the Back Country* (New York, 1970), 159–60. Joseph Holt Ingraham in *The Southwest. By a Yankee,* 2 vols. (New York, 1835), 2:205. James Stirling, *Letters from the Slave States* (London, 1857), 177. J. W. Dorr in Walter Prichard, ed., "A Tourist's Description of Louisiana in 1860," *Louisiana Historical Quarterly* 21 (October 1938): 1110–214.

Historians have offered a variety of explanations for why the South did not develop Northern-style cities. The problem lay in: the absence of markets in the cotton economy (Douglass C. North, *The Economic Growth of the United States, 1790–1860* (Englewood Cliffs, N.J., 1961), 52, 63–64); "The preponderance of agriculture" (Harold D. Woodman, *King Cotton and His Retainers: Financing and Marketing the Cotton Crop of the South, 1800–1925* (Lexington, 1968), 194); a distrust on the part of slaveholders of all things urban (Genovese, *The Political Economy of Slavery,* 24); slavery, which obstructed industrialization (Fred Bateman and Thomas Weiss, *A Deplorable Scarcity: The Failure of Industrialization in the Slave Economy* (Chapel Hill and London, 1981) and which limited Southern ties to a national market (Fox-Genovese, *Within the Plantation Household,* 74–75); and "the historical timing of the South's urbanization" relative to more advanced regions of the country (Don H. Doyle, *New Men, New Cities, New South: Atlanta, Nashville, Charleston, Mobile, 1860–1910* (Chapel Hill, 1990), 2).

4. Joseph J. Ernst and H. Roy Merrens, " 'Camden's turrets pierce the skies!': The Urban Process in the Southern Colonies during the Eighteenth Century," *William and Mary Quarterly* 30 (October 1973): 549–74; Leonard P. Curry, "Urbanization and Urbanism in the Old South: A Comparative View," *Journal of Southern History* 40 (February 1974): 43–60; Lyle W. Dorsett and Arthur H. Schaffer, "Was the Antebellum South Antiurban? A Suggestion," *Journal of*

Southern History 38 (February 1972): 93–100; David R. Goldfield, *Cotton Fields and Skyscrapers: Southern City and Region, 1607–1980* (Baton Rouge, 1982), 28–79; Rutman and Rutman, *A Place in Time,* 1:204–33.

5. For Warrenton, see *Statutes of the Mississippi Territory,* 98. For Hankinson, also known as Hankinsonville, see: *Port Gibson Correspondent,* 1821, January 10, 1823, November 11, 1824; Warren County Deed Book B, pp. 235–38, WCC; Gordon Cotton, "The New Town of Hankinson," *Vicksburg Sunday Post,* November 26, 1972. For Mount Vernon, see: Warren County Sectional Indexes, Township 14, Range 3 East, Section 26; *Port Gibson Correspondent,* September 27, 1828; "A New Map of Mississippi with its Roads and Distances" (ca. 1852; rpt., Jackson, Miss., 1974). For Carthage, or Redwood, see *Vicksburg Advocate and Register,* April 9, 1836. Data on the people who lived in Redwood and their occupations come from the Study Data. For Bridgeport and Tuscambia, see *Vicksburg Advocate and Register,* June 30, 1834. For DeSoto, see *Vicksburg Weekly Southern Sun,* January 24 and March 14, 1859. For Vicksburg, see: Will of Newit Vick, Wills and Bonds, August 1819, WCC; Warren County Deed Book B, p. 1, WCC; *John W. Vick et al. v. Mayor and Aldermen of Vicksburg* (1838), High Court of Errors and Appeals, RG 32, vol. 92, p. 527, MDAH. For Mississippi towns in general, see John Hebron Moore, *The Emergence of the Cotton Kingdom in the Old Southwest: Mississippi, 1770–1860* (Baton Rouge, 1988), 177–203.

6. David Goldfield, *Cotton Fields and Skyscrapers: Southern City and Region, 1607–1980* (Baton Rouge, 1982), 28–79, writes of "urbanization without cities." Darret B. Rutman emphasizes the village as central to the southern experience in *Small Worlds, Large Questions* (Charlottesville, 1994).

7. *Eliphalet Frazier v. Sinclair D. Gervais* (March 1819), Superior Court Record, OCHM. For a discussion of the Rapaljes' marketing activities and their connections with their neighbors, see Chapter 2.

8. Warren County Deed Book A, WCC pp. 75–78, 188–89, 229–30.

9. *Eliphalet Frazier v. Sinclair D. Gervais.* "A List of Balance Taken from the Books of E. Frazier Decd. up to the 6th of May, 1817," Elizabeth Frazier Papers, NTC. (The Natchez Trace Collection gives the wrong name to this collection. The papers are those of Eliphalet, not Elizabeth, Frazier). On the local activities of the Hunt brothers, see: William K. Thurston to Abijah Hunt (1804), Israel Loring to John Moore (January 16, 1804), Elijah Smith to [Abijah Hunt?] (September 1805), Hunt (Abijah and David) Papers, MDAH. Although the papers make no mention of a store on the Big Black River, Abijah Hunt owned 500 acres along both sides of the river: Warren County Deed Book B, pp. 235–38, WCC; Claiborne County Deed Book B, p. 336, Claiborne County Courthouse. Their main store in the region was located in Port Gibson.

10. Potter, *Passports,* 158. *John Duncan for use of Edmund Reeves v. Benjamin Steele* (March 1819), Superior Court Record, OCHM. Warren County Deed Book A, pp. 4–5, WCC. Reeves arrived in the U.S., probably from England, in February 1808, just before he showed up in Warren County. His mercantile connections may well have extended back to his port of entry, which could have been New Orleans or one of the ports in the Northeast. The size of his business was too small, however, to suggest direct ties to Europe, despite his recent emigration. Little is known about Thomas Grymes, except that he may have come from Virginia. How and when he linked up with Reeves is not known.

11. Warren County Tax Rolls, 1818, 1820, Warren County Records, MDAH. Warren County Deed Book C, pp. 162–63, 203–4, WCC. *John W. Vick et al. v. Mayor*

(1838), High Court of Errors and Appeals, RG 32, vol. 92, MDAH. *Durden, Vick and Wrenn v. John Huffman* (September 1819), Superior Court Record, OCHM.

12. McBee, *Natchez Court Records*, 438. Claiborne County Deed Book B, pp. 164–65, Claiborne County Courthouse.

13. *Vicksburg Register*, September 23, 1831.

14. Warren County Deed Book A, pp. 176–78, Book B, pp. 48–49, WCC. Warren County Tax Roll, 1820, Warren County Records, MDAH.

15. Francis Baily, *Journal of a Tour in Unsettled Parts of North America, in 1796 & 1797* (London, 1856), 147. Schultz, *Travels on an Inlands Voyage*, 2:127.

16. Warren County Deed Book B, pp. 50–56, WCC. E. H. Bay to Anthony Hutchins, December 17, 1802, Claiborne (J. F. H.) Collection, Book E, Group 4, Microfilm roll 7, MDAH. John Belton O'Neall, *Biographical Sketches of the Bench and Bar of South Carolina*, 2 vols. (Charleston, S.C., 1859), 1:53–65.

17. Zadok Cramer reported that Bay laid out town lots on a portion of his plantation. Cramer, *The Navigator*, 8th ed., (1814; Ann Arbor, 1966), 312. In 1804 Turnbull sent his brother John to manage his Walnut Hills plantation. Eliza Gould Memoir Letter, October 17, 1868, Marshall (Maria Chotard and family) Papers, Hill Memorial Library, LSU.

18. Cramer, *The Navigator*, 312.

19. Warren County Tax Rolls, 1818, 1820, Warren County Records, MDAH. Warren County Sectional Indexes for Range 4, Township 16, Section 2, Chancery Clerk's Office, WCC. *Vick et al. v. Mayor* (1838), Court Record, High Court of Errors and Appeals, RG 32, MDAH. *Gabriel Burnham v. E. D. Walcott and Foster Cook* (March 1821), Superior Court Record Book, OCHM. Will of Newit Vick, Wills and Bonds 1818–23, pp. 42–44, WCC.

20. In April 1823, John Lane, the administrator of Newit Vick's estate, advertised lots for sale in "Vicksburgh." Over the next year he sold 30. *Port Gibson Correspondent*, April 25, 1823. Warren County Deed Books B and C, WCC. In March 1826, Lane reported to the Probate Court "a true account of sales of all the lots that have been sold in Vicksburgh." The lots sold numbered 68. Orphans' Court Minute Book B, pp. 153–54, WCC.

21. Jones, *Methodism*, 1:348–49. *Port Gibson Correspondent*, June 12, 1823, and January 15, 1824.

22. *Vicksburg Advocate and Register*, September 11, 1834. Ingraham, *Southwest by a Yankee*, 169–70.

23. Howard G. Adkins, "Extinct Mississippi Towns," in Peggy W. Prenshaw and Jesse O. McKee, eds. *Sense of Place: Mississippi* (Jackson, 1979).

24. Herbert Anthony Kellar, ed., *Solon Robinson, Pioneer and Agriculturalist: Selected Writings, Volume 1, 1825–1845* (Indianapolis, 1936), 469.

25. Vicksburg Sentinel, December 30, 1844. See the advertisements of various fowarding agents in the Vicksburg newspapers.

26. MS Census, Warren County, 1820, 1850. Board of Police Minutes 1853–69, pp. 334, 353, 358, WCC. Study Data. The 1820 census lists persons engaged in commerce. Store locations were found by linking storekeepers with land records, or by linking persons named on the same census page as storekeepers with land records and the Study Data.

27. Ledger, Yokena, Mississippi (1852–56), in the W. S. Hankinson papers in the as yet uncatalogued Thomas D. Clark papers, Division of Special Collections and Archives, Margaret I. King Library, University of Kentucky, Lexington.

28. Hermann, *Pursuit of a Dream*, 9–12.

29. *Vicksburg Whig,* February 29, March 7, June 6, October 18, 1860. This method of sketching inter-urban connections is borrowed from Allan Pred, *Urban Growth and City-Systems in the United States, 1840–1860* (Cambridge, Mass., 1980), 156–64, who provides a discussion of the possible shortcomings of this method.

30. This corresponds with the pattern Allan Pred observed, which led him to conclude that there was no Southern city-system. See *Urban Growth and City-Systems,* 159. Clearly, however, there was a system, though it differed from the Northern one.

31. Harriet E. Amos found strong connections between Mobile, Alabama, and New York City. See her book *Cotton City: Urban Development in Antebellum Mobile* (Tuscaloosa, 1985).

Chapter 7

1. Clarke, *General Directory,* 73.
2. Ibid., passim.
3. Ibid., 74.
4. Study Data. The figure of 62 percent includes planters, farmers, and over-seers. The inclusion of those who gave their occupation as laborer, most of whom presumably worked on farms, would raise the figure to nearly 80 percent.
5. Artisans and mechanics expressed their fears of upriver competition in letters and articles written for local newspapers. See, for example, *Southern Mechanic* (Vicksburg), April 14, 1838.
6. Bettie to Will Gwin, April 13, 1860, Kiger Family Papers, box 2 E 516, folder 2, NTC. In January 1853, Basil Kiger paid $216 to an undisclosed number of Irishmen for completing $451\frac{1}{2}$ rods of ditch work. Buena Vista Plantation Record and Account Book, 1849–57, Kiger Family Papers, box 2 E 522, folder 3, NTC.
7. J. M. Gibson, *Memoirs of J. M. Gibson: Terrors of the Civil War and Reconstruction Days* (1929), 11.
8. Edwin L. Sabin, ed., "Vicksburg, and After: Being the Experience of a Southern Merchant and Non-Combatant during the Sixties," *Sewanee Review* 15 (October 1907): 484. Peter F. Walker, *Vicksburg: A People at War, 1860–1865* (Chapel Hill, 1960). Clarke, *General Directory,* 26, 29.
9. U. S. Census Office, *Seventh Census of the United States, 1850* (1853, rpt., New York 1976), 448. Bureau of the Census, *Population of the United States in 1860; compiled from the Original Returns of the Eighth Census* (Washington, 1864), 270–71. *Vicksburg Whig,* August 28, 1860. The significance of domestic service among slave occupations is suggested by the predominence of females. In 1850 female slaves outnumbered male slaves 636 to 540, and in 1860, 708 to 694. When Vicksburg's suburbs in 1860 are taken into account, to a three-quarter-mile radius of the courthouse, the slave population figures are 958 females and 908 males. In contrast, in the county beyond Vicksburg's suburbs, men outnumbered women 6,883 to 4,914.
10. Local artisans were much more likely to complain of competition from Northern manufacturers. See note 5 above.
11. Shugart (Henry Frederick) Account Book/Diary, January 3, 1839, and passim, microfilm, MDAH. Ingraham, *The South-west by a Yankee,* 2:170.
12. Vicksburg's permanent residents worried about controlling the strangers who filled the town during winter months. See, for example, *Vicksburg Advocate and Register,* September 16, 1831.

13. MS Census Population Schedules, Warren County 1850, 1860. The crude rate of persistence—the percentage of people present on the first census who are also present on the second—for Vicksburg household heads was 150 out of 535, or 28 percent. From the data used to create the mortality figures presented in Appendix E, Figures Tables E-1 and E-2, we can estimate that 146 heads of household died before the decade's end. Thus of the 389 who did not die, 39 percent ($150/389 \times 100$) persisted.

14. Ira Berlin and Herbert G. Gutman, "Natives and Immigrants, Free Men and Slaves: Urban Workingmen in the Antebellum American South," *Journal of American History* 88 (December 1983): 1182, argue that immigrants arrived in the South with a predisposition to oppose slavery. "Most urban workers," they write, "were born alien to the dominant characteristics of Southern culture," especially slavery. There is no evidence of immigrant opposition to slavery in Vicksburg, however. Indeed, they seemed to have adjusted as easily to Vicksburg as to any other American city.

15. MS Census, Free and Slave Population Schedules, 1850 and 1860.

16. MS Population Schedules for Warren County, 1850, 1860. *Vicksburg Register*, September 4, 1834. Although Smedes lived in Vicksburg in 1850 he owned a plantation on the south side of Vicksburg. See Sectional Indexes, Township 16, Range 3, sections 22, 25, 26, 29, 31, 32, 34.

17. *Vicksburg Advocate and Register*, September 16, October 7 and 14, 1831. *Vicksburg Whig*, December 18, 1860. Clarke, *General Directory*, 53–54.

18. *Woodville Republican*, July 18, 1835. L. S. Houghton to Henry Bosworth, July 10, 1835, transcribed copy on OCHM.

19. *Woodville Republican*, July 18, 1835.

20. L. S. Houghton to Henry Bosworth, July 10, 1835, transcribed copy in OCHM. This important document describes the crucial role of the local militia, which was probably responsible for minimizing hysteria and preventing the crisis from escalating into a bloody free-for-all.

21. *Vicksburg Advocate and Register*, January 29, 1834.

22. Harlan to Nell, November 24, 1848, Harlan Papers, box 2 D 270, Barker Texas History Collection, University of Texas, Austin.

23. *Vicksburg Advocate and Register*, April 9, 1836.

24. Ibid., April 13, 1836.

25. Ibid., April 9, 1836.

26. H. S. Fulkerson, *Random Recollections of Early Days in Mississippi* (Baton Rouge, 1937), 97–99. *Vicksburg Whig*, March 4 and April 9, 1840. *Harrison v. Mayor*, 3 Smedes and M. 581.

27. *Vicksburg Advocate and Register*, September 16, October 7, 1831; March 22, June 14, 1832; February 26, 1835. *Vicksburg Whig*, June 5, 1844; July 29, 1845; March 20, 1846; March 25, 1848; March 26, 1850; December 18, 1860. Clarke, *General Directory*, 48–54.

28. This profile of the voluntary association leadership is based on lists of officers printed in: Clarke, *General Directory*, 48–54, and in the *Vicksburg Whig*, December 18, 1860. Evidence for property-holding, occupation, and place of birth came from the MS Population Schedules for Warren County, 1860.

29. *Vicksburg Whig*, December 18, 1860.

30. Paul E. Johnson, *A Shopkeeper's Millennium: Society and Revivals in Rochester, New York, 1815–1837* (New York, 1978). Don Harrison Doyle, *The Social Order of a Frontier Community, Jacksonville, Illinois, 1825–70* (Urbana and Chicago, 1978).

31. On women and voluntary societies, see: William H. and Jane H. Pease, *The Web of Progress: Private Values and Public Styles in Boston and Charleston, 1828–1843* (New York, 1985), 147–52; Nancy A. Hewitt, *Women's Activism and Social Change: Rochester, New York, 1822–1872* (Ithaca, 1984); Suzanne Lebsock, *The Free Women of Petersburg: Status and Culture in a Southern Town, 1784–1860* (New York, 1984), 195–236; Mary P. Ryan, *Cradle of the Middle Class: The Family in Oneida County, New York, 1790–1865* (New York, 1981). All of these studies are of Eastern cities, whereas in Western cities, including those north of slavery, women were largely absent from voluntary societies. See, for example, Doyle, *Frontier Community*, 184–87.

32. Mahala Perkins Harding (Eggleston) Roach, diary, January 7, March, 19, 20, April 10, May 4, 8, 1851, Virginia Historical Society, Richmond.

33. See, for example, the entries in the Mahala Roach diary for June 18, September 24, and November 7, 1851, and March 2–8 and 12, 1852, Virginia Historical Society.

34. Mahala Roach, diary, December 27, and 31, 1851, Virginia Historical Society.

35. Clifford S. Griffin, *Their Brothers' Keeper: Moral Stewardship in the United States, 1800–1865* (New Brunswick, N.J., 1960); Charles I. Foster, *An Errand of Mercy: The Evangelical United Front, 1790–1837* (Chapel Hill, 1960); Johnson, *A Shopkeeper's Millennium.*

36. Mahala Roach, diary, May 4, 1851, Virginia Historical Society.

37. *Vicksburg Advocate and Register*, January 27, 1838. Frances and James Allen Cabaniss, "Religion in Antebellum Mississippi," *Journal of Mississippi History* 6 (January–October 1944), 202.

38. Johnson, *A Shopkeeper's Millennium.* The parallels between Vicksburg and Rochester are as intriguing as their differences. Both towns grew rapidly in large part because of their location on major waterways. The established citizenry of both places felt threatened by the large numbers of migrants and newcomers. But while Rochester responded with revivals, Vicksburg responded with militias.

39. *Vicksburg Whig*, March 14, 1840.

40. Ibid., December 18, 1860. In June 1848, a mob dealt with a thief by whipping him "nearly to death." *Vicksburg Whig*, June 6, 1848.

41. Cross-Tabulation of Organization Officers by Place of Birth

	Place of Birth	
Organization	South	Non-South
Militia	2	8
Temperance	8	5

$X^2 = 3.97; P < .05$

Source: U.S. Census, Population Schedules, Warren County, 1850 and 1860. Sons of Temperance officers in *Vicksburg Whig*, June 12, 1849, and Police Association Officers in same newspaper, December 18, 1860. Other militia officers listed in Clarke, *General Directory*, 53–54.

42. Pease and Pease, *Web of Progress*, 142–52.

43. The calculation of network density was made for a matrix created from the list of association officers of 1860 compiled from Clarke, *General Directory*, 48–54, and the *Vicksburg Whig*, December 18, 1860. On network analysis and the

calculation of density see Knoke and Kuklinski, *Network Analysis*. Kin-network density of rural neighborhoods is discussed in Chapter 6.

44. Welles (Edward R.) diary, 1854–56, pp. 78–79, typescript, MDAH.

45. Welles diary, p. 42.

46. Clarke, *General Directory*, 49, 53.

47. Mahala Roach, diary, volume 1, September 24, 1853, Roach-Eggleston Family Papers, Southern Historical Collection, University of North Carolina, Chapel Hill.

48. *Vicksburg Whig*, March 26, 1850. The Ladies' Benevolent Association received no mention alongside Vicksburg's other societies in the 1860 city directory, suggesting that it was gone by that date. See Clarke, *General Directory*, 75–76.

49. *Vicksburg Whig*, March 26, 1850. Mahala Roach, diary, volume 8, July 6, 1860, University of North Carolina.

50. *Vicksburg Whig*, October 2, 9, November 6, 1860.

51. Wilmuth S. Rutledge, "Dueling in Antebellum Mississippi," *Journal of Mississippi History* 26 (August 1964): 187, 189. Jack K. Williams, *Dueling in the Old South: Vignettes of Social History* (College Station, Texas, 1980), 32–33.

52. *Vicksburg Advocate and Register*, November 8, 1837.

53. Ibid. It is interesting to note that such defenses turned to accusations in comments on violent affairs in the surrounding countryside. After the lynching of a slave in Claiborne County the Vicksburg newspaper published an editorial that might have been written in the North: "The enormity of the guilt of the offender cannot be plead in palliation of the deep wound which such usurpations are calculated to inflict upon the free institutions of our beloved country." *Advocate and Register*, July 14, 1836.

54. Ibid., January 27, 1838. Joseph C. Passmore to George W. Hunter, December 16, 1842, Passmore letters, OCHM.

55. John Shannon, Jr., to Howard Morris, June 8, 1844, box 3, folder 28, Crutcher-Shannon Papers, MDAH. *Vicksburg Sentinel*, July 1 and 8, 1844. Williams, *Dueling in the Old South*, 32–33. A jury found Hagan's assailant not guilty on grounds of self-defense.

56. *Vicksburg Sentinel*, June 5, 1844.

57. Ibid.

58. Information on the pro- and anti-duelists was compiled for the Study Data. Vick was partner in a Texas land company. Another partner had ties to Cuba, and actually died there, thus there is the possibility that Vick invested in Cuba as well. On Vick's interests in botany, see Moore, *Emergence of the Cotton Kingdom*, 27, 29. On Seargent Prentiss see the romantic portrait by a contemporary, Joseph G. Baldwin, *The Flush Times of Alabama and Mississippi: A Series of Sketches*, with an Introduction and Notes by James H. Justus (1853; rpt., Baton Rouge, 1987), 197–222.

Chapter 8

1. Hutchinson, *Code of Mississippi*, 98. Warren County Deed Book A, pp. 34–35. State Legislature, Minutes, RG 47, MDAH. *The Republican* (Vicksburg), May 4, 1825.

2. Rutman, "The Social Web," 57–89, and Rutman, "Assessing the Little

Communities of Early America," *William and Mary Quarterly* 43 (April 1986): 175.

3. Port Gibson *Correspondent*, January 31, 1823. Vicksburg *Weekly Southern Sun*, November 25, 1858. John Hebron Moore, *The Emergence of the Cotton Kingdom in the Old Southwest: Mississippi, 1770–1860* (Baton Rouge, 1988), 166, 173. George Rogers Taylor, *The Transportation Revolution 1815–1860* (New York and Toronto, 1951).

4. Board of Police, Minutes, 1846, pp. 71–75.

5. *Vicksburg Advocate and Register*, December 1, 1834.

6. *Port Gibson Correspondent*, January 31, 1823.

7. Ibid., August 4, 1825.

8. Ibid., January 25, 1827. *Vicksburg Advocate and Register*, April 12, 1832.

9. In Mississippi, the land boom first began in 1820, following the Treaty of Doak's Stand, in which the Choctaw Nation ceded a large piece of territory to the United States. Most of the speculators and settlers, however, came from older regions in Mississippi, Natchez in particular. See Edwin Arthur Miles, *Jacksonian Democracy in Mississippi* (Chapel Hill, 1960), 19. By 1830, according to Miles, settlement and development of Choctaw lands had created in Mississippi a demand for more banking facilities, which the legislature met by chartering organizations like the Planters' Bank. The 1830s saw an even greater rush of population into new regions of Mississippi. For a description of the "flush times" by a contemporary see Joseph G. Baldwin, *The Flush Times of Alabama and Mississippi: A Series of Sketches*, with Introduction and Notes by James H. Justus (Baton Rouge, 1987), especially 82–83.

The reasons for the land boom and surge of westward migration in the 1830s are complex, and still debated by historians. The traditional view holds that a loosening of credit following Jackson's transfer of federal deposits from the Bank of the United States to various state banks made funds more available to Western speculators and homesteaders. An alternative view emphasizes the inflationary effects of foreign investment on increasing land sales. In the South, however, the price of cotton, combined with the productivity of the new land relative to older cotton lands in the East, in the words of economic historian Douglass North, "triggered a land boom." North, *The Economic Growth of the United States 1790–1860* (Englewood Cliffs, N.J., 1961), 73. See also Peter Temin, *The Jacksonian Economy* (New York, 1969). Historian Lacy Ford describes how during the 1830s people were leaving the upcountry region of South Carolina for the relatively more productive new lands to the west: Ford, *Origins of Southern Radicalism*, 37–43.

10. *Vicksburg Advocate and Register*, November 19, 1835.

11. Ibid., November 13, 1834. Section indexes, township 17, range 4, sections 3, 4, and 7, WCC.

12. Will Book A, WCC, pp. 78–80.

13. For the holdings of the Planters' Bank in Warren County, see the Section Indexes, particularly townships 16 and 17, range 3, WCC.

14. Halsell, "Vicksburg Speculator," 233–37.

15. *Vicksburg Advocate and Register*, January 15, 1834.

16. Ibid., January 15, 1834, March 29, 1832. Information on individual commissioners comes from the personal biographies compiled for the Study Data. Moore, *Emergence of the Cotton Kingdom*, 164–66.

17. When developers in the Natchez region announced their intentions to

build a railroad to Jackson, Vicksburg's merchants received added incentive to organize quickly before an alternative railroad could "ruin Vicksburg and reduce it to a Hamlet." *Vicksburg Advocate and Register,* October 2, 1834.

18. Board of Police, Minutes 1831–38, December 1835, pp. 200–201, January 1836, p. 204, OCHM.

19. Board of Police, Minutes 1838–45, February 1839, p. 41, January 1842, p. 219, OCHM. The county continued to grant monopoly privileges to transportation companies long after the famous U.S. Supreme Court case *Charles River Bridge v. Warren Bridge* (1837). While local and state governments in older areas of the country were curtailing monopoly privileges to permit competition and economic growth, newer locales in the West were granting such privileges to encourage developers to take risks. See Michael Dougan, "The Doctrine of Creative Destruction: Ferry and Bridge Law in Arkansas," *Arkansas Historical Quarterly* 39 (Summer 1980): 136–58.

20. Board of Police, Minutes 1838–45, May 1839, p. 67, May 1840, p. 124, OCHM.

21. On the laws regarding roads, see Hutchinson, *Code of Mississippi,* 251, 255, 257, 258.

22. For examples of fines levied on farmers for stringing fences across roads, see Board of Police, Minutes 1838, p. 354; 1842, p. 218; 1843, p. 501; 1844, p. 618; 1846, p. 31.

23. Board of Police, Minutes 1848, p. 129.

24. Hutchinson, *Code of Mississippi,* 258.

25. Board of Police, Minutes 1844, p. 608.

26. *Statutes of the Mississippi Territory* (Natchez, 1816), 427. Territorial Legislature, RG 5, vol. 27, Petitions to the General Assembly, 1810–16, untitled petition to keep the courthouse at Warrenton, 1815, MDAH. Petitions to the Legislature, container 17, January 1820. Board of Police, Minutes, January 1834, p. 94. Robert W. Harrison, "Levee Building in Mississippi before the Civil War," *Journal of Mississippi History* 12 (April 1950): 63. Monette, "Mississippi Floods," 443. During the first half of the nineteenth century "Extraordinary Floods" occurred twice each decade.

27. Study Data. Janet Sharp Hermann, *Joseph E. Davis: Pioneer Patriarch* (Jackson, Miss., 1990), 49–50.

28. Board of Police, Minutes, 1846, p. 32; 1853, p. 711; 1854, pp. 20, 28, 71; 1858, p. 274; 1859, p. 304; 1860, pp. 416, 422–23. Petitions to the Legislature, container 17, January 1820. *Papers of Jefferson Davis,* 3:119–20. The state legislature assessed a tax of $1,160 on Joseph Davis and $636 on Jefferson Davis. Turner's and Quitman's tax is not known, but surely took the total well over $2000, and the taxes on another neighbor, one Robert Wood, may have raised the total to near $3000.

29. *Report on the Mississippi River Floods by the Committee on Commerce, United States Senate,* 55th Cong., 3d Sess., Report No. 1433 (1898).

30. The expansion of government and law in Warren County during the antebellum years was part of a national pattern, as Charles Sellers has noted in his recent study of Jacksonian America. Sellers, however, argues that government was intrusive. He does not appreciate the extent to which the impetus and demand for increased governmental power came from *within* small communities, and from the supporters of Jackson. Sellers, *The Market Revolution,* 54.

31. Alice to Philan, n.d., Crutcher-Shannon Papers, box 1, folder 2, MDAH.

32. Board of Police, Minutes, February 1832, p. 27; May 1838, p. 354; October 1844, p. 623; 1854, p. 23. Carter Goodrich, "Local Government Planning of Internal Improvements," *Political Science Quarterly* 66 (1951): 411–45. Goodrich noted that the "intermixture of common and individual interests, and of government and private means . . . was particularly marked in the case of local aid" for internal improvements (p. 255). See also Carter Goodrich, *Government Promotion of American Canals and Railroads 1800–1890* (New York, 1960), 159–60, 170.

33. *Vicksburg Advocate and Register,* November 5, 1835. *Vicksburg Whig,* October 13, 1858.

34. *Port Gibson Correspondent,* August 14, 1823. Election Returns, RG 28, vol. 12a, 1823, MDAH.

35. *Port Gibson Correspondent,* August 14, 1823.

36. Freeland appears on the 1818 tax role for Warren County as part owner of a 1620-acre tract. Paul F. Bourke and Donald A. DeBats, "The Structure of Political Involvement in the Nineteenth Century: A Frontier Case," *Perspectives in American History* n.s. 3 (1987): 207–38. On the Oregon frontier while settlements were at best loosely integrated into the larger society, voting patterns varied from neighborhood to neighborhood, indicating that a political system had yet to evolve. Partisan loyalties in these conditions "arose not from systemwide variables such as wealth, ethnicity, occupation, or even religion" (p. 233) but from the "idiosyncratic" development of individual neighborhoods (p. 237). M. Philip Lucas, "Beyond McCormick and Miles: The Pre-partisan Political Culture of Mississippi," *Journal of Mississippi History* 44 (November 1982): 329–48, emphasizes the local orientation of Mississippi antebellum politics. See also Robert C. Kenzer, *Kinship and Neighborhood,* 52–70. Southern localism is central to William W. Freehling's recent reinterpretation of the Old South: *The Road to Disunion: Secessionists at Bay, 1776–1854* (New York, 1990), 298–99, 599–600.

37. Election Returns, Warren County, RG 28, MDAH. Vicksburg *Advocate and Register,* November 5, 1835, November 15, 1837. Vicksburg *Daily Whig,* November 8, 1841, November 11, 1843, November 7, 1845, November 5, 1847. Vicksburg *Weekly Whig,* November 14, 1849, November 12, 1851, November 12, 1853, October 13, 1858, October 12, 1859. Also see Appendix H.

38. In his study of politics in Cumberland County, North Carolina, Harry L. Watson concludes that economic interests and social status determined party preference in elections. Watson does not explore personal connections between elites and the voting masses who followed their lead regardless of economic interest or social status. Harry L. Watson, *Jacksonian Politics and Community Conflict: The Emergence of the Second American Party System in Cumberland County, North Carolina* (Baton Rouge, 1981). In nearby Orange County, North Carolina, Robert Kenzer found the influence of kinship to have been decisive in local elections. See Kenzer, *Kinship and Neighborhood,* 62–66. Kenzer asserts that neighborhood voting patterns based on the strength of kinship ties were peculiarly Southern, but then see the study of the Oregon frontier by Bourke and DeBats, "The Structure of Political Involvement," 207–38. Neighborhood voting patterns existed as well in Northern factory towns, owing to, among other things, the influence wielded by patriarchal bosses. See Ronald P. Formisano, *The Transformation of Political Culture: Massachusetts Parties, 1790s–1840s* (New York, 1983), 283–88. By 1830, however, patriarchal "influence" had weakened in Northeastern regions such as Massachusetts, where it was crosscut by growing religious and cultural divisions. Thus, in the South the so-called Second Party

System of Democrats and Whigs did not represent the break with eighteenth-century-style politics that it did in the North. The best description of eighteenth-century politics, much of it applicable to antebellum Warren County, remains Charles S. Sydnor, *Gentlemen Freeholders: Political Practices in Washington's Virginia* (Chapel HIll, 1952).

39. Precinct returns for the presidential election of 1844 are not available. In 1848 Milldale voted along with the rest of the county in favor of Taylor. *Vicksburg Whig*, November 5, 1840; November 9, 1848.

40. *Vicksburg Sentinel*, July 29, 1840.

41. *Vicksburg Whig*, December 2, 9, 23, 1844; April 22, 1845.

42. This discussion of Warren County politics confirms much of what Eugene D. Genovese suspected in his now classic essay "Yeoman Farmers in a Slaveholders' Democracy," originally published in *Agricultural History*, and revised and republished in Fox-Genovese and Genovese, *Fruits of Merchant Capital*, 249–64, esp. 262–63.

James Oakes, in *The Ruling Race*, argues for a Southern "middle-class politics that was as devoted to liberal democracy as it was to black slavery" (p. 143). However, patterns of election and office-holding do not point to a middle-class politics in Warren County. While Oakes does excuse the lower river counties of Mississippi as exceptional for their Whiggish "distaste for democracy" (p. 146)—a distaste he does not attempt to explain—the example of Warren County still presents difficulties for Oakes's efforts to generalize. The county led the democratic revolt against the Natchez Nabobs despite its deferential politics, despite becoming a Whig stronghold.

43. John H. Moore, "Local and State Governments of Antebellum Mississippi," *Journal of Mississippi History* 44 (May 1982): 105–6, 113–14.

44. Register of Appointments, County Officers, Warren County 1820, Series A, vol. N, roll 2108, MDAH.

45. *Vicksburg Advocate and Register*, November 5, 1835.

46. See Appendix H.

47. See Appendix H.

48. Formisano, *Transformation of Political Culture*, 131.

49. *Vicksburg Advocate and Register*, August 9, 1832. Miles, *Jacksonian Democracy in Mississippi*, 37.

50. *Port Gibson Correspondent*, January 22, 1824. Tax Rolls, Warren County, 1835.

51. Within local communities politics appear to have been much less democratic and ideological than they appear to observers of larger regions or states, for example, J. Mills Thornton III, *Politics and Power in a Slave Society: Alabama, 1800–1860* (Baton Rouge, 1978).

52. Miles, *Jacksonian Democracy in Mississippi*, 48–86.

53. The names of active party members collected from lists published in Vicksburg newspapers were linked with slaveholders listed on the 1835 tax roll and the 1850 census. During the 1830s Whigs owned on average 20 slaves, while Democrats owned on average only 10. Nevertheless a test of the relationship between party and slaveholding for 61 household heads active in party organizations produced an Eta (Eyx) of .20, which was not significant at the .05 level. In time differences in the size of slaveholding of active party members narrowed. By 1850 Whigs owned on average 18 slaves and Democrats owned 15.

54. *Vicksburg Sentinel,* October 21, November 8, 19, 1839, July 16, 1845. A split appeared in Vicksburg along ethno-cultural lines between native-born Protestant Whigs and immigrant Catholic Democrats, but the number of Catholic immigrants was too small to have made it the basis of party alignment. The insignificance of ethno-cultural voting patterns in the South relative to the North was a consequence of the region's smaller and less diverse immigrant population. Watson, *Jacksonian Politics,* 228. In Louisiana, however, Francophone Catholics in the southern parishes voted against the Protestant Anglophones to the north. Roger W. Shugg, *Origins of Class Struggle in Louisiana: A Social History of White Farmers and Laborers during Slavery and After, 1840–1875* (1939; Baton Rouge, 1968), 150.

55. *Vicksburg Sentinel,* November 11, 1839. As Colonel Howard of Vicksburg put it, Democrats were not opposed to all banks, only "fraudulent and rotten banks." The more fearful believed all banks were or would soon become hopelessly rotten to the core. Others, like Howard, had faith that, once exposed, corruptions could be remedied "through the majesty of the ballot box." See the *Sentinel,* November 16, 1839.

56. *Vicksburg Advocate and Register,* March 29, 1832; January 15, 1834. McNutt's efforts at bank reform are discussed in more detail in James Roger Sharp, *The Jacksonians versus the Banks: Politics in the States after the Panic of 1837* (New York, 1970), 60–84. Sharp sees McNutt as a hard money, anti-bank Democrat, but that analysis would seem to conflict with his activities as a banker, railroader, and land speculator. In any case, Sharp's account demonstrates that Democrats were rarely united against Whigs over the bank issue, but tended to fall on one side of the question or the other according to personal experience and interest. Few were ideologically opposed to banks.

57. Recent efforts to explain antebellum Southern politics in terms of commitment to "republican" ideals have been summarized by Harry L. Watson, "Conflict and Collaboration: Yeomen, Slaveholders, and Politics in the Antebellum South," *Social History* 10 (October 1985): 273–98. The historians discussed in Watson's article attribute such a wide variety of behavior to a single ideology so that it explains nothing. Moreover, much of the same behavior suggests an alternative ideology to some historians. For example, Oakes, *Slavery and Freedom,* sees in antebellum Southerners a commitment to "liberal" ideals.

58. *Vicksburg Sentinel,* February 9, 1848.

59. Arthur C. Cole, *The Whig Party in the South* (1914; Gloucester, Mass., 1962).

60. Thelma Jennings, *The Nashville Convention: Southern Movement for Unity, 1848–1851* (Memphis, 1980). Donald M. Rawson, "Party Politics in Mississippi, 1850–1860" (Ph.D. dissertation, Vanderbilt University, 1964), 24–52.

61. Jennings, *Nashville Convention,* 5.

62. The quotation is from the prospectus for a new Unionist newspaper printed in the *Vicksburg Whig,* August 6, 1851.

63. See Appendix H.

64. In the 1853 gubernatorial election all precincts gave a majority to the same candidate. A similar pattern prevailed in 1859 when all but one precinct gave a majority to the same candidate. The lone neighborhood to buck the countywide trend did so by only two votes. *Vicksburg Whig,* November 15, 1853, and October 12, 1859.

Chapter 9

1. James C. Cobb, *The Most Southern Place on Earth: The Mississippi Delta and the Roots of Regional Identity* (New York, 1992).

2. Herbert Anthony Kellar, ed., *Solon Robinson, Pioneer and Agriculturalist: Selected Writings* vol. 1: *1825–1845*, vol. 2: *1846–1851*, Indiana Historical Collections, vols. 21, 22 (Indianapolis, 1946), 2:127.

3. Kellar, ed., *Solon Robinson*, 1:467. Some farmers took Robinson's advice. The number of sheep in Warren County increased from 3,812 (1840) to 9,599 (1860), while the number of cattle remained constant. Nevertheless, the amount of unimproved land, which would have provided pasture for these animals, increased faster than the flocks and herds. In other words, by 1860 a greater amount of farm land was not used, presumably because it had been ruined by overuse and erosion. United States Census Office, *Compendium of the Sixth Census* (Washington, D.C., 1841), 227. United States Census Office, *The Seventh Census of the United States* (Washington, D.C., 1853), 456. United States Census Office, *Agriculture of the United States in 1860; Compiled from the Original Returns of the Eighth Census* (Washington, D.C., 1864), 84.

4. Kellar, ed., *Solon Robinson*, 1:473.

5. Ibid., 1:469. On the effects of European fauna on American flora see Crosby, *Ecological Imperialism*, 146–70.

6. *Vicksburg Weekly Southern Sun*, January 17, 1859.

7. Allen (James) Plantation Book, MDAH, typescript, pp. 3–4, 8, 32. Allen floated his timber to the mouth of the Big Black and disposed of it there. Basil Kiger stacked his at the river's edge. He also allowed some of his slaves to sell what they cut during off-times. Buena Vista Plantation Record and Account Book, 1859–60, Kiger Family Papers, box 2E522, folder 4, NTC.

Between 1850 and 1860 Warren County farmers brought 83,272 improved acres into production, while they retired 51,264 acres to unimproved status. By comparison, the new delta county of Coahoma brought 166,916 new acres into production but retired 121,670 acres. Farming in Warren County was considerably less extensive (or more intensive) than in Coahoma County, where new land was both brought into cultivation and discarded at a faster rate. But farming in Warren County was not as intensive as in Hinds County, where farmers actually reduced the number of acres they cultivated, reduced the number of unimproved acres as they brought formerly discarded land back into production, and still managed to increase cotton production. *Seventh Census*, 456, 458. *Agriculture of the United States in 1860*, 84, 85.

8. Buena Vista Plantation Record and Account Book, 1859–60, Kiger Family Papers, box 2E522, folder 4, NTC. Hill, McLean & Co. of New Orleans to William L. Sharkey, March 5, 1850, Sharkey (William Lewis) Papers, box 2E509, folder 1, NTC. Allen (James) Plantation Book, MDAH, typescript, p. 1. Sydnor, *Benjamin L. C. Wailes*, 99. These planters were importing pork even though the number of swine increased in Warren County. *The Seventh Census of the United States* (1853; rpt., New York, 1976), 456–60. *Agriculture of the United States in 1860*, 84–87. The 1860 published census reported a harvest of only 57,000 bushels of corn, an unbelievably low total. I suspect the correct figure was 570,000 bushels, representing a modest increase in line with neighboring counties.

9. High prices attracted the attention of farmers across the state. Cotton to corn ratios increased in every Mississippi county but one, excluding three coun-

ties for which their are no 1860 production figures and a forth county established after 1850. Cotton prices peaked in 1857, fell only slightly the next two years, then in 1860 fell dramatically. However, census data collected in 1860 represent production levels attained the previous year, when prices were high and had been so for two years before that. *The Seventh Census*, 457, 458. *Agriculture of the United States in 1860*, 85. Roger L. Ransom, *Conflict and Compromise: The Political Economy of Slavery, Emancipation, and the American Civil War* (Cambridge, 1989), 56, fig. 3.3.

10. Allen (James) Plantation Book, MDAH, typescript, p. 10. Wailes (B. L. C.) Diary, August 31, 1856, MDAH. Buena Vista Plantation Record and Account Book, 1859–60, Kiger Family Papers, box 2E522, folder 4, NTC.

11. See Appendix I: Wealth.

12. *The Seventh Census*, 322. *Agriculture of the United States in 1860*, 206.

The census did not count tenants, and so the number of farm families that did not own the land they worked or managed must be estimated from other figures the census did provide. In 1850, 520 people reported to the population census the occupations of farmer, planter, or overseer. That same year the agricultural census counted 435 farms. Thus, 85 farm workers did not own the land they planted. In 1860, 617 farmers/planters/overseers worked 396 farms, suggesting that 221 did not own the land they planted. Put another way, farm ownership rates declined from 84 to 64 percent of all farm households. These estimates, however, must be used cautiously, for unfortunately, though not unexpectedly, the numbers in the census do not add up the way they should. In 1850, for example, the population census counted 401 farmers and planters, of whom only 312 possessed real estate, and yet according to the agricultural census there were 435 farms. The discrepancy was probably caused by farm owners who lived in the city and reported a nonfarm occupation. If the census underreported farmers and planters them my estimates of tenancy are high. But the real estate holdings reported in the population census may also be misleading if tenants reported the value of the farms they worked as if they owned them. Thus, estimates of tenancy may be low.

The best way to avoid the problems with census data is to use only the figures most likely to be accurate. The surest figure for the number of farms is that provided by the agricultural census. And it is safe to assume that household heads who reported to the population census that they were farmers, planters, or overseers did in fact work or manage farms. Together these figures provide the most sound estimates of tenancy and landownership, the estimates reported above, and if anything are too conservative. In any case, the trend is clear: over time there were fewer farms and more nonlandowning farm families.

For a more complicated method of estimating farm ownership rates, see Frederick A. Bode and Donald E. Ginter, *Farm Tenancy and the Census in Antebellum Georgia* (Athens, 1986), figures for Mississippi on p. 203. Bode and Ginter's estimates for the region of Mississippi that included Warren County approximate the figures used here and show the same trend.

13. *Agriculture of the United States in 1860*, 206.

14. Osborn, "Clay Sharkey Papers," 285.

15. Study Data. In 1830, 67 household heads owned 19 or more slaves, enough to form one gang. How many of these planters—historians usually define planters as having 20 or more slaves—did not have to work in their own fields is not known. It seems unlikely, however, that those with only one gang could have afforded an overseer.

16. Joseph Holt to wife Mary, October 4, 1839, Joseph Holt Papers, Container 98, Manuscript Division, Libary of Congress. Hermann, *Joseph E. Davis*, 50–51. *Natchez Weekly Courier*, November 27, 1849. W. J. Cash pointed out the crudeness of plantation big houses, which could not have been much more comfortable than frontier log cabins, in his classic study *The Mind of the South*, reissued with a new introduction by Bertram Wyatt-Brown (New York, 1991), 15–16.

17. Basil Kiger to Carrie Kiger, December 4, 1852; January 1, 1853 (note that this letter is dated 1852, but Kiger had made a common mistake on the first day of the year); Carrie Kiger to Basil Kiger, January 12, 1853; Basil Kiger to Carrie Kiger, June 5, 1853; Carrie Kiger to Basil Kiger, June 9, 1853, Family Papers, box 2E516, folders 1 and 2, NTC.

18. Wailes (B. L. C.) diary, March 1861, MDAH.

19. *Vicksburg Whig*, May 29, 1860.

20. Ibid., September 29, 1860, reports that wife-beating was on the rise. Editors reported receiving news of one or two cases per week in Vicksburg and in the surrounding area just beyond the reach of municipal authorities. See also *Whig*, August 9, 1860. Kizer's story is reported in the *Vicksburg Weekly Southern Sun*, January 1, 1859. See the editorial, "A Woman or a Chattel?," in the *Weekly Southern Sun*, January 17, 1859.

21. Persistence Rates for Rural Household Heads Present in 1850

Slaveholders	44
Nonslaveholders	24
Landowners	43
Nonlandowners	25

N = 449

Source: Study Data.

Persistence Rates by Size of Slaveholding for All Warren County, Including Vicksburg

Number of slaves in 1850	0	1–5	6–10	11–20	21–50	50+
Rate of persistence	28	58	38	49	53	54

Source: Study Data.

Persistence Rates for Men by Age Group for All Warren County, Including Vicksburg

Age in 1850	16–29	30–39	40–49	50–59
Persistence rate	21	33	32	36

Source: Study Data.

22. Board of Police Minutes 1855, p. 84, Chancery Clerk's Office, WCC. U.S. Census, Population Schedules for Warren County, Mississippi, 1830.

23. Harlan to Nell, July 15, 1849, Harlan (Charles T.) Papers, box 2D270, Texas History Collection, Barker Library, University of Texas at Austin.

24. Asabel Gaylord to George Welles, November 29, 1851, Miscellaneous Manuscript Collection, box 2, folder 23, MDAH.

25. John Shannon, Jr., to Howard Morris, January 27, 1845, Crutcher-Shannon Family Papers, box 2E511, folder 1, NTC. Howard Morris to neice, December 6, 1851; Howard Morris to Marmaduke Shannon and Lavina Morris Shannon, December 5, 1852; Howard Morris to Lavina Morris Shannon, December 18, 1853, Crutcher-Shannon Papers, box 3, folder 28, MDAH.

26. Percentage of Rural Household Heads
Present in 1860 but Not in 1850

Slaveholders	30
Nonslaveholders	66
Landowners	34
Nonlandowners	70

N = 359

Source: Study Data.

27. Study Data.

28. For wealth-holding patterns in Vicksburg see Appendix I.

29. Moore, *Emergence of the Cotton Kingdom*, 173.

30. James Roach Diary, vol. 1, pp. 2, 26–27, 177. The entries for the winter of 1858 speak regularly of gloomy economic prospects.

31. *Vicksburg Weekly Southern Sun*, January 24, March 21, 1859. *Vicksburg Whig*, November 6, 1860.

32. *Vicksburg Weekly Southern Sun*, March 7, 1959.

33. *Vicksburg Southern Sun*, January 10, March 14, 1859.

34. *Vicksburg Whig*, September 13, 1855, January 22 and 25, September 19, October 7, 1856; November 20, 1857, March 10 and 17, September 29, 1858; March 21, 1860.

35. John Hebron Moore, ed., "The Textile Industry of the Old South as Described in a Letter by J. M. Wesson in 1858," *Journal of Economic History* 16 (1956): 200–205; Moore, *Emergence of the Cotton Kingdom*, 221–25.

36. Gavin Wright, *Old South, New South: Revolutions in the Southern Economy since the Civil War* (New York, 1986), 125–29.

37. *Vicksburg Weekly Sun*, April 4, 1859, reported that 12 slaves, including 6 or 7 males aged 9 to 21 years, recently smuggled into the United States from Africa, were being held in Vicksburg by a seller who wanted $400 for each. None of the slaves spoke English. A week earlier the same paper reported that "sixteen Africans evidently 'fresh caught' passed through" Jackson "on their way to some plantation in Madison County." *Weekly Sun*, March 28, 1859. On February 28, 1859, the *Weekly Sun* ran the following notice: "Congo Negroes—We are constantly in receipt of letter from planters desiring us to inform them where they can purchase Congo Negroes. We haven't any of 'em—wish we had. But if those desiring a few will address a certain good looking gentlemen who formerly represented the county of Claiborne in the Legislature at Port Gibson, they can obtain information."

38. Moore, ed., "Textile Industry," 203, 204. At the Vicksburg Southern Commercial Convention, one man dared to propose the use of nonslave labor in fac-

tories. The convention tabled the motion without discussion, and proceeded to take up the matter of repealing laws against the African slave trade. At that point nine Mississippians, at least four of whom were Vicksburgers, protested the motion, in part because they believed the matter would add to sectional tensions, but also in part because they saw nonslave factory labor as compatible with plantation slavery. Vicki Vaughn Johnson, *The Men and the Vision of the Southern Commercial Convention, 1845–1871* (Columbia, Mo., 1992), 121, 156–57. Herbert Wender, *Southern Commerical Conventions, 1837–1859* (Baltimore, 1930), 235.

39. Board of Police, minutes 1845–53, pp. 631–32, 634, 643, Chancery Clerk's Office, WCC.

40. See discussion of vagrants in Chapter 7.

41. Board of Police, minutes 1853–67, p. 292, Chancery Clerk's office, WCC.

42. *Vicksburg Whig,* May 25, November 1, 1860.

43. Ibid., August 28, 1860.

44. Ibid., May 22 and 25, September 21, 1860.

Chapter 10

1. Percy Lee Rainwater, *Mississippi: Storm Center of Secession 1856–1861* (1938; New York, 1969), 135–217. Peter F. Walker, *Vicksburg: A People at War, 1860–1865* (Chapel Hill, 1960), 13–34.

2. "The extension of state power," or integration of periphery into the center, "was the clearest possible indication of . . . a retreating frontier," write William Cronon, George Miles, and Jay Gitlan, in *Under an Open Sky,* 17. Robert Wiebe, *The Opening of American Society from the Adoption of the Constitution to the Eve of Disunion* (New York, 1984), has sketched a process of parallel sectional development whereby relatively autonomous communities and states merged economically, socially, culturally into North and South, which collided in the Western territories, and in the Civil War, as they merged into a single nation.

3. Nearly three decades ago David Potter complained that studies of the 1850s were "pregnant with the struggle which lay at the end," even though, in reality, "most human beings during these years went about their daily lives, preoccupied with their personal affairs, with no sense of impending disaster nor any fixation on the issue of slavery." Potter, *The Impending Crisis, 1848–1861* (New York, 1976), 145.

4. Allen (James) Plantation book, typescript, pp. 2, 23, MDAH.

5. Wailes (B. L. C.) diary, November 6 and 7, 1860, MDAH.

6. *Vicksburg Whig,* October 17, November 8, 1860. Percy Lee Rainwater, *Mississippi: Storm Center of Secession 1856–1861* (Baton Rouge, 1938), 176. Economic historian Gavin Wright has argued that prosperous planters favored secession to avoid Northern interference with slavery and escape the only threat to what they believed was a rosy future. Of course, claims Wright, they trusted the North would let them go peacefully. Wright, *Political Economy of the Cotton South,* 147. But surely the most confident of all planters were those who believed they could handle the worst Lincoln and the Republicans could throw at them.

7. I have in mind James Oakes's interpretation of the Old South, which he presents as an alternative to the Genovese thesis of a prebourgeois South. See in particular Oakes, *Slavery and Freedom,* but see also Oakes, *The Ruling Race.*

8. *Vicksburg Whig,* November 9, 1860. Rainwater, *Mississippi,* 162. Joseph Davis quoted in Janet Sharp Hermann, *Joseph E. Davis: Pioneer Patriarch* (Jackson, 1990), 97.

Unionists and Secessionists by Place of Residence,
Average Age, and Average Size of Slaveholding

	Unionists	*Secessionists*
Countryside		
Age	44	46
Slaveholding	25	31
N	59	10
Vicksburg		
Age	43	39
Slaveholding	6	7
N	31	12

Source: "Unionists" consist of active supporters of John Bell prior to the presidential election and active cooperationists, who may have supported Breckinridge but opposed secession after the election. "Secessionists" consist of active supporters of Breckinridge who also supported immediate secession after the presidential election. Politically active individuals were identified in newspapers and linked to the study data. Vicksburg *Weekly Southern Sun,* May 16, 1859; *Vicksburg Sun,* November 19, December 17, 1860; *Vicksburg Whig,* June 12, July 19, 21, August 3, 7, 18, September 11, October 2, November 21, December 5, 7, 11, 1860.

9. *Vicksburg Whig,* October 24, 1860. Patriarchs with less confidence in their status and authority, who felt challenged by slaves or nonslaveholding whites, might have taken the threat posed by Lincoln's election more seriously. See Michael P. Johnson, *Toward a Patriarchal Republic: The Secession of Georgia* (Baton Route, 1977).

10. *Vicksburg Whig,* December 7, 1860. Wailes (B. L. C.) Diary, February 10, 1861.

11. *Vicksburg Sun,* November 12, 1860. The evidence for Vicksburg raises questions about the political relationship between town and country during the secession crisis. Politics in Vicksburg, as in other Deep South urban areas, broke sharply from prevailing trends in surrounding plantation precincts, suggesting, among other things, the limits of planter leadership. Vicksburg, for example, gave 45% to Breckinridge, while Warren County as a whole gave only 39% to the same candidate. Similarly, Selma, Alabama, gave 27% to Breckinridge, while Dallas County, Alabama, as a whole gave 46% to Breckinridge. At least three other urban areas in Alabama and Mississippi bucked the rural trend. See William D. Barney, *The Secessionist Impulse: Alabama and Mississippi in 1860* (Princeton, N.J., 1974), Table 8, p. 128, and the tables in the appendix, pp. 317–20.

12. James Roach diary, pp. 104, 108–11, 124–25. *Vicksburg Whig,* October 13, 1858, discusses the fires but makes no mention of slaves.

13. At the heart of so many slave insurrection scares lay the question of control over certain white elements of society. See, for example, Christopher Morris, "An Event in Community Organization: The Mississippi Insurrection Scare of 1835," *Journal of Social History* 22 (Fall 1988): 93–111.

14. James Roach Diary, December 1859. *Vicksburg Whig*, October 10, 1860. Several Mississippi towns barred rural slaves during the Christmas holiday, when the suspected insurrection was supposed to occur. Donald M. Rawson, "Party Politics," 268.

15. *Vicksburg Whig*, August 29, September 6, December 27, 1860.

16. Ibid., October 30, December 25 and 27, 1860.

17. Ibid., November 1, December 11, 1860. Board of Police minutes, 1853–67, pp. 422, 425.

18. Roach Diary, December 1859.

19. *Vicksburg Whig*, October 18, 1860.

20. James Oakes has argued that as abolitionism questioned the legal and political legitimacy of slavery, slave resistance became political, that is, resistance could no longer be treated as existing outside the legal-political system. Although his point is well taken, Oakes underestimates the extent to which slave resistance always was political, the extent to which it became even more so as a consequence of Southern and local transformations, and the extent to which the slaves themselves acted upon the white legal-political system. Oakes, "The Political Significance of Slave Resistance," *History Workshop Journal* no. 22 (Autumn 1986): 89–107, and Oakes, *Slavery and Freedom*, 137–94.

21. *Vicksburg Whig*, September 25, October 3, November 15, 1860.

22. Ibid., July 11, August 1 and 28, October 9, 10, 16, 27, 30, November 6, 9, 10, 14, 28, December 4, 20, 22, 1860.

23. *Vicksburg Whig*, October 30, 1860.

24. Fear of slave insurrection, especially after John Brown's raid on Harpers Ferry, helped heat the secession crisis. See, for example, Steven A. Channing, *Crisis of Fear: Secession in South Carolina* (New York, 1970). But fear of insurrection does not explain why many who should have been most afraid did not support disunion.

25. Wailes (B. L. C.) diary, October 31, 1860, MDAH. Allen (James) plantation book, October 24, 1860, typescript, p. 22, MDAH.

26. January 1850, June 1859, Board of Police Minutes, Chancery Clerk's Office, WCC. *National Intelligencer*, August 29, 1817. U.S. Census, Population Schedules, 1850, 1860.

27. State Docket, 1856–60, OCHM.

28. Petition of Green, free black; Petition of Jordan Cheiwes, free black; Petition of William Newman and Candis Newman, free blacks; Petitions to the Legislature at the session of 1850–59, RG 47, vol. 27, MDAH.

29. Of the 22 secessionists, 9, or 41%, were born in Mississippi. Of the 90 unionists, 14, or 16%, were born in Mississippi. For source and further breakdown by age and slaveholding see table in note 8.

30. See table in note 8.

31. *Vicksburg Whig*, November 29, December 13, 1860.

32. *Vicksburg Sun*, November 19, December 16, 1860. *Vicksburg Whig*, July 28, December 18, 1860.

33.   November and December Elections Compared

		November		
	Bell	*Breckinridge*	*Douglas*	*Total*
Vicksburg	309	296	52	657
County	507	284	31	822

		December		
	Cooperationist		*Secessionist*	*Total*
Vicksburg	561		173	734
County	344		75	419

Source: Vicksburg Whig, November 9, December 8, 1860.

34. Rainwater, *Mississippi,* 192–200. David Potter noted the low turnout in convention elections across the South and attributed it to voter confusion amid an "atmosphere of excitement approaching hysteria." Potter, *Impending Crisis,* 500. Undoubtedly some voters were confused. But excited, nearly hysterical voters vote. The low turnout belied the drawing power of the secessionists. Unionists conceded without a fight.

35. For a brief survey of recent literature on secession, see Joe Gray Taylor, "The White South from Secession to Redemption," in Boles and Nolen, eds., *Interpreting Southern History,* 162–65.

Taylor says nothing of the emerging synthesis that began with J. Mills Thornton, *Politics and Power in a Slave Society: Alabama, 1800–1860* (Baton Rouge, 1978). Thornton traces secession in Alabama to the same process of nation-building that shaped events in Warren County, in particular to the state's integration into the market economy and "a national net of complex interrelationships" (p. 447). Alabamians, he argues, perceived the intrusion of the outside world as a threat to individual autonomy and democracy. Thus, in what Thornton interprets as the last act of the Jacksonian era, they turned on the Union, as they had the "monster" bank a generation earlier, to protect their freedoms, including their freedom to own slaves.

Thornton surely exaggerates the extent of democracy in antebellum Alabama and the commitment of Alabamians to personal autonomy. Assuming Mississippi was not too unlike its neighbor, what concerned so many in both states on the eve of the Civil War was too much democracy, not too little. The outside world, while it did indeed threaten the autonomy of individual communities, also undermined the authority of elites within those communities by loosening lower-class whites and slaves from their grasp. Vagrants, workers, immigrants, women, even the slaves were all freer in Vicksburg than in the surrounding countryside. This concerned the established citizens enough to cause them to consider breaking away from the Union so that they might take control of their city and the people in it. In the countryside, however, there was very little individual autonomy. Everyone had a place within a hierarchical, patriarchal order so entrenched that nothing, not even a Republican president, posed a threat to it, or so the planters believed. For an analysis similar to Thornton's but applied to another state, see Ford, *Origins of Southern Radicalism.*

36. This account of the war's coming to the Allen family is based on Allen (James) plantation book, typescript, pp. 23–41, quotations come from pp. 23, 24, 33, 34, 36, 38, 41, MDAH.

Epilogue

1. Allen (James) plantation book, November 27, 1861, April 17, 1862, typescript pp. 50, 64, 65, MDAH. Wailes (B. L. C.) diary, March 1, 26, 1862. James M. McPherson, *Battle Cry of Freedom: The Civil War Era* (New York, 1988), 405.

2. Allen (James) plantation book, typescript, 43.

3. Ibid., 52, 53 54, MDAH. Wailes (B. L. C.) diary, March 31, April 11, 1862, MDAH.

4. Allen (James) plantation book, typescript, 54, 67, 69, 87, 93.

5. Ibid., 1, 92, 93.

6. Ibid., 54, 87, 99.

7. Ibid., 91, 98, 99, 113. Wailes (B. L. C) diary, January 14, August 27, 29, 31, September 1, 24, 25, 27, 29, October 1, 1862.

8. Allen (James) plantation book, typescript, 73–74, 77–83. Wailes (B. L. C.) diary, May 18, June 14, August 23, 1862.

9. James T. Currie, *Enclave: Vicksburg and Her Plantations 1863–1870* (Jackson, 1980), 88–90, 95, 104.

10. Allen (James) plantation book, typescript, 69, 75–76, 78, 93. Wailes (B. L. C.) diary, May 6, 1862. Walker, *Vicksburg*, 89–114. McPherson, *Battle Cry of Freedom*, 420–21.

11. Allen (James) plantation book, typescript, 108, 112. Wailes (B. L. C.) diary, August 23, 1862.

12. Allan (James) plantation book, typescript, 73, 95, 101–2, 118. Wailes (B. L. C.) diary, November 16, 18, 1861, January 14, 1862.

13. Allen (James) plantation book, typescript, 121. Currie, *Enclave*, xxii, xxiii, 75. Tryphena Blanche Holder Fox, *A Northern Woman in the Plantation South: Letters of Tryphena Blanche Holder Fox, 1856–1876*, edited by Wilma King (Columbia, S.C., 1993), 134–35.

14. Currie, *Enclave*, 33. On life in Vicksburg during the siege, see Walker, *Vicksburg*, and the many diaries cited therein. For the military history of the siege, see Samuel Carter III, *The Final Fortress: The Campaign for Vicksburg 1862–1863* (New York, 1980).

15. Allen (James) plantation book, typescript, 121. On Reconstruction in the Vicksburg area, see Michael Wayne, *The Reshaping of Plantation Society: The Natchez District, 1860–1880* (Baton Rouge, 1983).

INDEX

Abolitionists: fear of, 123, 174–75
Abstractionist: approach to history, xv. *See also* Substantialist
Adams County, Mississippi, 150, 156, 160, 171
Africans: smuggled into U.S. and Warren County, 245. *See also* Slaves
Agriculture: seasonal cycles, 31–32; slash-and-burn, 30, 35. *See also* Cattle herding; Corn; Cotton; Economy; Erosion; Indigo; Internal economy; Land; Tobacco
Allen, Charly, 181, 182
Allen, James, 74, 154, 157, 170, 171, 172–73, 175, 180–81, 182–83
American Revolution, 6, 8, 13, 21–22, 37
Andrews, Ithamar, 10
Anti-Gambling Society, 121, 126
Arson, 77, 173–74, 175, 177
Authority, systems of: local vs. outside, 18–20, 120–23; county government, 138–43, 175; courts, 56–62, 95–96, 98, 100. *See also* Patriarchy; Voluntary associations

Baker, D. H., 97
Baker, Job, 137
Banks, 137, 150, 152; efforts to reform, 152
Barber, Benjamin, 10
Barclay, John, 29
Barkley, Samuel, 58
Baton Rouge, 15, 37, 38, 113
Bay, Elihu Hall, 20, 109
Beall, Thomas, 97
Beard, James, 88

Blackman, Mary, 54, 57
Board of police. *See* Authority, systems of
Boatmen, 122–23
Bodley, John, 129–30
Bolivar County, Mississippi, 80, 137
Bones, Tom, 75
Brady, Michael, 121
Brashears, Tobius, 11, 24, 26
British West Florida. *See* Lower Mississippi Valley; Chester, Peter
Brown, John: raid on Harpers Ferry, 174
Buena Vista plantation, 69, 75, 159, 160. *See also* Kiger, Basil

Calhoon, John, 12
Capital accumulation, 28, 159, 166
Capitalism, xiv, 17–18; transition to, 35–36, 153
Carellier family, 164
Caribbean: trade with, 23, 26, 27; slave trade, 64–65
Carondelet, Baron de, 24, 76
Cash: use and availability of, 15–17, 24, 28, 40, 110; paid to slaves, 75, 118
Caston, Green, 93
Caston, Seth, 92–93
Cattle herding, 23–26, 35, 41, 206–7
Censer, Jane Turner, 55
Chamberlain, Catherine, 92
Chamberlain, Ellen. *See* Hyland, Ellen Chamberlain
Chester, Peter, 8
Chewning, J. J., 137
Chickasaw, 4, 40–41, 156

Winans, William, 43, 61

Women: and local exchange, 17; household manufacturing, 45; as property-holders, 92; and urban context, 125, 127–28; and politics, 147; and patriarchy, 98–100, 162, 167–68; seen as threat to patriarchy, 177. *See also* Textile production; Plantation women; Wife-beating and wife-killing

Wood, Curtis, 79

Work: and the decision to plant cotton, 32–35, 36, 40; and the business of raising slaves, 72–74; of slaves, 74–75. *See also* Occupational groups

Work rhythms. *See* Cotton and work; Agriculture

Wright, Thomas, 48–49

Wyatt-Brown, Bertram, 55, 98

Yellow fever, 50, 127, 143, 173

Yeoman farmers. *See* Nonslave-holders

Yokena plantation, 111–12. *See also* Hyland, James; Hyland, Jacob